Combinatorial Programming: Methods and Applications

NATO ADVANCED STUDY INSTITUTES SERIES

Proceedings of the Advanced Study Institute Programme, which aims at the dissemination of advanced knowledge and the formation of contacts among scientists from different countries

The series is published by an international board of publishers in conjunction with NATO Scientific Affairs Division

A	Life Sciences	Plenum Publishing Corporation
B	Physics	London and New York
C	Mathematical and Physical Sciences	D. Reidel Publishing Company Dordrecht and Boston
D	Behavioral and Social Sciences	Sijthoff International Publishing Company Leiden
E	Applied Sciences	Noordhoff International Publishing Leiden

Series C – Mathematical and Physical Sciences

Volume 19 – Combinatorial Programming: Methods and Applications

Combinatorial Programming: Methods and Applications

Proceedings of the NATO Advanced Study Institute held at the Palais des Congrès, Versailles, France, 2–13 September, 1974

edited by

B. ROY

Professeur à l'Université de Paris
Conseiller Scientifique à la SEMA, France

Springer-Science+Business Media, B.V.

Library of Congress Cataloging in Publication Data

NATO Advanced Study Institute, Versailles, 1974.
Combinatorial programming.

(NATO advanced study institutes series : C, mathematical and physical sciences ; 19)
Bibliography: p.
1. Integer programming—Congresses. 2. Combinatorial analysis—Congresses.
I. Roy, Bernard, 1934– II. Title. III. Series: NATO advanced study institutes series : Series C, mathematical and physical sciences ; 19.
T57.7.N37 1974 519.7'7 75–17734
ISBN 978-94-011-7559-3 ISBN 978-94-011-7557-9 (eBook)
DOI 10.1007/978-94-011-7557-9

Originally published by D. Reidel Publishing Company, Dordrecht, Holland in 1975
Softcover reprint of the hardcover 1st edition 1975

CONTENTS

Alphabetical list of contributors XI

Preface XIII

PART I: GENERAL METHODOLOGY 1

MODELLING TECHNIQUES AND HEURISTICS FOR COMBINATORIAL PROBLEMS
Heiner Müller-Merbach 3
1. Objectives of the paper 3
2. Morphology of combinatorial problems 4
3. The general approach to solving combinatorial problems 6
4. Integer programming formulations 9
5. Explicit enumeration 14
6. Tree search (branch and bound) methods, implicit enumeration 16
7. Heuristic methods 22
8. Conclusions 25
References 26

LES PROCEDURES D'EXPLORATION ET D'OPTIMISATION PAR SEPARATION ET EVALUATION: a survey
Pierre Hansen 29
I. Classification et forme des tests 29
1. Introduction 29
2. Classification des tests 31
3. Formes des tests 34
Bibliographie 39
II. Séparations et formes standards 41
1. Introduction 41
2. Principe de séparation 42
3. Formes standards 44
4. Efficience et séparations 50
Bibliographie 52
III. Fonctions d'évaluation et pénalités 54
1. Introduction 54
2. Reformulation d'un problème 55

3. Obtention de fonctions d'évaluation et de pénalités en deux phases 58
4. Formulation implicite et relaxations 60
5. Choix des tests 62
Bibliographie 63

BOOLEAN ELEMENTS IN COMBINATORIAL OPTIMIZATION: a survey
Peter L. Hammer 67
Introduction 67
I. Elements of Boolean Algebra 69
II. The resolvent 71
III. Algorithms 72
IV. Equivalent forms of 0-1 programs 78
V. Packing and knapsack problems 79
VI. Coefficient transformation 80
VII. Polytopes in the unit cube 82
VIII. Pseudo-Boolean functions and game theory 83
References 89

FOURIER-MOTZKIN ELIMINATION AND ITS DUAL WITH APPLICATION TO INTEGER PROGRAMMING
George B. Dantzig and B. Curtis Eaves 93

PART II: PATHS AND CIRCUITS 103

CHEMINS ET CIRCUITS: ENUMERATION ET OPTIMISATION: a survey
Bernard Roy 105
I. Introduction 105
II. Procédures algébriques 107
1. Algèbre des chemins 107
a) Définition et interprétation de (L, *, E) 107
b) Hypothèses restrictives 112
c) Exemples 115
2. Principaux résultats 118
a) Structure matricielle ($\mathcal{M}_n$(L), *, E) 118
b) Résultats fondamentaux 120
c) A propos d'algorithmes 123
III. Procédures par séparation 124
1. Arborescence des chemins 124
a) Définition et propriété de χ 124
b) Sous-arborescences particulières 127
2. Fondements des principales procédures 127
a) Principe de séparation 129
b) Enchaînement des séparations 130
Références 133

PATH ALGEBRA AND ALGORITHMS
Michel Gondran 137
1. Path algebra 137

1.1. Definition of the algebra 137
1.2. Properties of the path algebra 139
2. General algorithms 141
2.1. Iterative methods 142
2.2. Direct methods 143
References 147

HAMILTONIAN CIRCUITS AND THE TRAVELLING SALESMAN PROBLEM: a survey
Nicos Christofides 149
1. Introduction 149
2. Hamiltonian circuits in a graph 150
2.1. The enumeration method of Roberts and Flores 151
2.2. The multi-path method 152
2.3. Computational results 154
3. The travelling salesman problem 156
4. The TSP and the SST 157
4.1. The vertex penalty algorithm for SST transformations 159
4.2. Convergence of the vertex-penalty method 162
4.3. The "closed" TSP 163
5. The TSP and AP 164
5.1. A tree-search algorithm for circuit elimination 165
5.2. A tighter bound from the AP 167
References 170

THE PERIPATETIC SALESMAN AND SOME RELATED UNSOLVED PROBLEMS
Jakob Krarup 173
1. Introduction 173
2. The peripatetic salesman problem 174
3. Hamiltonian numbers and perfect r-Hamiltonian graphs 174
4. PSP's with r=2 175
5. Minimum spanning trees 176
6. Discussion 177
7. Suggestions for future research 177
8. Acknowledgments 177
References 178

SOME RESULTS ON THE CONVEX HULL OF THE HAMILTONIAN CYCLES OF SYMETRIC COMPLETE GRAPHS
Jean-François Maurras 179

FINDING MINIMUM SPANNING TREES WITH A FIXED NUMBER OF LINKS AT A NODE
Fred Glover and Darwin Klingman 191
1. Introduction 191
2. Notation and results 193
3. Labeling procedures 197
4. Order-constrained one-trees and matroid extensions 199
References 200

PART III: SET PARTITIONING, COVERING AND PACKING 203

SET PARTITIONING: a survey
Egon Balas and Manfred W. Padberg 205
Introduction 206
1. Background 208
1.1. Set partitioning and its uses 208
1.2. Set packing and set covering 209
1.3. Edge matching and covering, node packing and covering 210
1.4. Node packing, set packing, clique covering 212
2. Theory 214
2.1. Facets of the set packing polytope 214
2.2. Facets of relaxed polytopes: cuts from Disjunctions 220
2.3. Adjacent vertices of the set partitioning and set packing polytopes 224
3. Algorithms 230
3.1. Implicit enumeration 231
3.2. Simplex-based cutting plane methods 235
3.3. A column generating algorithm 238
3.4. A symmetric subgradient cutting plane method 242
3.5. Set partitioning via node covering 247
References 251
Appendix: A bibliography of applications 255

AN ALGORITHM FOR LARGE SET PARTITIONING PROBLEMS
Roy E. Marsten 259
1. Introduction 259
2. Method of solution 260
2.1. Ordering the matrix 260
2.2. Separating the feasible solutions 261
2.3. Computing the lower bounds 264
2.4. The algorithm 265
3. Computational experience 265
References 267

LE PROBLEME DE PARTITION SOUS CONTRAINTE
Jean Fréhel 269
1. Introduction 269
2. Introduction d'une contrainte $\sum_{1}^{n} x_j = N$ 270
3. Introduction d'autres types de contraintes 273
Références 274

CHARACTERISATIONS OF TOTALLY UNIMODULAR, BALANCED AND PERFECT MATRICES
Manfred W. Padberg 275

SOME WELL-SOLVED PROBLEMS IN COMBINATORIAL OPTIMIZATION
Jack Edmonds 285

PART IV: OTHER COMBINATORIAL PROGRAMMING TOPICS 303

HOW TO COLOR A GRAPH: a survey
Dominique de Werra 305
1. Introduction and summary 305
2. Edge coloring 305
3. Node coloring 310
4. Hypergraph coloring 315
5. Balancing the colorings 318
References 323

PROBLEMES EXTREMAUX CONCERNANT LE NOMBRE DES COLORATIONS DES SOMMETS D'UN GRAPHE FINI
Ioan Tomescu 327

A FEW REMARKS ON CHROMATIC SCHEDULING
Dominique de Werra 337
1. Introduction and summary 337
2. Colorings of parallel nodes 337
3. Applications 341
References 342

MINIMIZING TOTAL COSTS IN ONE-MACHINE SCHEDULING
A.H.G. Rinnooy Kan, B.J. Lageweg, and J.K. Lenstra 343
1. Introduction 343
2. Description of the algorithm 344
3. Computational experiments 347
4. Concluding remarks 349
References 350

THE QUADRATIC ASSIGNMENT PROBLEM: A BRIEF REVIEW
Eugene L. Lawler 351
1. Problem statement 351
2. Applications and problem formulations 352
3. Methods of solution 355
4. One dimensional module placement problem 356
5. Special case due to Pratt 357
6. Another special case: network flows 357
7. The special case of trees 358
8. Rooted trees: a special case of Adolphson and Hu 358
References 359

FONCTIONS D'EVALUATION ET PENALITES POUR LES PROGRAMMES QUADRATIQUES EN VARIABLES 0-1
Pierre Hansen 361
1. Introduction 361
2. Fonctions d'évaluation et pénalités 362
3. Algorithmes et essais sur ordinateur 366
Bibliographie 369

SOLUTION OF THE MACHINE LOADING PROBLEM WITH BINARY VARIABLES
Claudio Sandi 371
1. Introduction 371
2. The problem 372
3. The method 373
4. Computational experience 376
5. Bibliograpy 378

THE ROLE OF PUZZLES IN TEACHING COMBINATORIAL PROGRAMMING
Heiner Müller-Merbach 379
1. The use of puzzles in teaching combinatorial programming 379
2. Number puzzles (arithmogriphs) 380
3. A discrete step dynamic process 383
4. Puzzles with true and false information (Liar puzzles) 384
5. Conclusions 385

ALPHABETICAL LIST OF CONTRIBUTORS

E. BALAS, M.W. PADBERG
Set partitioning : a survey (p. 205)

N. CHRISTOFIDES
Hamiltonian circuits and the travelling salesman problem : a survey (p. 149)

G.B. DANTZIG, B.C. EAVES
Fourier-Motzkin elimination and its dual with application to integer programming (p. 93)

B.C. EAVES
see G.B. DANTZIG, B.C. EAVES (p. 93)

J. EDMONDS
Some well-solved problems in combinatorial optimization (p. 285)

J. FREHEL
Le problème de partition sous contrainte (p. 269)

F. GLOVER, D. KLINGMAN
Finding minimum spanning trees with a fixed number of links at a node (p. 191)

M. GONDRAN
Path algebra and algorithms (p. 137)

P.L. HAMMER
Boolean elements in combinatorial optimization : a survey (p. 67)

P. HANSEN
Les procédures d'exploration et d'optimisation par séparation et évaluation : a survey (p. 29)

Fonctions d'évaluation et pénalités pour les programmes quadratiques en variables 0-1 (p. 361)

D. KLINGMAN
see F. GLOVER, D. KLINGMAN (p. 191)

J. KRARUP
The peripatetic salesman and some related unsolved problems (p. 173)

B.J. LAGEWEG
see A.H.G. RINNOOY KAN, B.J. LAGEWEG, J.K. LENSTRA (p. 343)

E.L. LAWLER
The quadratic assignment problem : a brief review (p. 351)

J.K. LENSTRA
see A.H.G. RINNOOY KAN, B.J. LAGEWEG, J.K. LENSTRA (p. 343)

R.E. MARSTEN
An algorithm for large set partitioning problems (p. 259)

J.F. MAURRAS
Some results on the convex hull of the hamiltonian cycles
of symetric complete graphs (p. 179)

H. MULLER-MERBACH
Modelling techniques and heuristics for combinatorial
problems (p. 3)

The role of puzzles in teaching combinatorial programming (p. 379)

M.W. PADBERG
see E. BALAS, M.W. PADBERG (p. 205)

Characterisations of totally unimodular, balanced and perfect
matrices (p. 275)

A.H.G. RINNOOY KAN, B.J. LAGEWEG, J.K. LENSTRA
Minimizing total costs in one-machine scheduling (p. 343)

B. ROY
Chemins et circuits : énumération et optimisation :
a survey (p. 105)

C. SANDI
Solution of the machine loading problem with binary
variables (p. 371)

I. TOMESCU
Problèmes extrémaux concernant le nombre des colorations des
sommets d'un graphe fini (p. 327)

D. de WERRA
How to color a graph : a survey (p. 305)

A few remarks on chromatic scheduling (p. 337)

PREFACE

"Combinatorial Programming" are two words whose juxtaposition still strike us as unusual, nevertheless their association in recent years adequately reflects the preoccupations underlying differing work fields, and their importance will increase both from methodology and application view points. To those who like definitions and consider the function of this book to furnish one for combinatorial programming, I will simply say that it is precisely this which is exclusively treated here and which in the eyes of the autors is the heart of this branch of applied mathematics. Such was the initial intention of those who in the spring of 1973 gathered together in Paris to state the work of the Advanced Study Institute from which this book arises. As young as combinatorial programming is, it was easy to see that a two week school was insufficient to cover the subject in an exhaustive manner. Finally the decision had to be taken to reduce to book form, and to organise within this particular means of expression, the essential syntheses and communications. Unfortunately the discussions, the round tables, and the majority of the case studies could not be included in this book which is more of a hand-book on the subject.

The choice and orientation of the surveys has been guided by two criteria : the importance of already accomplished work, and the originality of the survey to be undertaken. Accordingly since there is a rich supply of literature on integer programming surveys and shortest path algorithms these two topics have been excluded. On the other hand a new look at the set of branch and bound procedures, analysing them in a systematic way by using general concepts such as "separation principle", "evaluation function",... providing the means of conceiving new ones with respect to the specific problem to be resolved, seems to be self-imposing.

The communications complete the surveys on particular points or sketch the outlines where a survey may seem premature or even unjustifiable according to the two preceding self-imposed criteria.

If for the reasons cited above this book favours the methodology side of combinatorial programming, applications have not been totally neglected. Distribution and routing, investment and location, sequencing and scheduling are problems for which the reader will find throughout this book numerous methods of solution in the form of models, structural properties or even algorithms. Several of the papers included even go into numerical aspects (size of the problems resolved, comparison of algorithms, length and precision of the calculations, ...).

As editor of this book, if I had been confronted with a characteristic combinatorial programming problem this book itself would not really have helped me to solve it. It dealt with arrangement of problem material in such a way so as to form a coherent continuation, graduated in its difficulty, and easily understood by the non-specialist, even if in so doing it is rendered superficial through the eyes of the specialist (for whom in fact it little matters). The four part structure is closely related to the morphology of combinatorial programming problems presented in the first paper. Within each section the order adopted tends, without being too fragmented, to provide coverage of problems from a relatively vast domain to more specialised subjects. I in no way pretend that the solution finally adopted presents a marked character of optimality, nor even sub-optimality, but only a compromise which realises a satisfactory equilibrium between the antagonistic criteria which are nothing but weaker forms of incompatible constraints. Still one must admit that often the principal actors in a decision making process are confronted with problems formulated in this way (ill-defined in the eyes of certain people), but I leave them the responsibility of their own value of judgement. Thus we are led to predict that, with regard to new structures which are to be formalised and made operational relative to new enumeration generation and elimination procedures, or even to characterise and extract those solutions which appear balanced in the eyes of the expert in that they in no way sacrifice a particular aspect for another, combinatorial programming will undergo during the next few years important developments not only in algorithms and simple heuristics but in concepts and structures.

For this very reason I believe that I am able to say that this book is addressed to those, be they pure mathematicians or scientists, who are interested in the recent developments in this sector of applied mathematics which subtends what we call "operational research" or "decision aid" according to whether emphasis is centred on methods or applications.

I cannot complete this preface without expressing my deep obligation to all those who helped in making the school possible and in consequence this book. Thanks are due first to N.A.T.O. for their financial support and secondly to SEMA for having undertaken the secretarial duties. Although it may seem trivial to add, without the active participation of each one of the 98 who attended, lecturers or not, this book whould not have been possible, each one of these I would like to thank also for the confidence that they confided in me. Finally all those who organised and were responsible for the functioning of the school, the secretaries who typed and reproduced the lecture notes are especially thanked for the often "thankless" work they undertook. Last but nos least I am deeply indebted to Michel Gondran for the role he played in liaison with the authors, and for the continuous aid he provided in the realisation of this book. Here he will find the expression of my deep gratefulness.

Bernard Roy

P A R T I

GENERAL METHODOLOGY

MODELLING TECHNIQUES AND HEURISTICS FOR COMBINATORIAL PROBLEMS

H. Müller-Merbach

Fachgebiet Betriebswirtschaftslehre (Operations Research)
Technische Hochschule Darmstadt, D-61 Darmstadt, Germany

ABSTRACT. This paper will give a survey of the different methods to approach combinatorial optimization problems. The main emphasis will lie upon integer programming modelling, tree-search (branch and bound) methods, and heuristic methods. The paper is divided into the following sections: 1. Objectives of the paper; 2. Morphology of combinatorial problems; 3. The general approach to solving combinatorial problems; 4. Integer programming formulations; 5. Explicit enumeration; 6. Tree-search (branch and bound) methods; 7. Heuristic methods; 8. Conclusions.

1. OBJECTIVES OF THE PAPER

Actual combinatorial problems do not arise in mathematical departments, but rather in <u>real-life situations</u>. Two conclusions can be drawn from this statement: (1) Combinatorial programming research should not only treat well-defined problems; it should rather develop <u>tools and techniques</u> which are of <u>general use</u> for as many combinatorial problems as may arise. (2) As probably much more actual combinatorial problems arise than mathematicians (with experience in combinatorial programming) are available it is particularly necessary to make the developments in combinatorial programming as easily <u>accessible to non-mathematicians</u> as possible.

This paper is written for those who have to deal with actual combinatorial problems, but who need not necessarily be mathematicians. The reader should however be familiar with some combinatorial problems, with some integer programming models and methods including their limitations, with enumerative (tree-search or branch and bound) techniques and with heuristic methods.

B. Roy (ed.), Combinatorial Programming: Methods and Applications, 3–27.

This paper is to some extent morphological in that the author has tried to put up a morphological scheme of combinatorial problems, to suggest a general approach to solving combinatorial problems, to develop integer programming models of combinatorial problems in a somewhat general context, and to discuss morphological schemes of enumerative techniques and heuristic methods. The morphological schemes do not serve - in the first place - the purpose of giving a synopsis of today's knowledge in combinatorial programming. Rather, the main objective is to provide some kind of tool-boxes for solving real-world combinatorial problems. To put it differently, the morphological schemes are set up in order to be used as some sort of check-lists which are to be used when new methods for solving individual types of combinatorial problems are to be developed.

2. MORPHOLOGY OF COMBINATORIAL PROBLEMS

Before the methods for solving combinatorial problems can be considered, it is necessary to discuss briefly what combinatorial problems look like and which different types of combinatorial problems can be distinguished.

One can make a distinction between (1) combinatorial optimization problems and (2) those combinatorial problems for which only a feasible solution is seeked. This distinction, however, seems to be of little importance since (a) searching for a feasible solution can be interpreted as "minimizing infeasibility" and since (b) optimization can be interpreted as searching for feasible solutions subject to a constraint with an increasing (or decreasing, respectively) absolute coefficient. However, some problems (e.g. the traveling salesman problem) are usually considered as combinatorial optimization problems, while others (e.g. the school timetable problem and many job shop scheduling problems) tend to be taken as problems for which only a feasible solution is required.

More important seems to be the distinction between (1) sequencing problems, (2) selection problems, and (3) assignment problems as well as of combinations of these.

(1) In sequencing problems, a number of elements (or only a subset of them) have to be put into a feasible or optimal order (sequence). The most well-known problem of this type is the traveling salesman problem. Shortest route problems may also be considered to belong to this category.

(2) In selection problems, elements of a set have to be chosen such that certain requirements are fulfilled. The knapsack problem, the matching problem, the covering problem are the most well-known standard problems of this group.

(3) In assignment problems it is asked to assign elements of one set to elements of another set. Typical problems of this group are the linear assignment problem and the quadratic assignment problem.

Many real-world problems are combinations of these groups. So can the vehicle scheduling problem be taken as a combination of an assignment problem (customers to trucks) and of a sequencing problem (optimal route for each truck). And the school timetable problem can be considered as a combination of an assignment problem (which teacher to which class), of a selection problem (which hours for the single teachers), and of a sequencing problem (sequence of the teachers in the single classes as well as sequence of the classes for each teacher).

Although it seems prima facie as if there exists a fundamental distinction between sequencing, selection and assignment problems, it is to be emphasized that they can be converted into each other. A sequencing problem slips into the cover of a selection problem if subsequences are put up of which a full set has to be selected. The similar is true for the assignment problem since a selection of subassignments can be taken. Thirdly, sequencing problems can be considered as assignment problems, since the order of each element of a sequence can be interpreted as an assignment to the corresponding slot. Reversely to this, assignment problems can be taken as sequencing problems in that all the elements of one of the two sets are considered as slots for which the sequence of the elements of the other set (in relation to the slots) is seeked. Furthermore, it is in general possible to transvert selection problems into sequencing and assignment problems which, however, in many cases requires some arbitrariness in the argumentation.

It should be mentioned that integer programming models (particularly zero-one-models) in principle are selection problems. From this statement it follows that any combinatorial optimization problem turns into a selection problem as soon as it is modelled in integer programming terms.

After this brief morphology of combinatorial problems an attempt shall be made to give a definition of the term "combinatorial problem". One might define a combinatorial problem as any problem which can be represented by an integer programming model. This definition is not operational though. One might also say that the essence of combinatorial problems is that there are distinct elements of one or more sets which have to be put into an order, or which have to be divided into subsets (of selected and not selected elements), or which have to be assigned to each other in a certain way. More briefly, combinatorial problems can be understood as problems in which any particular kind of combination between distinct elements of one or more sets are seeked.

After the nature of combinatorial problems and a morphology have now been discussed, the next chapter will deal with a general procedure to treat combinatorial problems.

3. THE GENERAL APPROACH TO SOLVING COMBINATORIAL PROBLEMS

Since all combinatorial problems have certain properties in common, it is not surprising that a general approach to combinatorial problems can be suggested. It consists of the following 6 steps which can be used as a guideline or checklist to approach any combinatorial problem:

1) State the problem.
2) Build an integer programming model. If this model can successfully be handled by integer programming methods, then solve the problem and stop. Otherwise proceed to step 3.
3) Estimate the number of solutions.
4) Check whether explicit enumeration is an adequate method. If not, proceed to step 5, otherwise enumerate and stop.
5) Try to apply tree-search (implicit enumeration) methods, i.e. (i) branch and bound, (ii) dynamic programming, and (iii) bounded enumeration (branch and reject, branch and exclude, or whatever name is preferred). If tree-search methods are too time-consuming, then proceed to step 6.
6) Develop and apply heuristic methods (incomplete enumeration) which in general do not guarantee the optimal or any feasible solution but require little computation time.

These steps shall be considered in some more detail in the following.

3.1 State the problem

The first step means that a full verbal description of the problem shall be developed and checked with those individuals who are familiar with the details of the problem; this step includes the gathering of data, at least of sample data. In practice, it is very important to write all the details of the problem down and have the report signed by all those who are usually dealing with the problem.

3.2 Build an integer programming model

As second step, it is strongly suggested to build an integer programming model or - which is even better - several different programming models. This suggestion is kept in spite of the fact that integer programming algorithms are still highly inefficient.

The main benefit of integer programming models is that they provide an insight into the structure (and the size) of the problem. From this structure one may detect relations and similarities to any problems (e.g. standard problems) which were solved in the past; one may be able to apply the same methods or at least get stimulations for the development of new methods.

In addition, it might be possible that the particular integer programming model can efficiently be treated by integer programming methods (particularly in case of unimodularity).

As Williams (31) showed, many (if not all) combinatorial problems can be represented by several different integer programming models which differ from each other in the size and in the required computation time for the solution.

In general, however, integer programming models will only be of use for learning about the structure of the problem. Only in a very few cases general integer programming methods are more efficient than tree-search methods which are "directly" applied to the problem. This is almost obvious since most of the integer programming methods are also based on tree-searching.

3.3 Estimate the number of solutions

If - as in most cases - the integer programming model does not lead to a solution of the problem, enumerative or heuristic methods have to be applied. In order to select the appropriate method it is necessary to estimate the number of solutions. One should keep in mind though that "solution" may have different meanings with regard to the solution method. One may either consider all the feasible and infeasible solutions, or all the feasible solutions subject only to a subset of the constraints, or all the dual feasible solutions etc.

It may also be interesting to estimate the number of steps of computation which are required to yield all the solutions.

In connection with tree-search methods it should also be estimated how large (in both dimensions, succeeding nodes and parallel nodes) the tree would become and how many nodes are to be stored at the same time.

3.4 Check whether explicit enumeration is an adequate method

If it is found that the number of solutions is small, then explicit enumeration would be an appropriate tool to solve the problem. Here, the meaning of "small" depends upon the problem, e.g. the computation time required for each single solution. It is cheaper to write a computer program for explicit enumeration in one day and waste 15 or 30 minutes computer time than to program a more complicated tree-search method within four days and save up to half an hour computer time. But the more frequently the same type of combinatorial problem is to be solved the less explicit enumeration is the appropriate tool.

3.5 Try to apply tree-search (implicit enumeration) methods

If explicit enumeration tends to require too much computation time, then implicit enumeration or tree-searching could be an appropriate method. "Implicit enumeration" means that those branches of the enumeration tree are not considered any further the nonoptimality of which can be detected. Due to the organization of the enumerative process, three different principles can be distinguished:

(i) Branch and Bound. This is the most general approach with a mixed sequential and parallel organization. The branching process continues at uniquely chosen nodes of the tree.

(ii) Dynamic Programming. This is a parallel organization of the enumerative process where all the subsolutions (states) of a certain level (stage) are computed simultaneously.

(iii) Bounded Enumeration (branch and reject, branch and exclude etc.). This is a sequential organization of the enumerative process where only one sequence of succeeding branches is considered at the same time.

Generally speaking, dynamic programming is the appropriate method in cases where the enumeration tree is deep (many succeeding nodes) and narrow (only a few parallel nodes). In contrary, bounded enumeration is advantageous in cases with short (only a few succeeding nodes) but broad trees (many parallel nodes). Branch and bound requires that the number of "active nodes" does not exceed the storage capacity. The number of active nodes depends on the length as well as on the breadth of the enumeration tree. More details are given in section 6.

3.6 Develop and apply heuristic methods (incomplete enumeration)

In many real-life combinatorial problems even implicit enumeration would require much more computation time than appropriate. In these cases, heuristic methods are the only mean to treat the problem. Since heuristic methods are not subject to precise mathematical criteria (such as optimality etc.), there are almost no restrictions regarding the structure of heuristic approaches. This leads to the situation that heuristic methods are described in the literature without any justification why this or that way is walked upon. This is awkward.

Chapter 7 of this paper is dedicated to heuristic methods. A morphological scheme of these methods will be given there which can be used as frame or checklist for developing heuristic methods for specific problems.

4. INTEGER PROGRAMMING FORMULATIONS

As stated in section 3.2, it is suggested that integer programming models of combinatorial programs are to be built. Some details will be given in this chapter. It will be emphasized that usually several different integer programming models can be formulated for each combinatorial problem.

Sequencing, selection, and assignment problems will be considered individually in the sections 4.1 to 4.3.

4.1 Integer programming models of sequencing problems

Sequencing problems can be subdivided according to several criteria. There are problems where all given elements of a set have to be brought into an order. The traveling salesman problem which shall be considered in some more detail belongs to this class. In other cases only a not specified number of given elements of a specific set have to be ordered. The shortest route problem is of this kind. This class shall not be considered here any further.

Sequencing problems (where all the elements have to be ordered) can be subdivided into vicinal sequencing problems, see Jaeschke (19), and non-vicinal sequencing problems. "Vicinal" roughly means that the costs of the pair i-j is independent from the sequence of all the other elements. The traveling salesman problem is vicinal. The quadratic assignment problem (see section 4.3) is non-vicinal (if it is at all considered as a sequencing problem). Vicinal sequencing problems are much easier to solve than non-vicinal problems, and they can much easier be formulated in integer programming models.

The general integer programming formulation of vicinal sequencing problems consists of (i) a linear objective, (ii) constraints which say that each element (i.e. city) has to have a successor, (iii) constraints which say that each element has to have a predecessor, (iv) the 0,1-condition, and (v) the constraints which exclude cycles.

In the case of the traveling salesman problem the formulation reads:

$$x_{ij} = \begin{cases} 1, & \text{if } j \text{ succeeds } i \\ 0, & \text{otherwise} \end{cases}$$

c_{ij} = costs (or any other optimization criterion) for the sequence i-j

Minimize (or maximize, respectively)

$$\sum_i \sum_j c_{ij}\, x_{ij} \qquad (1)$$

$$\text{s.t.} \quad \sum_j x_{ij} = 1 \qquad \forall\, i=1,2,\ldots,n \qquad (2)$$

$$\sum_i x_{ij} = 1 \qquad \forall\, j=1,2,\ldots,n \qquad (3)$$

$$x_{ij} = 0 \text{ or } 1 \qquad \forall\, i,j=1,2,\ldots,n \qquad (4)$$

$$\sum_{i=1}^{k-1} x_{j_i j_{i+1}} + x_{j_k j_1} \le k-1 \qquad \text{for } k=1,2,\ldots,\tfrac{n}{2} \qquad (5)$$

and all $\binom{n}{k}\cdot k!$ possible sequences each.

The model (1) - (4) represents the linear assignment problem (section 4.3) with 2·n constraints one of which is redundant (due to linear dependence). Difficulties arise from eq.(5), firstly because it spoils the property of unimodularity and secondly because of the number of constraints. E.g. for n=15 elements the number of the constraints of this type reaches 36,432,075.

If one does however want to apply integer programming methods to this model, he can start with (1) - (4) and add only those constraints of type (5) which exclude the cycles of the solution to (1) to (4). This can be iteratively repeated until a solution without cycles is yielded. The early approach of Dantzig, Fulkerson and Johnson (6), (7) to the traveling salesman problem is similar to this iterative procedure.

A completely <u>different integer programming model</u> can be put up if subsequences of the elements are defined and a selection of these subsequences are to be put together to one complete route. However, the construction of the subsequences is not without arbitrariness. Therefore, this model is to some extent heuristic. Models of this type look like:

$$y_k = \begin{cases} 1, & \text{if the k-th subsequence is chosen} \\ 0, & \text{otherwise} \end{cases}$$

c_k = costs of the subsequence

$$a_{ik} = \begin{cases} 1, & \text{if element } i \text{ is an interior element of subsequence } k \\ 0.5, & \text{if element } i \text{ represents an end of subsequence } k \\ 0, & \text{otherwise} \end{cases}$$

Minimize (or maximize, respectively)

$$\sum_k c_k y_k \qquad (6)$$

$$\text{s.t.} \quad \sum_k a_{ik} y_k = 1 \qquad \forall\ i=1,2,\ldots,n \qquad (7)$$

$$y_k = 0 \text{ or } 1 \qquad \forall\ k=1,2,\ldots,K \qquad (8)$$

Further constraints which exclude cycles (9)

The approach (6) - (9) may have the advantage over (1) - (5) that in many cases it is much smaller (in terms of variables as well as in terms of constraints). This, however, depends very much upon the structure of the individual problem and upon the skill of selecting the subsequences. This selection is done by inspection and, therefore, does not even guarantee the optimal solution. For this reason, this model is only suggested for those problems where the costs can be well represented by a map.

As in the case of the traveling salesman problem all vicinal sequencing problems can be modeled in integer programming at least in two ways. One way is to let the variables represent the fact whether the element j follows immediately after the element i or not. In the second type of model, subsequences are defined a combination of which is seeked. In both cases, however, only small problems can be solved by means of integer programming methods.

4.2 Integer programming models of selection problems

It was seen that the integer programming models of the sequencing problems suffer from the many cycle constraints. In contrary to them, the models of selection problems tend to keep within moderate sizes.

Three standard selection problems shall be mentioned here, the knapsack problem, the matching problem, and the covering problem.

The knapsack problem consists of one objective and one constraint, as follows:

$$\text{Maximize} \quad \sum_j c_j x_j \qquad (10)$$

$$\text{s.t.} \quad \sum_j a_j x_j \le b \qquad (11)$$

$$x_j = 0 \text{ or } 1 \quad \forall\ j=1,2,\ldots,n \qquad (12)$$

This problem represents situations where one resource is limited (b) and each of the single choices $j=1,2,\ldots,n$ requires a_j units of the resource and spends a benefit of c_j.

Today, knapsack problems can be solved efficiently up to sizes of 1000 or more variables. Algorithms were suggested by Kolesar (20), Greenberg and Hegerich (13), Ingargiola and Korsh (18), Müller-Merbach (25), and Gerhardt (11).

The second standard selection problem is the matching problem. Its integer programming representation looks as follows:

$$\text{Maximize} \quad \sum_j c_j x_j \tag{13}$$

$$\text{s.t.} \quad \sum_j a_{ij} x_j \leq 1 \qquad \forall\ i=1,2,\ldots,m \tag{14}$$

$$x_j = 0 \text{ or } 1 \qquad \forall\ j=1,2,\ldots,n \tag{15}$$

with $a_{ij} = 0$ or 1.

Related to the matching problem is the covering problem. Its integer programming representation looks as follows:

$$\text{Minimize} \quad \sum_j c_j x_j \tag{16}$$

$$\text{s.t.} \quad \sum_j a_{ij} x_j \geq 1 \qquad \forall\ i=1,2,\ldots,m \tag{17}$$

$$x_j = 0 \text{ or } 1 \qquad \forall\ j=1,2,\ldots,n \tag{18}$$

with $a_{ij} = 0$ or 1.

Although there are not many real-life problems which immediately have the structure of the matching or the covering problem, many problems can be formulated in similar models. For example, the model (6) - (9) has a very similar shape. It can be considered as a combination of a matching problem and a covering problem.

Since matching and covering problems will be discussed in this Advanced Study Institute in great detail by Balas and Edmonds, they shall not be considered here any further. But since there exist many problems with a similar structure to these standard problems it is emphasized that everybody who is involved in combinatorial problems has to be familiar with the state of the art of the solution techniques for these problems.

4.3 Integer programming models of assignment problems

As the third group of combinatorial problems, assignment problems and their integer programming representations shall be discussed now. In particular, the linear and quadratic assignment problems will be considered.

The typical questions of assignment problems is to assign elements of one set individually to elements of another set.

In the linear case the assignment of the element i of set 1 to the element j of set 2 causes the costs c_{ij}, independently from all the other assignments. The well-known problem can be formulated in a model which is identical with the model (1) - (4), i.e. with the first four types of equations of the traveling salesman problem, where $x_{ij} = 1$, if element i of set 1 is assigned to element j of set 2, and $x_{ij} = 0$, otherwise.

Due to unimodularity, this problem can be solved very easily by means of linear programming or - even more efficiently - by means of network flow algorithms, see e.g. Ford, Fulkerson (9).

The linear assignment problem is not only closely related to the traveling salesman problem, as stated in section 4.1. It is also closely related to the "simple matching problem" which is a matching problem with only two $a_{ij} = 1$ in each column j, see Müller-Merbach (27). The simple matching problem can be transformed into the linear assignment problem simply by "symmetrical complementation", where in addition the constraint $x_{ij} = x_{ji}$ must hold for all i and j.

The relationship of a problem to the linear assignment problem can be used successfully in any tree-search method.

Much more difficult to solve than the linear assignment problem is the quadratic assignment problem. It differs from the latter only by the objective function which is quadratic of the form, see e.g. Lawler (22) and Müller-Merbach (26):

Minimize (or maximize, respectively)

$$\sum_i \sum_j \sum_k \sum_l c_{ik} f_{jl} x_{ij} x_{kl} \qquad (19)$$

This type of problem will be discussed by Lawler in the course of this Advanced Study Institute. Therefore, it shall not be discussed in great detail here. However, one different approach by Beale and Tomlin (1) shall be mentioned here. They define the variables x_{ijkl} which are taken as 1 if i is located at j and k is located at 1. In their actual problem the number of variables was kept low since many assignments of facilities to locations needed not be considered.

4.4 Conclusions

As conclusions from the section 4.1 - 4.3, the following statements shall be made:

(i) Sequencing problems frequently tend to require a great number of constraints to exclude cycles. This may make it advisable to apply integer programming methods iteratively (if at all integer programming methods are applied) in that one starts with no cycle conditions, computes a solution, inserts those conditions which exclude the present cycles, and starts again etc.

(ii) Many combinatorial problems are related to (or can be formulated as) selection problems the most common standard problems of which are the knapsack problem, the matching problem, and the covering problem. The experience from the state of the art regarding the standard problems can be used to develop specific methods for solving actual problems.

(iii) The linear assignment problem (as well as other problems with the property of unimodularity) is related to many difficult combinatorial problems and can be solved easily. This property can be taken advantage of in constructing special algorithms.

(iv) Most real-life problems can be formulated in more than one integer programming model which was shown by means of the traveling salesman problem and the quadratic assignment problem.

(v) Even if the integer programming model is too large or ill-structured so that integer programming methods cannot efficiently be applied to them, the advantage of these models is that the problemsolver gets insight into the structure of the model and perhaps finds relations or similarities to standard problems which may put him on the right track to develop an individual algorithm on the basis of existing algorithms for these standard problems.

5. EXPLICIT ENUMERATION

Independently from any integer programming model, it can be tried to solve combinatorial problems by explicit enumeration. Even though explicit enumeration is not at all a sophisticated approach, it can be the most efficient approach to a problem. The advantage of explicit enumeration over integer programming models, tree-searching etc. is the simplicity of the method. On the other hand, explicit enumeration has its limitations in the number of steps which are required to search for all solutions. Therefore, the number of steps has to be estimated before a decision is made whether explicit enumeration is an appropriate method or not.

Although the number of solutions and the number of steps of enumeration have to be estimated for each individual type of problem, there exist some general formulas for sequencing problems, selection problems, and assignment problems.

If in a sequencing problem a (due to the objective) particular order of n elements is seeked and if each order is permitted, then there exist n! different sequences. To enumerate the n! sequences, approximately e·n! (with e=2,71828...) steps of enumeration are necessary, see Müller-Merbach (26), p.7-9. The numbers of solutions and steps can be smaller in cases where certain subsequences are not permitted. The numbers can be larger if the single elements are sets of subelements.

Similar as for sequencing problems are the numbers for assignment problems. If n elements of one set have to be individually assigned to n elements of another set and if all the elements differ from each other, then the number of solutions is n! while the number of steps again is approximately e·n!. The numbers are smaller in cases where the single elements of the first set are not allowed to be assigned to every element of the other set.

Much smaller are the corresponding numbers for enumerating selection problems. If a specific number of m elements have to be chosen out of n elements (with $m<n$) then only $\binom{n}{m}$ solutions have to be enumerated. The number of steps is not larger than $m\cdot\binom{n}{m}$. If, however, the number of selected elements is not specified, the number of solutions is 2^n, as is the number of steps.

If one considers 10^7 steps of enumeration as the limitation to solve a problem by explicit enumeration, then sequencing problems and assignment problems of the size of not more than n=10 elements can be solved by enumeration, since there exist n!=3,628,800 solutions, and the number of steps is 9,864,100. But selection problems of even n=23 elements can be solved by enumeration, since 2^{23}=8,388,608. The selection problems can be even larger if the number m of selected elements is defined before. For instance, for the selection of m=5 elements out of n=50 elements, there exist $\binom{50}{5}$=2,118,760 solutions while the number of steps will be close to 10^7.

If the sizes of the problems increase further, then the amount of computation for carrying out the explicit enumeration process tends to explode. Therefore, switching to implicit enumeration is necessary.

6. TREE SEARCH (BRANCH AND BOUND) METHODS, IMPLICIT ENUMERATION

6.1. General requirement

Implicit enumeration (also called tree-searching, branch and bound etc.) differs from explicit enumeration in that a branch of the enumeration tree is not considered any further as soon as it is recognized that it does not include the optimal solution. The difficulty in developing implicit enumeration methods for specific problems arises from the necessity that a tremendously large percentage of the branches have to be cut off.

For instance, a sequencing problem with n=20 elements may have 20! or roughly $2.4 \cdot 10^{18}$ solutions. Their enumeration might require roughly $6.5 \cdot 10^{18}$ steps. Even if implicit enumeration succeeds to cut off 99.999999 percent of the branches, there remain roughly $6.5 \cdot 10^{10}$ branches which is much too large a number to be computed within a reasonable amount of time. And if for instance a selection problem with n=100 elements is to be solved, at least 99.99999999999999999999 percent of the 2^{100} or roughly $1.3 \cdot 10^{30}$ possible solutions have to be cut off by the implicit enumeration process such that not more than 10^7 solutions have to be explicitly computed.

It is surprising that in spite of such tremendous requirements even larger problems can be solved efficiently by implicit enumeration approaches. For instance, random number traveling salesman problems with up to n=40 cities did not require more than 4 minutes on an IBM 7040, see Müller-Merbach (26), p.133 f; the number of nodes did not exeed 375 (in 35 examples) while the number of different solutions is 40! or roughly 10^{48}. "Geographic" traveling salesman problems are much harder to solve; however, Held and Karp (16), (17) report very reasonable computation times for geographic traveling salesman problems (with sparse distance matrices) of even larger sizes. It is also surprising that, for instance, knapsack problems with n=1000 and even more variables were efficiently solved by tree-searching, even if the number of potential solutions is in the order of 2^{1000} or roughly 10^{301}.

On the other hand, there are combinatorial problems for which implicit enumeration is not able to yield solutions within a reasonable computation time, even if the size of the problem is small. This is partly due to the general structure of a problem type, and partly to the special structure of a specific problem. For instance, implicit enumeration could not as yet successfully be applied to quadratic assignment problems with more than some n=10 different elements of either set. And there exist ill-conditioned knapsack problems with only some n=50 variables the solution of which by implicit enumeration causes computational problems; this is particularly so if the ratios c_j/a_j (see eq.(10) and (11)) are within a very small range.

Since the efficiency of implicit enumeration differs from one type of combinatorial problem to another and even from one problem of a specific type to another problem, it is very important to have a morphological scheme of implicit enumeration in mind when such a method is to be developed for a certain type of problem or even for a specific problem of a certain type. Such a scheme will be outlined in section 6.2.

6.2 Morphological scheme of tree-search methods

Implicit enumeration or tree-search methods can be divided into the three commonly known groups (i) dynamic programming which is characterized by a parallel organization of the enumeration tree; (ii) bounded enumeration (also called branch and reject, branch and exclude etc.) with a sequential organization of the enumerative process; and (iii) branch and bound which, in general, continues from the "champion" node of the tree (see also section 3.5). These types of organization are mentioned in line 1 of the morphological box of table 1.

The following paragraphs refer to line 2 - 15 of table 1.

Line 2: Tree-search methods can also be divided according to the general branching principle. "Force" means that each branch represents a variable or an element etc. which is forced into a solution; e.g. cities can be forced into a sequence while solving the traveling salesman problem. "Exclude" means that each branch corresponds with an exclusion of a variable or an element from a solution; e.g. loops of cities can be broken up by excluding certain connections while solving a traveling salesman problem, see Eastman (8), Bellmore and Nemhauser (4), Müller-Merbach (26) pp. 112-117, (25). "Force and exclude" characterizes those trees where one branch forces a certain element into the solution while the opposite branch excludes that very element; e.g. this is realised by Little et al. (24) for the traveling salesman problem. "Force or exclude" finally means that each branch may either correspond with a variable which is forced into the solution or with a variable which is excluded from the solution. In integer programming for example, the algorithm by Land and Doig (21) uses the "force" principle while the algorithm of Dakin (5) is based on the "exclude" principle.

Line 3: Implicit enumeration methods also differ from each other by the number of branches which leave from each node. The

1	General organization of enum.tree	parallel (Dynamic Progr.)	sequential (Bounded Enum.)	"Continue from the Champ" (Branch & Bound)				
2	General branching principle	force	exclude	force & exclude	force or exclude			
3	Number of branches from each node	h=2	h>2; (fixed h)	h=f(stage) (Dyn.Progr.)	open, flexible			
4	Branch on	single variables	combinations of variables					
5	Sets represented by nodes are	disjunct	non-disjunct; no memory	non-disjunct; plus memory				
6	Branching strategy	small sets vs. large sets	good sols. vs. poor sols.	small+ good vs. large+ poor	fixed order	critical variable	random	formal criterion
7	Objective	Maximum	Minimum	Minimal infeasibility				
8	Bounds	simple	look ahead					
9	Computation of bounds by relaxation of	non-negativity	constraints a,b,c,...	integer condition	objective	completeness		
10	Comparison of	bounds with best sol.so far (Bounded Enum.)	bounds of every active node (Branch&Bound)	bounds of comparable states (Dyn.Progr.)				
11	Stop	at last node (Dyn.Progr.)	at end (Bounded Enum.)	when a sol. of a subset is known which dominates each active node (Branch&Bound)				
12	Branching subject	city	loop/cycle	etc., due to type of problem				
13	Heuristic methods	no	once, before start	repeatedly				
14	Use of heuristic methods	reject non-optimal solutions	aid for branching strategy					
15	General philosophy	sets of unknown sols. (B & B)	partial sols. (Bounded Enum.)	states at stages (Dyn.Progr.)				

Table 1: Morphological box of tree-search methods (implicit enumeration)

Dakin-algorithm (5) for integer programming and the Little et al. algorithm (24) for the traveling salesman problem are examples for binary enumeration trees with exactly <u>h=2</u> branches from each node. It is also possible to develop enumeration trees with a <u>fixed number h>2</u> of branches from each node. In many dynamic programming algorithms the number h of branches from the single nodes are defined by the <u>stage</u> of the solution process, e.g. in the traveling salesman problem, see Bellman (2) and Held and Karp (14), (15) and others. The same holds for bounded enumeration approaches to many problems. Very often the number of branches from the single nodes is <u>not defined beforehand</u> and is due to the solution process; e.g. this holds for the Land and Doig algorithm (21) for integer programming.

<u>Line 4</u>: Usually implicit enumeration methods enumerate on <u>single variables</u> or <u>single elements</u> etc. In many cases, however, it is also possible to enumerate on <u>combinations of variables</u>, e.g. force and exclude subsequences of cities while solving a traveling salesman problem or force and exclude subsets of variables in integer programming problems.

<u>Line 5</u>: Usually, enumeration trees are organized in such a way that the parallel nodes represent <u>disjunct subsets</u> of solutions; see the Land and Doig approach (21) and the Dakin approach (5) to integer programming, the Little et al. approach (24) to the traveling salesman problem, the Kolesar approach (20)to the knapsack problem etc. It can be advantageous though to work with nodes of <u>non-disjunct subsets</u> of solutions; in this case a <u>special memory</u> may or may not be developed which is to prevent from computing any solution twice.

<u>Line 6</u>: Of particular importance for the efficiency of tree-searching is the <u>branching strategy</u>. One may try to split a subset of a <u>few</u> solutions from a subset of <u>many</u> solutions. One may also define a strategy which separates a set of <u>good</u> solutions from a set of <u>poor</u> solutions. It may be even more worthwhile to separate a <u>small</u> set of <u>good</u> solutions from a <u>large</u> set of <u>poor</u> solutions; e.g. the Little et al. algorithm (24) tends to work in this direction. Simply to branch according to a <u>fixed order</u> of the elements is another possibility; the Kolesar algorithm (20) for the knapsack problem is an example. In some problems it is possible to branch on a "<u>critical variable</u>"; this procedure is followed by Greenberg and Hegerich (13) for the knapsack problem. A <u>random choice</u> is another branching strategy which should only be applied if no arguments for any goal-oriented strategy can be found. Finally, many algorithms are using "<u>formal criteria</u>" as e.g. in dynamic programming.

<u>Line 7</u>: As far as an <u>objective</u> is concerned, <u>maximization</u> and <u>minimization</u> problems can be distinguished. In addition, there are

problems where only a <u>feasible solution</u> or a solution with <u>minimal infeasibility</u> is seeked.

<u>Line 8</u>: In most implicit enumeration processes, <u>bounds</u> are computed for the subsets of solutions which are represented by the nodes. These bounds can be "<u>simple</u>" in that only the obvious costs etc. are summed up; this is typically done in dynamic programming; see e.g.Bellman's approach (2) to the traveling salesman problem. Branch and bound procedures and bounded enumeration procedures usually work with advanced <u>look ahead rules</u> which try to yield bounds as high as possible (in minimization problems, or as low as possible in maximization problems, respectively).

<u>Line 9</u>: The <u>look ahead rules</u> generally consist of the <u>solution of auxiliary problems</u> which are closely related to the real problem which has to be solved. The auxiliary problems are derived from the real problem by <u>relaxing</u> components or conditions of the real problem. The auxiliary problems have to have such a structure that they can be solved within a very short computation time. E.g. the <u>non-negativity</u> conditions can be relaxed. It is also possible to relax <u>constraints</u> of any type; it is e.g. commonly known that the relaxation of the cycle conditions, see eq.(5), of the traveling salesman problem leads to the easily solvable linear assignment problem; furthermore, Held and Karp (16), (17) have shown that the traveling salesman problem is also closely related to the spanning 1-tree, which is also based on a relaxation of constraints In integer programming problems it is common to relax the <u>integer conditions</u>; this is particularly easy and efficient to carry out for the knapsack problem, see e.g. Kolesar (20) as well as Greenberg and Hegerich (13). It is also a possibility to relax or to modify the <u>objective</u> function; this is e.g. done in several approaches to the fixed charge problem, see the survey by Gallus (10). Finally the requirements of completeness of the variables or elements can be given up which e.g. is usually done in dynamic programming (except for the final state).

<u>Line 10</u>: Once the <u>bounds</u> are computed, they can be used for comparison in different ways. In <u>bounded enumeration</u> the bounds are being compared with the <u>best solution</u> found so far. In <u>branch and bound</u> processes a comparison is made between all the active nodes; "active" means that no or at least not all branches were drawn from the node. In <u>dynamic programming</u> the bounds of <u>comparable states</u> (at the same stage) are compared; "comparable" means here that e.g. two sequences lead from the same start to the same destination via the same set of intermediate elements.

<u>Line 11</u>: Following from line 10, the <u>stop rules</u> depend also upon the general organization of the enumeration tree. <u>Dynamic programming</u> processes stop at the <u>final node</u> which is the best state at the final stage. <u>Bounded enumeration</u> processes terminate

when no further bound can be found which dominates the best solution so far. Branch and bound processes terminate when a solution of a subset is explicitly known the value of which is not less (in maximization problems, or not greater in minimization problems, respectively) than any bound of the active nodes.

Line 12: Due to the type of problem, different branching subjects can be chosen. In traveling salesman problems, for example, the branching subjects can be the single cities as in the Little et al. approach (24) or can be the loops or cycles of cities which are to be broken as in the Eastman approach (8) and the Müller-Merbach approach (25), (26) pp. 112-117; again different is the branching subject of the Held and Karp approach (16), (17). In the traveling salesman problem the different branching subjects lead to tremendous differences of the computation times.In many other problems there exists also a choice between different branching subjects.

Line 13: It is possible to combine heuristic methods with tree-search methods. Heuristic methods can be applied once to the problem before the enumeration process starts. They can also be repeatedly applied during the enumeration process.

Line 14: The results of the heuristic methods can as well be used to reject non-optimal solutions (as preferably done in bounded enumeration) or be used as an aid for carrying out the branching strategy (line 6).

Line 15: Finally, the general philosophy of the three basic groups of tree-search methods shall be outlined. Branch and bound processes are based on the picture of a set of all the (unknown) solutions which is divided into subsets as long until the optimal solution according to line 11 is found. In contrary, bounded enumeration is derived from complete enumeration and builds up the single solutions step by step starting from scratch via partial solutions to complete solutions. Finally, dynamic programming is based upon stages (levels) each of which may have several states. The states correspond to some extent to the partial solution of bounded enumeration.

As the content of the morphological box of table 1 is explained as yet, the use of it shall be briefly mentioned. As each morphological box, see Zwicky (32), also this box shall serve the purpose of (i) showing implicitly the whole range of possibilities (here of assembling a tree-search algorithm for any combinatorial problem) and (ii) being a checklist for the development of tree-search algorithms for specific problems.

It should be emphasized that the effective use of the morphological box requires a great deal of knowledge and experience with special tree-search methods for a variety of problems. The morphological box is more or less worthless without this knowledge and experience. On the other hand, knowledge and experience from special problems do not guarantee the ability of developing efficient methods for new combinatorial problems; the morphological box shall serve the purpose of enlarging this ability. The use of the morphological box as some sort of checklist contributes to the probability that good methods are developed right in the beginning.

That the more or less random-dependent development of tree-search methods for specific problems may result in time lags of many years can be shown by many examples, e.g. the traveling salesman problem, see Dantzig, Fulkerson, Johnson (6), (7), Bellman (2), Gonzales (12), Held and Karp (14), (15), Little et al. (24), Eastman (8), Müller-Merbach (26) pp. 112-117, Lawler and Wood (22), Bellmore and Nemhauser (4), and Held and Karp (16), (17). Another example is the knapsack problem, see Bellman and Dreyfus (3), Gerhardt (11), Kolesar (20), Müller-Merbach (25), Greenberg and Hegerich (13), and Ingargiola and Korsh (18).

As mentioned in section 6.1, by far not every combinatorial problem can be solved by implicit enumeration. The enumeration tree for these problems becomes too large, i.e. the number of nodes exceed 10^7 by far. In these cases, there exist no methods which guarantee the optimal solution. On the other hand, in most cases heuristic methods (approximation methods) can be developed which are able to yield good, but not necessarily optimal solutions. A morphological scheme of heuristic methods will be given in section 7.

7. HEURISTIC METHODS

7.1 General requirements

Heuristic methods can be considered as incomplete enumeration methods in that single branches of the enumeration tree are cut off even if it is not sure that they do not contain the optimal solution.

Good heuristic methods should have the following three properties: (i) They should yield solutions within a reasonable amount of computation time. (ii) The solutions should be close to the optimum, in the average. (iii) The probability of single solutions which are far below the optimum should be small. The conditions (ii) and (iii) are not identical (although related) since good average solutions do not exclude the possibility of poor solutions in certain instances. How good these requirements are met by a certain heuristic method can in general only be judged after numerical tests. There are, however, different types of heuristic methods which can well be distinguished from each other and which have characteristic properties. The knowledge of these basic types is important for the development of heuristic methods for any problem.

7.2 Morphological scheme of heuristic methods

The discussion of the single types of heuristic methods is based upon the morphological scheme given in table 2. Similar schemes were suggested by the author in three other papers and explained by means of the traveling salesman problem in (28), a resource scheduling problem in (29), and the knapsack problem in (30).

First Feasible Solution (FFS)	Decreasing Degrees of Freedom (DDF), using Priority Rules (PR)	Decreasing Degrees of Freedom (DDF), using Look Ahead Rules (LAR)	Increasing Degrees of Freedom (IDF)
Iteratively Improved Solution (IIS)	Eager But Tedious (EBT)	Reflected and Skillful Seeking (RSS)	

Table 2: Morphological scheme of heuristic methods

On a first level, heuristic methods can be divided in those yielding a first feasible solution (FFS-methods) and those which - hopefully - improve a given solution iteratively (IIS-methods).

If one starts to develop FFS-methods for a certain problem, he will in most cases begin to search for priority rules (PR-methods). One example is the "nearest neighbour" rule for the traveling salesman problem; it starts from any city, goes to the nearest neighbour, from here to its nearest neighbour etc. A PR-method for the knapsack problem would be to select the variables in the order of decreasing ratios c_j/a_j, see eq.(10) and (11). Most of the simple job shop scheduling methods like "shortest operation", "earliest date of completion", "greatest value" etc. are also PR-methods.

The general disadvantage of the PR-methods is due to the fact that the criterion of selection is short-sighted. From this it follows immediately that look ahead rules (LAR-methods) would do much better. LAR-methods are based on the question: "What are the minimal cost (profit or any other optimization criterion) consequences that follow from the selection of a certain variable or element etc.?" To answer this question, relaxed problems (compare line 9 of table 1) can be solved. For instance, if the cost consequences of the connection i-j on the solution of the traveling salesman problem are asked for, the corresponding assignment problem can be solved after row i and column j (except for i-j), and (to prevent loops) the element j-i have been erased from the cost matrix. Similarly, the selection of a variable x_j of a knapsack problem would be accompanied by solving the remaining problem under relaxation of the integer condition.

Both, the PR-method and the LAR-method are characterized by decreasing degrees of freedom. This means that the number of choices decreases with the continuation of the solution process. For instance, the solution of a traveling salesman problem with n cities starts with (n-1) choices, then continues with (n-2) choices,..., and terminates with steps of 3 choices, 2 choices, and finally only one choice. Similarly, the solution of a knapsack problem starts with the selection of 1 out of n variables, then 1 out of (n-1) variables etc.

Therefore, both, the PR-method and the LAR-method, will be called DDF-methods (with DDF = Decreasing Degrees of Freedom).

The poorer the selection rule of a DDF-method is the greater is the danger of extremely poor selections at the final steps of the method. This leads to the following suggestions: (i) Either try to replace simple PR-methods by advanced LAR-methods, or (ii) try to replace DDF-methods by IDF-methods (with IDF = Increasing Degrees of Freedom).

IDF-methods are characterized by increasing degrees of freedom during the procedure of the method. This sounds difficult, but it is doubted that any combinatorial problem exists for which not an IDF-method can be developed. For instance, an IDF-method for the traveling salesman problem can start from a loop of two cities and fit in a third city at the best of the two possibilities. Then a fourth city will be inserted at the best of the three positions etc. Finally there will be (n-1) different positions for the n-th city. Numerical experience with this method tells that IDF-methods yield much better routes than a simple PR-method, see Müller-Merbach (26) pp. 125 ff.

For many combinatorial problems it is possible to develop several different PR-methods, LAR-methods, and IDF-methods. As long as they work quickly, it is recommended to use several of them in parallel and to choose the best solution provided by them.

In addition, many FFS-methods allow to begin at different starting points (e.g. cities). In this case it is recommended to apply the most efficient FFS-methods repeatedly, each time with another starting point.

Yet, the first feasible solutions may not meet the requirements. Therefore, it can be tried to improve a solution iteratively. These heuristic methods are called IIS-methods. Two groups of them shall be distinguished, namely the EBT-methods (with EBT= Eager But Tedious) and the RSS-methods (with RSS = Reflected and Skillful Seeking).

EBT-methods work with standard modification schemes which are applied to every part of a solution. For instance, a solution of a traveling salesman problem can be modified by taking one city out of the sequence and place it alternatively at any of the other (n-1) positions. Since this can be carried out for each of the n cities, the total of $n \cdot (n-1)$ different solutions has to be considered. Although each solution itself does not require much computation time, the total number of solutions is quite large. And if an EBT-method starts with a good first feasible solution, the percentage of the improved solutions among the computed solutions will be very low. Therefore, it tends to be a waste of time to compute that many solutions.

Rather, it should be tried to find criteria which can be used to recognize in advance those modifications which are likely to improve a solution and those which can certainly not cause an improvement. Although the accomplishment of such criteria requires computation time, the number of alternative solutions can often remarkably be reduced. The solution of a traveling salesman problem can e.g. be used for a reduction of the cost matrix in that constants are subtracted from the rows and columns such that the c_{ij} corresponding to the $x_{ij}=1$ become zero. Now it is obvious that the $c_{ij} \geq 0$ would not yield improvements while the $c_{ij} < 0$ may do so. Therefore, one need to consider only the negative reduced cost elements. This is done in the two RSS-methods called three-item-exchange and four-item-exchange, see Müller-Merbach (26) pp. 77 ff and 125 ff, (28).

It was found by the author that the morphological scheme of table 2 was extremely helpful when heuristic methods had to be developed for any combinatorial problem. The application of table 2 as some sort of checklist leads to much broader and more flexible heuristic concepts than the one-method-approaches which are found in the literature so frequently.

8. CONCLUSIONS

Three conclusions shall bring this paper to its end.

(i) The number of different combinatorial problems is very large. Each type requires its own tailor-made method. In order to develop such methods for solving specific combinatorial problems,

(ii) a broad knowledge and experience from as many as possible different combinatorial problems (including the standard problems) as well as

(iii) a morphological view of the methods are required.

In this paper, only very few standard combinatorial problems could be mentioned, due to the limited space. Therefore, many important publications were not quoted here, e.g. on zero-one-programming (Balas, Burdet, Glover, Hammer, Korte, Spielberg etc.), on vehicle scheduling (Clark and Wright), on assembly line balancing (Salveson, Helgeson and Bernie, Klein, Mertens etc.), on job shop scheduling(S.M. Johnson, Conway, Maxwell and B.M. Johnson, Eilon, Mitten, Story and Wagner, Hoss, Ignall and Schrage, Lomnicki, Manne, and many others) etc.

REFERENCES

1. E.M. Beale, J.A. Tomlin, An Integer Programming Approach to a Class of Combinatorial Problems, Mathematical Programming (3), 3 (1972), pp. 339-344.
2. R.E. Bellman, Dynamic Programming Treatment of the Traveling Salesman Problem, J. ACM (1), 9 (1962), pp. 61-63.
3. R.E. Bellman, S.E. Dreyfus, Applied Dynamic Programming, Princeton University Press, Princeton, 1962.
4. M. Bellmore, G.L. Nemhauser, The Traveling Salesman Problem: A Survey, Opns. Res. (3), 16 (1968), pp.538-558.
5. R.J. Dakin, A Tree-Search Algorithm for Mixed Integer Programming Problems, Comput. J. (3), 8 (1963), pp. 250-255.
6. G.B. Dantzig, D.R. Fulkerson, S.M. Johnson, Solution of a Large-Scale Traveling-Salesman Problem, Opns. Res. (4) 2 (1954), pp. 393-410.
7. G.B. Dantzig, D.R. Fulkerson, S.M. Johnson, On a Linear-Programming, Combinatorial Approach to the Traveling-Salesman Problem, Opns. Res. (1), 7 (1959), pp. 58-66.
8. W.L. Eastman, Linear Programming with Pattern Constraints (Diss.), Harvard University, Cambridge, 1958.
9. L.R. Ford, D.R. Fulkerson, Flows in Networks, Princeton University Press,Princeton, 1962.
10. G. Gallus, Die Erweiterung linearer Optimierungsmodelle um fixe Grundkosten (Diss.), Darmstadt, 1974.
11. C. Gerhardt, Gedanken zur Lösung des Knapsack-Problems, Ablauf- und Planungsforschung (2), 11 (1970), pp. 69-83.
12. R.H. Gonzales, Solution of the Traveling Salesman Problem by Dynamic Programming on the Hypercube, Interim Technical Report No. 18, OR Center, MIT, Cambridge, 1962.
13. H. Greenberg, R.L. Hegerich, A Branch Search Algorithm for the Knapsack Problem, Mgmt. Sci. (5), 16 (1970), pp. 327-332.

14. M. Held, R.M. Karp, A Dynamic Programming Approach to Sequencing Problems, SIAM J. Appl. Math. (1), 10 (1962), pp. 196-210.
15. M. Held, R.M. Karp, The Construction of Discrete Dynamic Programming Algorithms, IBM Systems J. (2), 4 (1965),pp. 136-147.
16. M. Held, R.M. Karp, The Traveling-Salesman Problem and Minimum Spanning Trees, Opns. Res. (6), 18 (1970), pp. 1138-1162.
17. M. Held, R.M. Karp, The Traveling-Salesman Problem and Minimum Spanning Trees: Part II, Math. Prog. (1), 1 (1971), pp. 6-25.
18. G.P. Ingargiola, J.F. Korsh, A Reduction Algorithm for the Zero-One Knapsack Problems, Mgmt. Sci. (4), 20 (1973), pp. 460-463.
19. G. Jaeschke, Vicinal Sequencing Problems, Opns. Res. (5), 20 (1972), pp. 984-992.
20. P. Kolesar, A Branch and Bound Algorithm for the Knapsack Problem, Mgmt. Sci. (9), 13 (1967), pp. 723-735.
21. A.H. Land, A.G. Doig, An Automatic Method of Solving Discrete Programming Problems, Econometrica (3), 28 (1960), pp. 497-520.
22. E.L. Lawler, The Quadratic Assignment Problem, Mgmt. Sci. (6), 9 (1963), pp. 586-599.
23. E.L. Lawler, D.E. Wood, Branch and Bound Methods: A Survey, Opns. Res. (4), 14 (1966), pp. 699-719.
24. J.D.C. Little, K.G. Murty, D.W. Sweeney, C. Karel, An Algorithm for the Traveling Salesman Problem, Opns. Res. (12), 11 (1963), pp. 972-989.
25. H. Müller-Merbach, Operations Research, Vahlen-Verlag, Berlin 1969, 3rd ed., Munich 1973.
26. H. Müller-Merbach, Optimale Reihenfolgen, Springer-Verlag, Berlin/Heidelberg/New York, 1970.
27. H. Müller-Merbach, The Minimal Cost Maximum Matching of a Graph (Supplementary Remarks), Unternehmensforschung (3), 15 (1971), pp. 211-213.
28. H. Müllèr-Merbach, Heuristic Methods: Structures, Applications, Computational Experience, Optimization Methods for Resource Allocation (ed. R. Cottle, J. Krarup), English Universities Press, London, 1974, pp. 401-416.
29. H. Müller-Merbach, Heuristische Verfahren, Management Enzyklopädie (Ergänzungsband), Verlag Moderne Industrie, München, 1973, pp. 346-355.
30. H. Müller-Merbach, Heuristische Verfahren und Entscheidungsbaumverfahren des Operations Research, Handwörterbuch der Betriebswirtschaft (4th ed.; ed. E. Grochla, W. Wittmann), Poeschel Verlag, Stuttgart, 1974, to appear.
31. P.Williams, Experiments in the Formulation of Integer Programming Problems, Mathematical Programming, to appear.
32. F. Zwicky, Discovery, Invention, Research, Mac Millan, New York, 1968.

LES PROCEDURES D'EXPLORATION ET D'OPTIMISATION PAR SEPARATION ET EVALUATION

P. Hansen
Institut d'Economie Scientifique et de Gestion, Lille

I. CLASSIFICATION ET FORME DES TESTS

RESUME. Afin de caractériser les procédures d'exploration et d'optimisation par séparation et évaluation, on pose les cinq questions suivantes: a) quand un ensemble de solutions doit-il être séparé? b) comment les séparations doivent-elles être faites? c) comment les séparations doivent-elles s'enchaîner? d) quelles sont les formes des tests qu'on peut utiliser? e) comment faut-il construire les tests et choisir ceux qui seront appliqués? Afin de répondre, dans ce premier article aux questions a) et d), on présente une classification des tests et on décrit les formes principales que peuvent prendre les tests de chaque classe.

1. INTRODUCTION

Apparues vers 1960, [7][18][25],les procédures d'exploration et d'optimisation par séparation et évaluation (branch-and-bound methods) constituent actuellement un des principaux outils de la programmation combinatoire. Les articles décrivant des procédures particulières se comptent par centaines; par contre, les articles consacrés à la théorie des procédures de séparation sont rares. Les travaux de Bertier et Roy [4][22][23], Balas [2], Mitten [20], Rinnooy Kan [21] et d'autres auteurs [1][11][15][17][19] ont permi de dégager certains concepts fondamentaux, de définir de grandes classes de procédures de séparation et évaluation et d'établir sur une base axiomatique la convergence des procédures appartenant à ces classes. D'au-

B. Roy (ed.), Combinatorial Programming: Methods and Applications, 29–65.

tres aspects des procédures d'exploration et d'optimisation par séparation et évaluation comme, par exemple, la forme des tests utilisés ou le problème de la sélection des tests ne semblent pas encore avoir fait l'objet d'études systématiques.
Etant donné un problème de programmation combinatoire, on peut obtenir à l'aide d'une procédure de séparation et évaluation

α) une solution optimale,
β) toutes les solutions optimales,
γ) une solution proche de l'optimum,
δ) un ensemble de solutions optimales ou proches de l'optimum.

Dans les trois premiers cas on parlera de procédure d'optimisation par séparation et évaluation, exacte (cas α et β) ou approchée (cas γ); dans le quatrième cas on parlera de procédure d'exploration par séparation et évaluation. Les modifications à apporter à une procédure de séparation pour l'adapter à l'une ou l'autre des quatre problématiques α) à γ) sont minimes.
On sait que la résolution d'un problème P_0 à l'aide d'une procédure de séparation et évaluation consiste à séparer séquentiellement l'ensemble I_0 des solutions* de P_0 et à appliquer des tests aux sous-problèmes obtenus par ces séparations. La procédure de résolution peut être représentée sur une arborescence**: l'ensemble I_0 est associé à la racine de cette arborescence et les ensembles de solutions I_1, I_2, ... obtenus en cours de résolution sont associés aux autres sommets; les arcs de l'arborescence relient les sommets associés aux ensembles de solutions séparés aux sommets associés aux ensembles de solutions obtenus par ces séparations.
Afin de caractériser les procédures d'exploration et d'optimisation par séparation et évaluation on pose les cinq questions suivantes:

a) quand un ensemble de solutions doit-il être séparé?
b) comment les séparations doivent-elles être faites?
c) comment les séparations doivent-elles s'enchainer?
d) quelles sont les formes des tests qu'on peut utiliser?
e) comment faut-il construire les tests et choisir ceux qui seront appliqués?

On verra dans la suite de cet article que les concepts d'ensemble de solutions sondable [9], partiellement

---

**La terminologie utilisée lorsqu'il est fait appel à la théorie des graphes est celle de C. Berge [3].
*Plus précisement, l'ensemble des solutions candidates de P_0; cf. ci-dessous.

sondable et faiblement sondable permettent de répondre à la question a). Une classification des tests suivie d'une description des principales formes qu'ils peuvent prendre permettra de répondre en même temps à la question d). L'étude des conditions auxquelles doit satisfaire un principe de séparation [4] et de la convergence des procédures de séparation en parallèle [4], en série [10][24] et en parallèle-série [10][24] permettra de répondre aux questions b) et c) dans un second article. Enfin, l'étude des fonctions d'évaluation [4] et des pénalités [6] apportera des éléments de réponse à la question e) dans un troisième article.

2. CLASSIFICATION DES TESTS

Considérons un problème de programmation combinatoire P_0 à résoudre par une procédure d'optimisation par séparation et évaluation. Un tel problème peut être exprimé, explicitement ou implicitement*, sous la forme d'un programme mathématique, c'est-à-dire d'un problème d'optimisation d'une fonction de plusieurs variables soumise à des contraintes. Ecrivons donc P_0 sous la forme:

$$\mathrm{Min}\{f(X):g_t(X)\geq 0 \quad t=1,2,\ldots,m, X\in \prod_{j=1}^{n} D_j\} \qquad (1)$$

où D_j représente l'ensemble des valeurs admissibles de la variable x_j et $I_0 = \prod_{j=1}^{n} D_j$ l'ensemble des solutions candidates de P_0, c'est-à-dire l'ensemble des vecteurs satisfaisant les contraintes impropres $x_j \in D_j$ pour $j=1,2,\ldots,n$. $f(X)$ et les $g_t(X)$ sont des applications de I_0 dans R. Désignons par F_o l'ensemble des solutions admissibles de P_0, c'est-à-dire l'ensemble des solutions candidates de P_0 satisfaisant les contraintes propres $g_t(X)\geq 0$ pour $t=1,2,\ldots,m$.
A une itération courante de la résolution de P_0 on considèrera un sous-problème P_k obtenu en fixant certaines

---

* Pour certains problèmes, comme par exemple les problèmes de plus court chemin dans les graphes, il n'est pas utile d'introduire explicitement des variables et des contraintes, la formulation devenant dans ce cas très lourde. Pour d'autres problèmes, comme par exemple le problème du voyageur de commerce, les contraintes sont trop nombreuses pour pouvoir être toutes écrites explicitement.

des variables de P_o à des valeurs particulières ou encore en imposant des bornes aux valeurs que ces variables peuvent prendre. Généralement, P_k aura la même forme que P_o. Désignons par I_k l'ensemble des solutions candidates et par F_k l'ensemble des solutions admissibles de P_k. Les tests de la procédure d'optimisation par séparation et évaluation utilisée seront alors appliqués à l'ensemble I_k de solutions candidates de P_k. L'information fournie par un test à une itération courante dépendra de l'ensemble I_k de solutions candidates auquel il est appliqué, du test lui-même, et, dans certains cas, de l'information préalablement obtenue avant ou au cours de la résolution. On dira qu'un ensemble I_k de solutions candidates est <u>sondable</u> (fathomable) [9] si les tests de la procédure de séparation utilisé fournissent à l'itération courante toute l'information requise en ce qui le concerne pour la résolution de P_o. Un ensemble de solutions sondable ne devra plus être séparé. I_k sera sondable si les tests permettent de montrer que

α) une solution admissible particulière $\tilde{X}_k \in F_k$ est une solution optimale de P_k:

$$f(\tilde{X}_k) \leq f(X) \qquad \forall X \in F_k, \tag{2}$$

ou bien,

β) P_k n'a pas de solution admissible:

$$F_k = \emptyset, \tag{3}$$

ou bien,

γ) P_k n'a pas de solution admissible donnant à la fonction économique une valeur inférieure à la valeur f_{opt} de la meilleure solution précédemment obtenue:

$$\nexists\ \tilde{X}_k \in F_k : f(\tilde{X}_k) < f_{opt}. \tag{4}$$

Notons que les deux premiers cas correspondent aux deux cas dans lesquels la résolution d'un programme mathématique en variables continues, par exemple dans le cas linéaire par l'algorithme du simplexe, est terminée; le troisième cas s'ajoute du fait des séparations. Notons aussi que si l'on désire obtenir toutes les solutions optimales de P_o et non une seule d'entre elles, l'inégalité stricte (4) doit être remplacée par une inégalité non stricte.

Les tests d'une première classe, qu'on appelera <u>tests directs</u> ont pour but de montrer qu'un ensemble de solutions candidates I_k est sondable. Aux trois cas α), β) et γ) dans lesquels I_k peut être sondable correspondent respectivement les tests directs de résolution, les tests directs d'admissibilité et les tests directs d'optimalité*. Un test direct de résolution est donc basé sur une condition suffisante pour qu'une solution admissible particulière soit la solution optimale du sous-problème considéré. Un test direct d'admissibilité est basé sur une condition suffisante pour que le sous-problème considéré n'ait pas de solution admissible. Un test direct d'optimalité est basé sur une condition suffisante pour que le sous-problème considéré n'ait pas de solution admissible donnant à la fonction économique une valeur inférieure à celle de la meilleure solution précédemment obtenue. Les conditions suffisantes sur lesquelles les tests directs sont basés ne sont en général pas nécessaires; c'est pourquoi, par exemple, l'ensemble F_k de solutions admissibles d'un sous-problème P_k peut être vide sans que le test direct d'admissibilité utilisé permette de le montrer. Il se pourrait qu'un autre test direct d'admissibilité utilisé à sa place puisse le faire. Lorsqu'un ensemble de solutions candidates n'est pas sondable les tests de la procédure d'optimisation par séparation et évaluation utilisée peuvent fournir une information utile en montrant qu'une partie de cet ensemble I_k est sondable. On dira qu'un ensemble I_k de solutions candidates est partiellement sondable si les tests de la procédure d'optimisation par séparation et évaluation utilisée permettent de montrer qu'une partie de I_k spécifiée par une contrainte d'égalité ou d'inégalité portant sur une seule variable est sondable. On dira qu'une ensemble I_k de solutions candidates est faiblement sondable si les tests de la procédure d'optimisation par séparation et évaluation utilisée permettent de montrer qu'une partie de I_k spécifiée par une contrainte linéaire d'inégalité portant sur plusieurs variables est sondable. Un ensemble de solutions partiellement sondable ou faiblement sondable devra être séparé de manière particulière, en un ensemble de solutions sondable (et qui, en fait, a déjà été sondé) et en un autre ensemble de solutions.

Les tests d'une deuxième classe, qu'on appelera tests conditionnels, ont pour but de montrer qu'un ensemble

---

* Comme l'on remarqué Garfinkel et Nemhauser [8] un test direct d'admissibilité peut être considéré comme un test direct d'optimalițé particulier; la distinction entre ces deux classes de tests est cependant commode, notamment dans l'étude de leur formes.

I_k de solutions candidates èst partiellement sondable. On distinguera des <u>tests conditionnels d'admissibilité</u> et des <u>tests conditionnels d'optimalité</u> selon qu'ils permettent de montrer que la partie de I_k qui est sondable (s'il y en a une) l'est dans le cas β) ou dans le cas γ). Les tests d'une troisième classe, qu'on appelera <u>tests relationnels</u> ont pour but de montrer qu'un ensemble I_k de solutions candidates est faiblement sondable. Comme dans le cas précédent, on distinguera des <u>tests relationnels d'admissibilité</u> et des <u>tests relationnels d'optimalité</u>.
Enfin les tests d'une quatrième classe, qu'on appelera <u>tests auxiliaires</u> ne sont pas utilisés seuls mais en conjonction avec un test direct, conditionnel ou relationnel et ont pour but d'en éviter un usage inutile. Un test auxiliaire est donc basé sur une condition suffisante pour que le test auquel il est associé ne fournisse pas ou probablement pas d'information utile; dans le premier cas on parlera de <u>test auxiliaire déterministe</u> et dans le second de <u>test auxiliaire probabiliste</u>.

3. FORMES DES TESTS

Les concepts de <u>relaxation</u> [10][12] et de <u>minoration</u> [15] d'un programme mathématique sont essentiels dans l'exposé de la forme des tests des procédures d'exploration et d'optimisation par séparation et évaluation. Une relaxation P'_k d'un programme P_k est un programme mathématique ayant la même fonction économique que P et dont l'ensemble de solutions admissibles contient strictement celui de P_k. Si f'(X) désigne la fonction économique et F'_k l'ensemble des solutions admissibles de P'_k on a donc

$$f'(X) = f(X) \quad \forall X \in F_k; \; F_k \subset F'_k. \qquad (5)$$

Une minoration P''_k d'un programme P_k est un programme mathématique ayant les mêmes contraintes et donc le même ensemble de solutions admissibles que P_k et dont la fonction économique prend une valeur inférieure ou égale à celle prise par la fonction économique de P_k pour toute solution admissible. On a donc

$$f''(X) \leq f(X) \quad \forall X \in F_k; \; F_k = F''_k \; . \qquad (6)$$

3.1. Test directs

On peut distinguer trois formes de tests directs de résolution:

$1^{\text{ère}}$ forme:

- Construire une relaxation P'_k du problème P_k considéré.
- Déterminer la solution optimale $\tilde{X}'_k$ de P'_k.
- Si $\tilde{X}'_k \in F_k$ et $f(\tilde{X}'_k) < \tilde{f}_{opt}$, remplacer f_{opt} par $f(\tilde{X}'_k)$ et conserver $\tilde{X}'_k$.

Cette première forme est très fréquemment utilisée.

$2^{\text{ème}}$ forme:

- Construire une minoration P''_k du problème P_k considéré.
- Déterminer la solution optimale $\tilde{X}''_k$ de P''_k.
- Si $f''(\tilde{X}''_k)=f(\tilde{X}''_k)$ et $f(\tilde{X}''_k) < f_{opt}$ remplacer f_{opt} par $f(\tilde{X}''_k)$ et conserver $\tilde{X}''_k$.

Certains sous-problèmes peuvent être résolus sans séparation: dans les tests de résolution de troisième forme, on suppose qu'une condition suffisante pour qu'il en soit ainsi est connue.

$3^{\text{ème}}$ forme:

- Examiner si la condition suffisante pour que P_k puisse être résolu sans séparation est vérifiée.
- Si c'est le cas, déterminer $\tilde{X}_k$.
- Si $f(\tilde{X}_k) < f_{opt}$ remplacer f_{opt} par $f(\tilde{X}_k)$ et conserver $\tilde{X}_k$.

Cette forme peut être utilisée, par exemple, dans une procédure d'optimisation par séparation et évaluation pour déterminer le nombre chromatique d'un graphe [5]; la condition suffisante est que les degrés des sommets restants à colorier soient inférieurs au nombre de couleurs déjà utilisées. Une condition plus forte peut être obtenue en considérant le graphe réduit obtenu en condensant les sommets de même couleur.

On peut distinguer trois formes de test direct d'optimalité:

$1^{\text{ère}}$ forme:

- Construire une relaxation P'_k ou une minoration P''_k du problème P_k considéré.
- Déterminer la valeur $\underline{z}'_k$ ou $\underline{z}''_k$ de la solution optimale de P'_k ou de P''_k.
- Si $\underline{z}'_k$ ou $\underline{z}''_k > f_{opt}$ passer à l'examen du sous-problème suivant.

Cette première forme est très fréquemment utilisé; dans certains tests directs d'optimalité le procédé utilisé pour obtenir un minorant $\underline{z}_k'$ ou $\underline{z}_k''$ des valeurs de $f(X)$ pour $X \in F_k$ est plus complexe que ceux décrits ci-dessus. $\underline{z}_k'$ ou $\underline{z}_k''$ est une évaluation par défaut de la valeur de la solution optimale de P_k.

<u>2ème forme:</u>

- Calculer à l'aide d'un théorème la valeur d'un minorant $\underline{z}_k$ des valeurs de $f(X)$ pour $X \in F_k$.
- Si $\underline{z}_k > f_{opt}$ passer à l'examen du sous-problème suivant.

<u>3ème forme:</u>

- Examiner si P_k est isomorphe à un problème précédemment étudié. Si c'est le cas passer à l'examen du sous-problème suivant.

Ces deux dernières formes peuvent être utilisées dans une procédure d'optimisation par séparation et évaluation pour déterminer le nombre chromatique d'un graphe [3][5].

Les tests directs d'admissibilité s'appliquent à des problèmes P_{kt}^*, $t=1,2,\ldots,m$ associés au sous-problème P_k courant, dans lesquels on ajoute une contrainte sur la fonction économique et où le membre de gauche de la $t^{\text{ème}}$ contrainte sert de fonction économique:

$$\operatorname{Max}\{g_t(X) : f(X) \leq f_{opt}, g_{t'}(X) \geq 0 \quad t'=1,2,\ldots,m, \quad t' \neq t, \; X \in \prod_{j=1}^{n} D_j\} \tag{7}$$

La forme de ces problèmes est semblable à celle du problème (1). On peut construire des test directs d'admissibilité de première, seconde et troisième forme en raisonnant sur le problème (7) comme on l'a fait sur le problème (1) dans les tests directs d'optimalité. Le plus souvent les tests d'admissibilité seront de première forme.

<u>1ère forme:</u>

- Construire une relaxation $P_{kt}^{*\prime}$ ou une majoration $P_{kt}^{*\prime\prime}$ du problème P_{kt}^* considéré.
- Déterminer la valeur $\bar{g}_t'$ ou $\bar{g}_t''$ de la solution optimale de $P_{kt}^{*\prime}$ ou de $P_{kt}^{*\prime\prime}$.
- Si $\bar{g}_t'$ ou $\bar{g}_t'' < 0$ passer à l'examen du sous-problème suivant.

3.2. Tests conditionnels

On peut distinguer deux formes de tests conditionnels d'optimalité. Dans la première forme on fait usage de <u>pénalités</u> associées à une évaluation par défaut $\underline{z}'_k$ ou $\underline{z}''_k$ de la valeur de la solution optimale de P_k, obtenue par un test direct. Une pénalité est un accroissement qui peut être donné à cette évaluation si on impose une contrainte supplémentaire à une variable <u>libre</u>, c'est-à-dire à une variable non encore fixée à une valeur donnée. Désignons par p_j^u et p_j^d les pénalités associées à un couple de contraintes complémentaires imposées à la variable x_j.

<u>1ère forme</u>:

- Calculer pour toutes les variables libres x_j les pénalités p_j^u et p_j^d.
- Si $\underline{z}'_k+p_j^u>f_{opt}$ ajouter au problème P_k la contrainte associée à p_j^d. Si $\underline{z}'_k+p_j^d>f_{opt}$ ajouter au problème P_k la contrainte associée à p_j^u.

Cette première forme est très fréquemment utilisée. Dans la seconde forme, on exploite des conditions locales d'optimalité, c'est-à-dire des conditions suffisantes pour qu'à toute solution admissible dans laquelle une variable x_j ne prend pas la valeur $\tilde{x}_j$ il corresponde une solution admissible de valeur inférieure ou égale dans laquelle $x_j=\tilde{x}_j$.

<u>2ème forme</u>:

- Examiner si la condition pour qu'à toute solution admissible X_1 telle que $x_j\neq\tilde{x}_j$ corresponde une solution admissible X_2 telle que $x_j=\tilde{x}_j$ et $f(X_2)\leq f(X_1)$ est satisfaite.
- Examiner si la fixation de $\tilde{x}_j$ à la valeur x_j rend toutes les contraintes moins serrées que la fixation de x_j à une autre valeur.
- Si ces deux conditions sont satisfaites, fixer x_j à la valeur $\tilde{x}_j$.

Une version moins forte de ce test s'applique dans le cas où la fixation de x_j à la valeur $\tilde{x}_j$ rend toutes les contraintes plus serrées que la fixation de x_j à une autre valeur, comme l'ont noté Ibaraki, Liu, Baugh et Muroga [16]. Si x_j est d'abord fixée à une autre valeur que $\tilde{x}_j$ et que la suite de la résolution montre que le sous-problème obtenu n'a pas de solution admissible, il n'est plus nécessaire d'étudier le sous-problème dans lequel $x_j=\tilde{x}_j$.
Les tests conditionnels d'admissibilité sont semblables

aux tests conditionnels d'optimalité de première forme; on associe à l'évaluation par excès $\bar{g}_t'$ ou $\bar{g}_t''$ de la valeur de la solution optimale de (7) des pénalités qui seront soustraites si des contraintes sont imposées aux variables libres.

3.3. Tests relationnels

On peut distinguer trois formes de tests relationnels d'optimalité. Les deux premières s'appliquent dans le cas où le problème considéré est exprimé sous forme de programme linéaire ou non linéaire en variables 0-1 [13][14]. La première forme fait usage de pénalités (dont la somme constitue une pénalité valable).

$1^{\underline{\text{ère}}}$ forme:

- Calculer pour toutes les variables libres x_j les pénalités p_j^0 et p_j^1 associées à la fixation de ces variables à 0 et à 1.
- Si $\underline{z}_k' + p_j^0 + p_k^0 > f_{opt}$ ajouter à P_k la contrainte $x_j + x_k \geq 1$, etc.

Dans la deuxième forme on exploite des conditions locales d'optimalité portant sur deux variables à la fois. Par exemple:

$2^{\underline{\text{ème}}}$ forme:

- Examiner si une condition suffisante pour qu'à toute solution admissible X_1 dans laquelle $x_j = x_k = 0$ corresponde une solution admissible X_2 telle que $x_j = 1$ ou $x_k = 1$ et $f(X_2) \leq f(X_1)$ est satisfaite.
- Examiner si la fixation de x_j et x_k à 0 rend toutes les contraintes plus serrées que la fixation de x_j et x_k à tout autre couple de valeurs.
- Si ces deux conditions sont satisfaites ajouter à P_k la contrainte $x_j + x_k \geq 1$.

La troisième forme constitue un pont entre les algorithmes de plan de coupure de la programmation en entiers [8] et les procédures de séparation.

$3^{\underline{\text{ème}}}$ forme:

- Engendrer un plan de coupure et l'ajouter à P_k.
- Déterminer la solution optimale du problème ainsi obtenu et l'accroissement de valeur de la fonction économique dû à la nouvelle contrainte.
- Si cet accroissement dépasse un seuil donné réitérer le test.

3.4. Tests auxiliaires

On peut concevoir un grand nombre de tests auxiliaires déterministes ou probabilistes. Une première forme permet d'éviter dans certains cas l'emploi inutile des tests directs et conditionnels d'admissibilité.

1ère forme:

- Calculer la valeur d'un minorant g_t des valeurs du membre de gauche de la $t^{ème}$ contrainte pour $X \in F_k$.
- Si $g_t > 0$ supprimer la $t^{ème}$ contrainte du sous-problème courant.

Une deuxième forme permet d'éviter l'emploi inutile d'un test conditionnel d'optimalité.

2ème forme:

- Calculer la valeur d'un majorant $\bar{p}$ des pénalités p_j^u et p_j^d pour toute variable libre x_j.
- Si $\bar{p} < f_{opt} - \underline{z}_k$ omettre le test conditionnel d'optimalité.

Dans un test auxiliaire probabiliste on peut remplacer $\bar{p}$ par $\alpha\bar{p}$ ou la valeur du paramètre α, comprise entre 0 et 1, sera choisie d'après des résultats empiriques. Une autre forme de test auxiliaire consiste à noter après combien de séparations les tests directs ou conditionnels deviennent utiles au début de la résolution et à omettre ensuite ces tests lorsque le nombre de séparations ayant conduit au sous-problème courant est nettement plus faible.

BIBLIOGRAPHIE

1. N. Agin, Optimum Seeking with Branch and Bound, Manag. Sci. **13**, 176, 1966.
2. E. Balas, A Note on the Branch-and-Bound Principle, Oper. Res., **15**, 915, 1968.
3. C. Berge, Graphes et hypergraphes, Dunod, Paris, 1970.
4. P. Bertier et B. Roy, Procédure de résolution pour une classe de problèmes pouvant avoir un caractère combinatoire, Cahiers CERO, **6**, 202, 1964.
5. J.R. Brown, Chromatic Scheduling and the Chromatic Number Problem, Manag. Sci., **19**, 456, 1972.
6. N.J. Driebeek, An Algorithm for the Solution of Mixed Integer Programming Problems, Manag. Sci., **12**, 576, 1966.
7. W.L. Eastman, A Solution to the Travelling Salesman Problem, Econometrica, **27**, 282, 1959.

8. R.S. Garfinkel and G.L. Nemhauser, Integer Programming, Wiley, New-York, 1972.
9. A.M. Geoffrion, Integer Programming by Implicit Enumeration and Balas'Method, SIAM Rev., 7, 178, 1967.
10. A.M. Geoffrion and R.E. Marsten, Integer Programming: A Framework and State-of-the-Art Survey, Manag. Sci., 18, 465, 1972.
11. S.W. Golomb and L.D. Baumert, Backtrack Programming, JACM, 12, 516, 1965.
12. G. Gorry, J. Shapiro and L. Wolsey, Relaxation Methods for Pure and Mixed Integer Programming Problems, Manag. Sci., 18, 229, 1972.
13. P.L. Hammer and S. Nguyen, APPOSS, A Partial Order in the Solution Space of Bivalent Programs, Univ. Montréal CRM 186, 1972.
14. P.L. Hammer and P. Hansen, Quadratic 0-1 Programming, CORE Discussion Paper 7219, 1972.
15. P. Hansen, Les procédures d'optimisation par séparation: présentation générale, Revue Belge Stat. Rech. Opér., 11, 35, 1971.
16. T. Ibaraki, T.K. Liu, C.R. Baugh and S. Muroga, Implicit Enumeration Program for Zero-One Programming, University of Illinois, 1969.
17. W.M. Kohler and K. Steiglitz, Characterization and Theoretical Comparison of Branch-and-Bound Algorithms for Permutation Problems, JACM, 21, 140, 1974.
18. A.H. Land and A.G. Doig, An Automatic Method for Solving Discrete Programming Problems, Econometrica, 28, 497, 1960.
19. E.L. Lawler and D.E. Wood, Branch-and-Bound Methods: A Survey, Oper. Res., 14, 699, 1966.
20. L.G. Mitten, Branch-and-Bound Methods: General Formulation and Properties, Oper. Res., 18, 24, 1970.
21. A.H.G. Rinnooy Kan, On Mitten's Axioms for Branch-and-Bound, Graduate School of Management, Delft, 1974.
22. B. Roy, Procédures d'exploration par séparation et évaluation (P.S.E.P. et P.S.E.S.), Revue Fr. Infor. Rech. Opér., 1, 61, 1969.
23. B. Roy, Algèbre Moderne et Théorie des Graphes, Dunod, Paris, tome 1, 1969 et tome 2, 1970.
24. B. Roy, R. Benayoun et J. Tergny, From S.E.P. Procedure to the Mixed Ophelie Program, in Integer and Nonlinear Programming, ed. by J. Abadie, North-Holland, 1970.
25. R.S. Walker, An Enumerative Technique for a Class of Combinatorial Problems, AMS Symp. On Applied Math. Proc., 10, 91, 1960.

II. SEPARATIONS ET FORMES STANDARDS

RESUME : Afin de répondre aux questions b) et c) de l'introduction concernant la manière dont les séparations doivent être faites et doivent s'enchaîner, on présente un théorème de convergence valable pour toutes les procédures d'optimisation par séparation et évaluation finies, pour lesquelles le cyclage est exclu. On définit ensuite trois formes standards, correspondant aux P.S.E.P., aux P.S.E.S. et aux P.S.E.P.S. (ou procédures mixtes) et on montre que les procédures mises sous ces formes sont convergentes. On étudie enfin divers problèmes liés à l'efficience des procédures de séparation : choix du sous-problème à examiner dans une P.S.E.P., choix de la variable à utiliser pour une séparation, modification de l'ordre des variables choisies dans une P.S.E.S., relocalisation de l'origine et emploi d'un algorithme heuristique auxiliaire.

1. INTRODUCTION

Dans cet article, on étudie les questions b) et c) de l'introduction concernant la manière dont les séparations doivent être faites et doivent s'enchaîner dans une procédure d'exploration ou d'optimisation par séparation et évaluation. Il est nécessaire qu'une telle procédure soit convergente, c'est-à-dire qu'elle donne en un temps fini la solution optimale de tout problème de la classe pour laquelle elle est construite ou la preuve que ce problème n'a pas de solution admissible; de plus elle doit être efficiente, c'est-à-dire ne pas

prendre un temps de calcul prohibitif pour résoudre un problème donné.
On présente dans la section suivante trois conditions à vérifier par le principe de séparation d'une procédure d'exploration ou d'optimisation par séparation et évaluation, suffisantes pour assurer la convergence s'il n'y a pas de possibilité de cyclage, c'est-à-dire de reproduction d'une même situation à différentes itérations de la résolution. Aux différentes manières dont les séparations peuvent s'enchaîner correspondent trois classes de procédures de séparation, décrites dans la section 3; pour chaque classe on propose une forme standard précisant la succession des tests et l'enchaînement des séparations et excluant le cyclage.
Plusieurs facteurs autres que les tests utilisés ont une grande influence sur l'efficience des procédures de séparation : on examine dans la section 4 le choix du sous-problème à étudier dans une P.S.E.P. et le choix de la variable utilisée dans les séparations.
Enfin, on étudie divers procédés destinés à augmenter l'efficience des procédures de séparation : fixation préalable de certaines ou de toutes les variables à une valeur donnée, "relocalisation de l'origine", modification de l'ordre des variables choisies dans une P.S.E.S. et emploi d'un algorithme heuristique.

2. PRINCIPE DE SEPARATION

La manière dont les séparations doivent être faites dans une procédure d'exploration ou d'optimisation par séparation et évaluation sera précisée en un principe de séparation [4] [15] [16]. Plusieurs auteurs ont proposé des ensembles de conditions à vérifier par un tel principe et assurant la convergence (en l'absence de cyclage) [2] [4] [12] [14].
Les trois conditions proposées ci-dessous, proches de celles proposées par Bertier et Roy [4], sont simples et vérifiées par un grand nombre de procédures de séparation. Rappelons que les séparations se font sur l'ensemble des solutions candidates du problème considéré ou sur une partie de cet ensemble*.
Condition C1: La réunion des ensembles de solutions obtenus lors d'une séparation doit être égale à l'ensemble séparé.

---

* Plusieurs auteurs supposent que les séparations se font sur l'ensemble des solutions admissibles du problème considéré ou sur une partie de cet ensemble; cela entraîne des paradoxes comme de devoir séparer un ensemble vide.

<u>Condition C2</u> : Lorsqu'un ensemble de solutions ne peut plus être séparé il doit être sondable.
<u>Conditions C3</u> : Le nombre de séparations possibles doit être fini.
Dans la plupart des procédures de séparation les ensembles de solutions obtenus lors d'une séparation constituent une partition de l'ensemble de solutions séparé ; la condition C1 exige seulement qu'ils constituent un recouvrement de cet ensemble.
La condition C2 est souvent vérifiée de manière triviale les ensembles de solutions qui ne peuvent plus être séparés ne contenant qu'un seul vecteur. Pour certaines procédures de séparation, qui seront dites infinies, la condition C3 n'est pas vérifiée; la démonstration de la convergence repose alors sur des résultats classiques d'analyse [12] [14].
On dira qu'un ensemble de solutions candidates a été <u>sondé</u> si l'on a montré qu'il ne contient pas de solution admissible, qu'il ne contient pas de solution admissible de valeur inférieure à celle de la meilleure solution précédemment obtenue ou qu'une solution particulière de cet ensemble est la meilleure solution connue.
<u>Théorème 1</u>. <u>Toute procédure d'optimisation par séparation et évaluation telle que</u>
- <u>les tests utilisés prennent un temps de calcul fini</u>,
- <u>l'enchaînement des tests et des séparations exclut le cyclage</u>,
- <u>le principe de séparation vérifie les conditions C1 à C3</u>,

<u>est convergente</u>.
<u>Démonstration</u> : Considérons un problème P_o à résoudre par une procédure de séparation vérifiant les conditions du théorème 1. Comme le nombre de séparations est fini (C3), le nombre d'ensembles de solutions candidates obtenu l'est aussi, et comme tout ensemble de solutions qui ne peut être séparé est sondable (C2) on n'aura à un moment donné que des ensemble sondables. De plus cette situation sera atteinte en un temps fini car les tests prennent un temps de calcul fini et l'enchaînement des tests et des séparations exclut le cyclage. Désignons par G = (X, Γ) l'arborescence correspondant à l'application de cette procédure de séparation; les ensembles de solutions associés aux sommets pendants de G sont sondables et ont été sondés. Si G n'est pas trivial, il contient au moins un sommet qui n'est pas un sommet pendant et dont tous les suivants sont des sommets pendants. Comme la réunion des ensembles de solutions obtenus lors d'une séparation contient l'ensemble séparé (C1) l'ensemble de solutions associé.

à ce sommet a été sondé. Par récurrence, on voit que l'ensemble de solutions associé à la racine de G, qui n'est autre que I_0, a été sondé. On a donc obtenu la solution optimale ou montré que le problème n'a pas de solution admissible.

3. FORMES STANDARDS

On distingue trois grandes classes de procédures de séparation : les procédures d'exploration ou d'optimisation par séparation et évaluation en parallèle (P.S.E.P.) [4], les procédures d'exploration ou d'optimisation par séparation et évaluation en série (P.S.E.S.) [1] [8] et les procédures d'exploration ou d'optimisation par séparation et évaluation en parallèle-série (P.S.E.P.S.) [17]. *

Dans les P.S.E.P., les sous-problèmes obtenus lors d'une séparation sont ajoutés à une liste de problèmes courants; après cette séparation ou après avoir sondé le sous-problème courant on sélectionne d'après une règle donnée un des problèmes de cette liste comme nouveau sous-problème courant.

Dans les P.S.E.S. on conserve comme sous-problème courant après une séparation un des problèmes obtenus par cette séparation; lorsqu'on a sondé le sous-problème courant on sélectionne le problème non encore sondé qui est le plus proche de ce sous-problème. Dans les P.S.E.P.S. on procède comme dans les P.S.E.P. jusqu'à ce que la liste de problèmes courants ait atteint une taille maximum, on poursuit ensuite la résolution comme dans les P.S.E.S. tant que la liste de problèmes courants a cette taille; sinon on procède à nouveau comme dans les P.S.E.P.

En d'autres termes, dans les P.S.E.P. on sélectionne à chaque itération un sous-problème correspondant à l'un des sommets pendants de l'arborescence associée à la procédure de séparation. Dans les P.S.E.S. on parcourt une des branches de l'arborescence jusqu'à un sommet correspondant à un ensemble sondable puis on revient sur ses pas jusqu'au premier sommet dont un des suivants correspond à un ensemble de solutions non encore sondé et on examine cet ensemble. Il est toujours

* Ces trois classes ont aussi été appelées procédures par séparation et évaluation progressives, procédures par séparation et évaluations séquentielles et procédures mixtes. Les nouveaux noms ont été proposés par B. Roy (communication personnelle).

possible de représenter l'arborescence associée à la procédure de séparation de sorte qu'on explore toujours en premier lieu en un sommet la branche non explorée située la plus à droite : l'ordre de parcours est alors l'ordre de Tarry [21] introduit pour l'étude des labyrinthes.

Dans les P.S.E.P.S. on sélectionne à chaque itération un sous-problème correspondant à l'un des sommets pendants de l'arborescence si le nombre de ces sommets ne dépasse pas une limite donnée et sinon on examine la sous-arborescence dont le dernier sommet choisi est la racine suivant l'ordre de Tarry.

L'organigramme de la forme standard 1, qui correspond aux P.S.E.P. se trouve sur la figure 1. On suppose que la procédure de séparation comprend t_{max} tests directs et autant de tests conditionnels. (Si le nombre de tests conditionnels est inférieur au nombre de tests directs on peut introduire des tests fictifs pour lesquels I_k n'est jamais partiellement sondable). t est l'indice des tests, ℓ l'indice des sous-problèmes engendrés en cours de résolution et k l'indice du sous-problème courant. Si une solution admissible X_h est connue préalablement à la résolution elle est conservée dans X_{opt} et sa valeur est la première valeur de f_{opt}. Les tests directs et conditionnels sont appliqués en séquence sauf si I_k est sondable ou partiellement sondable. Si c'est un test de résolution qui a permi de sonder I_k et si $f(X) < f_{opt}$, X_{opt} et f_{opt} sont mis à jour puis on examine le sous-problème suivant, s'il en reste; si ce n'est pas le cas on passe directement à l'examen du sous-problème suivant.

Si I_k a été partiellement sondé on fixe les variables ou on ajoute les nouvelles contraintes imposées par le test conditionnel puis on retourne au premier test direct. Si aucun des tests ne permet de sonder partiellement ou complètement I_k on procède à une séparation, on ajoute les nouveaux sous-problèmes $P_{\ell+1}$ et $P_{\ell+2}$ à la liste et on passe à l'étape de sélection.

Lorsque la liste de problèmes est vide on imprime les résultats.

Supposons que les ensembles de solutions candidates obtenus lors d'une séparation constituent une partition de l'ensemble séparé (ce qui est presque toujours le cas); l'absence de cyclage d'une procédure de séparation sous forme standard 1 est alors facile à démontrer.

Théorème 2. Toute procédure d'optimisation par séparation et évaluation en parallèle mise sous la forme standard 1 exclut le cyclage.

Démonstration : Les sous-problèmes obtenus par les séparations ont des ensembles de solutions candidates

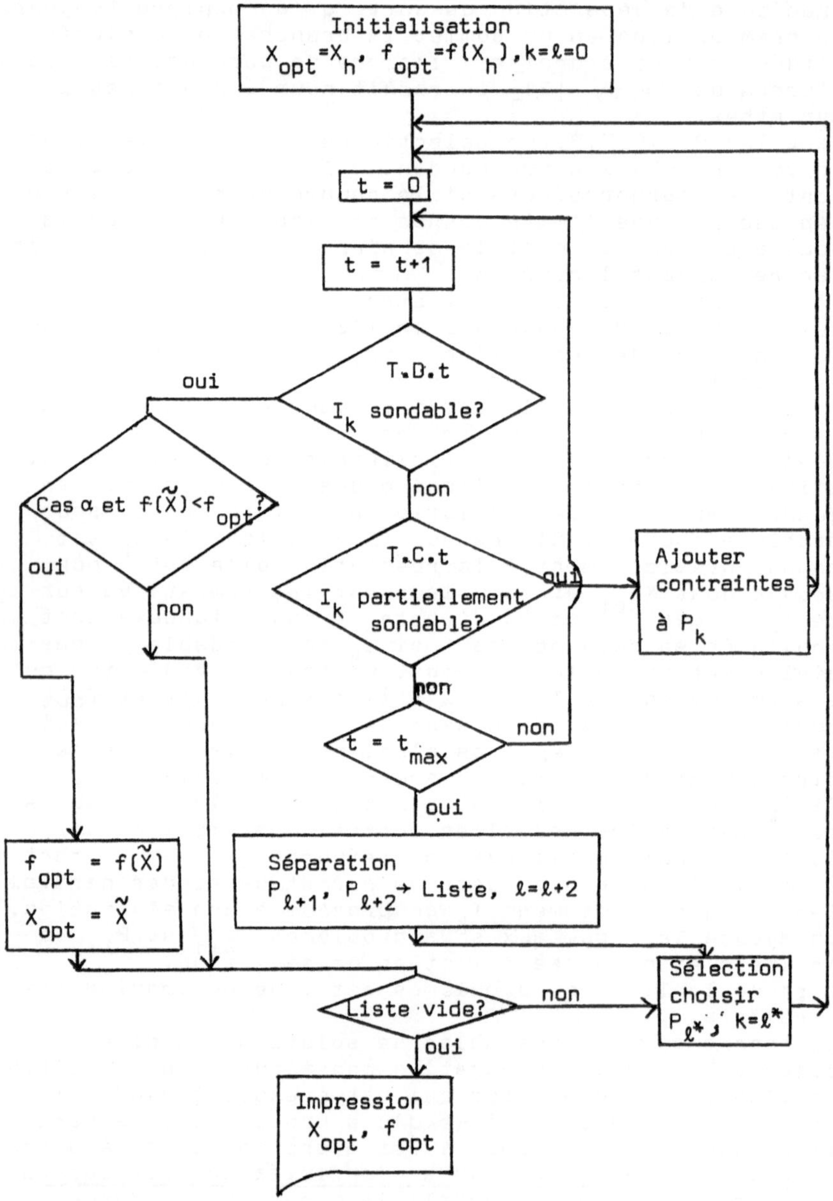

Forme Standard 1 (P.S.E.P)

Figure 1

disjoints et les variables fixées en cours de résolution dans un sous-problème ne sont jamais libérées (ou les contraintes sur les valeurs des variables supprimées); les sous-problèmes obtenus en cours de résolution sont donc tous différents. De plus, on ne retourne à un test qui en précède un autre que par les deux chemins à droite de la figure 1, c'est-à-dire après avoir modifié le sous-problème courant ou après avoir sélectionné un nouveau sous-problème; on ne peut donc appliquer deux fois le même test au même sous-problème. Notons que si les ensembles de solutions obtenus lors d'une séparation constituent un recouvrement et non une partition de l'ensemble séparé le même sous-problème peut être obtenu à plusieurs itérations différentes; comme ceci ne peut se produire qu'un nombre fini de fois la procédure est quand même convergente. Si la P.S.E.P. étudiée comporte des tests relationnels l'organigramme de la figure 1 peut être modifié en ajoutant les tests relationnels à la suite de tests conditionnels; si I_k est faiblement sondable on ajoute les nouvelles contraintes imposées par le test relationnel et on retourne au premier test direct.
La démonstration de la convergence est semblable à celle donnée plus haut pourvu que le nombre de contraintes qui peuvent être ajoutées soit fini.
Après avoir montré que I_k est partiellement sondable on peut ne pas retourner au premier test direct mais retourner à un des tests directs ou conditionnels précédant celui qui vient d'être appliqué, ou encore continuer en séquence. En particulier, on peut réitérer un test qui a permi de sonder partiellement I_k jusqu'à ce qu'il ne donne plus d'information utile puis continuer en séquence ou retourner à un test précédant.
L'organigramme de la forme standard 2, qui correspond aux P.S.E.S. se trouve sur la figure 2. Les différences entre les formes standards 1 et 2 portent sur la manière de stocker l'information relative à la résolution et sur les étapes de séparation et de régression.
Dans une P.S.E.S.on met constamment à jour le problème courant en lui ajoutant ou retranchant des contraintes; l'ensemble des contraintes imposées à l'itération courante définit une <u>solution partielle</u> notée dans un vecteur X (ou plusieurs vecteurs si c'est nécessaire).
L'ordre dans lequel les contraintes sont ajoutées est noté dans un vecteur M de longueur variable : l'indice j est ajouté à M par la droite si une contrainte est imposée à la variable x_j et souligné si c'est du fait d'un test conditionnel. A l'étape de régression on cherche dans M de droite à gauche un indice j^+ non souligné, on supprime les contraintes correspondants aux

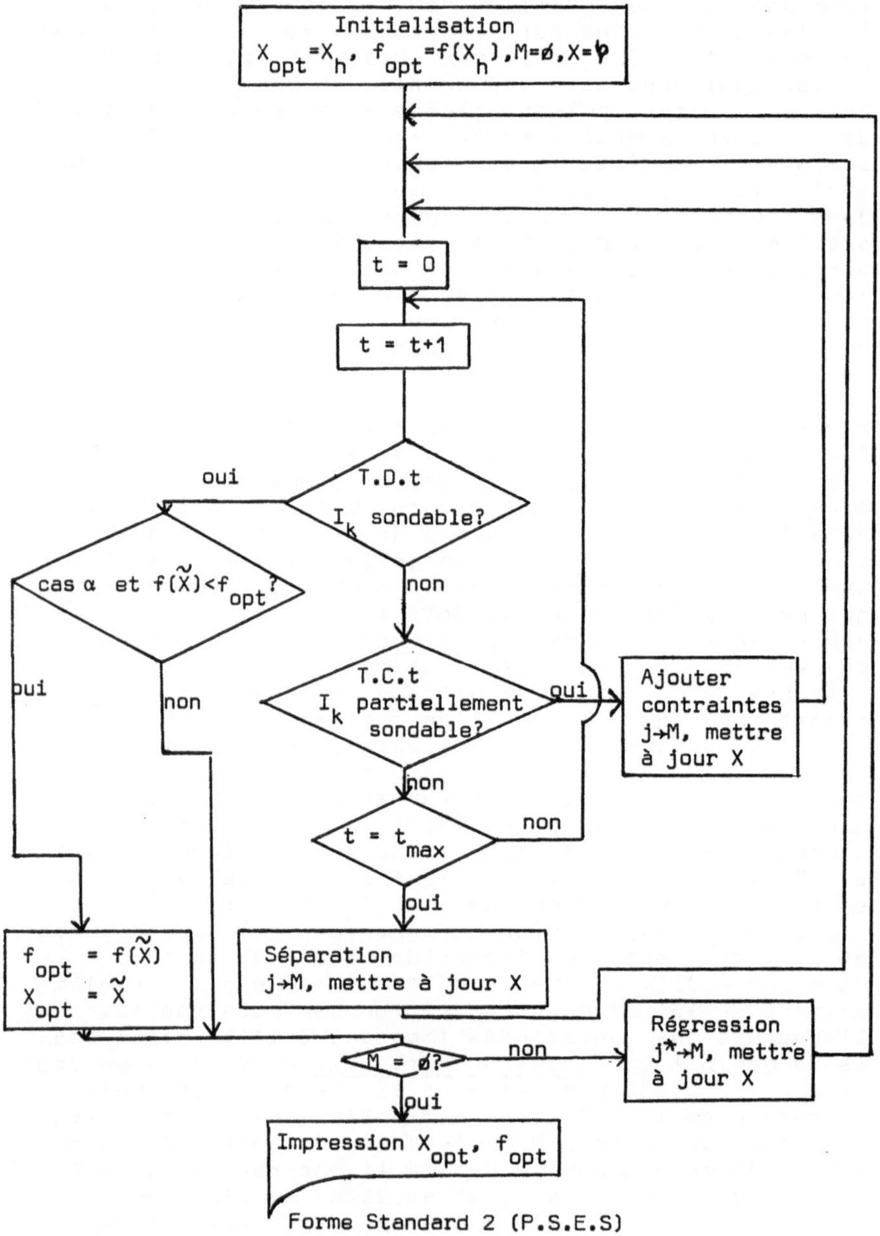

Forme Standard 2 (P.S.E.S)

Figure 2

indices à droite de j^+ dans M et on efface ces indices, on impose à x_{j^+} la contrainte complémentaire (ou une des contraintes complémentaires non encore imposée) de celle qui lui était imposée et on souligne j^+. S'il n'y a plus d'indice j^+ la résolution est terminée. Un organigramme pour la forme standard 3 qui correspond aux P.S.E.P.S., peut être construit sans difficulté à partir des deux organigrammes précédents, en insérant des tests pour voir si la liste de problèmes courants a atteint ou non la taille maximum. Comme les P.S.E.S. et les P.S.E.P.S. peuvent être considérées comme des cas particuliers de P.S.E.P., dans lesquelles une règle de sélection du sous-problème courant est imposée durant une partie ou durant toute la résolution, le théorème 2 montre que toute P.S.E.S. ou P.S.E.P.S. mise sous la forme standard 2 ou la forme standard 3 exclut le cyclage.

Les P.S.E.P. et les P.S.E.S. présentent des avantages et des inconvénients complémentaires. A l'actif des P.S.E.P., notons que la règle de sélection du sous-problème à examiner est très souple et se prête bien à l'exploitation d'information préalable sur le problème à résoudre. On n'examinera que très peu de problèmes auxquels correspond une évaluation supérieure à la valeur de la solution optimale (et selon certaines règles, aucun). Au passif, notons qu'une solution admissible n'est souvent obtenue qu'en fin de résolution; si l'on doit interrompre la résolution le temps de calcul devenant trop élevé, on ne dispose pas d'une bonne solution dont on pourraît se contenter. Ensuite, comme f_{opt} aura une valeur très élevée en début de résolution les tests conditionnels d'optimalité seront alors inutiles : on ne pourra écarter rapidement des ensembles de solutions correspondant à des valeurs très défavorables de certaines variables. De plus, si la liste des sous-problèmes courants s'allonge la conservation des informations pose des problèmes; pour résoudre de grands problèmes il faudra recourir à la mémoire externe d'un ordinateur et les fréquents transferts entre mémoire interne et mémoire externe allongent la résolution.

Dans les P.S.E.S. une solution admissible est généralement obtenue rapidement. Comme on travaille en mettant à jour le problème courant un petit nombre de mémoires sont requises; on pourra résoudre de grands problèmes sur ordinateur en utilisant seulement la mémoire interne. Enfin, les P.S.E.S. sont plus faciles à programmer que les P.S.E.P. ou les P.S.E.P.S.

Par contre quelques choix malencontreux en début de résolution peuvent entraîner l'examen inutile d'un grand nombre de sous-problèmes. Dans les P.S.E.P.S.

on évite dans une certaine mesure à la fois les inconvénients dus à de mauvais choix initiaux et ceux dus au trop grand nombre de mémoires requises.

4. EFFICIENCE ET SEPARATIONS

L'efficience d'une procédure d'exploration ou d'optimisation par séparation et évaluation dépend très fortement des tests qu'on choisit d'y inclure et des règles précisant comment doivent se faire et s'enchaîner les séparations. Après avoir choisi les tests et décidé d'utiliser une P.S.E.P., une P.S.E.S. ou une P.S.E.P.S. il faut encore préciser dans le premier et le troisième cas la règle de sélection du sous-problème courant, dans le second cas quel sous-problème doit être examiné en premier parmi ceux obtenus lors de la dernière séparation et dans les trois cas la règle de choix de la variable utilisée dans les séparations.
En général, on ne possède pas de règles optimales pour guider ces choix. Des études empiriques approfondies ont été faites par Forrest, Hirst et Tomlin [6] pour le cas des programmes mixtes, par Khumawala [9] pour le cas des problèmes de localisation d'entrepôts ; pour beaucoup d'autres classes de problèmes on ne dispose que de résultats disparates.
Un règle proposée déjà en 1960 par Land et Doig [10] pour la sélection du sous-problème courant dans une P.S.E.P. ou dans la première phase d'une P.S.E.P.S. consiste à choisir toujours le sous-problème auquel correspond la plus petite évaluation. En suivant cette règle, on n'examine jamais de sous-problème dont l'évaluation dépasse la valeur de la solution optimale mais on n'obtient pas rapidement de solution admissible. Cette règle semble bonne si une bonne solution est connue a priori et qu'on a décidé de trouver la solution optimale et de prouver son optimalité. Comme les évaluations augmentent au fur et à mesure des séparations, on peut tenir compte, comme l'on proposé Roy, Benayoun et Tergny [17] à la fois de l'évaluation et du nombre de séparations effectuées. Une alternative, qui tient compte de ce que l'effet des différentes séparations n'est pas nécessairement le même consiste à tenir compte de l'évaluation et de la distance de la solution optimale de la relaxation du sous-problème courant à une solution admissible [6] [14]. Lorsque la relaxation est un problème en variables continues et que la solution du problème à résoudre doit être en entiers, la somme des écarts des variables de la solution optimale

de la relaxation et des entiers immédiatement supérieurs ou inférieurs constitue une bonne estimation de cette distance. Si l'on dispose d'informations sur la signification des variables du problème à résoudre on peut aussi pondérer ces écarts [3]. Une telle information peut également être utilisée pour indiquer quels problèmes doivent être examinés en premier, éventuellement dans une procédure interactive, le choix se faisant après l'examen des solutions optimales des relaxations des sous-problèmes courants.

En ce qui concerne le choix des variables à utiliser dans les séparations un accord assez large semble s'être fait pour choisir la variable qui donne, dans un des sous-problèmes la plus grande augmentation de valeur de la fonction économique [11]. Dans les P.S.E.S. on examine d'abord le sous-problème, complémentaire, dans l'espoir de ne pas devoir examiner le sous-problème rejeté ensuite une solution de valeur inférieure à son évaluation ayant été obtenue. Si les pénalités associées aux variables sont précises, on peut faire le choix d'après leurs valeurs; si elles sont imprécises on peut calculer des pénalités plus précises (notamment dans une P.S.E.S. pour voir quel problème doit être examiné en premier) ou employer une évaluation heuristique. Forrest, Hirst et Tomlin [6] ont analysé en détails ces techniques dans le cas des programmes mixtes.

Dakin [5], Geoffrion [7], Nghiem [13] et d'autres auteurs ont noté que si l'on n'utilise pas de tests conditionnels dans une P.S.E.S., l'ordre dans lequel les contraintes ont été ajoutées au sous-problème courant peut être modifié avant de passer à l'étape de régression; si l'on utilise des tests conditionnels l'ordre des contraintes ajoutées à l'étape de séparation entre des contraintes ajoutées par des tests conditionnels peut être modifié avant de passer à l'étape de régression.

Il est aussi possible dans une P.S.E.S. d'imposer a priori certaines contraintes ou de fixer certaines variables à des valeurs données, les cas complémentaires étant examinées ensuite. Comme on introduit de la sorte une certaine rigidité dans la procédure et qu'on néglige d'employer les tests conditionnels durant cette première phase, de telles contraintes ne devraient être imposées qu'avec prudence. Certains auteurs ont supposé que dans les P.S.E.S. pour les programmes en variables 0-1 toutes les variables devraient initialement être fixées à 0, ce qui semble inutile. En liaison avec cette hypothèse, la procédure de relocalisation de l'origine de Salkin [18] et Spielberg [19] consiste à obtenir une bonne solution puis à reformuler le problème de façon à ce que cette solution coïncide avec la solution obtenue en annulant toutes les variables dans le problème reformulé. L'intérêt de cette procédure semble être surtout lié à la connaissance d'une bonne solution qui rend les tests d'optimalités plus efficaces dans le problème reformulé. Une bonne solution peut souvent être obtenue aussi par un algorithme heuristique auxiliaire avant d'entamer la résolution. S'il est difficile d'obtenir une bonne solution a priori, on peut recourir à la méthode suivante, proposée par Tang et Wong : on se donne un seuil pour les valeurs de la fonction économique et on applique la procédure de séparation; si on obtient une solution optimale, la résolution est terminée. Si on n'obtient pas de solution admissible on relève le seuil et on recommence. De la sorte on utilise très efficacement les tests directs et conditionnels d'optimalité mais on risque d'effectuer de nombreuses itérations si les seuils successifs sont mal choisis.

BIBLIOGRAPHIE

1. E. Balas, An Additive Algorithm for Solving Linear Programs with Zero-One Variables, Oper. Res., 13, 517, 1965.
2. E. Balas, A Note on the Branch-and-Bound Principle, Oper. Res., 16, 442, 1968.
3. M. Benichou, J.M. Gauthier, P. Girodet, G. Hentges, G. Ribière and D. Vincent, Experiments in Mixed Integer Linear Programming, Math. Prog., 1, 76, 1971.
4. P. Bertier et B. Roy, Procédure de résolution pour une classe de problèmes pouvant avoir un caractère combinatoire, Cahiers CERO, 6, 202, 1964.
5. R.J. Dakin, A Tree-Search Algorithm for Mixed Integer Programming Problems, Comp. J., 8, 250, 1965.
6. J.J.H. Forrest, J.P.H. Hirst and J.A. Tomlin, Practical Solution of Large Mixed Integer Programming Problems with Umpire, Manag. Sci., 20, 736, 1974.
7. A.M. Geoffrion, Integer Programming by Implicit Enumeration and Balas' Method, SIAM Review, 7, 178, 1967.
8. S.W. Golomb and L.D. Baumert, Backtrack Programming, JACM, 12, 516, 1965.
9. B.M. Khumawala, An Efficient Branch-and-Bound Algorithm for the Warehouse Location Problem, Manag. Sci., 18, 718, 1972.

10. A.H. Land and A.G. Doig, An Automatic Method for Solving Discrete Programming Problems, Econometrica, 28, 497, 1960.
11. J.D.C. Little, K.G. Murty, D.W. Sweeney and C. Karel, An Algorithm for the Travelling Salesman Problem, Oper. Res., 11, 972, 1963.
12. L.G.Mitten, Branch-and-Bound Methods : General Formulation and Properties, Oper. Res., 18, 24, 1970.
13. Ph. T. Nghiem, A Flexible Tree-Search Method for Integer Programming Problems, Oper. Res., 19, 115, 1971.
14. A.H.G. Rinnooy Kan, On Mitten's Axioms for Branch-and-Bound, Graduate School of Management, Delft, 1974.
15. B. Roy, Procédures d'exploration par séparation et évaluation (P.S.E.P. et P.S.E.S.), Revue Fr. Infor. Rech. Oper., 1, 61, 1969.
16 B. Roy, Algèbre Moderne et théorie des graphes, Dunod, Paris, Tome 1, 1969 et tome 2, 1970.
17. B. Roy, R. Benayoun and J. Tergny, From S.E.P. Procedure to the Mixed Ophelic Program in Integer and Nonlinear Programming, ed. by J. Ababie, 419, 1970.
18. M.M. Salkin, On the Merit of the Generalized Search Origin, Manag. Sci., 16, 165, 1969.
19. K.Spielberg, Plant Location with Generalized Search Origin, Manag. Sci., 16, 165, 1969.
20. S.Tang and C.Wong, A Strategy for Branch-and-Bound Programming, IBM, 1973.
21. G. Tarry, Le problème des labyrinthes, Nouvelles Annales de Math., 14, 1895.

III. FONCTIONS D'EVALUATION ET PENALITES

RESUME. Afin de répondre à la question e) de l'introduction concernant la manière de construire et de choisir les tests on examine d'abord comment reformuler un programme combinatoire. On montre ensuite comment des fonctions d'évaluations et des pénalités peuvent être obtenues en deux phases : après avoir construit une relaxation ou une minoration initiale qui donne une première fonction d'évaluation, on impose à nouveau une partie des contraintes supprimées, ce qui permet le calcul de pénalités et d'une nouvelle fonction d'évaluation. Une procédure en deux phases semblables s'applique dans le cas où la formulation du programme est implicite. On examine enfin comment le choix des tests peut être éclairé par deux relations de dominance entre tests.

1. INTRODUCTION

Dans cet article on étudie la question e) de l'introduction concernant la manière de construire et de sélectionner les tests à inclure dans une procédure d'exploration ou d'optimisation par séparation et évaluation. Une reformulation préalable du problème permet souvent d'obtenir des évaluations précises; on examine dans la section suivante comment éliminer des contraintes redondantes, modifier les coefficients des contraintes ou de la fonction économique, remplacer plusieurs contraintes par une contrainte équivalente et construire de nouvelles contraintes qui sont des conséquences de la conjonction des contraintes du problème considéré. L'obtention de fonctions d'évaluation et de pénalités se fait en deux phases, étudiées dans la section 3. Dans une première phase, on construit une relaxation ou une minoration du problème considéré; dans une seconde phase on impose à nouveau une partie des contraintes supprimées et on étudie l'accroissement de valeur de la fonction économique résultant. Ceci permet fréquemment d'obtenir des pénalités et une nouvelle fonction d'évaluation; cette dernière sera particulièrement précise si les pénalités sont additives. Si la formulation du problème considéré est implicite on peut encore appliquer une procédure en deux phases, sans expliciter la formulation; cette démarche est illustrée dans la section 4 dans le cas du problème du voyageur de commerce. Le problème du choix des tests à inclure dans une procédure de séparation est difficile; on montre dans la section 5 comment deux relations de dominance entre tests, au sens mathématique et au sens empirique apportent des élements de réponse.

2. REFORMULATION D'UN PROBLEME

Avant de construire une relaxation ou une minoration du problème considéré, il est très souvent utile de le reformuler. En premier lieu, on peut éliminer les <u>contraintes redondantes</u>, qui ne sont pas rares dans les problèmes pratiques, tels par exemple ceux de Petersen |38|. Certaines contraintes peuvent être toujours vérifiées quand d'autres contraintes le sont; dans le cas d'un programme linéaire en variables 0-1, la contrainte

$$\sum_j a_{1j}x_j - b_1 \geq 0 \qquad (1)$$

sera redondante si le minimum du membre de gauche de (1) sous les contraintes

$$\sum_j a_{2j}x_j - b_2 \geq 0 \qquad (2)$$

et $x_j \in \{0,1\}$ pour tout j est positif ou nul. Ce résultat s'étend sans difficulté au cas où les variables x_j sont entières et bornées. On peut aussi modifier les coefficients de la fonction économique ou des contraintes : Bradley, Hammer et Wolsey [8] ont proposés des techniques pour remplacer une contrainte du type(1) par une contrainte équivalente, c'est-à-dire vérifiée par le même ensemble de vecteurs, dans laquelle les coefficients sont plus petits. Plusieurs contraintes peuvent également être remplacées par une seule contrainte équivalente d'après une généralisation d'un résultat classique de Matthews [36], comme l'on montré Elmaghraby et Wig [13], Bradley [7], Glover et Wolsey [20], Padberg [37] et Anthonisse [1]; si α et β sont des entiers suffisamment grands et premiers entre eux, deux contraintes d'égalité du type (1) et (2) peuvent être remplacées par la contrainte

$$\alpha\sum_j a_{1j}x_j + \beta\sum_j a_{2j}x_j - \alpha b_1 - \beta b_2 = 0 \ ; \qquad (3)$$

ce résultat s'étend au cas où les variables sont entières et bornées et au cas où les contraintes sont non linéaires. En appliquant itérativement ce résultat on peut remplacer plusieurs contraintes par une seule; les coefficients de cette nouvelle contrainte peuvent être très grands, ce qui limite l'applicabilité de cette méthode. Comme l'ont montré Fayard et Plateau [14] elle est intéressante pour agréger des contraintes simples, par exemple du type à choix multiples :

$$\sum_{j\in J} x_j = 1 \qquad (4)$$

où $x_j \in \{0, 1\}$ pour $j \in J$.

Des contraintes du type (4) se rencontrent dans de très nombreux problèmes combinatoires en variables 0-1; si la fonction économique est linéaire une réduction d'une quantité a de tous les coefficients c_j pour $j \in J$ aura pour effet de diminuer de a les valeurs de cette fonction économique. En effectuant itérativement de telles réductions et en maintenant les $c_j \geq 0$, Little, Murty, Sweeney et Karel [35] ont obtenu une assez bonne fonction d'évaluation pour le problème du voyageur de commerce. Gondran et Laurière [23] ont utilisé la même procédure pour le problème de partitionnement.

On a vu que les tests relationnels de première forme permettent d'obtenir des relations logiques entre variables 0-1, qui doivent être vérifiées par toutes les solutions optimales du problème considéré. Hammer et Nguyen [24] ont proposé de combiner les relations entre couples et entre triplets de variables ainsi obtenues pour obtenir de nouvelles relations. Après avoir obtenu toutes les relations découlant des relations de départ on peut examiner si les relations entre couples de variables impliquent des conclusions; ces relations seront de la forme

$$x_i \leq x_j \quad , \quad x_i \leq \bar{x}_j \quad , \quad \bar{x}_i \leq x_j \quad , \quad \bar{x}_i \leq \bar{x}_j \qquad (5)$$

où $\bar{x}_i$ désigne la variable complémentaire de x_i. On montre aisément que 4 relations entre x_i et x_j impliquent une contradiction, 3 relations permettent de fixer x_i et x_j à 0 et à 1, 2 relations permettent de fixer x_i ou x_j à 0 ou à 1 ou d'identifier x_i et x_j ou x_i et $\bar{x}_j$.
On peut également déduire de nouvelles contraintes d'une des contraintes du problème et d'une relation logique renforçante; [25], la relation

$$x_j + x_k \geq 1 \qquad (6)$$

sera renforçante par rapport à la contrainte (1) si $a_{1j} < 0$ et $a_{1k} < 0$. Alors, la contrainte

$$\sum_{j \neq k,\, \ell} a_{1j} x_j + \max(a_{1k}, a_{1\ell}) - b_1 \geq 0 \qquad (7)$$

peut être ajoutée aux contraintes du problème considéré.
Dans plusieurs algorithmes, les tests s'appliquent à chacune des contraintes individuellement; c'est pourquoi Glover [18] a proposé d'utiliser des contraintes composites, combinaisons linéaires à poids positifs des contraintes du problème considéré, afin d'obtenir une information qui ne peut être obtenue en considérant les contraintes individuellement mais qui est néanmoins une conséquence de leur conjonction. Balas [4], Glover [19] et Geoffrion [17] ont étudié le problème du choix des poids à donner aux contraintes dans le cas des programmes linéaires en variables 0-1.
La solution retenue par Balas et Geoffrion consiste à prendre les valeurs optimales des variables duales du programme linéaire en variables continues obtenu en relachant les contraintes d'intégralité des variables.
On peut également ajouter au problème courant une ou plusieurs contraintes obtenues par une des très nom-

breuses méthodes de plan de coupure de la programmation en nombres entiers; pour la description de telles contraintes, on peut se reporter à Balas [5] [6], Garfinkel et Nemhauser [15] et Gomory et Johnson [21] [22].

3. OBTENTION DE FONCTIONS D'EVALUATION ET DE PENALITES EN DEUX PHASES

Les fonctions d'évaluation et les pénalités utilisées dans les procédures d'exploration et d'optimisation par séparation et évaluation s'obtiennent d'habitude en deux phases. Dans une première phase, on construit une relaxation ou une minoration du problème considéré qui fournit une première fonction d'évaluation; dans une seconde phase on impose à nouveau une partie des contraintes omises afin de calculer des pénalités et/ou d'obtenir une nouvelle fonction d'évaluation.
Dans la première phase, il faut tenir compte de la précision des évaluations qui seront obtenues et de la facilité de déterminer la solution optimale de la relaxation ou de la minoration considérée. Les procédés les plus couramment employés pour construire une relaxation sont d'omettre une partie des contraintes propres ou des contraintes d'intégralité des variables. Dans le cas des programmes linéaires en variables 0-1, Balas [4] a proposé d'omettre l'ensemble des contraintes propres dans la relaxation utilisée dans un test direct d'optimalité. Une évaluation imprécise est obtenue sans aucun calcul. Petersen [38] a proposé de conserver une des contraintes propres ce qui donne avec peu de calculs une meilleure évaluation. Balas [6], Geoffrion [17] et Glover [19] ont proposé de conserver toutes les contraintes propres (ainsi que certaines contraintes logiques déduites de ces contraintes et des contraintes d'intégralité des variables, selon Glover) et de remplacer les contraintes $x_j \in \{0, 1\}$ par $x_j \in [0, 1]$; le programme linéaire ainsi obtenu fournit une évaluation précise.
De nombreux problèmes combinatoires ont une structure particulière qui peut être exploitée pour obtenir des évaluations précises avec assez peu de calculs. Dans certains cas une relaxation qui a la forme d'un programme linéaire peut être résolue beaucoup plus rapidement que par l'algorithme du simplexe ou une de ses variantes. Efroymson et Ray [12] ont montré que c'est le cas pour le problème de la localisation des entrepôts.
Dans la seconde phase, on réimpose le plus fréquemment les contraintes portant sur une variable à la fois, ce qui fournit des pénalités. Si la relaxation du problème

considéré est un programme linéaire on considérera une variable x_ℓ en base dans la solution optimale et prenant la valeur fractionnaire $x_{\ell o}$; cette variable devra vérifier l'une des deux contraintes $x_\ell \leq [x_{\ell o}]$ ou $x_\ell \geq [x_{\ell o}] + 1$, où $[x_{\ell o}]$ est la partie entière de $x_{\ell o}$, dans toute solution admissible du problème considéré. Driebeek [10] a montré que l'accroissement de la fonction économique de la relaxation dû à la première itération duale simplexe suivant l'imposition d'une de ces contraintes constitue une pénalité p_ℓ^d ou p_ℓ^u valable. Tomlin [39] et Armstrong et Sinha [2] ont montré que des pénalités plus fortes pouvaient être obtenues en tenant compte à la fois des contraintes d'intégralité des variables en base et des variables hors-base. Si $\underline{z}$ est la valeur de la solution optimale du programme linéaire et J l'ensemble des indices des variables en base

$$\underline{z}' = \underline{z} + \max_{j \in J} \min (p_j^d, p_j^u) \qquad (8)$$

est une nouvelle évaluation par défaut de la valeur de la solution optimale du problème considéré.
Une formule semblable peut être obtenue lorsque le problème considéré est exprimé sous forme de programme en variables 0-1; désignons par K_0, K_1 et K_2 les ensembles d'indices des variables fixées à 0, à 1 et des variables libres du sous-problème courant. Désignons par $F(K_0, K_1, K_2)$ l'ensemble des solutions admissibles de ce problème et par $\underline{z}$ une évaluation par défaut de la valeur de la solution optimale :

$$\underline{z} \leq f(X) \quad \forall X \in F(K_0, K_1, K_2) \quad . \qquad (9)$$

Si p_j^0 et p_j^1 sont des pénalités liées à la fixation de la variable x_j à 0 et à 1 et associées à $\underline{z}$,

$$\underline{z}' = \underline{z} + \max_{j \in K_2} \min(p_j^0, p_j^1) \qquad (10)$$

est une évaluation par défaut de la valeur de la solution optimale du sous-problème considéré. Un résultat plus fort peut être obtenu si les pénalités sont <u>additives</u> [26], c'est-à-dire si la somme des pénalités encourues lors de la fixation simultanée de plusieurs variables à 0 ou à 1 constitue une pénalité valable. Donc si pour tout couple d'ensembles d'indices K'_o et $K'_1 \subset K_2$ tels que $K'_o \cap K'_1 = \emptyset$

$$\underline{z} + \sum_{j \in K'_o} p^o_j + \sum_{j \in K'_1} p^1_j \leq f(X)$$

$$\forall X \in F(K_o \cup K'_o,\ K_1 \cup K'_1, K_2 \setminus (K'_o \cup K'_1)) \tag{11}$$

les pénalités p^o_j et p^1_j sont additives. Alors

$$\underline{z}'' = \underline{z} + \sum_{j \in K_2} \min(p^o_j,\ p^1_j) \tag{12}$$

est une évaluation par défaut de la valeur de la solution optimale du sous-problème considéré.
Des pénalités additives ont été obtenues notamment pour le problème de la localisation des entrepôts [27] [28] et pour les programmes quadratiques et non linéaires en variables 0-1 [29] [30].

4. FORMULATION IMPLICITE ET RELAXATIONS

Pour certains problèmes de programmation combinatoire une formulation mathématique explicite de toutes les contraintes s'avère trop lourde et une formulation implicite est préférable; c'est notamment le cas d'un grand nombre de problèmes exprimés en termes de graphes. Il est alors possible de raisonner sur cette formulation implicite pour construire des relaxations : on établit la liste des propriétés mathématiques qui, collectivement, définissent une solution optimale et on examine les problèmes obtenus en omettant ou en affaiblissant une ou plusieurs de ces propriétés. Si une des relaxations ainsi obtenues correspond à un problème suffisamment aisé à résoudre on l'utilise pour construire une fonction d'évaluation. Eventuellement, dans une seconde phase, on améliore cette fonction d'évaluation en raisonnant sur les conséquences de la réintroduction de la ou des propriétés omises.
Considérons par exemple le problème du voyageur de commerce. Soit un graphe G = (X, U) aux arcs duquels sont

associés des nombres réels positifs appelés longueurs. Un circuit hamiltonien de G est un circuit passant une et une seule fois par tout sommet de G. Un cycle hamiltonien de G est un cycle passant une et une seule fois par tout sommet de G. Le problème du voyageur de commerce consiste à déterminer un circuit hamiltonien de G de longueur minimum, ou, si G est symétrique, un cycle hamiltonien de longueur minimum.
Un circuit hamiltonien C est caractérisé par les propriétés suivantes :

- C est connexe,
- C contient $n = |X|$ arcs,
- le demi-degré intérieur de x_j (c'est-à-dire le nombre d'arcs de C dont l'extrémité terminale est x_j) $d^-_C(x_j) = 1$ pour tout $x \in X$,
- le demi degré extérieur de x_j (c'est-à-dire le nombre d'arcs de C dont l'extrémité initiale est x_j) $d^+_C(x_j) = 1$ pour tout $x_j \in X$.

Un cycle hamiltonien D est caractérisé par les propriétés suivantes :

- D est connexe,
- D contient $n = |X|$ arêtes,
- le degré de x_j (c'est-à-dire le nombre d'arêtes incidents à x_j) $d_C(x_j) = 2$ pour tout $x_j \in X$.

Eastman [11] a noté que si l'on abandonne la restriction que C est connexe, on obtient un problème d'affectation [34] qui peut être aisément résolu. A la solution optimale de ce problème d'affectation correspondront un ou plusieurs circuits partitionnant l'ensemble X des sommets de G. S'il y a un seul circuit le problème du voyageur de commerce est résolu; s'il y en a plusieurs le coût de la solution du problème d'affectation est une évaluation par défaut du coût de la solution optimale du problème du voyageur de commerce. Cette évaluation peut être améliorée en raisonnant dans une seconde phase comme le fait Christofides [9] sur les conséquences d'une réimposition de la contrainte de connexité de C : désignons par $X_1, X_2, \ldots, X_\ell$ les ensembles des sommets appartenant au 1er, 2ème, ... ℓème circuit; la solution optimale du problème du voyageur de commerce doit être connexe et comprendre, outre certains des arcs des ℓ circuits obtenus ℓ chemins issus chacun d'un des ensembles de sommets $X_1, X_2, \ldots, X_\ell$ et allant chacun à l'un de ces ensembles. On peut donc définir un nouveau problème du voyageur de commerce avec ℓ sommets $x'_1, x'_2, \ldots, x'_\ell$ correspondants à $X_1, X_2, \ldots, X_\ell$, les longueurs entre paires de sommets x'_i, x'_j, étant les plus courtes distances entre paires des sommets de X_i et X_j, calculées d'après le tableau optimal du problème d'affectation. Une évaluation de la longueur du plus court circuit hamiltonien dans ce nouveau problème peut être obtenue comme plus haut et ajoutée à l'évaluation précédente. Cette procédure peut être itérée jusqu'à l'obtention d'une solution optimale pour le problème d'affectation et les évaluations sommées.

Dans le cas où G est symétrique le problème obtenu en remplaçant les contraintes $d_D(x_j) = 2$ pour tout $x_j \in X$ par les contraintes plus faibles $d_D(x_j) \geq 1$ peut être aisément résolu comme l'a montré Kruskal [33] : c'est le problème de la recherche d'un 1-arbre minimum dans un graphe (c'est-à-dire d'un arbre auquel on adjoint l'arête la plus courte qu'il ne comprend pas). Si $d_D(x_j) = 2$ pour tout $x_j \in X$ dans le 1-arbre optimal la solution optimale du problème du voyageur de commerce a été obtenue. Si ce n'est pas le cas, on peut améliorer l'évaluation donnée par la longueur de cet 1-arbre en modifiant les longueurs de toutes les arêtes incidentes à un sommet x_j d'une même quantité; comme $d_D(x_j)$ doit être égal à 2 on sait de combien la longueur de la solution optimale du problème du voyageur de commerce sera modifiée et cette solution elle-même ne sera pas modifiée. Si le degré de x_j dans le 1-arbre n'est pas égal à 2 ce 1-arbre sera modifié si la variation est assez grande et l'évaluation pourra, dans certains cas, être rendue plus précise. Si, par exemple le degré de x_j dans le 1-arbre vaut 1 et reste égal à 1 tant que les longueurs des arêtes incidentes à x_j ne sont pas réduites de plus de a, l'évaluation est améliorée de cette quantité a. Une fonction d'évaluation très précise pour le problème de voyageur de commerce a été obtenue par Held et Karp [31] [32] en utilisant systématiquement de telles modifications des longueurs des arêtes de G.

5. CHOIX DES TESTS

Dans le choix des tests, il faut tenir compte de la précision des évaluations et du temps de calcul nécessaire à les obtenir : deux critères généralement divergents. Selon le premier critère on peut dire qu'un test en domine un autre s'il fournit au moins autant d'information pour tout problème de la classe auquel il s'applique. Pour certains couples de tests une telle relation de dominance peut être prouvée mathématiquement : ce sera le cas si la relaxation utilisée dans le second test est une relaxation de celle utilisée dans le premier. La dominance au sens mathématique engendre généralement un ordre partiel sur l'ensemble des tests. On peut aussi comparer la précision des tests expérimentalement et dire qu'un test en domine au autre au sens empirique si pour tous les problèmes considérés dans une série d'expériences il fournit au moins autant d'information, ce qui donne un nouvel ordre partiel. De manière moins certaine, on peut aussi ordonner complètement les test d'après la précision moyenne de leurs évaluations. Il faudra ensuite tenir compte du temps de calcul nécessaire à obtenir les évaluations. Une décision rationnelle serait basée sur une étude systématique des effets de ces deux paramètres sur le temps global de calcul. Des expériences faites en ajoutant ou retranchant des tests dans un même programme montrent que les meilleures performances sont très souvent obtenues avec les évaluations les plus précises.

BIBLIOGRAPHIE

1. J. Anthonisse, A Note on Equivalent Systems of Linear Diophantine Equations, Zeitschrift für Oper. Res., 17, 167, 1973.
2. R.D. Armstrong and P. Sinha, Improved Penalty Calculations for a Mixed Integer Branch and Bound Algorithm, Math. Prog., 6, 1974.
3. E. Balas, An Additive Algorithm for Solving Linear Programs with Zero-One Variables, Oper. Res., 13, 517, 1965.
4. E. Balas, Discrete Programming by the Filter Method, Oper. Res., 15, 915, 1967.
5. E. Balas, The Intersection Cut-A New Cutting Plane for Integer Programming, Oper. Res. 19, 19, 1971.
6. E. Balas, Integer Programming and Convex Analysis : Intersection Cuts from Outer Polars, Math. Prog. 2, 330, 1972.
7. G.H. Bradley, Transformation of Integer Programs to Knapsack Problem, Discrete Math., 1, 29, 1971.
8. C.H. Bradley, P.L. Hammer and L. Wolsey, Coefficient Reduction for Inequalities in 0-1 Variables, Research Report CORR 73-6, University of Waterloo
9. N. Christofides, Bounds for the Travelling Salesman Problem, Oper. Res., 20, 1044, 1972.
10. N.J. Driebeek, An Algorithm for the Solution of Mixed Integer Programming Problems, Manag. Sci., 12, 576, 1966.
11. W.L. Eastman, A Solution to the Travelling Salesman Problem, Econometrica, 27, 282, 1959.
12. M.A. Efroymson and T.L. Ray, A Branch and Bound

Algorithm for Plant Location, Oper. Res., 14, 361, 1966.
13. S.E. Elmaghraby and M.K. Wig, On the Treatment of Stock Cutting Problems as Diophantine Programs, North Carolina State University, 1970.
14. D. Fayard et G. Plateau, Résolution d'un problème d'affectation, Bulletin de la Direction des Etudes de Recherches, EDF, 83, 1973.
15. R.S. Garfinkel and G.L. Nemhauser, Integer Programming, Wiley, New York, 1972.
16. A.M. Geoffrion, Integer Programming by Implicit Enumeration and Balas'Method, SIAM Rev., 7, 178, 1967.
17. A.M. Geoffrion, An Improved Implicit Enumeration Approach for Integer Programming, Oper. Res., 17, 437, 1969.
18. F. Glover, A Multiphase-Dual Algorithm for the Zero-One Integer Programming Problem, Oper. Res., 13, 879, 1965.
19. F. Glover, Surrogate Constraints, Oper. Res., 16, 741, 1968.
20. F. Glover and R.E. Wolsey, Aggregating Diophantine Equations, Zeitschrift für Oper. Res., 16, 1, 1972.
21. R. Gomory and E.L. Johnson, Some Continuous Functions Related to Corner Polyhedra, Math. Prog., 3, 23,1972.
22. R. Gomory and E.L. Johnson, Some Continuous Functions Related to Corner Polyhedra II, Math. Prog., 3, 359, 1972.
23. M. Gondran et J.L. Laurière, Un algorithme pour le problème de partitionnement, Revue Fr. Auto. Infor. Recherche Opér., 8, 27, 1974.
24. P.L. Hammer and S. Nguyen, APPOSS, A Partial Order in the Solution Space of Bivalent Programs, Univ. de Montréal, CRM 186, 1972.
25. P.L. Hammer and P. Hansen, Quadratic 0-1 Programming, CORE Discussion Paper, 7219, 1972.
26. P. Hansen, Pénalités additives pour les programmes en variables 0-1, Comptes Rendus Acad. Sci. Paris, 273, 175, 1971.
27. P. Hansen, Pénalités additives pour le problème de la localisation des entrepôts, Comptes Rendus Acad. Sci., 273, 252, 1971.
28. P. Hansen, Two Algorithms for the Simple Plant Location Problem Using Additive Penalties, soumis pour publication.
29. P. Hansen, Fonctions d'évaluation et pénalités pour les programmes quadratiques en variables 0-1, dans ce volume.

30. P. Hansen, Programmes Mathématiques en Variables 0-1, thèse d'agrégation de l'enseignement supérieur, Université Libre de Bruxelles, 1974.
31. M. Held and R.M. Karp, The Travelling Salesman Problem and Minimum Spanning Trees, Oper. Res. 18, 1138, 1970.
32. M. Held and R.M. Karp, The Travelling Salesman Problem and Minimum Spanning Trees, Part.II, Math. Prog., 1, 1971.
33. J.B. Kruskal, On the Shortest Spanning Subtree of a Graph and the Travelling Salesman Problem, Proc. Amer. Math. Soc. 2, 48, 1956.
34. H. Kuhn, The Hungarian Method for the Assigment Problem, Naval Res. Logist. Quart., 2, 1965.
35. J.D.C. Little, K.G. Murty, D.W. Sweeney and C. Karel, An Algorithm for the Travelling Salesman Problem, Oper. Res. 11, 972, 1963.
36. G.B. Matthews, On the Partition of Numbers, Proc. Lond. Math. Soc., 28, 486, 1896.
37. M. Padberg, Equivalent Knapsack-type Formulations of Bounded Integer Linear Programs, Naval Res. Log. Quart., 19, 699, 1972.
38. C.C. Petersen, Computational Experience with Variants of the Balas Algorithm Applied to the Selection of R. and D. Projects, Manag. Sci., 13, 736, 1967.
39. J. Tomlin, An Improved Branch-and-Bound Method for Integer Programming, Oper. Res. 19, 1070, 1971.

BOOLEAN ELEMENTS IN COMBINATORIAL OPTIMIZATION

Peter L. Hammer

Department of Combinatorics and Optimization
University of Waterloo
Waterloo, Ontario, Canada

TABLE OF CONTENTS. Introduction; I. Elements of Boolean Algebra; II. The Resolvent; III. Algorithms; IV. Equivalent Forms of 0-1 Programs; V. Packing and Knapsack Problems; VI. Coefficient Transformation; VII. Polytopes in the Unit Cube; VIII. Pseudo-Boolean Functions and Game Theory; References.

INTRODUCTION

The possibility of using Boolean elements in the formulation and interpretation of combinatorial optimization problems has been first pointed out by R. Fortet [12], [13]. This approach was continued by P. Camion [5], R. Faure and Y. Malgrange [11], P.L. Hammer (Ivanescu), I. Rosenberg and S. Rudeanu [29]. A monograph [31] on this subject has appeared in 1968, and since then numerous publications have been devoted both to theoretical and to practical (algorithmic) aspects of this topic. Rudeanu's recent monograph [44] is devoted to the problems of Boolean equations.

Most of the generally available algorithms for the solution of discrete optimization problems are based either on implicit enumeration, or on linear algebra. The use of linear algebra is motivated by the excellent results it yields in the solution of (continuous) linear programming problems, and by the possibility of "relaxing" a typical discrete condition of the form $x \in \{0,1\}$ to its continuous counterpart $0 \le x \le 1$. However, in this relaxation one risks to lose essential features of the original discrete problem. (Consider for example the system $2x - 6y \ge -5$, $2x + 6y \ge 1$, with $x, y \in \{0,1\}$; this system obviously implies

B. Roy (ed.), Combinatorial Programming: Methods and Applications, 67–92.

$x = 1$. If we relax $x, y \in \{0,1\}$ to $0 \leq x, y \leq 1$ and examine *all* the possible surrogates of the above two inequalities, i.e. all inequalities of the form $(2 + 2\lambda)x + (-6 + 6\lambda)y \geq -5 + \lambda$, we see that they have the following 0-1 solutions: (0,0), (1,0), (1,1) for $0 \leq \lambda \leq 1/5$, (0,0), (0,1), (1,0), (1,1) for $1/5 \leq \lambda \leq 5$, and (0,1), (1,0), (1,1) for $\lambda \geq 5$. In other words, there is no surrogate of our problem implying $x = 1$). On the other hand, the degree of implicitness of an enumeration-type algorithm depends heavily on the art of using it. The interaction of constraints being usually hard to realize (unless it is strong enough to be detected in the continuous relaxation of the problem) is bypassed and taken care of only at later steps when sufficient variables have been fixed to arrive at conclusions from one of the particular constraints of the problem (e.g. how "implicit" is the enumeration which tells us that in every solution of the above problem $x = 1$, while y is arbitrary?). The difficulties arising in connection with discrete nonlinear problems are even greater.

The necessity of complementing rather than replacing the presently utilized methods with other ones seems obvious and Boolean algebra appears to be a likely candidate for this task. In our above discussed example, it would tell that the first inequality is equivalent to $\bar{x}y = 0$, the second to $\bar{x}\bar{y} = 0$, and the system to $\bar{x}y \vee \bar{x}\bar{y}(=\bar{x}) = 0$, i.e. to $x = 1$).

On the other hand, the role of a Boolean viewpoint in combinatorial optimization does not reduce to that of assiting the computations. Boolean procedures can be used to transform problems to simpler ones and to get a better insight into their structure. Irrelevant elements can be disposed of (in the above example the variable y was irrelevant, since our problem did not depend on it), inessential data simplified (e.g. the inequality $2x + 6y \geq 1$ can be reduced to $x + y \geq 1$). Further, some familiar problems can be given new and possibly advantageous formulations (e.g. see [48] for a new formulation of the plant-location problem). Moreover one can expect connections to be established between apparently different questions and structural results to be obtained (e.g. "almost" every 0-1 programming problem can be reduced to a covering problem in the original variables, there is a strong connection between prime implicants of threshold functions and facets of the polytope of 0-1 solutions of knapsack problems, different concepts of value in n-person characteristic function games can be viewed as linear approxamations of nonlinear pseudo-Boolean functions, etc.)

The aim of this survey is not to present a comprehensive bibliography of all pertinent developments, but rather to discuss a relatively small (and subjective) selection of possibly useful ideas which have been reported in the literature of the last few years.

I. ELEMENTS OF BOOLEAN ALGEBRA

Let $B = \{0,1\}$. For $x \in B$ we shall denote $\bar{x} = 1 - x$ its *complement* or *negation*. We shall also write frequently $x^\alpha = x$ if $\alpha = 1$, and $x^\alpha = \bar{x}$ if $\alpha = 0$. This notation can cause no confusion, because the regular powers of $x \in B$ being all equal to x (idempotency of multiplication) we shall never use them.

For any $x, y \in B$, we shall define their *union* $x \vee y$ by $x \vee y = x + y - xy$.

Some of the most commonly utilized properties of the above defined operations are the following: $x \vee y = y \vee x$ (commutativity), $x \vee (y \vee z) = (x \vee y) \vee z$ (associativity), $x \vee x = x$ (idempotency), $x \vee y = 0$ if and only if $x = y = 0$, $x \vee 0 = x$, $x \vee 1 = 1$, $x \vee \bar{x} = 1$, $x \vee yz = (x \vee y)(x \vee z)$ and $x(y \vee z) = xy \vee xz$ (distributivities), $x \vee xy = x$ (absorption), $x \vee \bar{x}y = x \vee y$, $\overline{xy} = \bar{x} \vee \bar{y}$ and $\overline{x \vee y} = \bar{x}\cdot\bar{y}$ (De Morgan's Laws), $\bar{\bar{x}} = x$ (double negation), $x \le y$ if and only if $xy = x$, $x \le y$ if and only if $x\bar{y} = 0$, $x = y$ if and only if $x\bar{y} \vee \bar{x}y = 0$.

A function $f(x_1,\ldots,x_n)$ whose variables and values belong to B, will be called a *Boolean function*. Examples of such functions are $x \vee yz$, $x \vee yz \vee \bar{x}\bar{z}$, $(x \vee \bar{y})(\overline{y \vee xz})$, etc. The algebraic expression of a Boolean function is not unique, e.g. the expressions $x \vee y \vee \bar{z}$ and $x \vee yz \vee \bar{x}\bar{z}$ define the same function (this can be seen either by giving to x, y, z all 2^3 possible combinations of values, or noticing that $x \vee yz \vee \bar{y}\bar{z} = x \vee yz \vee \bar{z}$. $= x \vee y \vee \bar{z}$.

A variable x, or its negation $\bar{x}$ will be called a *literal* X. A finite product of literals will be called an *elementary conjunction* $C = \prod_{j \in S} x_j^{\alpha_j}$ by convention, we shall consider sometimes also the constant $\underline{1}$ as being an elementary conjunction (with $S = \emptyset$). A finite union of elementary conjunctions $E = C_1 \vee C_2 \vee \ldots \vee C_m$ will be called a *disjunctive form*. It can be shown easily that every Boolean function can be expressed in a disjunctive form.

We shall say that an elementary conjunction C is *contained* in the elementary conjunction C' if every literal appearing as a factor in C is also a factor of C'. e.g. $x\bar{y}$ is contained in $x\bar{y}zu$, also in $x\bar{y}$, but is not contained in xz or in xyz .

An elementary conjunction I is said to be an *implicant* of the Boolean function $f(x_1,\ldots,x_n)$, if $I = 1$ implies $f(x_1,\ldots,x_n) = 1$. For example, $x\bar{y}$ is an implicant of

$x\bar{y} \vee \bar{y}z(x \vee \bar{z})$. Also, $x\bar{y}$ is an implicant of $xz \vee \bar{y}\bar{z}$ (indeed, if $x\bar{y} = 1$, then $x = 1$, $y = 0$, and hence $xz \vee \bar{y}\bar{z}$ becomes $z \vee \bar{z}$ which is equal to 1).

An implicant P of a Boolean function $f(x_1,\ldots,x_n)$ is said to be a *prime implicant* if there is no other implicant P' of f contained in P. For example, $x\bar{y}$ is a prime implicant of $f = xz \vee \bar{y}\bar{z}$, but $x\bar{y}z$ is a non-prime implicant of f. If all the prime implicants of a Boolean function f are $P_1,\ldots,P_t$, then it is easy to see that $f = P_1 \vee \ldots \vee P_t$.

We shall see later that the knowledge of the prime implicants of a given Boolean function is extremely useful. A way of finding all the prime implicants is offered by the so-called *consensus* method.

Given two elementary conjunctions C and C', such that there is precisely one variable (x_o) appearing unnegated (x_o) is one of them, and negated $(\bar{x}_o)$ in the other, then the elementary conjunction obtained from the juxtaposition CC' of C and C' after deleting x_o, $\bar{x}_o$ and repeated literals, will be called the *consensus* of C and C'. For example, let $C = x\bar{y}\bar{z}u$ and $C = \bar{y}zu\bar{w}$; then their consensus is $C'' = x\bar{y}u\bar{w}$.

The *consensus method* consists in applying as many times as possible the following two operations to a disjunctive form of a Boolean function:

(i) eliminate any elementary conjunction which contains another one;
(ii) add as a new elementary conjunction the consensus of two elementary conjunctions, provided this consensus does not include any of the listed (undeleted elementary conjunctions.

All the different expressions obtained along this process represent the same Boolean function, and the elementary conjunctions appearing in the final form at the end of this (finite, but long) process are exactly the prime implicants of the given functions.

It is likely that in practical problems finding all the prime implicants of a Boolean function might require an excessive amount of computation. Therefore, in the more practical procedures described in Section III, we shall work with implicants which are not necessarily prime, but which allow an efficient solution of many 0-1 programs. A particular way of finding them is described in [20], and numerous other alternatives are easy to describe.

II. THE RESOLVENT

Let $S \subseteq B^n$ be the set of solutions of the system Σ of pseudo-Boolean inequalities $f(X) \leq 0$ $(i = 1,\ldots,m)$ and let $\rho(X)$ be a Boolean function which takes the value 0 iff $X \in S$. The function ρ will be called the *resolvent* of Σ, and also the resolvent of S.

Let us consider the linear inequality

$$(1) \quad \sum_{j=1}^{n} a_j x_j \leq a_0$$

and let $\mathcal{C}$ be the family of all *minimal covers* of (1), i.e. the family of all the minimal sets $C \subseteq \{1,\ldots,n\}$ with the property $\sum_{j \in C} |a_j| > a_0 - \sum_{j=1}^{n} \min(0, a_j)$. It can be seen ([19]) that the function

$$(2) \quad \phi(X) = \bigvee_{C \in \mathcal{C}} \prod_{j \in C} x_j^{\alpha_j}$$

(where $\alpha_j = 1$ if $a_j \geq 0$ and $\alpha_j = 0$ if $a_j < 0$) is the resolvent of (1).

It has been shown in [29] (see also [31]) that every pseudo-Boolean function $f(X)$ has a polynomial expression, which is linear in each variable. Hence, every pseudo-Boolean inequality can be written in the form

$$(3) \quad \sum_{h=1}^{\ell} b_h y_h \leq b_0$$

where

$$(4) \quad y_h = \prod_{j \in H_h} x_j \quad (h = 1,\ldots,k)$$

are themselves taking only the values 0 and 1. If $\psi(Y)$ is the resolvent of (3) (viewed as a linear inequality in the y_h's), then it is easy to see that the resolvent $\phi(X)$ of (3) (viewed as an inequality in the x_j's) can be obtained from $\psi(Y)$ by simply substituting (4) into it.

Further, if $\phi_i(X)$ are the resolvents of the pseudo-Boolean inequalities $f_i(X) \leq 0$ $(i = 1,\ldots,m)$ then $\phi(X) = \bigvee_{i=1}^{m} \phi_i(X)$ will be the resolvent of the system Σ.

Consider for example the system consisting of $x_j \in B(j = 1,\dots,6)$ and

$$(5\text{-}1) \quad 5x_1 - 4x_2 - 2x_3 - x_4 - 4x_5 + 3x_6 \leq -2$$

$$(5\text{-}2) \quad -5x_2 + 6x_2x_6 - 8x_1x_3x_4 - 4x_2x_4 \leq -7$$

or

$$(5\text{-}1)' \quad 5x_1 + 4\bar{x}_2 + 2\bar{x}_3 + \bar{x}_4 + 4\bar{x}_5 + 3x_6 \leq 9$$

$$(5\text{-}2)' \quad 5\bar{x}_2 + 6x_2x_6 + 8\overline{x_1x_3x_4} + 4\overline{x_2x_4} \leq 10$$

The resolvents of these inequalities are, respectively.

$$(6\text{-}1) \quad \phi_1 = x_1\bar{x}_2\bar{x}_3 \vee x_1\bar{x}_2\bar{x}_4 \vee x_1\bar{x}_2\bar{x}_5 \vee x_1\bar{x}_2x_6 \vee x_1\bar{x}_3\bar{x}_5 \vee x_1\bar{x}_4\bar{x}_5 \vee x_1\bar{x}_5x_6 \vee x_1\bar{x}_3x_6 \vee \bar{x}_2\bar{x}_3\bar{x}_5 \vee \bar{x}_2\bar{x}_5x_6 \vee \bar{x}_2\bar{x}_3\bar{x}_4x_6 \vee \bar{x}_3\bar{x}_4\bar{x}_5x_6 ,$$

$$(6\text{-}2) \quad \phi_2 = \bar{x}_1\bar{x}_2 \vee \bar{x}_2\bar{x}_3 \vee \bar{x}_1x_6 \vee \bar{x}_3x_6 \vee \bar{x}_4 ,$$

while the resolvent of the system (5-1) - (5-2) is

$$(7) \quad \phi = \phi_1 \vee \phi_2 = \bar{x}_1\bar{x}_2 \vee \bar{x}_1x_6 \vee x_1\bar{x}_3\bar{x}_5 \vee \bar{x}_2\bar{x}_3 \vee \bar{x}_2\bar{x}_5 \vee \bar{x}_2x_6 \vee \bar{x}_3x_6 \vee \bar{x}_4 \vee \bar{x}_5x_6 ,$$

(showing in particular that in every solution of (5-1) - (5-2), $x_4 = 1$).

III. ALGORITHMS*

Due to the fact that the resolvent of a system of inequalities might involve an excessive number of (prime) implicants, practical algorithms based on the ideas outlined in the previous section can utilize only partially the information contained in it. Spielberg's minimal preferred inequalities method [44] belongs essentially to this class. Another example, APOSS (A Partial Order in the Solution Space), an algorithm given in [32] for solving linear 0-1 programs, utilizes only those minimal covers of the individual constraints which involve at most 3 elements. The corresponding implicants are combined to produce more implicants of lengths 1, 2 and 3. To every implicant of length 2 an order relation between variables is naturally associated ($x\bar{y} = 0$ means $x \leq y$, $xy = 0$ means $x \leq \bar{y}$, $\bar{x}\bar{y} = 0$ means $\bar{x} \leq y$).

* A survey on Boolean-based algorithms is given in [20].

If two binary relations involving the same pair of variables can be detected, then one of the variables can be eliminated ($xy = x\bar{y} = 0$ implies $x = 0$, $\bar{x}y = \bar{x}\bar{y} = 0$ implies $x = 1$, $xy = \bar{x}\bar{y} = 0$ implies $x = \bar{y}$, $x\bar{y} = \bar{x}y = 0$ implies $x = y$). When all these informations are exhausted, the same binary relations are re-used as cuts in the associated linear program, and finally, if no further use of the binary relations is apparent, a branching tehnique is applied.

Consider for example a problem involving the constraints

$$8x_1 + 7x_2 + 5x_3 + 4x_4 + 2x_5 + 2x_6 \le 14$$

$$4x_1 + 2x_2 + 6x_3 + 3x_4 + x_5 + 5x_6 \ge 12$$

The minimal covers of lengths not exceeding 3 give rise to the "partial resolvents"

$$\psi_1 = x_1x_2 \vee x_1x_3 \vee x_1x_4 \vee x_2x_3x_4$$

$$\psi_2 = \bar{x}_1\bar{x}_3 \vee \bar{x}_2\bar{x}_3\bar{x}_4 \vee \bar{x}_2\bar{x}_4\bar{x}_6 \vee \bar{x}_3\bar{x}_4\bar{x}_5 \vee \bar{x}_3\bar{x}_6$$

From $x_1x_3 = \bar{x}_1\bar{x}_3 = 0$ it follows that $x_3 = \bar{x}_1$. Substituting we get

$$\psi_1' = x_1x_2 \vee x_1x_4 \vee x_2x_4$$

$$\psi_2' = x_1\bar{x}_2\bar{x}_4 \vee \bar{x}_2\bar{x}_4\bar{x}_6 \vee x_1\bar{x}_4\bar{x}_5 \vee x_1\bar{x}_6 ,$$

hence $\psi' = \psi_1' \vee \psi_2' = x_1 \vee x_2x_4 \vee \bar{x}_2\bar{x}_4\bar{x}_6$, implying in particular $x_1 = 0$, and hence $x_3 = 1$. Substituting $x_1 = 0$, $x_3 = 1$ into our original system, we get $7x_2 + 4x_4 + 2x_5 + 2x_6 \le 9$, $2x_2 + 3x_4 + x_5 + 5x_6 \ge 6$, the partial resolvents of which are

$$\psi_1'' = x_2x_4 \vee x_2x_5x_6$$

$$\psi_2'' = \bar{x}_2\bar{x}_6 \vee \bar{x}_4\bar{x}_6 \vee \bar{x}_5\bar{x}_6 \vee \bar{x}_2\bar{x}_4\bar{x}_5;$$

hence $\psi'' = \psi_1'' \vee \psi_2'' = \bar{x}_6 \vee x_2x_4 \vee x_2x_5 \vee \bar{x}_2\bar{x}_4\bar{x}_5$ showing that $x_6 = 1$ in every feasible solution.

This algorithm has been coded on a CDC-6600 and a few hundred test problems involving up to 200 variables have been solved; the execution times (varying from .35 up to 65 sec.) compare favourably with those given by other methods.

The special case of quadratic 0-1 programs has been examined in [21], [30]. Consider a quadratic function in 0-1 variables

$$f = \sum_{j=1}^{n} c_j x_j + \sum_{\substack{i,j=1 \\ i<j}}^{n} d_{ij} x_i x_j ,$$

and let us put

$$\Delta_j = c_j + \sum_{i=1}^{j-1} d_{ij} x_i + \sum_{i=j+1}^{n} d_{ji} x_i \quad (j = 1,\ldots,n)$$

$$\Delta_{jk} = \Delta_j - \Delta_k - d_{jk} x_k + d_{kj} x_j \quad (j,\ k = 1,\ldots,n;\ j < k).$$

It is easy to see that in every minimizing point of f, $\Delta_j > 0$ ($\Delta_j < 0$) implies $x_j = 0$ ($x_j = 1$), while $\Delta_{jk} > 0$ ($\Delta_{jk} < 0$) implies $x_j \le x_k$ ($x_j \ge x_k$). These relations can be exploited exactly as in the linear case to obtain information about variables with fixed values and about equal or complementary variables. If for example,

$$f = -x_1 + 3x_2 + x_1x_4 - 3x_1x_3 + 2x_2x_4 + 3x_3x_4 - 4x_2x_3$$

then from $\Delta_1 = -1 - 3x_3 + x_4$ we get $x_4 = 0 \to \Delta_1 < 0 \to x_1 = 1$, and from $\Delta_4 = x_1 + 2x_2 + 3x_3$ we get $x_1 = 1 \to \Delta_4 > 0 \to x_4 = 0$, i.e. $\bar{x}_1\bar{x}_4 = x_1x_4 = 0$, or $x_4 = \bar{x}_1$. Replacing now x_4 by $1 - x_1$ in f gives

$$f' = -x_1 + 5x_2 + 3x_3 - 2x_1x_2 - 6x_1x_3 - 4x_2x_3 ;$$

now $\Delta_1 < 0$, and hence $x_1 = 1$; f' becomes

$$f'' = -1 + 3x_2 - 3x_3 - 4x_2x_3 ,$$

where $\Delta_3 < 0$, showing that $x_3 = 1$; finally, f'' becomes

$$f''' = -4 - x_2 ,$$

showing that $x_2 = 1$, and the minimum (-5) is obtained in (1, 1, 1, 0).

Another device which gives some insight into the problem is the examination of a "penalty relaxation inequality". This inequality has the form $\ell(x) \le b^*$, where $\ell(x)$ is a linear lower bound of the quadratic function $f(x)$, and b^* is an upper bound of the minimum of $f(n)$; the rôle of b^* can be played by the value of $f(x)$ in an arbitrary 0-1 point, while the construction of $\ell(\mathbf{x})$ (see [21]) is based on Hansen's additive penalties [34]. Such an $\ell(x)$ for our function is

$-6 + \frac{5}{2}\bar{x}_1 + x_2 + \frac{7}{2}\bar{x}_3$, and if we take as b* the value $f(1\ 0\ 1\ 0) = -4$, we find that $\frac{5}{2}\bar{x}_1 + x_2 + \frac{7}{2}\bar{x}_3 \leq 2$, i.e. $x_1 = x_3 = 1$.

Of course, the examination of the Δ_j's, Δ_{ij}'s and of the penalty-relaxation inequalities does not usually solve the entire problem, but can give valuable information when coupled with branch-and-bound type method. Since every quadratic 0-1 problem can be brought to a form where the quadratic form is positive (negative) definite (see [30]), there are possibilities of "bounding" by the use of continuous quadratic programming.

A special case of quadratic 0-1 programming has been studied in [15]. The question of maximizing a quadratic function with a single linear constraint ("quadratic knapsack problem") arose in connection with a location problem for airports in Italy, and the method suggested in [15] for its solution consists in determining linear upper bounds of the objective function and solving a sequence of associated (linear) knapsack problems.

A question which arises frequently in applications is that of minimizing an unconstrained polynomial in 0-1 variables. A method of successive elimination of variables has been given in [29] (see also [31]) for its solution. Branch-and-bound methods for the same problem have been devised in [3], [25], [33], [47], [51]; the main characteristic of these methods is the fact that branching is not performed according to single variables, but according to the 0-1 values of the nonlinear terms appearing in the polynomial. A variant of these procedures (see [25]) has been programmed on an IBM 360/50; problems with 10-30 variables, involving 10-50 nonlinear terms required between 0.48 and 239 seconds of execution time (including input-output time).

An efficient method for minimizing quotients of linear functions in 0-1 variables has been given by M. Florian and P. Robillard [41], [42]. (see also [31]).

Another question which has been examined was that of constraint pairing and its application to knapsack problems. Single linear constraints can be used in a straightforward way for deriving bounds on the variables of discrete optimization problems from the examination of all the surrogate constraints associated to pairs of constraints. Different surrogates might be helpful in fixing the values (or at least improving the bounds) of different variables; it might of course happen that no surrogate constraint fixes a variable, although the system does. It was however shown in [24] that if any variables can be fixed (or its bounds improved) by using arbitrary surrogates, then the same conclusion can also be obtained from the examination of n + 2 "special" surrogates (n of which correspond to those multipliers for which the coefficient of one of the variables in ths surrogate is 0). R. Dembo [9] shows that many of the conclusions so obtainable, are also available from the "best" surrogate. A. Charnes, D. Granot and F. Granot [6] show how to extend these ideas to the case of more than two constraints.

An efficient application of this approach to knapsack problems [10]

$$(KP)\begin{cases}\text{maximize } \sum_{j=1}^{n} a_j x_j \\ \text{subject to } \sum_{j=1}^{n} b_j x_j \le b_0 \\ x_j \in \{0, 1\}, \quad j = 1,\dots,n \; .\end{cases}$$

associates to (KP) a pair of constraints and derives conclusions from the resulting system.

Let us assume that $\frac{a_1}{b_1} \ge \dots \ge \frac{a_n}{b_n}$. Let $\Xi = (\xi_1,\dots,\xi_n)$ be the optimal solution of (KP'), obtained from (KP) by replacing all the constraints $x_j \in \{0, 1\}$ by $0 \le x_j \le 1$ $(j = 1,\dots,n)$. If Ξ is not an integer vector, then we have $\xi_j = 1$ $(j = 1,\dots,t)$, $\xi_j = 0$ $(j = t + 2,\dots,n)$, and $0 < \xi_{t+1} < 1$. A very good (frequently optimal) solution is obtained by fixing $x_j^* = 1$ $(j = 1,\dots,t)$, $x_{t+1}^* = 0$, and re-solving a new KP' for b_0 replaced by $b_0 - \sum_{j=1}^{t} b_j$, etc., until arriving to a problem with x_j fixed for $j = 1,\dots,t^*$, and such that all the b_j's $(j = t^* + 1,\dots,n)$ are larger than the remaining b_0. Then the already fixed values x_j^* $(j = 1,\dots,t^*)$ together with $x_j^* = 0$ $(j = t^* + 1,\dots,n)$ form a good initial solution: let $a^* = \sum_{j=1}^{n} a_j x_j^*$. If the data are integer, than any better solution will have $a^* + 1$ as a lower bound, An upper bound to it is $\hat{a} = \sum_{j=1}^{t} a_j + [a_{t+1}\, \xi_{t+1}]$, (where $[\alpha]$ means the integer part of α). Hence if X^* is not an optimal solution, then any better solution satisfies

$$\sum_{j=1}^{n} a_j x_j = a^* + p + 1 ,$$

where p is a nonnegative integer not exceeding $\hat{a} - a^* - 1$. Pairing this with the constraint

$$\sum_{j=1}^{n} b_j x_j + s = b_0 \quad (s \geq 0)$$

usually supplies enough information to fix at least some of the variables. These informations can be supplemented by those given by the binary and ternary relations among the variables.

Consider for example the 0-1 knapsack problem of maximizing

$$15x_1 + 16x_2 + 13x_3 + 9x_4 + 17x_5 + 11x_6$$

subject to

$$9x_1 + 10x_2 + 11x_3 + 8x_4 + 16x_5 + 11x_6 \leq 29$$

Here $\Xi = (1, 1, \frac{10}{11}, 0, 0, 0)$, $X^* = (1, 1, 0, 1, 0, 0)$, $\hat{a} = 42$, $a^* = 40$. Hence, if X^* is not optimal, then any optimal solution satisfies

$$15x_1 + 16x_2 + 13x_3 + 9x_4 + 17x_5 + 11x_6 = 41 + p$$
$$(0 \leq p \leq 1)$$

$$9x_1 + 10x_2 + 11x_3 + 8x_4 + 16x_5 + 11x_6 + s = 20$$
$$(s \geq 0)$$

Multiplying the first equation by 11, the second one by 13 and subtracting, we get

$$48x_1 + 46x_2 - 5x_4 - 21x_5 - 22x_6 - 13s = 74 + 11p$$

or

$$48x_1 + 46x_2 + 5\bar{x}_4 + 21\bar{x}_5 + 22\bar{x}_6 + 11\bar{p} = 133 + 13s,$$

implying $x_1 = 1$, $x_2 = 1$, $x_5 = 0$, $x_6 = 0$, and the last relation reduces to $5\bar{x}_4 + 11\bar{p} = -4 + 13s$, which obviously has no nonnegative integer solutions, showing that X^* was the optimal solution of our problem.

Experiments carried out with this idea show that it is

extremely useful for fixing variables in 0-1 knapsack problems. In experiemnts carried out on an IBM 370/145 it turned out that in randomly generated problems involving 50-10,000 variables, the average number of fixed variables was between 74% and 93% of the total number of variables, while the computing time was less then one second.

IV. EQUIVALENT FORMS OF 0-1 PROGRAMS

Let us rewrite the resolvent $\phi(X)$ of a system Σ of linear or nonlinear inequalities, in the form

$$(8)\quad \phi(X) = \bigvee_{t=1}^{T} \left(\prod_{j\in U_t} x_j\right)\left(\prod_{j\in V_t} \bar{x}_j\right)$$

where U_t, V_t $(t = 1,\ldots,T)$ are disjoint subsets of $\{1,\ldots,n\}$. Then, it is easy to see that $\phi(X) = 0$ iff X is a solution of the following *generalized covering problem*

$$(9)\quad \sum_{j\in V_t} x_j - \sum_{j\in U_t} x_j \geq 1 - |U_t| \quad (t = 1,\ldots,T)$$

Hence ([19])* every linear or nonlinear 0-1 programming problem is *strongly equivalent* to (i.e. has the same set of feasible solutions as) a generalized covering problem.

Consider now the problem (PI) of minimizing a pseudo-Boolean function $f(X)$ subject to Σ. Assume that f_0 is *strictly monotonic*, i.e. changing any 1 of any $X \in B^n$ to a 0 strictly decreases the value of f_0. This assumption holds for example for all linear f_0's having only positive coefficients. Specializing (8) to the case where $(\prod_{j\in U_t} x_j)(\prod_{j\in V_t} x_j)$ $(t = 1,\ldots,T)$ are the prime implicants of $\phi(X)$, and assuming that $U_t = \emptyset$ for $t = 1,\ldots,T_0$ and $U_t \neq \emptyset$ for $t = T_0 + 1,\ldots,T$, it can be shown ([22]) that (PI) is *equivalent* to (i.e. has the same optimal solutions as) the problem (PII) of minimizing $f_0(X)$ subject to $\phi'(X) = 0$, where

---

*This remark appears in a somewhat stronger form for the special case of a single linear pseudo-Boolean inequality in [2].

$$(10)\qquad \phi'(X) = \bigvee_{t=1}^{T_0} \prod_{j\in V_t} \bar{x}_j \ ,$$

i.e. to the *covering problem*: minimize $f_0(X)$ subject to $\sum_{j\in V_t} x_j \geq 1$ $(t = 1,\dots,T_0)$.

This equivalence holds because every feasible solution of PI is a feasible solution of the covering problem, while a feasible solution of the covering problem cannot be optimal unless it is feasible for PI too.

For example minimizing $\sum_{j=1}^{6} c_j x_j$ $(c_j > 0,\ j = 1,\dots,6)$ subject to (5-1) - (5-2) is strongly equivalent to the generalized covering problem: minimize $\sum_{j=1}^{6} c_j x_j$ subject to $x_4 = 1$ and to $x_1 + x_2 \geq 1$, $x_1 - x_6 \geq 0$, $-x_1 + x_3 + x_5 \geq 1$, $x_2 + x_3 \geq 1$, $x_2 + x_5 \geq 1$, $x_2 - x_6 \geq 0$, $x_3 - x_6 \geq 0$, $x_5 - x_6 \geq 0$ and is equivalent to the covering problem: minimize $\sum_{j=1}^{6} c_j x_j$ subject to $x_4 = 1$ and to $x_1 + x_2 \geq 1$, $x_2 + x_3 \geq 1$, $x_2 + x_5 \geq 1$ (x_6 does not appear in any of the constraints, hence $x_6 = 0$ in any optimal solution).

Numerous equivalences between different forms of 0-1 programs have been described in [28].

V. PACKING AND KNAPSACK PROBLEMS

By a *packing problem* we shall mean a set of linear inequalities in 0-1 variables of the form $x_i + x_j \leq 1$ $((i, j) \in \Gamma)$. A linear inequality $\sum_{j=1}^{n} a_j x_j \leq a_0$ $(a_j \geq 0$, $j = 0, 1,\dots,n)$ is equivalent to a packing problem iff all its minimal covers contain exactly two elements.

The converse problem, of characterizing those packing problems which are equivalent to a single linear inequality, has been examined in [7]. It has been shown that the following two characterizations follow from the theory of threshold functions.

I. PP is not 0-1 equivalent to a single linear inequality iff it is possible to find 4 distinct indices h, i, j, k such that

$$(h, i) \in \Gamma, (h, j) \notin \Gamma, (h, k) \notin \Gamma, (i, j) \notin \Gamma,$$
$$(i, k) \notin \Gamma, (j, k) \in \Gamma,$$

or such that

$$(h, i) \in \Gamma, (h, j) \notin \Gamma, (h, k) \notin \Gamma, (i, j) \in \Gamma,$$
$$(i, k) \notin \Gamma, (j, k) \in \Gamma,$$

or such that

$$(h, i) \in \Gamma, (h, j) \notin \Gamma, (h, k) \in \Gamma, (i, j) \in \Gamma,$$
$$(i, k) \notin \Gamma, (j, k) \in \Gamma .$$

II. PP is 0-1 equivalent to a single linear inequality iff there exists a partitioning of $\{1,\ldots,n\}$ into two subsets N' and N'' and a permutation $(j_1,\ldots,j_r)$ of the elements of N'' such that

i) $\forall\, i, j \in N', \quad (i, j) \in \Gamma$

and

ii) $\forall\, i, j \in N'', \quad (i, j) \notin \Gamma$

iii) $\forall\, j_s, j_t \in N'', \quad (s < t), \forall i \in N', \quad (i, j_t) \in \Gamma$ implies $(i, j_s) \in \Gamma$.

An efficient algorithm was also presented in [7] for finding such a 0-1 equivalent single linear inequality, if any, or otherwise to find a "small" system of linear inequalities equivalent to the given PP. Peled studies in a recent paper the more general question of reducing the number of linear constraints in an arbitrary system of inequalities involving only 0-1 variables.

VI. COEFFICIENT TRANSORMATION

It is obvious that different linear inequalities may have the same 0-1 solutions, and it might be useful to be able to transform a given inequality to an equivalent one which has a "better" form. For example $x + y \leq 1$ seems to be a better form than $173x + 89y \leq 244.5$, but obviously the two inequalities have the same 0-1 solutions. This problem is studied in [4] and it is shown that the "optimal" coefficients (according to a large variety of criteria) can be determined by solving an associated linear program.

Let us consider a linear inequality

$$(11) \quad \sum_{j=1}^{n} a_j x_j \le a_0 ,$$

where $a_1 \ge \dots \ge a_n \ge 0$. A minimal cover $R \subseteq \{1,\dots,n\}$ such that $\sum_{j\in R} a_j - a_r + a_{r'} \le a_0$ holds for any $r \in R$, $r' \notin R$, $r < r'$, is called a *roof* of (11). Similarly a set $C \subseteq \{1,\dots,n\}$, maximal with the property that $\sum_{j\in C} a_j \le a_0$, and such that $\sum_{j\in C} a_j - a_c + a_{c'} > a_0$ holds for any $c \in C$, $c' \notin C$, $c > c'$, is called a *ceiling* of (11). It is shown that every inequality

$$(12) \quad \sum_{j=1}^{n} b_j x_j \le b_0$$

0-1 equivalent to (11) and such that $b_1 \ge \dots \ge b_n \ge 0$, is proportional to a solution of the system

$$\sum_{j\in R} b_j \ge b_0 + 1 \quad \text{(for all roofs } R \text{ of (12))}$$

$$\sum_{j\in C} b_j \le b_0 \quad \text{(for all ceilings } C \text{ of (12))}$$

$$b_1 \ge \dots \ge b_n \ge 0.$$

For example all the inequalities 0-1 equivalent to

$$7x_1 + 5x_2 + 3x_3 + 3x_4 + x_5 \le 10$$

and having the coefficients ordered in the same way, are characterized by the system

$$b_1 + b_2 \ge b_0 + 1, \qquad b_1 + b_3 \le b_0,$$

$$b_1 + b_4 + b_5 \ge b_0 + 1, \quad b_2 + b_3 + b_5 \le b_0,$$

$$b_2 + b_3 + b_4 \ge b_0 + 1,$$

$$b_1 \ge b_2 \ge b_3 \ge b_4 \ge b_5 \ge 0.$$

If the criterion is to minimize b_0, the optimal solution is (4, 3, 2, 2, 1; 6), i.e. the inequality

$$4x_1 + 3x_2 + 2x_3 + 2x_4 + x_5 \leq 6.$$

Numerous problems of similar nature have been studied in threshold logic (e.g. see [35], [36]). The usefulness of such transformations for increasing the efficiency of branch-and-bound methods is pointed out in [49].

VII. POLYTOPES IN THE UNIT CUBE

The convex hull $\hat{S}$ of a set S of vertices of the unit cube can be characterized by its facets. The set S is characterized by a Boolean Function $\delta_S(X)$ equal to 0 for $X \in S$ and to 1 elsewhere. The question of relating the Boolean and the geometric structures of a system of inequalities in 0-1 variables arises naturally. M.A. Pollatschek [40] seems to have been the first to examine such questions. M.W. Padberg [39] has given a procedure for producing facets of $\hat{S}$. A systematic investigation of this topic has been attempted in [23]. Some of the results of [23] overlap with those of [1], [17], [18], [37], [39], [50].

It was noticed in section IV that every 0-1 programming problem with a strictly monotone objective function can be reduced to a covering problem. Therefore in this section we shall mainly deal with facets of covering problems. For notational convenience we shall put $y_j = \bar{x}_j$ $(j = 1,\ldots,n)$; thus the constraints $\sum_{j \in T_i} x_j \geq 1$ $(i = 1,\ldots,h)$ of the given covering problem become

$$(13) \quad \sum_{j \in T_i} y_j \leq t_i - 1 \quad (i = 1,\ldots,h)$$

where $t_i = |T_i|$. Let S be the set of 0-1 solutions of (13), and $\hat{S}$ its convex hull. We shall assume that $\hat{S}$ is n-dimensional. It can be seen easily that $-y_j \leq 0$ is a facet of $\hat{S}$ for all $j = 1,\ldots,n$, but $y_j \leq 1$ is a facet of $\hat{S}$ iff $t_1 = 2$ implies that $j \notin T_i$.

It has been shown in [23] that the constraint [13] is a facet of $\hat{S}$ iff for any $k \notin T_j$, the intersection of all those T_j which are contained in $\{k\} \cup T_i$ is nonempty. Further, if (13) is not a facet of $\hat{S}$, a procedure was given for strengthening it to a facet (by changing the coefficients of the variables $y_k (k \notin T_i)$ from 0 to certain positive values. The procedure becomes particularly efficient for an apparently special class of covering problems, the so-called *regular covering problems*, i.e. those covering problems where the feasibility of any point $(y_1^*,\ldots,y_n^*)$ (where $y_{j_1}^* =\ldots= y_{j_s}^* = 1$, the other components are 0) implies the feasibility of any point $(y_1^{**},\ldots,y_n^{**})$ having the same number of 1 components $(y_{\ell_1}^{**} =\ldots= y_{\ell_s}^{**} = 1$, the other components are 0) when $j_1 \le \ell_1,\ldots,j_s \le \ell_s$. However (see [22]), a very wide class of covering problems can be brought to such a form.

The extension procedure becomes extremely simple for the case of regular covering problems and it can be shown that there is a 1-1 correspondence between those factors of $\hat{S}$ which have only 0-1 coefficients and those sets T_i which have the following two properties: (i) if $u_i = \min\{j \mid j \in T_i\}$, $w_i = \min\{j \mid j \notin T_i,\ j > u_i\}$ (if any), and if $P_i \in B^n$ is the point whose 1-components are all the elements of the set

$$\begin{cases} (\{w_i\} \cup T_i) - \{u_i\} & \text{(if } w_i \text{ is defined)} \\ T_i - \{u_i\} & \text{(otherwise)}, \end{cases}$$

then $P_i \in S$; (ii) if $v_i = \min\{j \mid j \in T_i,\ j \ne u_i\}$ and $R_i \in S$ is the point whose 1-components are all the elements of the set $(\{1\} \cup T_i) - \{u_i, v_i\}$, then $R_i \in S$.

The most common case of a regular covering problem corresponds to knapsack problems, when the T_i's are its minimal covers. A list of all the facets of all the knapsack problems with at most 5 variables is given in [23].

VIII. PSEUDO-BOOLEAN FUNCTIONS AND GAME THEORY.*

A *characteristic function game* (N, W) is a set of "players" $N = \{1, 2,\ldots,n\}$ and a real-valued function $W: 2^N \to R$ (called the *characteristic function*), defined for all subsets T of N. If T is a "coalition", then W(T) is the "payoff" it can secure. It is clear that 2^N is mapped in a 1-1 way onto B^n by mapping a subset T of N to its *characteristic vector* X, defined by $x_k = 1$ for $k \in T$ and $x_k = 0$ for $k \notin T$. Hence as

*See [26].

remarked by Owen ([38]) a characteristic function game is actually the same as a pseudo-Boolean function.

It is well known [31] that every pseudo-Boolean function f in n variables has a unique polynomial expression of the form

$$f(x) = \sum_{T\subseteq N} [a_T \prod_{k\in T} x_k] ,$$

called its *canonical form*. The corresponding characteristic function game (N, W) then satisfies

$$W(T) = \sum_{S\subseteq T} a_S , \quad T \subseteq N .$$

Shapley ([45]) has shown that this relation gives

$$a_T = \sum_{S\subseteq T} (-1)^{t-s} W(S) , \quad T \subseteq N ,$$

where t and s are the cardinalities of T and S, respectively. Thus the a_T's can be found from the function $f(x)$.

As an example let us consider the 3-person characteristic function game defined by the following table:

T	∅	{1}	{2}	{3}	{1, 2}	{1, 3}	{2, 3}	{1,2,3}
W(T)	0	0	0	0	3	2	2	4

The corresponding pseudo-Boolean function on B^3 is $f(X) = 3x_1x_2\bar{x}_3 + 2x_1\bar{x}_2x_3 + 2\bar{x}_1x_2x_3 + 4x_1x_2x_3$. By replacing each $\bar{x}_j$ by $1 - x_j$ and simplifying, we obtain the canonical expression:

$$(14) \quad f(X) = 3x_1x_2 + 2x_1x_3 + 2x_2x_3 - 3x_1x_2x_3 .$$

A game (N, W) is said to be *superadditive* if for any disjoint sets S, T of N, we have $W(S) + W(T) \le W(S \cup T)$ (i.e. it always "pays" to form a larger coalition). It can be easily seen that the game of the example in section 1 is superadditive. The following result holds:

Let f be the pseudo-Boolean function corresponding to the game W. Then the following are equivalent: (a) W is superadditive, (b) $X + Y \le 1$ implies $f(X) + f(Y) \le f(X + Y)$ for all $X, Y \in B^n$, (c) $XY = 0$ implies $f(X) + f(Y) \le f(X + Y)$

for all $X, Y \in B^n$, (d) $f(XY) + f(X\bar{Y}) \le f(X)$ for all $X, Y \in B^n$ (here $\bar{Y} = \underline{1} - Y$, $\underline{1} = (1,\ldots,1)$).

The goal of n-person characteristic function game theory is to find a "solution", i.e. a value for each player based upon the coalitions he may join. If a game (N, W) satisfies $W(\emptyset) = 0$ then, as Shapley [45] mentions, we may regard a solution as an inessential game (N, Z) which "approximates" (N, W) by some method and which assigns a value $Z(\{j\})$ to each player j. In this paper we discuss a few specific solutions in terms of pseudo-Boolean functions. Since such a function defines a game we can speak about the core and the Shapley value of a function. Throughout this section let f be a pseudo-Boolean function with $f(0) = 0$. A *core element* of f is a linear pseudo-Boolean function $h(X)$ satisfying $h(X) \ge f(X)$ for all $X \in B^n$ and $h(1) = f(1)$. We shall also say that the vector h of coefficients of $h(X)$ is a *core element* of f. The polyhedron of all the core elements of f is called the *core* of f. It may be empty for some f. In this selection we construct another polyhedron (the *selectope*) and show that it contains the core of f.

Consider the canonical form of the pseudo-Boolean function f. We denote $T^+ = \{T \subseteq N: a_T > 0\}$, $T^- = \{T \subseteq N: a_T < 0\}$, $\mathcal{T} = T^+ \cup T^-$. The *incidence graph* of f is a directed bipartite graph $G = (\mathcal{T}, N; E)$ in which an edge $e \in E$ is directed from $T \in T^+$ to $j \in N$ if $j \in T$, and an edge $e \in E$ is directed from $j \in N$ to $T \in T^-$ if $j \in T$. For any node $T \in \mathcal{T}$, $I(T)$ denotes the set of edges $e \in E$ incident with T. For any node $j \in N$, $I^+(j)$ denotes the set of edges $e \in E$ directed to j, $I^-(J)$ denotes the set of edges $e \in E$ directed away from j and $I(j) = I^+(j) \cup I^-(j)$. For each edge $e \in E$, $T(e)$ denotes its end in $\mathcal{T}$ and $j(e)$ its end in N. The edge $e \in E$ corresponds to the occurence of the variable $x_{j(e)}$ in the term $a_{T(e)} \cdot \prod_{j \in T(e)} x_j$ of f. Figure 1 illustrates the incidence graph of our pseudo-Boolean function (14) with the values a_T displayed next to the nodes T.

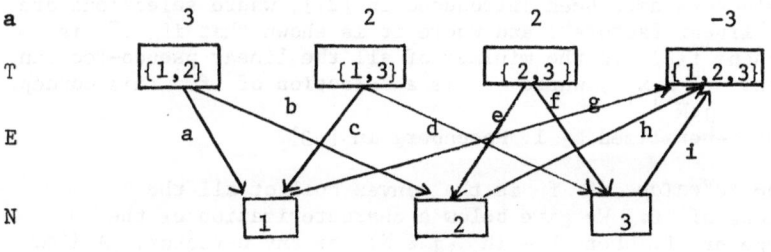

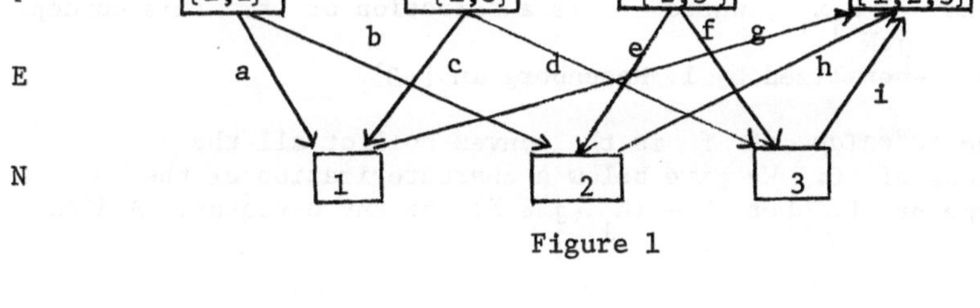

Figure 1

A *selector* of f is a vector $s = (e_T, T \in \mathcal{T})$, such that $e_T \in I(T)$, $\forall\, T \in \mathcal{T}$. The corresponding *selection* of f is the vector $h(s) = (h_j, j \in N)$, where $h_j = \sum_{e_T \in I(j)} a_T$. S will denote the set of all selectors of f. In our example there are $\prod_{T \in \mathcal{T}} |T| = 2 \cdot 2 \cdot 2 \cdot 3 = 24$ selectors, which are listed below along with the corresponding selections (of which only 20 are distinct).

	Selectors				Selections		
	$e_{\{1,2\}}$	$e_{\{1,3\}}$	$e_{\{2,3\}}$	$e_{\{1,2,3\}}$	h_1	h_2	h_3
1	a	c	e	g	2	2	0
2	a	c	e	h	5	-1	0
3	a	c	e	i	5	2	-3
4	a	c	f	g	2	0	2
5	a	c	f	h	5	-3	2
6	a	c	f	i	5	0	-1
7	a	d	e	g	0	2	2
8	a	d	e	h	3	-1	2
9	a	d	e	i	3	2	-1
10	a	d	f	g	0	0	4
11	a	d	f	h	3	-3	4
12	a	d	f	i	3	0	1
13	b	c	e	g	-1	5	0
14	b	c	e	h	2	2	0
15	b	c	e	i	2	5	-3
16	b	c	f	g	-1	3	2
17	b	c	f	h	2	0	2
18	b	c	f	i	2	3	-1
19	b	d	e	g	-3	5	2
20	b	d	e	h	0	2	2
21	b	d	e	i	0	5	-1
22	b	d	f	g	-3	3	4
23	b	d	f	h	0	0	4
24	b	d	f	i	0	3	1

Selectors have been introduced in [27], where selections are called "linear factors", and where it is shown that if $\mathcal{T}^-$ is empty then $f(X)$ is the minimum of all the linear pseudo-Boolean functions $\sum_{j \in N} h_j x_j$, where h is a selection of f. This concept has been generalized by I. Rosenberg in [43].

The *selectope* of f is the convex hull of all the selections of f. We give below a characterization of the selectope of f. Let $h = (h_j, j \in N)$ be any n-vector. A *flow* for h in G is a non-negative vector $z = (z_e, e \in E)$ satisfying the node equations

$$\sum_{e \in I(T)} z_e |a_T|, \quad T \in \mathcal{T}$$

$$\sum_{e \in I^+(j)} z_e - \sum_{e \in I^-(j)} z_e = h_j , \quad j \in N.$$

Then:

(1) The selectope of f is the set of those n-vectors h for which there exists a flow in G.

(2) The selectope of f contains the core of f, equality holding if and only if all the nonlinear terms in (1) have nonnegative coefficients.

We remark that from here we obtain an efficient partial test for a non-negative vector h satisfying $h(1) = f(1)$ to be a core element of an unlinear pseudo-Boolean function f. Apply the maximal flow algorithm to G. If the value of this flow is less than $\sum_{T \in T^+} a_T$, h cannot be a core element of f. However if the value is $\sum_{T \in T^+} a_T$, we do not have any conclusion. (For example, of all the 20 selections of the pseudo-Boolean function f in (14), only $(2, 2, 0)$ is a core element of f.) It would be of interest to refine the test for that case.

A vector $Y \in B^n$ is said to be a *carrier* of a pseudo-Boolean function f on B^n if $f(X) = f(XY)$ for all $X \in B^n$. The product of carriers of f is a carrier of f, hence the product Y^* of all the carriers of f is the unique minimal carrier of f, and f effectively depends on x_j if and only if $y_j^* = 1$.

A mapping $\pi: B^n \to B^n$ is an *automorphism* if it is one-one and onto, and also conserves the operations $\vee$, $\cdot$ and $^-$, i.e. $\pi(X \vee Y) = \pi(X) \vee \pi(Y)$, $\pi(XY) = \pi(X)\pi(Y)$, $\pi(\bar{X}) = \overline{\pi(X)}$. For convenience we shall write πX for $\pi(X)$. For any automorphism π on B^n and for any function f on B^n we define the function πf by $\pi f(X) = f(\pi^{-1} X)$ or equivalently by $\pi f(\pi X) = f(X)$. It can be seen that if π is an automorphism of B^n and X is a unit vector of B^n, then πX is a unit vector of B^n. Hence π permutes the unit vectors of B^n and permits us to view π as a permutation of the variables $j \in N$ themselves. For $j \in N$, $k = \pi(j)$ is defined so that if X is the unit vector with $x_j = 1$, then πX is the unit vector with

$(\pi X)_k = 1$. Thus $(\pi X)_k = x_{\pi^{-1}_k}$ for all $X \in B^n$.

We can now state the axiomatic definition of the Shapley value ([45]). Let F be the set of all pseudo-Boolean functions f on B^n such that $f(0) = 0$. A *Shapley value* is a mapping $\eta: F \to R^n$ satisfying the following axioms:

Axiom 1. For each automorphism π of B^n and for each $f \in F$,

$$\eta_{\pi(k)}[\pi f] = \eta_k[f], \quad k = 1,\ldots,n.$$

Axiom 2. For each $f \in F$ and for each carrier Y of f,

$$\sum_{k=1}^{n} \eta_k[f] y_k = f(1).$$

(in particular then $\sum_{k=1}^{n} \eta_k[f] = f(1)$).

Axiom 3. For each $f, g \in F$

$$\eta[f + g] = \eta[f] + \eta[g].$$

The following theorem is due to Shapley ([45]):

There exists a unique Shapley value, and it is given by the formula

$$\eta_k[f] = \sum_{\substack{T \subseteq N \\ k \in T}} \frac{a_T}{|T|}.$$

As an illustration, the Shapley value of (14) is:

$$\eta[f] = (\frac{3}{2} + \frac{2}{2} - \frac{3}{3}, \frac{3}{2} + \frac{2}{2} - \frac{3}{3}, \frac{2}{2} + \frac{2}{2} - \frac{3}{3}) = (\frac{3}{2}, \frac{3}{2}, 1).$$

Let f be a pseudo-Boolean function with $f(0) = 0$. Then the Shapley value of f is the arithmetic mean, over all the selectors of f, of the corresponding selections, i.e.

$$\frac{1}{|S|} \sum_{s \in S} h(s).$$

Also the following result holds: Let $f(0) = 0$. If $a_T \geq 0$ for all $T \subseteq N$ then f is superadditive and every selection of f as well as the Shapley value of f are core elements of f.

ACKNOWLEDGEMENTS

Sincere acknowledgements are due to the National Research Council of Canada for partial support (Grant A-8552) of this work and to the organizers of the NATO Advanced Study Institute in Combinatorial Programming for their kind invitation and support at the meeting. Special acknowledgements are due to the Mathematisch Centrum, Amsterdam, The Netherlands, where this survey has been discussed and prepared.

REFERENCES

1. Balas, E., Facets of the Knapsack Problem. Carnegie-Mellon University, Management Science Research Report, No. 323, September 1973.
2. Balas, E., R. Jeroslow, Canonical Cuts on the Unit Hypercube. Carnegie-Mellon University, Management Science Research Report No. 198, August-December 1969.
3. Berman, G., A Branch-and-Bound Method for the Maximization of a Pseudo-Boolean Function. Technical Report, Faculty of Mathematics, University of Waterloo.
4. Bradley, G., P.L. Hammer, L.A. Wolsey, Coefficient Reduction in 0-1 Programming. Mathematical Programming (forthcoming).
5. Camion, P., Une méthode de résolution par l'algèbre de Boole des problèmes combinatoires ou interviennent des entiers. Cahiers Centre Etudes Recherche Opér., 2, 1960, pp. 234-289.
6. Charnes, A., D. Granot, F. Granot, On Improving Bounds for Variables in Linear Integer Programs by Surrogate Constraints. Center for Cybernetic Studies Report, The University of Texas, Austin, Texas, September 1973.
7. Chvátal, V., P.L. Hammer, Set Packing Problems and Threshold Graphs. University of Waterloo, Combinatorics and Optimization, Research Report CORR 73-21, August 1973.
8. Colijn, A.W., Pseudo-Boolean Programming, Ph.D. Thesis, University of Waterloo, Department of Combinatorics and Optimization, July 1973.
9. Dembo, R., A Note on Constraint Pairing in Integer Linear Programming. University of Waterloo, Department of Management Science, Working Paper, April 1974.
10. Dembo, R., P.L. Hammer, A Reduction Algorithm for Knapsack Problems. University of Waterloo, Combinatorics and Optimization Research Report CORR 74-11, April 1974.
11. Faure, R., Y. Malgrange, Une méthode booléenne pour la résolution des programmes linéaires en nombres entiers. Gestion, Numéro Spécial, April 1963.
12. Fortet, R., L'algèbre de Boole et ses applications en recherche opérationnelle. Cahiers Centre Etudes Recherche Opér., 1, No. 4, 1959, pp. 5-36.
13. Fortet, R., Applications de l'algèbre de Boole en recherche opérationnelle. Rev. Francaise Recherche Opér., 4, 1960, pp. 17-26

14. Gale, D., A Theorem on Flows in Networks, Pacific Journal of Mathematics, 7, 1957, pp. 1073-1082.
15. Gallo, G., P.L. Hammer and B. Simeone, Quadratic Knapsack Problems. Instituto per le Applicazione del Calcolo, Roma, 1974.
16. Geoffrion, A.M., Lagrangean Relaxation for Integer Programming, University of California at Los Angeles, Western Management Science Institute, Working Paper No. 195, December 1973.
17. Glover, F., Unit-Coefficient Inequalities for Zero-One Programming, University of Colorado, Management Science Report Series, No. 73-7, July 1973.
18. Glover, F., Polyhedral Annexations in Mixed Integer Programming. University of Colorado, Management Science Report Series, No. 73-9, August 1973.
19. Granot, F., P.L. Hammer, On the Use of Boolean Functions in 0-1 Programming, Technion Mimeograph Series on Operations Research, Statistics and Economics, No. 70, August 1970.
20. Hammer, P.L., Boolean Procedures for Bivalent Programming. In: Mathematical Programming in Theory and Applications, (P.L. Hammer and G. Zoutendijk, editors), North-Holland Publishing Company, Amsterdam, 1974.
21. Hammer, P.L., P. Hansen, Quadratic 0-1 Programming. Management Science (forthcoming).
22. Hammer, P.L., E.L. Johnson, U.N. Peled, Regular 0-1 Programs. Cahiers du Centre d'Etudes de Recherche Operationnelle (forthcoming).
23. Hammer, P.L., E.L. Johnson, U.N. Peled, Facets of Regular 0-1 Polytopes. Mathematical Programming (forthcoming).
24. Hammer, P.L., M.W. Padberg, U.N. Peled, Constraint Pairing in Integer Programming. INFOR (forthcoming).
25. Hammer, P.L., U.N. Peled, On the Maximization of a Pseudo-Boolean Function. Journal of the Association for Computing Machinery, 19, 1972, pp. 265-282.
26. Hammer, P.L., U.N. Peled, S. Sorensen, Pseudo-Boolean Functions and Game Theory I. Core Elements and Shapley Value. University of Waterloo, Combinatorics and Optimization Research Report CORR 73-26, October 1973.
27. Hammer, P.L., I.G. Rosenberg, Linear Decomposition of a Positive Group-Boolean Function, University of Waterloo, Department of Combinatorics and Optimization, Research Report, CORR No. 73-25, October 1973.
28. Hammer, P.L. and I.G. Rosenberg, Equivalent Forms of Zero-One Programs. In: "Applications of Number Theory to Numerical Analysis" (S. Zaremba, editor), Academic Press, New York and London, 1972, pp. 453-463.
29. Hammer, P.L., I.G. Rosenberg, S. Rudeanu, On the Minimization of Pseudo-Boolean Functions. Stud. Cerc. Matem., 14, 1963, No. 3, pp. 359-364. (In Romanian).

30. Hammer, P.L., A.A. Rubin, Some Remarks on Quadratic Programming with 0-1 Variables. Revue Francaise d'Informatique et de Recherche Opérationelle, 4, 1970, V-3, pp. 67-79.
31. Hammer, P.L., S. Rudeanu, Boolean Methods in Operations Research and Related Areas. Springer-Verlag, Berlin/Heidelberg/New York, 1968, French edition: Dunod, Paris, 1970.
32. Hammer, P.L., Sang Nguyen, APOSS - A Partial Order in the Solution Space of Bivalent Programs. Université de Montréal, Centre de rechérches mathématiques. Publication 163, April 1972.
33. Hansen, P., Un Algorithme SEP pour les Programmes Pseudo-Booléens Nonlinéaires. Cahiers du Centre d'Etudes de Recherche Opérationnelle, 11, 1969, pp. 26-44.
34. Hansen, P., Pénalités Additives pour les Programmes en Variables Zéro-Un. C.R. Acad. Sci. Paris, 273, 1971, pp. 175-177.
35. Hu, S.T., Threshold Logic. University of California Press, Berkeley and Los Angeles, 1965.
36. Muroga, S., Threshold Logic and its Applications. Wiley-Interscience, New York, 1971.
37. Nemhauser, G.L., L.E. Trotter, Jr., Properties of Vertex Packing and Independence Systems Polyhedra. Department of Operations Research, Cornell University, Technical Report No. 179, March 1973.
38. Owen, G., Multilinear Extensions of Games, Management Science, 18(5), January 1972, pp. 64-79.
39. Padberg, M.W., A Note on Zero-One Programming. University of Waterloo, Combinatorics and Optimization Research Report CORR No. 73-5, March 1973.
40. Pollatschek, M.A., Algorithms on Finite Weighted Graphs. Ph.D. Thesis, Technion-Israel Institute of Technology, Faculty of Industrial and Management Engineering, 1970. (in Hebrew, with English synopsis).
41. Robillard, P., (0, 1) Hyperbolic Programming Problems. Nav. Res.Log.Quart., 18, 1971, No. 1, pp. 47-57.
42. Robillard, P., M. Florian, Note concernant la programmation hyperbolique en variables bivalentes. Université de Montréal, Département d'Informatiques, Publication 41, June 1971.
43. Rosenberg, I.G., Decomposition of a Positive Group-Boolean Function into Linear Factors, Université de Montréal, Centre de recherches mathématiques, Publication 345, October 1973.
44. Rudeanu, S., Boolean Functions and Equations, North-Holland Publishing Company, Amsterdam, 1974.
45. Shapley, L.S., A Value for n-Person Games, in Contributions to the Theory of Games, Vol. II, ed. H.W. Kuhn and A.W. Tucker, Annals of Mathematics Studies, No. 28, Princeton University Press, Princeton, N.J., 1953, pp. 307-317.

46. Spielberg, K., Minimal Preferred Variable Reduction Methods in Zero-One Programming. IBM Philadelphia Scientific Center Report No. 320-3013, July 1972, Revized, 1973.
47. Taha, H.A., A Balasian-Based Algorithm for Zero-One Polynomial Programming, Management Science. 18, 1972, pp. 328-343.
48. Warszawski, A., Pseudo-Boolean Solutions to Multidimensional Location Problems, Operations Research, 22, 1974, pp. 1081-1085.
49. Williams, H.P., Experiments in the Formulation of Integer Programming Problems. University of Sussex, March 1973.
50. Wolsey, L.A., Faces for Linear Inequalities in 0-1 Variables. Centre for Operations Research and Econometrics, Louvain, 1973.
51. Yoshida, Y., Y. Inagaki and T. Fukumura, Algorithms of Pseudo-Boolean Programming Based on the Branch and Bound Method, J. Inst. Elec. and Commun. Engs. Japan, 50, 1967, pp. 277-285.

FOURIER-MOTZKIN ELIMINATION AND ITS DUAL WITH APPLICATION TO INTEGER PROGRAMMING*

George B. Dantzig and B. Curtis Eaves

Department of Operations Research, Stanford University, Stanford, California 94305

Dedicated to the Memory of Theodore S. Motzkin

Research on linear inequalities systems prior to 1947 consisted of isolated efforts by a few investigators. A case in point is the elimination technique for reducing the number of variables in the system. A description of the method can be found in Fourier [1], Dines [2], and Motzkin [3]. It differs from its analog for systems of equations in that (unfortunately) each step in the elimination can greatly increase the number of inequalities in the remaining variables. For years the method was referred to as the Motzkin Elimination Method. However, because of the odd grave-digging custom of looking for artifacts in long forgotten papers, it is now known as the Fourier-Motzkin Elimination Method and perhaps will eventually be known as the Fourier-Dines-Motzkin Elimination Method.

Given a system of linear inequalities: Find $x = (x_1,\ldots,x_n)$ such that

$$\sum_{j=1}^{n} a_{ij}x_j \geq b_i, \qquad i = (1, \ldots, m). \tag{1}$$

*Research and reproduction of this report was partially supported by U.S. Office of Naval Research under contract N-00014-67-A-0112-0011, U.S. Atomic Energy Commission Contract AT(04-3)-326 PA No. 18, National Science Foundation Grants GP 31393, and GP 34559, and Army Research Office--Durham DAHC-71-C-0041. Originally published in Journal of Combinatorial Theory, Vol. 14, No. 3, 1973, 288-297.

B. Roy (ed.), Combinatorial Programming: Methods and Applications, 93–102.

One may partition it into three sets of inequalities according to whether the coefficients of x_1 are positive, negative, or zero. This permits rewriting (1) in the form:

$$\begin{cases} x_1 \geq D_1(\bar{x}) \\ \vdots \\ x_1 \geq D_p(\bar{x}) \end{cases} \qquad \begin{cases} x_1 \leq E_1(\bar{x}) \\ \vdots \\ x_1 \leq E_q(\bar{x}) \end{cases} \qquad \begin{cases} 0 \leq F_1(\bar{x}) \\ \vdots \\ 0 \leq F_r(\bar{x}) \end{cases} \tag{2}$$

where $D_i(\bar{x})$, $E_j(\bar{x})$, $F_k(\bar{x})$ are linear functions of $\bar{x} = (x_2,\ldots,x_n)$. It may be solved by first solving the reduced system: Find $\bar{x}$ satisfying

$$D_i(\bar{x}) \leq E_j(\bar{x}), \quad i = (1,\ldots,p),\ j = (1,\ldots,q),\ k = (1,\ldots,r),$$
$$0 \leq F_k(\bar{x}), \tag{3}$$

and then finding an x_1, satisfying

$$\max_i D_i(\bar{x}) \leq x_1 \leq \min_j E_j(\bar{x}), \tag{4}$$

where x_1 always exists providing there exists an $\bar{x}$ satisfying (3).

Proof. Given any $(x_1,\bar{x})$ satisfying (2), it is clear that (3) and (4) must hold. Conversely, given any $\bar{x}$ satisfying (3), then $\max_i D_i(\bar{x}) \leq \min_j E_j(\bar{x})$ and we can always find an x_i satisfying (4); hence $(x_1,\bar{x})$ satisfies (1).

System (3) is said to be the result of "eliminating" x_1 from system (2). If $p + q \leq 4$, the reduced system contains one less variable and no more inequalities. If $p > 2$, $q > 2$, $r = 0$, however, the process of elimination will greatly increase the number of inequalities. This is the chief reason given why it is not used as a practical solution method. It is worth noting, however, that (3) has special structure and that this might be used to advantage to develop it into a practical computational procedure.

Since (3) is a linear inequality system also, one could next proceed to eliminate x_2, etc., until one has eliminated all but a single variable, say x_n. The original system is solvable if and only if the final system $x_n \leq \alpha_i$, $x_n \geq \beta_j$, $0 \leq \gamma_k$ for $i = 1,\ldots,p'$, $j = 1,\ldots,q'$, $k = 1,..,r'$ is consistent, i.e., iff $\alpha_i - \beta_j \geq 0$ and $\gamma_k \geq 0$ for all i, j, k. Another way to state this is:

FEASIBILITY THEOREM. A necessary and sufficient condition that system (1) is solvable, is there exist no set of weights $(y_1 \geq 0,\ y_2 \geq 0,\ \ldots,\ y_m \geq 0)$ such that

$$\sum_{i=1}^{m} y_i b_i > 0 \quad \text{and} \quad \sum_{i=1}^{m} y_i a_{ij} = 0, \quad \text{for} \quad j = (1,\ldots,n) . \tag{5}$$

Proof. Assume a solution x to (1) exists and there exists weights $y_i \geq 0$ satisfying (5), then (1) implies

$$\sum_{j=1}^{n}\left(\sum_{i=1}^{m} y_i a_{ij}\right) x_j \geq \sum_{i=1}^{m} y_i b_i, \qquad y_i \geq 0, \tag{6}$$

or $0x \geq \Sigma\, y_i b_i > 0$, a contradiction. Thus the condition is necessary.

Assume no solution x to (1) exists, then note each system generated by the elimination process, for example (3) from (2), is formed by nonnegative linear combinations of the inequalities of the previous system which in turn were formed by nonnegative linear combinations of the system one before that, etc., back to the original system (1). Thus the condition for non-solvability, $\alpha_i - \beta_j < 0$ or $\gamma_k < 0$ for some i, j or k (referred to earlier), could be derived directly by some nonnegative linear combination of the inequalities of the original system.

This remarkably simple proof of the feasibility theorem based on Fourier-Motzkin elimination is due to Kuhn [4]. From it one can derive easily (by trival algebraic manipulations) the fundamental Duality Theorem of linear programming, Farkas Lemma, the various theorems of the alternatives, and the well-known

MOTZKIN TRANSPOSITION THEOREM. Given the dual homogeneous linear program in partitioned form

$$\begin{aligned} &\text{Primal:} \quad A_I x_I + A_{II} x_{II} = 0, \qquad (x_I, x_{II}) \geq 0, \\ &\text{Dual:} \quad yA_I \leq 0, \quad yA_{II} \leq 0, \end{aligned} \tag{7}$$

then either there exists a solution to the dual such that $yA_1 < 0$ (i.e., holds strictly in all components) or there exists a solution to the primal such that $x_I \neq 0$.

Proof. A solution to the dual such that $yA_I < 0$ implies there exists a y such that

$$\begin{aligned} &yA_I \leq -e, \qquad e = (1, 1, \ldots, 1), \\ &yA_{II} \leq 0. \end{aligned} \tag{8}$$

If no such y exists satisfying (8), then by the feasibility theorem, there exists weights $x_I \geq 0$, $x_{II} \geq 0$ such that $A_I x_I + A_{II} x_{II} = 0$ and $-ex_I < 0$, i.e., $x_I \neq 0$.

THE DUAL OF FOURIER-MOTZKIN ELIMINATION. Suppose we are given the homogeneous linear program

$$\begin{aligned} x_1 - D_i\bar{x} &\geq 0, \qquad i = (1, \ldots, p), \\ -x_1 + E_j\bar{x} &\geq 0, \qquad j = (1, \ldots, q), \\ F_k\bar{x} &\geq 0, \qquad k = (1, \ldots, r), \end{aligned} \tag{9}$$

where $\bar{x} = (x_2, \ldots, x_n)$ and D_i, E_j, F_k are $1 \times n\text{-}1$. The elimination of x_1 from (9) yields

$$\begin{aligned} (E_j - D_i)\bar{x} &\geq 0, \qquad \text{for all } i, j \\ F_k\bar{x} &\geq 0, \qquad \text{for all } k. \end{aligned} \tag{10}$$

On the other hand the homogeneous dual of (9) is: to find $u_i \geq 0$, $v_j \geq 0$, $w_k \geq 0$ such that

$$\begin{aligned} &(a) \qquad \sum_{i=1}^{p} u_i - \sum_{j=1}^{q} v_j = 0, \\ &(b) \qquad -\sum_{i=1}^{p} u_i D_i + \sum_{j=1}^{q} v_j E_j + \sum_{k=1}^{r} w_k F_k = 0; \end{aligned} \tag{11}$$

and the homogeneous dual of (10) is: to find $\lambda_{ij} \geq 0$, $w_k \geq 0$ such that:

$$\sum_{i=1}^{p} \sum_{j=1}^{q} \lambda_{ij}(E_j - D_i) + \sum_{k=1}^{r} w_k F_k = 0. \tag{12}$$

Since (9) and its eliminated form (10) are in a sense equivalent systems, it seems natural to expect that their duals (11) and (12), are also equivalent in the same sense; i.e., from any solution to (11) we can derive a solution to (12) and conversely. Note that (11) has n equations corresponding to the n components of x_j whereas (12) has $n\text{-}1$ equations but would have (in general) far more variables. This suggests we have at hand a technique for reducing the number of equations in a linear program. Let us give a direct proof of this for the <u>non</u>-homogeneous system:

Find $u_i \geq 0$, $v_j \geq 0$, $w_k \geq 0$ satisfying:

$$\begin{aligned}
&\text{(a)} \quad \sum_{i=1}^{p} u_i - \sum_{j=1}^{q} v_j = 0, \\
&\text{(b)} \quad -\sum_{i=1}^{p} u_i D_i + \sum_{j=1}^{q} v_j E_j + \sum_{k=1}^{r} w_k F_k = g.
\end{aligned} \tag{13}$$

Let us introduce pq new variables $\lambda_{ij} \geq 0$ by setting

$$\begin{aligned}
u_i &= \sum_{j=1}^{q} \lambda_{ij}, \qquad i = (1, \ldots, p), \\
v_j &= \sum_{i=1}^{p} \lambda_{ij}, \qquad j = (1, \ldots, q).
\end{aligned} \tag{14}$$

Note that, if u_i and v_j satisfy (13a), it is always easy to find $\lambda_{ij} \geq 0$ satisfying (14). Even if $u_i \geq 0$ and $v_j \geq 0$ are constrained to be <u>integers</u>, it is easy to find <u>integer</u> $\lambda_{ij} \geq 0$ satisfying (14). Substituting (14) into (13) we note that (13a) is automatically satisfied and we obtain the reduced system:

Find $\lambda_{ij} \geq 0$, $w_k \geq 0$ such that

$$\sum_{i=1}^{p} \sum_{j=1}^{q} \lambda_{ij}(E_j - D_i) + \sum_{k=1}^{r} w_k F_k = g. \tag{15}$$

Conversely note that, if we have a solution to (15), we can, by regrouping the terms and substituting u_i and v_j for the resulting λ_{ij}. obtain a solution to (13). The solution will be in integers if λ_{ij} is integral.

To apply the technique to a system of equations in nonnegative variables, it is necessary to have one equation with a zero constant term to play the role of (13a) or to create an equation with a zero constant term by replacing one of the equations by some appropriate linear combination of the equations of the system. This will yield an equation of the form

$$\sum_{i=1}^{p} \alpha_i u_i - \sum_{j=1}^{q} \beta_j v_j = 0, \qquad \alpha_i \geq 0, \qquad \beta_j \geq 0, \tag{16}$$

and we could obtain a system of form (13) by a change of units. This may conveniently be done by replacing (14) by

$$\alpha_i u_i = \sum_{j=1}^{q} \lambda_{ij}, \qquad i = (1, \ldots, p),$$
$$\beta_j v_j = \sum_{i=1}^{p} \lambda_{ij}, \qquad j = (1, \ldots, q), \tag{17}$$

where $\alpha_i \geq 0$, $\beta_j \geq 0$, $\lambda_{ij} \geq 0$, $u_i \geq 0$, $v_j \geq 0$.

APPLICATION OF THE DUAL OF THE MOTZKIN ELIMINATION TO INTEGER PROGRAMS: Given the system

$$\sum_{j=i}^{n} a_{ij}x_j = b_i \qquad i = (1, \ldots, m)$$
$$x_i \geq 0 \qquad j = (1, \ldots, n) \tag{18}$$

where the a_{ij}'s and b_i's are integer we describe two schemes, 1 and 2, for generating all solutions $x = (x_1, \ldots, x_n)$ which are integer, that is, have integer components. Scheme 1 requires that the a_{ij} be nonnegative, whereas, Scheme 2 requires no additional assumptions.

Scheme 1 for Generating all Integer Solutions

First let us assume that system (18) is 0-1, that is, all a_{ij}'s and b_i's are 0 or 1; hence we can assume that all b_i's are 1, since otherwise, we obviously have an infeasible or redundant system.

If $m = 1$, the set of solutions is evident; if $a_j = 1$ for some j, a typical solution is

$$x_i = \begin{cases} 1 & \\ 0 & \text{if} \\ \text{arbitrary} & \end{cases} \begin{array}{c} i = j \\ i \neq j \\ a_{1i} = 0 \end{array} \quad \text{and} \quad a_{1i} \neq 0. \tag{19}$$

Now assume $m > 1$. Subtract row one from row two to obtain an equation of form

$$\sum_I x_i = \sum_J x_j \qquad I \cap J = \Phi\ . \tag{20}$$

Introduce the variables λ_{ij} for $(i,j) \in I \times J$ and replace x_i for $i \in I$ and x_j for $j \in J$ in the system (18) by

$$x_i = \sum_{j \in J} \lambda_{ij}\ , \qquad x_j = \sum_{i \in I} \lambda_{ij}. \tag{21}$$

If some λ_{ij} has a coefficient exceeding 1, clearly $\lambda_{ij} = 0$ in a solution. Finally delete the first row (i = 1) in (18). We have now reduced the original 0-1 system in m rows to a 0-1 system in m-1 rows. Repeating this process until there is but one row, then, by generating all solutions, and by back-substitution, one gets all solutions to the original system (18).

This scheme for the 0-1 system, if properly implemented, appears to yield a reasonable technique for enumerating all solutions (especially if there are not too many solutions and equations).

If the a_{ij}'s and b_i's of (18) are merely nonnegative integers then we can, as is demonstrated in the appendix, transform the problem to an equivalent 0-1 system. We then proceed to use the above elimination scheme to generate all solutions for the 0-1 system which in turn yields all solutions for (18).

Scheme 2 for Generating all Integer Solutions

We suppose that the data of (18) is integer. Either some b_i is 0, or one can scale (with integers) rows one and two and subtract them to get an expression of form

$$\sum_{i \in I} \alpha_i x_i = \sum_{j \in J} \beta_j x_j \qquad I \cap J = \Phi . \tag{22}$$

Suppose for (22) that we have the following example:

$$(u_1 + 2u_2) - (v_1 + v_2 + v_3) = 0. \tag{23}$$

Let us rewrite this

$$(u_1 + u_2 + u_3) - (v_1 + v_2 + v_3) = 0. \tag{24}$$

where $u_2 = u_3$ and set as above

$$\begin{aligned} u_i &= \sum_{j=1}^{3} \lambda_{ij}, \qquad j = (1, 2, 3), \\ v_j &= \sum_{i=1}^{r} \lambda_{ij}, \qquad i = (1, 2, 3). \end{aligned} \tag{25}$$

The resulting integer reduced system is in $\lambda_{ij} \geq 0$ (as before) except we have the additional condition $u_2 = u_3$ which, in terms of λ_{ij}, becomes

$$(\lambda_{21} + \lambda_{22} + \lambda_{23}) - (\lambda_{31} + \lambda_{32} + \lambda_{33}) = 0. \tag{26}$$

But (26) is in exactly the form we need for the integer reduction. We accordingly can introduce additional integer variables $\mu_{ij} \geq 0$, where

$$\lambda_{2i} = \sum_{j=1}^{3} \mu_{ij}, \qquad i = 1, 2, 3,$$
$$\lambda_{3j} = \sum_{i=1}^{3} \mu_{ij}, \qquad j = 1, 2, 3. \tag{27}$$

Back-substituting into (25), we have the desired integer substitution in terms of 12 auxiliary variables:

$$\begin{aligned} u_1 &= \sum_{j=1}^{3} \lambda_{1j}, \\ u_2 (= u_3) &= \sum_{i=1}^{3} \sum_{j=1}^{3} \mu_{ij}, \\ v_1 &= \lambda_{11} + \sum_{j=1}^{3} \mu_{1j} + \sum_{i=1}^{3} \mu_{i1}, \\ v_2 &= \lambda_{12} + \sum_{j=1}^{3} \mu_{2j} + \sum_{i=1}^{3} \mu_{i2}, \\ v_3 &= \lambda_{13} + \sum_{j=1}^{3} \mu_{3j} + \sum_{i=1}^{3} \mu_{i3}. \end{aligned} \tag{28}$$

By setting $\mu_{12} + \mu_{21} = \bar{\mu}_{12}$, $\mu_{13} + \mu_{31} = \bar{\mu}_{13}$, $\mu_{32} + \mu_{23} = \bar{\mu}_{23}$ we could simplify the above substitution to one involving nine nonnegative integer variables λ_{1i}, μ_{ii}, $\bar{\mu}_{ij}$, where $i, j = 1, 2, 3$ $i \neq j$.

The problem in general of finding substitutions to replace (14) so as to reduce a linear system in nonnegative integer variables to fewer equations is under study and will be the subject of a subsequent paper.

APPENDIX

Our purpose here is to show that a system of form (18) where the a_{ij}'s and b_i's are nonnegative integers has an equivalent 0-1 system.

Consider the system with one equation:

$$4x + 3y + 2z = y$$
$$x \geq 0, \quad y \geq 0, \quad z \geq 0 \tag{29}$$

and the corresponding system in detached coefficient form:

$$\begin{array}{cccccccccccc} x_1 & x_2 & x_3 & y_1 & y_2 & y_3 & y_4 & z_1 & z_2 & z_3 & z_4 & z_5 \end{array}$$
$$\begin{bmatrix} 1 & 0 & 0 & 1 & 0 & 0 & 0 & 1 & 0 & 0 & 0 & 0 \\ 1 & 1 & 0 & 1 & 1 & 0 & 0 & 1 & 1 & 0 & 0 & 0 \\ 1 & 1 & 1 & 1 & 1 & 1 & 0 & 0 & 1 & 1 & 0 & 0 \\ 1 & 1 & 1 & 0 & 1 & 1 & 1 & 0 & 0 & 1 & 1 & 0 \\ 0 & 1 & 1 & 0 & 0 & 1 & 1 & 0 & 0 & 0 & 1 & 1 \\ 0 & 0 & 1 & 0 & 0 & 0 & 1 & 0 & 0 & 0 & 0 & 1 \end{bmatrix}$$

$$= \begin{bmatrix} 1 \\ 1 \\ 1 \\ 1 \\ 1 \\ 1 \end{bmatrix} \qquad \begin{array}{l} x_i \geq 0 \\ i = (1, \ldots, 3) \\ y_i \geq 0 \\ i = (1, \ldots, 4) \\ z_i \geq 0 \\ i = (1, \ldots, 5) \end{array} \tag{30}$$

We will call (30) the 0-1 form of (29). Note that (30) is generated so that the number of equations, 6, is equal to the right-hand side of (29), and so that the column corresponding to x_i has 1's in positions i to $i + a$ where $1 + a = 4$ is the coefficient of x in (29), and $i = 1, \ldots, k$ where $k + a = 6$, etc., for y_i and z_i. One can readily see that if (20) is solved with integer x_i, y_i, and z_i's then

$$x = \Sigma x_i, \qquad y = \Sigma y_i, \qquad z = \Sigma z_i \tag{31}$$

is an integer solution of (29). Further if (x,y,z) is an integer solution of (29) then there is an integer solution of (30) where (31) holds.

THEOREM. The expanded 0-1 form of a linear equation with nonnegative integer data and variables is totally unimodular. All extreme solutions are integral.

Proof. By totally unimodular we mean that each submatrix of the coefficient matrix (as that in (30)) has determinant of 0 or $\pm$ 1. Consider a submatrix, by subtracting row $j + 1$ from j for $j = 1, \ldots,$ we get a network matrix; it is well known that such matrices are totally unimodular and the result follows. (Veinott and Wagner [5] made extensive use of this feature. Note that if we augment the system by including an $i = 0$ equation which is the negative sum of equations $i = 1, \ldots,$ we see that a solution corresponds to a directed path from $i = 0$ to $i = 6$.)

Next consider the example

$$4x_1 + \sum_{i=2}^{n} a_i x_i = 6$$
$$1x_1 + \sum_{i=2}^{n} \bar{a}_i x_i = 2 \tag{32}$$

one could proceed much as above to generate a 0-1 system for (32) as (30) was for (29). Here we get in detached form

$$\begin{matrix} x_1 & x_2 & x_3 & x_4 & x_5 & x_6 \end{matrix}$$
$$\begin{pmatrix} 1 & 0 & 0 & 1 & 0 & 0 \\ 1 & 1 & 0 & 1 & 1 & 0 \\ 1 & 1 & 1 & 1 & 1 & 1 \\ 1 & 1 & 1 & 1 & 1 & 1 \\ 0 & 1 & 1 & 0 & 1 & 1 \\ 0 & 0 & 1 & 0 & 0 & 1 \end{pmatrix} + \cdots = \begin{pmatrix} 1 \\ 1 \\ 1 \\ 1 \\ 1 \\ 1 \end{pmatrix} \quad x_i \geq 0 \quad i = (1, \ldots, 6) \tag{33}$$
$$\begin{pmatrix} 1 & 1 & 1 & 0 & 0 & 0 \\ 0 & 0 & 0 & 1 & 1 & 1 \end{pmatrix} \qquad \begin{pmatrix} 1 \\ 1 \end{pmatrix}$$

These techniques of generating (30) and (33) from (29) and (32) can be applied in general to get a 0-1 system from a system with integer $a_{ij} \geq 0$ and b_i. Observe that the derived 0-1 system can be arbitrary orders of magnitude larger than the initial system. Unfortunately, it is easy to construct examples where (33) has nonintegral extreme points; hence (33) is not in general unimodular.

REFERENCES

1. J.B.J. Fourier, Solution d'une question particuliere du calcul des inégalités, (1826), and extracts from "Histoire de l' Académie" (1823, 1824), Oeuvres II, pp. 317-328 (French Academy of Sciences).
2. L.L. Dines, Systems of Linear Inequalities, Ann. of Math. **20** (1918-1919).
3. T.S. Motzkin, Beitrage zur theorie der linearen Ungleichungen, Doctoral Thesis, University of Basel, 1936.
4. H.W. Kuhn, Solvability and Consistency for Linear Equations and Inequalities, Amer. Math. Monthly **43** (1956).
5. Arthur F. Veinott, Jr., and Harvey M. Wagner, Optimal Capacity Scheduling, Operations Res. **10** (1962), 518-532.

P A R T I I

PATHS AND CIRCUITS

CHEMINS ET CIRCUITS : ENUMERATION ET OPTIMISATION

B. Roy

Univ. Paris-Dauphine - Direction Scientifique METRA

I - INTRODUCTION

L'importance et la diversité des problèmes mettant en cause des familles particulières F de chemins dans un graphe G sont bien connues dès l'instant où il est question d'itinéraires de véhicules ou de messages, d'horaires en matière de transport public ou de gestion d'équipes, de circuits de distribution ou de ramassage, de séquence de fabrication ou de montage, d'ordonnancement de chantiers ou de production, de rotation d'engins ou d'équipages, de filières administratives ou financières...

Nous n'aborderons ici qu'occasionnellement les problèmes très classiques, tels ceux du "plus court chemin" ou du "plus court circuit hamiltonien" pour lesquels nous renvoyons à DREYFUS (69), ROY (70), YEN (75), CHRISTOFIDES (ce livre). Notre propos vise des problèmes dans lesquels l'objectif ne se ramène pas nécessairement à l'optimisation d'une somme de nombres affectés aux arcs formant le chemin et/ou mettant en jeu des familles F dont la caractérisation peut être liée à d'autres propriétés que "avoir les mêmes extrémités" ou "être hamiltonien".

Voici quelques exemples qui serviront de support pour la suite (cf. notamment tableaux 1 et 2).

Exemple 1 : Génération (1) de chemins vérifiant une propriété P

(1) Le terme "génération" n'implique pas ici l'exhaustivité contrairement au terme "énumération".

B. Roy (ed.), Combinatorial Programming: Methods and Applications, 105–136.

- passer au plus (au moins) α fois par un même sommet (ou un même arc) ;

- ne pas passer par des sommets (ou des arcs) incompatibles dans une relation d'exclusion ;

- passer par au moins p sommets (ou arcs) d'un sous-ensemble donné ;

- partir d'un sommet pour y revenir en respectant diverses contraintes portant sur l'ensemble des arcs empruntés.

Exemple 2 : Calcul des valeurs des K "meilleurs" chemins

Le critère $\mathcal{C}$ définissant un meilleur chemin est généralement défini dans les applications en attribuant à tout chemin $c \in F$ une "valeur" $\mathcal{C}(c) \in L$ ensemble ordonné (le plus souvent $L \subset R$). $\mathcal{C}(c)$ se déduit de valeurs élémentaires affectées aux arcs, et ce par addition, multiplication, minimisation...

Exemple 3 : Dénombrement des chemins "voisins" d'un meilleur

La relation de voisinage entre deux chemins est susceptible de définition variée faisant intervenir la différence symétrique des familles d'arcs, un indice de proximité des familles de sommets, ou encore l'écart entre les valeurs selon un critère $\mathcal{C}$.

Exemple 4 : Enumération des chemins efficaces

Lorsque chaque arc u de G est porteur d'un vecteur à ν composantes $a(u) \in L$, on peut en déduire un vecteur de même nature $a(c) \in L$ pour tout chemin c de F dès l'instant où L est muni d'une opération binaire (1).

Supposons que pour $i = 1, \ldots, \nu$, deux vecteurs quelconques de L soient comparables d'après leur $i^{\text{ème}}$ composante selon un ordre complet $\leqq^i$ (ex. : $L \subset R^\nu$). On dit alors d'un chemin $c \in F$ qu'il est efficace dans F s'il n'existe aucun chemin $c' \in F$ vérifiant :

$$a^i(c) \leqq^i a^i(c') \quad \text{pour } i = 1, \ldots, \nu$$
$$a^i(c) \neq a^i(c') \quad \text{pour au moins un } i.$$

(1) même si elle n'est pas associative ; ce cas ne semble guère avoir été étudié bien qu'il se présente dans certaines applications.

En résumé, dans ces problèmes, il s'agit d'EXTRAIRE de F certains chemins "intéressants" ou certaines informations (labels) les concernant.

Les procédures proposées dans la littérature à propos de tels problèmes relèvent presque exclusivement des deux catégories étudiées ci-après et dont on a cherché à donner une présentation aussi synthétique que possible en dégageant les concepts et résultats fondamentaux qui les sous-tendent.

II - PROCEDURES ALGEBRIQUES

1. Algèbre des chemins

a) Définition et interprétation de $(L, \star, E)$

La formatisation des problèmes de cheminement, en termes de structures algébriques a préoccupé de nombreux auteurs (voir BERGE (58), FORTET (59), ROY (59 et 70), WARSHALL (62), MAGHOUT (63), KUNTZMAN (66), TOMESCU (66 et 68), PETEANU (67 et 69-70), BENZA KEN (68), PICHAT (68), ROBERT et FERLAND (68), CARRE (71), PAIR et DERMIAME (71), GONDRAN (74)). Nous nous inspirons ici principalement de la formulation donnée par GONDRAN (74) ainsi que, pour certains aspects, des travaux de PETEANU (69).

Soit $G = (X, U, a)$ un graphe de n sommets dont chaque arc u est doté d'un "<u>label</u>" $a(u) \in L$.

Les familles finies formées de un ou plusieurs labels (distincts ou non mais considérés indépendamment de leur ordre) sont appelés des "tas" (bag ou multiset) ; on notera $\underline{L}$ l'ensemble des tas. On utilisera généralement une lettre minuscule soulignée pour désigner un tas ; toutefois, le tas formé du seul label m non répété pourra être noté tout simplement m $(L \subset \underline{L})$. $\{\underline{m}\}$ désignera l'ensemble des labels figurant dans $\underline{m}$ et $|\underline{m}|$ le nombre d'éléments formant le tas $\underline{m}$ $(|\underline{m}| \neq |\{\underline{m}\}|)$. On pose :

$\underline{m} \cup \underline{p} = \{\underline{m}\} \cup \{\underline{p}\}$ tas formé de labels tous distincts

$\underline{m} \vee \underline{p} =$ tas formé des labels de $\underline{m}$ et de ceux de $\underline{p}$ avec un nombre de répétition égal pour chaque label à la somme des nombres de répétitions dans $\underline{m}$ et $\underline{p}$. L'opération $\vee$ ainsi définie sur $\underline{L}$, appelée "<u>vrac</u>" est commutative, associative.

On suppose maintenant $\underline{L}$ muni de 2 opérations $\star$ et E définies comme suit :

1) Soit $\star$ une opération associative définie sur L, appelée "concaténation" dont l'élément neutre e (s'il n'existait pas on l'ajouterait) est dit "unité". On étend la définition de la concaténation à $\underline{L}$ en posant :

$$(m_1, \ldots, m_i, \ldots) \star (p_1, \ldots, p_j, \ldots) = (m_1 \star p_1, \ldots, m_1 \star p_j, \ldots, m_i \star p_1, \ldots, m_i \star p_j, \ldots).$$

$\star$ reste associative sur $\underline{L}$ avec e comme élément neutre. De plus, $\star$ est distributive (à droite et à gauche) par rapport à V et U.

2) Soit ε un élément particulier de L dit élément "nul". Désignons par :

. E une opération (dite "d'extraction") définie sur $\underline{L}$ et vérifiant :

$$\left.\begin{array}{lll} E \text{ associative} & & \\ m\, E\, \varepsilon = m & \forall\, m \in L & (\alpha) \\ \underline{m}\, E\, \underline{p} = (\underline{m}\, V\, \underline{p})\, E\, \varepsilon & \forall\, \underline{m}, \underline{p} \in \underline{L} & (\beta) \end{array}\right\} \qquad (II.1.1)$$

(E est donc commutative).

. $\hat{E}$ une application (dite "d'extraction") définie sur $\underline{L}$ à valeur dans $\underline{L}$ et vérifiant :

$$\left.\begin{array}{lll} \hat{E}(m\, V\, \varepsilon) = \hat{E}(m) = m & \forall\, m \in L & (\hat{\alpha}) \\ \hat{E}[\hat{E}(\underline{m})\, V\, \underline{p}] = \hat{E}[\underline{m}\, V\, \underline{p}] & \forall\, \underline{m}, \underline{p} \in \underline{L} & (\hat{\beta}) \end{array}\right\} \qquad (II.1.\hat{1})$$

Théorème 1

A toute opération d'extraction, on peut associer une application d'extraction, et réciproquement, en posant :

$$\underline{m}\, E\, \underline{p} = \hat{E}(\underline{m}\, V\, \underline{p}) \quad \forall\, \underline{m}, \underline{p} \in \underline{L} \qquad (II.1.2)$$

On a alors :

$$\hat{E}(\underline{m}) = \underline{m}\, E\, \varepsilon \qquad \forall\, \underline{m} \in \underline{L} \qquad (II.1.3)$$

$$\underline{m}\, E\, \underline{p} = \hat{E}(\underline{m})\, E\, \underline{p} \qquad \forall\, \underline{m}, \underline{p} \in \underline{L} \qquad (II.1.4)$$

(Démonstration : voir ROY (74)).

Faisons $\underline{p} = \varepsilon$ dans (II.1.4), il vient :

$$\hat{E}[\hat{E}(\underline{m})] = \hat{E}(\underline{m}) \quad \forall\, \underline{m} \in \underline{L}$$

ces éléments seront qualifiés de "fermés" et notés $\hat{\underline{m}}$. Soit $\hat{\underline{L}}$ l'ensemble des éléments fermés, on a :

$$\underline{m} \; E \; \underline{p} \in \hat{\underline{L}} \quad \forall \underline{m}, \underline{p} \in \underline{L} \qquad \underline{m} \in \hat{\underline{L}} \quad \forall m \in L.$$

Les hypothèses faites s'expliquent par l'interprétation que l'on souhaite donner de $*$ et de $\hat{E}$ relativement aux chemins finis de G. Un chemin c sera défini par la suite (non nécessairement sans répétitions mais nécessairement finie) des arcs qui le compose (1) ; c_{ij} désignera un chemin allant du sommet x_i (extrémité initiale du 1er arc) au sommet x_j (extrémité terminale du dernier arc). C(G) désignera l'ensemble des chemins de G et C_{ij} le sous-ensemble de ceux allant de x_i à x_j. Un circuit est un chemin de la forme c_{ii}, x_i est le sommet de fermeture. Deux circuits parcourant dans le même ordre les mêmes arcs mais à partir d'origines différentes seront regardés comme distincts puisque n'ayant pas même sommet de fermeture.

L'opération de concaténation sert à déduire des labels des arcs, un label a(c) $\forall c \in C$:

$$a(c) = a(u_1, \ldots, u_t) = a(u_1) * \ldots * a(u_t) = \mathop{*}_{h=1}^{h=t} a(u_h).$$

L'associativité est nécessaire pour que, quel que soit le sommet intermédiaire x_k ($\neq x_i$ et x_j) sur un chemin c_{ij}, on ait :

$$a(c_{ij}) = a(c_{ik}, c_{kj}) = a(c_{ik}) * a(c_{kj}).$$

Deux circuits ne différant que par leur sommet de fermeture ont donc même label si $*$ est commutative.

Soit F une famille de chemins, on notera $\underline{a}(F)$ le tas de labels défini par les labels des chemins formant F. Lorsque F est le produit cartésien de deux familles de chemins $F_{ik} \subset C_{ik}$ et $F_{kj} \subset C_{kj}$, l'extension de $*$ à $\underline{L}$ permet d'écrire :

$$a(F) = \underline{a}(F_{ik} \times F_{kj}) = \underline{a}(F_{ik}) * \underline{a}(F_{kj}).$$

(1) Rappelons que, pour former un chemin, l'extrémité terminale de chaque arc doit coïncider avec l'extrémité initiale de l'arc suivant dans la suite.

L'application d'extraction (dont l'interprétation en termes d'optimisation, d'énumération, de dénombrement... est souvent plus claire que celle de l'opération, cette dernière étant mieux adaptée au formalisme des calculs) sert à passer de $\underline{a}(F)$ à un ou plusieurs labels :

$$\hat{E}[\underline{a}(F)] = \underline{\hat{r}}(F),$$

$\underline{\hat{r}}(F)$ apparaissant comme un "résumé exhaustif" de l'information souhaitée relativement à F. Imposer $\hat{E}(m) = m \ \forall m \in L$ équivaut à l'hypothèse naturelle dans cette interprétation :

$$\text{si } F = \{c\} \text{ alors } \underline{\hat{r}}(F) = a(c).$$

De même, la substitution de $\underline{\hat{r}}(F)$ à $\underline{a}(F)$ doit apparaître comme légitime dans certains calculs, c'est précisément ce que traduit $\hat{\beta}$ dans (II.1.1) qui s'écrit :

$$\hat{E}[\underline{a}(F) \vee \underline{a}(H)] = \hat{E}[\underline{\hat{r}}(F) \vee \underline{a}(H)] = \underline{\hat{r}}(F \vee H)$$

(H étant une famille de chemins). Enfin ε s'interprète comme un label ne véhiculant aucune information significative en ce sens qu'il jouit de la propriété caractéristique suivante : l'adjonction à une famille F de un ou plusieurs chemins de label ε, formant une famille F_ε n'influence pas le résumé exhaustif :

$$\hat{r}(F) = \hat{r}(F \vee F_\varepsilon) \qquad \text{(II.1.5)}$$

Nous appellerons "<u>algèbre des chemins</u>" la structure $(\underline{L}, \star, E)$ lorsqu'elle possède les propriétés supplémentaires suivantes :

3) ε est absorbant pour $\star$:

$$\varepsilon \star \underline{m} = \underline{m} \star \varepsilon = \varepsilon \qquad \forall \underline{m} \in \underline{L}$$

ce qui implique que l'on pose :

$$\varepsilon = (\varepsilon, \varepsilon) = \dots = (\varepsilon, \varepsilon, \dots, \varepsilon)$$

identification légitime car (comme on vient de le souligner) :

$$\underline{m} \mathrel{E} (\varepsilon, \dots, \varepsilon) = \underline{m} \mathrel{E} \varepsilon \qquad \forall \underline{m} \in \underline{L}$$

$$\hat{E}(\underline{m} \vee (\varepsilon, \dots, \varepsilon)) = \hat{E}(\underline{m} \vee \varepsilon) \qquad \forall \underline{m} \in \underline{L}.$$

4) La concaténation jouit d'une certaine forme de distributivité par rapport à l'extraction, définie par l'une des 2 propriétés équivalentes ci-après :

Théorème 2

$$\left.\begin{array}{l} [\underline{m} \star (\underline{p} \mathrm{E} \underline{r})] \mathrm{E} \varepsilon = (\underline{m} \star \underline{p}) \mathrm{E} (\underline{m} \star \underline{r}) \\ [(\underline{p} \mathrm{E} \underline{r}) \star \underline{m}] \mathrm{E} \varepsilon = (\underline{p} \star \underline{m}) \mathrm{E} (\underline{r} \star \underline{m}) \end{array}\right\} \forall \ \underline{m}, \underline{p}, \underline{r} \in \underline{L}$$

$$\left.\begin{array}{l} \hat{\mathrm{E}}[\underline{m} \star \hat{\mathrm{E}}(\underline{p})] = \hat{\mathrm{E}}(\underline{m} \star \underline{p}) \\ \hat{\mathrm{E}}[\hat{\mathrm{E}}(\underline{p}) \star \underline{m}] = \hat{\mathrm{E}}(\underline{p} \star \underline{m}) \end{array}\right\} \forall \ \underline{m}, \underline{p} \in \underline{L}$$

(Démonstration : voir ROY (74)).

Soit alors $G' = (X, U')$ un graphe déduit de G par une simple adjonction d'arcs $(U' \supset U)$ dits "arcs artificiels" auxquels on attribue le label $a(u') = \varepsilon \ \forall u' \in U' - U$. Si F désigne une famille de chemins de G et c' un chemin de G' empruntant au moins un arc artificiel, la famille $F \cup \{c'\}$ de chemins de G' est telle que :

$$\hat{\underline{r}}(F \cup \{c'\}) = \hat{\underline{r}}(F) \qquad \text{(II.1.5')}$$

si $a(c') = \varepsilon$. Pour qu'il en soit ainsi dès que c' contient un arc artificiel, il faut et il suffit que la propriété 3) soit vérifiée. Ainsi, il n'est nullement restrictif de supposer le graphe G complet car, lorsqu'il ne l'est pas, l'adjonction d'arcs artificiels de label ε engendre des chemins artificiels qui n'influent pas les résumés exhaustifs.

Considérons maintenant une famille $F = F_{ik} \times F_{kj}$ avec $F_{ik} \subset C_{ik}$ et $F_{kj} \subset C_{kj}$. La propriété de distributivité équivaut, en terme de résumés exhaustifs, à :

$$\left.\begin{array}{l} \hat{\underline{r}}(F) = \hat{\underline{r}}(F_{ik} \times F_{kj}) = \hat{\mathrm{E}}[\underline{a}(F_{ik}) \star \underline{a}(F_{kj})] \\ = \hat{\mathrm{E}}[\hat{\underline{r}}(F_{ik}) \star \underline{a}(F_{kj})] = \hat{\mathrm{E}}[\hat{\underline{r}}(F_{ik}) \star \hat{\underline{r}}(F_{kj})] \end{array}\right\} \qquad \text{(II.1.6)}$$

L'algèbre des chemins est partiellement ordonnée par la relation que nous appellerons "<u>dominance</u>" définie par :

$$\underline{m} \succ \underline{p} \Longleftrightarrow \hat{\mathrm{E}}(\underline{m} \vee \underline{p}) = \underline{m}.$$

En effet, il est clair que $\underline{m} \succ \underline{p}$ et $\underline{p} \succ \underline{m}$ sont incompatibles pour $\underline{p} \neq \underline{m}$ (antisymétrie) ; d'autre part, si $\underline{r} \succ \underline{m}$ et $\underline{m} \succ \underline{p}$, alors (du fait de l'associativité) : $\underline{r} \succ \underline{p}$ (transitivité).

Faisons observer que, $\forall \ \underline{m} \in \underline{L}$, $\hat{\underline{m}} \succ \varepsilon$, mais en général $\underline{m}$ n'est comparable ni à $\hat{\underline{m}}$ ni à ε. En dépit de ce caractère partiel, la dominance a une interprétation intéressante dans de nombreux exemples (cf. II.1.c). Elle jouît en outre de quelques propriétés remarquables relativement aux deux opérations (voir ROY (74)) et permet en particulier une extension importante des propriétés (II.1.5) et (II.1.5'). Pour l'énoncer, introduisons la définition suivante : une famille de chemins D(c) domine un chemin c si $\hat{\underline{f}}[D(c)] \succ a(c)$.

Théorème 3

Si H est une sous-famille de F telle que :

$$\forall c \in H \quad \exists D(c) \subset F - H \text{ tel que } D(c) \text{ domine } c$$

alors :

$$\hat{\underline{f}}(F) = \hat{\underline{f}}(F - H).$$

b) Hypothèses restrictives

Tous les travaux cités en référence définissent une algèbre telle que $\hat{\underline{f}}(F)$ soit un label :

$$\hat{E}(\underline{m}) \in L \quad \forall \underline{m} \in \underline{L} \quad \text{OU} \quad \hat{\underline{L}} \subset L \qquad (II.1.\hat{7})$$

Les exemples 1 à 4 du tableau ci-après sortent de ce cas particulier (1). Il est généralement introduit différemment : $\underline{L}$ n'intervient pas explicitement et l'algèbre est restreinte à L, autrement dit :

$$m \, E \, p \in L \quad \forall m, p \in L \qquad (II.1.7)$$

(il est facile de vérifier que (II.1.$\hat{7}$)$\Longleftrightarrow$(II.1.7)). De plus, les problèmes étudiés se rapportent principalement aux cas où l'extraction s'opère par Max, Min ou réunion, donc dans lesquels :

$$m \, E \, m = m \quad \forall m \in L \qquad (II.1.8)$$

Cette "idempotence" de E peut être considérée indépendamment de l'hypothèse précédente. Elle est en fait équivalente à l'une des suivantes (voir ROY (74)) :

$$\underline{m} \, E \, \underline{m} = \hat{E}(\underline{m}) \quad \forall \underline{m} \in \underline{L} \qquad (II.1.8')$$

$$\hat{E}(\underline{m}) \succ \underline{m} \quad \forall \underline{m} \in \underline{L} \qquad (II.1.8'')$$

$$e \succ e \qquad (II.1.8''')$$

(1) On peut évidemment les y faire rentrer au prix d'une définition moins naturelle de L.

Une autre hypothèse importante concerne les labels des circuits et leur incidence sur l'extraction. Quelques définitions supplémentaires s'imposent pour énoncer une intéressante forme particulière du théorème 3.

Soit c_{ij} un chemin non élémentaire de G, c'est-à-dire tel que la suite d'arcs le définissant puisse, d'une façon au moins, se mettre sous la forme :

$$c_{ij} = c_{ih}, \sigma_{hh}, c_{hj}$$

σ_{hh} étant un circuit non vide différent de c_{ij}, c_{ih} et c_{hj} étant deux chemins, l'un d'eux pouvant être vide lorsque $i = h$ ou $h = j$. Le circuit σ_{hh} est dit <u>supprimable</u> dans c_{ij} et c_{ih}, c_{hj} est le chemin résultant de sa suppression.

Un chemin <u>élémentaire</u> est un chemin sans circuit supprimable, c'est-à-dire ne passant pas 2 fois par un même sommet, sauf par le sommet de fermeture lorsque ce chemin est un circuit.

Considérons un circuit c tel que :

σ^1 supprimable dans c, chemin résultant c^1
σ^2 supprimable dans c^1, chemin résultant c^2
....
σ^λ supprimable dans $c^{\lambda-1}$, chemin résultant c^λ ;

les circuits $\sigma^1, \sigma^2, \ldots, \sigma^\lambda$ sont dits <u>progressivement supprimables</u> et chacun des chemins résultant $c^1, c^2, \ldots, c^\lambda$ est appelé un <u>support</u> de c.

Enfin R est un <u>résidu</u> pour une famille F de chemins de G si :

- $R \subset F$;
- $\forall c \in F - R \;\exists Z(c) \subset \{c' \,/\, c' \in F,\ c'$ support de $c\}$ tel que $Z(c)$ domine c.

<u>Théorème 3'</u>

Si F admet un résidu R, alors :

$$\underline{\hat{f}}(F) = \underline{\hat{f}}(R).$$

Démonstration : Voir ROY (74), ainsi que pour la démonstration des 2 corollaires qui suivent.

Posons :

$$\overset{*}{F} = \{c' \;/\; c' \text{ support d'au moins } 1 \text{ chemin de } F\}$$

$$\overset{\ominus}{F} = \{c' \;/\; c' \in \overset{*}{F},\ c' \text{ est élémentaire}\}.$$

Corollaire 1

Si $F \in \overset{\ominus}{F}$ et si chaque circuit élémentaire emprunté par un chemin F a un label ω sous-unitaire $(\omega \prec e)$, alors :

$$\underline{\hat{f}}(\overset{\ominus}{F}) = \underline{\hat{f}}(F) = \underline{\hat{f}}(\overset{*}{F}).$$

Les circuits dont le label n'est pas sous-unitaire sont habituellement qualifiés d'absorbants. Ce corollaire explique pourquoi l'hypothèse d'absence de circuits absorbants simplifie l'étude de nombreux problèmes de cheminement.

Notons Ω l'ensemble des labels des circuits élémentaires de G. Voici une hypothèse moins restrictive que l'absence de circuit absorbant : Ω est K-stable si $\forall$ K-tuple $\omega_1, \ldots, \omega_K$ d'éléments de Ω :

$$e \mathrel{E} \omega_1 \mathrel{E} \ldots \mathrel{E}(\omega_1 * \ldots * \omega_{K-1}) \succ \omega_1 * \ldots * \omega_K$$

(être 1-stable $\Longleftrightarrow e \succ \omega \quad \forall\, \omega \in \Omega$).

Appelons enfin λ-élémentaire un chemin sans suite $\sigma^1, \sigma^2, \ldots, \sigma^\lambda$ progressivement supprimable, et posons :

$$\overset{\lambda\ominus}{F} = \{c' \;/\; c' \in \overset{*}{F},\ c' \ \lambda\text{-élémentaire}\}.$$

Faisons observer que :

$$1\text{-élémentaire} \Longleftrightarrow \text{élémentaire} \qquad \overset{1\ominus}{F} = \overset{\ominus}{F}.$$

Corollaire 2

Si $F \supset \overset{K\ominus}{F}$, si Ω est K-stable et si $*$ est commutative, alors :

$$\underline{\hat{f}}(\overset{K\ominus}{F}) = \underline{\hat{f}}(F) = \underline{\hat{f}}(\overset{*}{F}).$$

c) Exemples

Le tableau 1 (pages suivantes), complété par les précisions ci-après, décrit 9 exemples d'algèbres des chemins.

1er exemple

D'après la définition de L, la propriété P doit être vérifiée pourtous les chemins réduit à un seul arc. Il en est ainsi avec :

"être élémentaire", "avoir k-arcs en plus" ou encore avec les deux premières propriétés citées en introduction exemple 1.

On remarquera le caractère artificiel de e et ε, ainsi que l'idempotence de l'extraction. Enfin l'absence de circuit absorbant est synonyme de : aucun circuit de G ne vérifie P.

2e exemple

Pour que l'extraction (non idempotente) jouisse des propriétés requises, il faut définir K-min. comme suit. Posons :

$\underline{m} = (m_1, m_2, \ldots, m_t)$ avec $m_1 \leqq m_2 \leqq \cdots \leqq m_t$

Si $m_1 = +\infty$ K-min. $(\underline{m}) = +\infty$

Si $m_1 \neq +\infty$ K-min. $(\underline{m}) = (m_1, m_2, \ldots, m_h)$

h étant le plus grand indice tel que $h \leqq K$, $m_h \neq +\infty$.

Dans cette formulation, l'absence de circuit absorbant est synonyme de "aucun circuit de longueur $\neq +\infty$". Mais :

$\omega \leqq 0 \quad \forall \omega \in \Omega \Longleftrightarrow \Omega$ K-stable.

En outre $\star$ est commutative. Ainsi dès l'instant où G est sans circuit élémentaire de longueur négative, le corollaire 2 peut être appliqué. Faisons observer que la présence de circuits de longueur négative engendre des chemins de longueur aussi petite que l'on veut.

3e exemple

Avec les mêmes notations que dans l'exemple précédent, l'extraction (non idempotente) est définie par :

$\text{Min } \Delta(\underline{m}) = (m_1, m_2, \ldots, m_h)$

h étant le plus grand indice tel que $m_h \leqq m_1 + \Delta$.

Tableau I : Exemples d'algèbres des chemins

N°	L	$m * p$	$\underline{m}$ E $\underline{p}$	e	ε	Problèmes étudiés
1	C (P) = { chemins vérifient P }.	m.p si m.p $\in$ C(P) ∅ sinon	$\underline{m}$ U $\underline{p}$	Ψ chemin sans arc avec 1er sommet indéterminé	∅ chemin sans arc et sans 1er sommet	énumération des chemins ayant une propriété p
2	$\vec{R}$ = R ∪ {+ ∞}	m + p	K-min ($\underline{m}$V$\underline{p}$)	0	+ ∞	K plus courts chemins ; si K = 1 longueur des plus courts chemins
3	$\vec{R}$ = R ∪ {+ ∞}	m + p	Min_{Δ}($\underline{m}$ V $\underline{p}$)	0	+ ∞	chemins proches du plus court ; si Δ = 0 : longueur et nombre des plus courts chemins
4	$\overleftarrow{R}^{\nu}$ $\overleftarrow{R}$ = R ∪ {- ∞ }	m + p	D($\underline{m}$ U $\underline{p}$)	(0,...,0)	(-∞,..., -∞)	chemins efficaces ; si ν = 1 longueur des plus longs chemins

Tableau I (suite)

N°	L	m * p	$\underline{m}$ E $\underline{p}$	e	ε	Problèmes étudiés
5	N	m x p	$\|\underline{m}\| + \|\underline{p}\|$ $\|m_1,\ldots,m_h\| = m_1+\ldots+m_h$	1	0	dénombrement de chemins
6	$R^+ \cup \{+\infty\}$	Min(m, p)	Max($\underline{m}$ V $\underline{p}$)	$+\infty$	0	chemins de capacité maximale
7	[0, 1] (segment réel)	m + p - m . p	Min($\underline{m}$ V $\underline{p}$)	0	1	probabilité d'existence du chemin le moins probable
8	$\{-\infty, [0, 1]\}$	m + p - m . p	Max($\underline{m}$ V $\underline{p}$)	0	$-\infty$	probabilité d'existence du chemin le plus probable
9	$\mathcal{P}(\lambda)$	$m \cap p$	$\{\underline{m}\} \Delta \{\underline{p}\}$ Δ : différence symétrique	λ	∅	λ = ensemble de caractères ; chemins qui sont les seuls à être formés d'arcs possédant tous un certain sous-ensemble de caractères

Les circuits sous-unitaires sont ceux de longueur supérieure à Δ. Si $\omega > 0$ $\forall \omega \in \Omega$, Ω est K-stable avec

$$K = \text{plus petit entier} \geqq / \eta = \min_{\omega \in \Omega} \omega.$$

<u>4e exemple</u>

Reprenons les notations de l'introduction exemple 4 et posons :

$$L = R^{\nu} \quad \leqq^{i} = \leqq \text{ sur } R \text{ pour } i = 1, \ldots, \nu$$

$$D(\underline{m}) = \{m \in \underline{m} \text{ efficaces dans } \underline{m}\}.$$

L'ordre $\prec$ est ici l'ordre habituellement appelé (en économie ou en analyse multi-critères) "dominance". Les solutions efficaces sont donc celles qui ne sont pas dominées strictement.

<u>5e et 6e exemples</u>

Ils sont classiques et vérifient $\underline{\hat{m}} \in L$ $\forall \underline{m} \in \underline{L}$.

<u>7e et 8e exemples</u>

Ils sont plus connus avec des formulations différentes ($* = \times$).

<u>9e exemple</u>

Les labels sont ici des groupes de caractères, d'attributs. Le label d'un chemin comporte les caractères communs à tous ses arcs.

L'extraction révèle tout chemin ayant la propriété suivante : "être le seul dont le label renferme un certain groupe de caractères".

2. <u>Principaux résultats</u>

a) <u>Structure matricielle $(\mathcal{M}_n(\underline{L}), *, E)$</u>

Désignons par $\mathcal{M}_n(\underline{L})$ l'ensemble des matrices carrées d'ordre n à éléments dans $\underline{L}$. Soit :

$$M = (\underline{m}_{ij}), \ P = (\underline{p}_{ij})$$

deux éléments de $\mathcal{M}_n(\underline{L})$. Posons :

$$M \mathrm{E} P = (\underline{m}_{ij} \mathrm{E} \underline{p}_{ij}) = \hat{\mathrm{E}}(\underline{m}_{ij} \vee \underline{p}_{ij}) \qquad \text{(II.2.1)}$$

$$M \star P = \Big(\mathop{\mathrm{E}}_{h=1}^{h=n} \underline{m}_{ih} \star \underline{p}_{hj} \Big)$$

La structure ainsi définie jouit alors à des nuances près (en toute rigueur dans sa restriction aux éléments fermés) des mêmes propriétés que $(\underline{L}, \star, \mathrm{E})$ avec :

$$\Sigma = \begin{bmatrix} \varepsilon & \cdots & \varepsilon \\ \vdots & & \vdots \\ \varepsilon & \cdots & \varepsilon \end{bmatrix} \quad \text{élément nul}$$

$$I = \begin{bmatrix} e & \varepsilon & \cdots & \varepsilon \\ \varepsilon & e & & \\ \vdots & & & \\ \varepsilon & & & e \end{bmatrix} \quad \text{élément unité}$$

$$\hat{\mathrm{E}}(M) = (\hat{\mathrm{E}}(\underline{m}_{ij})) = M \mathrm{E} \Sigma$$

$$M \star I = I \star M = \hat{\mathrm{E}}(M) \qquad M \star \Sigma = \Sigma \star M = \Sigma$$

Considérons maintenant une famille quelconque F de chemins de G, F_{ij} désignera la sous-famille de F formée des seuls chemins allant de x_i à x_j (1). Associons à F les matrices :

$$M[\underline{a}(F)] = (\underline{f}_{ij}) \qquad f_{ij} = \begin{cases} \underline{a}(F_{ij}) & \text{si } F_{ij} \neq \emptyset \\ \varepsilon & \text{sinon} \end{cases}$$

$$M[\hat{\underline{r}}(F)] = (\hat{\underline{f}}_{ij}) = \hat{\mathrm{E}}(M[\underline{a}(F)])$$

Etant donné deux familles F et H de chemins, on notera $F \star H$ la famille obtenue par concaténation (au sens des chemins), c'est-à-dire constituée des chemins de la forme :

$$(C_{ih}, C_{hj}) \text{ avec } C_{ih} \in F_{ih}, C_{hj} \in H_{hj}.$$

Il découle des interprétations du (II.1.a) et plus particulièrement de (II.1.6) que :

---

(1) F_{ii} est formé des seuls circuits ayant x_i pour sommet de fermeture.

$$\left.\begin{array}{l} M[\underline{a}(F)] \star M[\underline{a}(H)] = M[\underline{\hat{r}}(F)] \star M[\underline{a}(H)] \\ = M[\underline{\hat{r}}(F)] \star M[\underline{\hat{r}}(H)] = M[\underline{\hat{r}}(F \star H)] \end{array}\right\} \quad (II.2.2)$$

Ceci montre que la signification de résumé exhaustif est attribuée aux tas du type $\underline{\hat{r}}(F)$ demeure valable dans le calcul matriciel, lequel élimine automatiquement l'information superflue et se borne très rapidement à ne manipuler que des éléments fermés (les seuls véritablement intéressants).

Intéressons-nous maintenant aux familles particulières que sont :

C^k = {chemins de k arcs exactement}

$C^{(k)}$ = {chemins de k arcs au plus}

${}^{\lambda}_{C}^{\ominus}{}^{(k)}$ = {supports λ-élémentaires des chemins de $C^{(k)}$}
= {chemins λ-élémentaires de k arcs au plus}.

Notons :

$$B_k = M[\underline{\hat{r}}(C^k)],\ B_{(k)} = M[\underline{\hat{r}}(C^{(k)})],\ {}_{\lambda}B_{(k)} = M[\underline{\hat{r}}({}^{\lambda\ominus}C^{(k)})]$$

pour $k = 1$: $B_1 = B_{(1)} = {}_{\lambda}B_{(1)} = A = M[\underline{a}(U)]$, (cette dernière égalité définissant A).

Ces définitions introduisent évidemment des arcs artificiels et des chemins artificiels de label ε (du moins si G n'est pas complet), mais nous avons vu que, compte-tenu des hypothèses faites, cette adjonction laissait les résultats invariants - cf. (II.1.5).

L'introduction et les exemples du (I.1.c) montrent que de nombreux problèmes de cheminement peuvent se formuler comme suit dans la structure matricielle $(\mathcal{M}_n(\underline{L}), \star, E)$:

G étant caractérisé par la matrice A, calculer B_k et/ou $B_{(k)}$ et/ou ${}_{\lambda}B_{(k)}$ pour certaines valeurs de k ($k = n$, $k \to \infty$, ...).

b) Résultats fondamentaux

B^k désignera la puissance $k^{\text{ième}}$ de la matrice B selon l'opération $\star$; il est clair que :

$$B^k \star B^r = B^{k+r}.$$

Théorème 4

Quel que soit G :

$$B_k = A^k,\ B_{(k)} = A\ E\ A^2 \ldots E\ A^k \qquad k = 1, 2 \ldots$$

et lorsque E est idempotente :

$$I\ E\ B_{(k)} = (I\ E\ A)^k.$$

Démonstration : voir ROY (74).

Théorème 5

S'il existe $D^{(k)} \subset C^{(k)}$ tel que

$$\forall c \in C_{ij}^{(k)} - D_{ij}^{(k)}\ \exists D(c) \subset D_{ij}^{(k)} \text{ vérifiant } D(c) \text{ domine } c$$

alors

$$M[\underline{\hat{f}}(D^{(k)})] = A\ E\ A^2 \ldots E\ A^k.$$

S'il existe $\tilde{k}$ tel que les conditions ci-dessus soient remplies pour $k = \tilde{k}$ et $k = \tilde{k} + 1$ avec en outre

$$I\ E\ M[\underline{\hat{f}}(D^{(\tilde{k})})] = I\ E\ M[\underline{\hat{f}}(D^{(\tilde{k}+1)})] = \tilde{A}$$

alors :

$$\tilde{A} = I\ E\ A * \tilde{A} = I\ E\ A \ldots E\ A^{\tilde{k}+h} \qquad \forall h \geqq 0$$

Lorsque E est idempotente :

$$\tilde{A} = (I\ E\ A)^{\tilde{k}+h} \qquad \forall h \geqq 0$$

Ces résultats sont des conséquences directes des théorèmes 3 et 4. Pour la démonstration du théorème suivant et de ses 2 corollaires, voir ROY (74).

Théorème 5'

Si pour tout chemin c non λ-élémentaire de $C^{(k)}$ il existe une famille Z(c) de supports de c qui domine c, alors :

$$_{\lambda}B_{(k)} = A \; E \; A^2 \ldots E \; A^k.$$

Si ces conditions sont remplies pour $k = n.\lambda$ et $k = n.\lambda + 1$, alors la matrice $M[\underline{\hat{r}}(\overset{\lambda\theta}{C})] = \tilde{A}$ vérifie :

$$\tilde{A} = I \; E \; \tilde{A} * A = I \; E \; A \ldots E \; A^{n.\lambda+h} \qquad \forall h \geqq 0$$

Corollaire 1

Si $\forall \omega \in \Omega \quad \omega \prec e$, alors :

$$_{1}B_{(k)} = A \; E \; A^2 \ldots E \; A^k \qquad \forall k \geqq 1$$

$$M[\underline{\hat{r}}(\overset{1\theta}{C})] = \tilde{A} = I \; E \; A * \tilde{A} = I \; E \; A \ldots E \; A^{n+h} \qquad \forall h \geqq -1$$

Corollaire 2

Si Ω est K-stable et $*$ commutative, alors :

$$_{k}B_{(k)} = A \; E \; A^2 \ldots E \; A^k \qquad \forall k \geqq 1$$

$$M[\underline{\hat{r}}(\overset{nK\theta}{C})] = \tilde{A} = I \; E \; A * \tilde{A} = I \; E \; A \ldots E \; A^{n.K+h} \qquad \forall h \geqq 0$$

Les exemples 2 et 3 du tableau 1 montrent l'intérêt de ces 2 corollaires.

Soit $P = (\underline{p}_{ij}) \in \mathcal{M}_n(\underline{L})$, considérons la famille de transformation suivante :

$$\Theta_t : P \rightarrow \Theta_t \, . \, P = (\underline{p}_{ij} \; E \; (\underline{p}_{it}) * p_{tj}) \qquad t = 1, \ldots, n$$
$$\Theta_{t,s} : P \rightarrow \Theta_s \, . \, \Theta_t \, . \, P \qquad s = 1, \ldots, n$$

Théorème 6

Si $\omega \prec e \quad \forall \omega \in \Omega$:

$$M[\underline{\hat{r}}(\overset{1\theta}{C})] = \Theta_{1,2,\ldots,n} \; . \; A = \Theta_n \, . \, \Theta_{n-1} \, . \, \Theta_1 \, . \, A$$

Démonstration : voir ROY (74).

c) A propos d'algorithmes

Les résumés exhaustifs que sont, pour l'étude (énumération, dénombrement, optimisation) des chemins (et circuits) de G les matrices B_k, $B_{(k)}$, $\lambda B_{(k)}$ et $\tilde{A}$ peuvent, conformément aux théorèmes 4, 5, 5' et 6, être construites en ayant recours à l'un des trois types de procédures algorithmiques envisagées ci-après.

1) Calcul des puissances successives

Selon le problème, il s'agit de construire A^k, $(I \mathrm{E} A)^k$ et ce pour une ou plusieurs valeurs de k. Il est souvent avantageux (pour réduire le nombre des produits matriciels) d'exploiter la décomposition de k en base 2 et le fait que :

$$B^{2^{r-1}} * B^{2^{r-1}} = B^{2^r}.$$

2) Résolution de l'équation $\tilde{A} = I \mathrm{E} (A * \tilde{A})$

Il y a là une équation matricielle linéaire vis-à-vis de laquelle différents auteurs (notamment CARRE (71, 74), GONDRAN (74)) ont songé à appliquer les techniques classiques de résolution des systèmes d'équations (méthodes de JORDAN, GAUSS, GAUSS-SEIDEL, JACOBI, ...).

L'article de GONDRAN (ce livre) contient une étude systématique des algorithmes ainsi obtenus ; plusieurs algorithmes classiques apparaissent ainsi sous un jour un peu nouveau.

3) Application des transformations $\Theta_1, \ldots, \Theta_n$

Le passage de P à Θ_t . P est très simple (cf. ROY (59)et (70 Tome 1 p. 254)) et beaucoup plus rapide qu'un produit matriciel (n fois moins d'opérations $*$ et n fois moins d'opérations E). En l'absence de circuit absorbant, le théorème 6 fournit donc un moyen efficace de calculer $M[\hat{r}(C)]$ (y compris sa diagonale relative aux circuits) qui accroît considérablement la portée de l'algorithme proposé par l'auteur en 59, puis indépendamment par WARSHALL en 62 et déjà généralisé en 68 séparément par TOMESCU et ROBERT etFERLAND. D'autres généralisations sont encore à faire. Il semble en particulier que les applications Θ_t puissent permettre un calcul rapide de :

$$M[\underline{\hat{r}}(C)^{\lambda\ominus}] \quad \text{pour} \quad \lambda > 1$$

sous des hypothèses telles que :

Ω est K-stable
$\ast$ est commutative
$\lambda_C^{\ominus}$ est un résidu pour C
E est idempotente.

III - PROCEDURES PAR SEPARATION

1. Arborescence des chemins

a) Définition et propriété de χ

Etant donné un graphe, on peut associer à chaque sommet x l'ensemble S(x) de ses suivants, c'est-à-dire des sommets y tels que (x, y) soit un arc. La donnée de l'ensemble des sommets et de l'application S suffit à définir le graphe.

Soit Ω un ensemble (fini ou infini dénombrable) et Δ une application de Ω dans l'ensemble des parties finies de Ω. On définit ainsi un graphe χ ayant pour sommets les éléments ω de Ω, $\Delta(\omega)$ définissant l'ensemble des suivants de ω. χ est une arborescence de racine ω_1 si : $\forall \omega \in \Omega$ il existe dans χ un chemin (1) et un seul allant de ω_1 à ω. Ce chemin sera désigné par $\gamma(\omega)$.

Considérons une règle (exemple : être plus à droite sur la figure) permettant de ranger selon un ordre complet les sommets de $\Delta(\omega)$ et ce $\forall \omega \in \Omega$. Nous parlerons alors d'ordre transverse sur l'arborescence χ. Etant donné un ordre transverse, Ω peut être doté d'un ordre complet τ, compatible avec lui et appelé ordre de Tarry. Par définition, τ prescrit de ranger le sommet ω' avant le sommet ω'' si (et seulement si), ω_d désignant le dernier sommet commun à $\gamma(\omega')$ et $\gamma(\omega'')$, l'une des deux conditions suivantes est remplie :

---

(1) Même lorsque Ω est infini dénombrable, un chemin reste ici défini par une suite nécessairement finie.

- $\omega_d = \omega'$;
- $\omega_d \neq \omega'$, $\omega_d \neq \omega''$ et la comparaison dans l'ordre transverse des deux éléments de $\Delta(\omega_d)$ que sont ω'_d suivant de ω_d sur $\gamma(\omega')$ et ω''_d suivant de ω_d sur $\gamma(\omega'')$, place ω'_d avant ω''_d.

Revenons maintenant à un graphe (cf. II.1.a) $G = (X, U, a)$, $a(u) \in L$ muni de l'opération $\star$ (concaténation associative ou non avec élément neutre à droite e). Choisissons dans G un <u>sommet origine</u>, par exemple x_1 ; au couple (G, x_1) associons l'arborescence $\chi = (\Omega, \Delta)$ - encore notée $\chi(G, x_1)$ - dont chaque sommet ω est étiqueté par un sommet $x_{i_\omega} \in X$, celle-ci étant définie de façon récursive comme suit :

1) la racine de l'arborescence ω_1 est étiquetée x_1 ;
2) si ω Ω étiqueté x_{i_ω}, alors :
   $\Delta(\omega)$ contient autant d'éléments que x_{i_ω} a de suivants dans G et leurs étiquettes définissent une bijection entre ces deux ensembles.

Affectons de plus un label $a(\omega) \in L$ à chaque sommet de χ en posant (λ désignant le précédent de ω) :

$$a(\omega_1) = e \qquad a(\omega) = a(\lambda) \star a_{i_\lambda i_\omega} \qquad \omega \in \Omega - \{\omega_1\}.$$

L'arborescence étiquetée χ ainsi définie est évidemment finie si G est sans circuit (cf. par exemple figure 1). Qu'elle soit finie ou non, il est clair que, à tout chemin c issu de x_1 dans G correspond un sommet ω unique de Ω tel que la suite d'étiquettes portée par le chemin $\gamma(\omega)$ (joignant dans $X\omega_1$ à ω) soit précisément la suite de sommets définissant c.

Réciproquement, quel que soit ω Ω la suite d'étiquettes portées par le chemin $\gamma(\omega)$ définit dans G une suite $\mu(\omega)$ de sommets formant un chemin c de G issu de x_1. Ainsi :

<u>Proposition 1</u>

L'application $\mu : \omega \rightarrow \mu(\omega)$: définit une bijection entre Ω et l'ensemble C_1 des chemins de G issus de x_1 avec $a(\mu(\omega)) = a(\omega)$. De plus, il existe un ordre transverse tel que μ applique l'ordre de Tarry correspondant sur un ordre complet introduit a priori sur C_1 si et seulement si ce dernier vérifie :

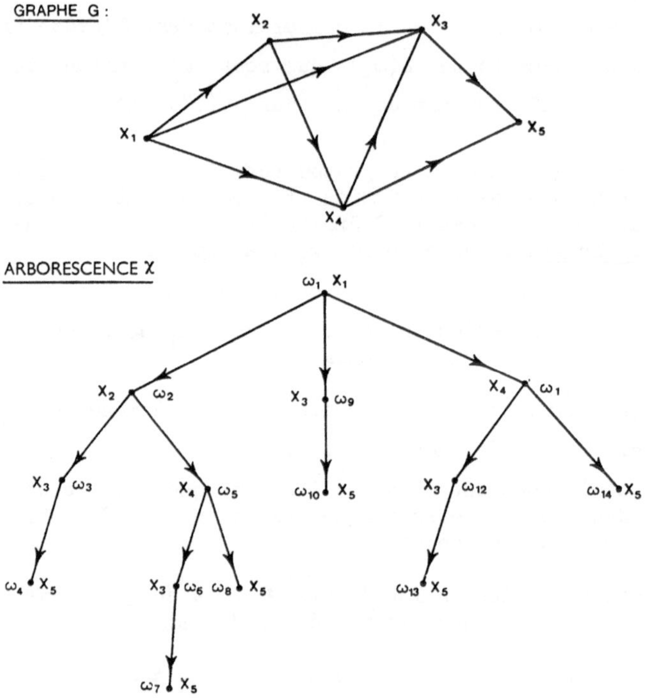

Figure 1
Arborescence des chemins

$$c \subsetneq d \quad (\text{c'est-à-dire } d = c\ c') \Longrightarrow c \text{ avant } d$$

$$c \subset d,\ c \not\subset d',\ c \text{ avant } d' \Longrightarrow d \text{ avant } d'.$$

(il est clair que la condition est nécessaire ; si elle est vérifiée, C_1 induit sur tout ensemble de chemins du type $(c(\omega), u)$ avec $u = (x_{i\omega}, y) \in U$ un ordre complet définissant un ordre transverse qui répond à la question).

En particulier, si l'ordre introduit sur C_1 correspond à l'ordre lexicographique des suites de sommets (resp. d'arcs) déduit d'un numérotage des sommets (resp. des arcs), alors (cf. figure 1) l'ordre transverse respectant le numérotage induirait un ordre de Tarry conforme à l'ordre lexicographique.

b) Sous-arborescences particulières

Soit $\omega^{\ominus}$ un sommet particulier ($\neq \omega_1$) de χ et $D(\omega^{\ominus})$ l'ensemble de ses descendants, c'est-à-dire des sommets ω tels qu'il existe un chemin allant dans χ de $\omega^{\ominus}$ à ω. Le sous-graphe de χ ayant pour sommets $D(\omega^{\ominus})$ et pour arcs tous ceux de χ ayant leurs deux extrémités dans $D(\omega^{\ominus})$ forme une sous-arborescence de χ dite sous-arborescence de racine $\omega^{\ominus}$.

Si l'on supprime dans χ l'arc admettant $\omega^{\ominus}$ comme extrémité terminale et la sous-arborescence de racine $\omega^{\ominus}$, il reste encore une arborescence dite déduite de χ par coupure de la branche $\omega^{\ominus}$.

Sauf peut-être pour un graphe G sans circuit, les procédures par séparation ne concernent pas χ dans sa totalité, mais des sous-arborescences finies déduites de χ en coupant certaines branches. Ces coupures ont lieu dès qu'un certain test T - dit test de coupure - effectué en ω fournit un résultat positif. Notons $\chi^T = (\Omega^T, \Delta^T)$ la sous-arborescence étiquetée définie de façon récursive comme suit :

1) la racine ω_1 est étiquetée x_1 ;

2) si $\omega \in \Omega^T$ étiqueté x_{i_ω}, alors :

$$\Delta^T(\omega) = \Delta(\omega) \quad \text{pour} \quad T(\omega) \leqq 0$$
$$\Delta^T(\omega) = \phi \quad \text{pour} \quad T(\omega) > 0.$$

Le test T est généralement constitué de divers tests élémentaires et il est positif dès l'instant où l'un de ses tests élémentaires l'est.

Le tableau 2 indique les types de tests élémentaires les plus courants.

2. Fondements des principales procédures (1)

---

(1) Pour tout complément relatif aux procédures par séparation en général, nous renvoyons le lecteur à HANSEN (ce livre).

Tableau II : Exemples de tests de coupure

N°	Définition	Cas particulier
1	Le sommet x_{i_ω} vérifie-t-il la propriété P ?	P : l'ensemble de ses descendants dans un sous-graphe partiel de G a une intersection vide avec $Y \subset X$
2	Le label $a(\omega)$ vérifie-t-il la propriété Q ?	Q : $a(\omega) * b(\omega) \in L_Q \subset L$ $b(\omega)$ = résultat d'un calcul effectué en ω
3	L'ensemble $\Gamma(\omega)$ des étiquettes portées par $\gamma(\omega)$ vérifie-t-il la propriété R ?	R : - $\Gamma(\omega) \supset Y \quad (Y \subset X)$ - $r' \leqq \|\Gamma(\omega)\| \leqq r''$ - le sous-graphe engendre par $X - \Gamma(\omega)$ remplit une certaine condition (comme : aucun des suivants de x_{i_ω} n'a de descendant dans Y).
4	La suite $\mu(\omega)$ des étiquettes portée par $\gamma(\omega)$ vérifie-t-elle la propriété S ?	S : - chaque élément de $\mu(\omega)$ figure au plus α fois - chaque arc de la forme (x_{i_ω}, y) satisfait relativement à $\mu(\omega)$ une certaine relation d'incompatibilité.

a) Principe de séparation

Soit F une famille de chemins de G d'origine x_1 ($F \subset C_1$). A de très rares exceptions près (notamment LITTLE and alt. (63)), les procédures par séparation proposées dans la littérature relatives aux problèmes "d'extractions" (visant à l'énumération ou à l'optimisation) se fondent (généralement sans l'expliciter) sur l'arborescence des chemins $\chi(G, x_1)$ ou, plus précisément, sur une des sous-arborescences de type χ^T.

Au fur et à mesure des séparations successives, tout sommet supplémentaire (venant développer la partie déjà construite de χ^T) doit être regardé comme représentatif de la famille $F(\omega)$:

$$F(\omega) = \{c \mid c \in F,\ c \supset \mu(\omega)\}.$$

Par définition, le sous-ensemble $F(\omega)$ est dit sondable (à un instant donné du déroulement de la procédure) si on est en mesure :

- soit de prouver que $F(\omega) = \phi$ ou que les chemins qu'il renferme sont sans intérêt compte-tenu de ceux déjà extraits ;
- soit d'extraire de $F(\omega)$ tous les chemins présumés intéressants compte-tenu de ceux déjà extraits.

Les tests élémentaires constitutifs du test de coupure T doivent être tels que :

$$\Delta^T(\omega) = \phi \Longrightarrow F(\omega) \text{ est sondable} \qquad \text{(III.2.1)}$$

(ce qui n'implique pas $\mu(\Omega^T) \supset F$, bien que de nombreuses procédures se soient imposées cette condition).

L'examen de sondabilité peut avoir lieu soit au moment d'inscrire ω sur la liste $\mathcal{L}$ des candidats aux séparations ultérieures, soit au moment de réaliser la séparation en ω. La liste $\mathcal{L}$ résume à tout instant l'information nécessaire à la poursuite de la procédure.

Quoi qu'il en soit, ω^o désignant le sommet sélectionné en vue de la prochaine séparation, celle-ci n'a lieu que si ω^o n'est pas sondable et elle a alors pour résultat l'introduction des sommets supplémentaires formant $\Delta^T(\omega^o)$.

On appellera représentant en ω un chemin particulier $r(\omega) \in F(\omega)$ facile à exhiber (par exemple en recherchant le complément le plus "naturel" a $\mu(\omega)$). Que ce soit en relation avec

T (cf. propriétés P ou Q du tableau 2) ou avec la sondabilité ($|F(\omega)| = 1$) ou pour organiser l'enchaînement des séparations (cf. b ci-après), il est souvent commode d'introduire un (éventuellement plusieurs) représentant(s).

Plus encore que le rôle précis dévolu aux représentants ou encore que la nature et l'emplacement des tests, c'est l'enchaînement des séparations successives qui différencie les procédures.

b) Enchaînement des séparations

C'est ici qu'intervient l'ordre transverse $<_t$. Etant donné $\Delta^T(\omega^o)$, $<_t$ est habituellement défini par référence à l'ordre :

- des étiquettes x_{i_ω} résultant d'un numérotage originel des sommets de X ;
- des arcs $(x_{i_{\omega^o}}, x_{i_\omega})$ résultant d'un numérotage originel des arcs de U ;
- des représentants $r(\omega)$ résultant d'un ordre originel sur les labels $a(r(\omega)) \in L$;
- des $F(\omega)$ résultant d'une évaluation optimiste $\mathfrak{V}(\omega)$ des "meilleurs chemins de $F(\omega)$ selon un certain critère $\mathfrak{C}(c)$:

$$\mathfrak{V}(\omega) \geqq \mathfrak{C}(c) \quad \forall c \in F(\omega) \qquad \text{(III.2.2)}$$

si "meilleur" = max.

Les séparations successives sont normalement enchaînées conformément à l'un des deux schémas types indiqués figure 2. On peut également concevoir des procédures mixtes panachant :

- sélection du 1er suivant de ω^o et sélection du 1er dans $\mathcal{L}$ interclassé ;
- rangement en tête de la suite ordonnée par $<_t$ ou interclassement dans $\mathcal{L}$ selon un ordre compatible avec $<_t$, des suivants de ω^o (autres que le 1er s'il est sélectionné).

Dans les P.S.E.S. (Procédures par Séparation et Evaluation en Série), les sélections en vue de la séparation sont conformes à l'ordre τ de Tarry restreint à Ω^T. Or, la proposition 1 jointe à la propriété (III.2.1) montrent qu'il est généralement facile de concevoir une P.S.E.S. dont le déroulement conduise à énumérer les éléments de F conformément à un ordre de type lexicographique introduit a priori sur F. Ainsi pour F = {circuits élémentaires passant par x_1} et $<_t$ défini par référence à un numé-

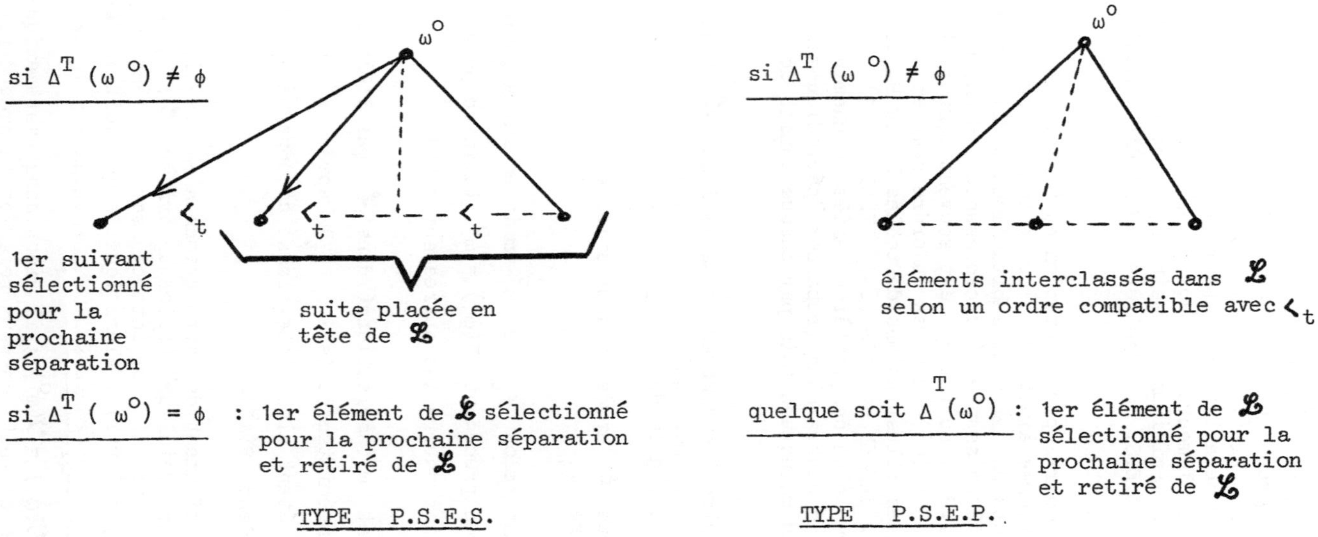

Figure 2

schémas classiques d'enchaînement des séparations

rotage des sommets on obtient l'algorithme d'énumération des circuits élémentaires d'un graphe proposé par TIERNAN (70). Ceux décrits par FLORIAN et ROBERT (71) pour l'obtention des circuits élémentaires de longueur négative, WEINBLATT (72) à nouveau pour la totalité des circuits élémentaires, ROY et GALLAND (73) pour l'énumération de chemins ε-minimum admissibles, et beaucoup d'autres sont en fait des P.S.E.S. particulières du modèle exposé cidessus.

Dans les P.S.E.P. (Procédures par Séparation et Evaluation en Parallèle), l'ordre transverse ainsi que l'ordre complet servant à interclasser les éléments de $\mathcal{L}$ sont habituellement définis par référence aux valeurs décroissantes (ou croissantes) d'une évaluation optimiste (cf. III.2.2) ou (ce qui est souvent compatible) au classement des labels a $(r(\omega))$ d'après un ordre complet sur L. On trouvera de nombreuses illustrations de telles P.S.E.P. notamment dans BERTIER (66), HANSEN et MAES (69), LEMAIRE (71) relativement à l'optimisation selon des critères variés de chemins devant satisfaire diverses contraintes (repasser "périodiquement" en un sommet, passer au moins une fois par chaque sommet de $Y \subset X$, ...).

Il est possible de réduire l'encombrement de la liste $\mathcal{L}$ ainsi que le travail d'interclassement qui suit chaque séparation en modifiant comme suit les règles de la figure 2 :

- inscrire sur la liste $\mathcal{L}$ après la séparation en ω^o en plus un sommet supplémentaire ω_1 :

  ω_1 = le 1er suivant selon $<_t$ de ω^o mais en lui associant la référence de son précédent $\nabla(\omega_1) = \omega^o$ (afin de pouvoir le cas échéant réintroduire les autres suivants) ;

- remplacer tout sommet ω^o sélectionné dans $\mathcal{L}$ par l'élément (s'il existe) venant immédiatement (selon $<_t$) après ω^o dans $\Delta^T[\bar{}(\omega^o)]$, cet élément étant alors interclassé accompagné de la référence de son précédent $\nabla(\omega^o)$.

Il est clair que l'enchaînement des séparations n'est en rien modifié. Si $r(\omega)$ est le "meilleur" (selon un critère $\mathcal{C}$) chemin de $F(\omega)$ et si l'ordre utilisé pour interclasser les éléments de $\mathcal{L}$ est défini par $\mathcal{V}(\omega) = \mathcal{C}(r(\omega))$, alors (quelle que soit la séparation) l'unique suivant supplémentaire ω_1 introduit à la séparation ω^o vérifie : $\mathcal{V}(\omega_1) = \mathcal{V}(\omega^o)$; il vient donc systématiquement en tête de $\mathcal{L}$. De ce fait, on peut regarder la procédure ainsi définie comme une procédure mixte : ω_2 second suivant selon $<_t$ de ω^o étant seul inscrit sur $\mathcal{L}$ après la séparation et ce avec la référence de ω^o pour pouvoir opérer le remplacement comme indiqué plus haut. Avec F = {chemins élémentaires joignant x_1 à x_n}, $\mathcal{C}$ = longueur du plus court chemin, on retrouve (aux détails des tests près) les algorithmes proposés par YEN (71) et LAWLER (72) pour l'énumération des K plus courts chemins élémentaires.

Quel que soit le type de procédure (en série, en parallèle ou mixte), les tests requis nécessitent fréquemment des calculs (cf. tableau 2) que les résultats de la section II permettent d'accélérer. Par exemple, l'exclusion d'un sous-ensemble Y de sommets conduit (cf. LAWLER (72)) à s'intéresser à des matrices du type $M[\underline{\hat{f}}(C'_Y)]$ avec C'_Y = {chemins élémentaires n'ayant aucun sommet intermédiaire dans Y}. Or il découle de la démonstration du théorème 6 que en l'absence de circuit absorbant :

$$M[\underline{\hat{f}}(C'_Y)] = \left(\prod_{x_t \in X-Y} \Theta_t\right) . A.$$

En conclusion, les procédures par séparation sont très bien adaptées à l'étude de nombreux problèmes concrets de génération de chemins devant satisfaire à des contraintes complexes.

En revanche, les procédures algébriques conviennent souvent mieux à l'égard de structures moins anarchiques et cette complémentarité peut être exploitée dans la résolution d'un même problème.

REFERENCES

BACKHOUSE R.C. and CARRE B.A., (75), "Regular algebra applied to path finding problems", J. Inst. Maths. Applics., (1975).

BENZAKEN C., (68), "Structures algébriques des cheminements : pseudo-treillis, gerbier de carré nul", in Network and Switching Theory, edited by G. BIORCI, Academic Press, (1968), p. 40-47.

BERGE C., (58), "Théorie des graphes et ses applications", Dunod, Paris, (1958).

BERTIER P., (66), "Procédures pour élaborer des tournées de distribution", METRA Série Spéciale n° 8, (1966).

CARRE B.A., (71), "An algebra for network routing problems", J. Inst. Maths. Applics., 7 (1971), p. 273-294.

CLARKE S., KRIKORLAN A. and RAUSEN J., (63), "Computing the N best loopless paths in a network", Journal of the Society for Industrial and Applied Mathematics, (1963), 11, 1096-1102.

DANTZIG G.B., BLATTNER W.O. and RAO M.R., (67), "All shortest routes from a fixed origin in a graph", Théorie des graphes, Journées Internationales d'Etudes, Rome, 1966 (Dunod, Paris, 1967).

DREYFUS S.E., (69), "An appraisal of some shortest path algorithms", Operations Research, vol. 17, n° 3, (1969).

ELLON S., WATSON-GANDY C.D.T. and CHRISTOFIDES N., (71), "Distribution Management", Griffin, London, (1971).

FLORIAN M. et ROBERT P., (71), "Search method to locate negative cycles", Management Science, vol. 17, number 5, (January 1971), p. 307 à 310.

FLOYD R.W., (62), "Algorithm 97 : Shortest path", Communication of ACM, Vol. 5 (1962), p. 345.

FORTET R., (59), "L'algèbre de Boole et ses applications en Recherche Opérationnelle", Cahier du Centre d'Etudes de R.O., Bruxelles, (1959), n° 4.

GONDRAN M., (74), "Problèmes combinatoires et programmation en nombres entiers", Thèse d'Etat, Université de Paris, (1974).

HAMMER and RUDEANU S., (68), "Boolean methods in operational research", Berlin, Springer-Verlag, (1968).

HANSEN P., (74), "Programmes mathématiques en variables 0-1", Thèse, Université Libre de Bruxelles, (mars 1974).

HANSEN P. et MA S J.M., (69), "Parcours d'un graphe", Cahiers du Centre d'Etudes de Recherche Opérationnelle - Université Libre de Bruxelles, vol. 11, n° 3, (1969).

HOFFMAN A.J. and WINOGRAD S., (73), "Finding all shortest distances in a directed Network", IBM J. Res. Develop., (1973).

KAUFMAN A. et MALGRANGE Y., (63), "Recherche des chemins et circuits hamiltoniens d'un graphe", Revue Française de R.O., 7e année, (1963), n° 26, p. 61-73.

KUNTZMANN J., (66), "Théorie des relations et des réseaux", Cours, Université de Grenoble, (1966).

LAWLER E.L., (72), "A procedure for computing the K best solutions to discrete optimization problems and its application to the shortest path problem", Management Science, vol. 18, n° 7, (Mars 1972).

LAWLER E.L. and WOOD D.E., (66), "Branch and bound methods : a survey", The University of Michigan, Ann Arbor, Michigan, Operations Research, (July-August 1966), V. 14 N. 4.

LEMAIRE, (71), "Problèmes de tournées avec contraintes multiples", Thèse 3e cycle, Université de Paris, (Décembre 1971).

LITTLE J.D.C., MURTY K.G., SWEENEY D.W. and KAREL C., (63), "An algorithm for the travelling salesman problem", Operations Research, 11, n° 6, pp. 972-989, (1963).

MAGHOUT K., (63), "Applications de l'algèbre de Boole à la théorie des graphes et aux problèmes linéaires et quadratiques", Cahiers du Centre d'Etudes et de R.O., Bruxelles, Tome 5, (1963), n° 1-2, p. 21-99.

MINIEKA E., (74), "On computing sets of shortest paths in a graph", Communications of the ACM, (June 1974), Vol. 17 - number 6.

MINIEKA E. and SHIER D.R., (73), "A note on an algebra for the K best routes in a Network", J. Inst. Maths. Applics., (1973), 11, 145-149.

PAIR C. et DERNIAME J.C., (71), "Problèmes de cheminement dans les graphes", Monographies d'informatique, Dunod, (1971).

PETEANU V., (67), "An algebra of the optimal path in networks", Mathematica, Vol. 9 (1967), n° 2, p. 335-342.

PETEANU V., (70), "Optimal paths in networks and generalizations", Mathematica, Vol. 11 (34) 2, pp. 311-327, 1ère partie : 1969-Vol. 12 (35), 1, pp. 159-186, 2e partie : 1970.

PICHAT E., (68), "Algorithms for finding the maximal elements of a finite universal algebra", Proc. IFIP Congress 1968, Edinburg, Booklet A, p. 96-101.

PICHAT E., (70), "Contribution à l'algorithmique non numérique dans les ensembles ordonnés", Thèse, Université de Grenoble, (1970).

ROBERT P. and FERLAND J., (68), "Généralisation de l'algorithme de WARSHALL", Rev. RIRO (janvier-février 1968), n° 7, p. 71-85.

ROY B., (59), "Transitivité et connexité", C.R. Acad. Sciences Paris, Tome 249 (1959), p. 216.

ROY B., (70), "Algèbre moderne et Théorie des Graphes orientées vers les sciences économiques et sociales", (Dunod, Paris, 1er tome : 1969, 2e tome : 1970).

ROY B., (74), "Chemins et circuits : Enumération et optimisation", Cahier de Mathématiques de la Décision, n° 74-18, Université Paris IX Dauphine.

ROY B. et GALLAND D., (73), "Enumération des chemins ε-minimum admissibles entre deux points", R.A.I.R.O., (septembre 1973), V-3, p. 3 à 20.

SAKAROVITCH M., (68), "The K shortest chains in a graph", Transportation Research, (1968), 2, 1-11.

SVESTKA J.A. and HUCKFELDT V.E., (73), "Computational experience with an m-salesman traveling salesman algorithm", Management Science - Vol. 19, n° 7, (March 1973).

TABOURIER Y., (73), "All shortest distances in a graph. An improvement to Dantzig's inductive algorithm", Discrete Mathematics, 4, (1973), p. 83-87.

TIERNAN J.C., (70), "An efficient search algorithm to find the elementary circuits of a graph", Comm. A.C.M. 13,12 (Dec. 1970).

TOMESCU I., (66), "Sur les méthodes matricielles dans la théorie des réseaux", C.R. Acad. Sci. Paris, Tome 263 (1966), p. 826-829.

TOMESCU I., (68), "Sur l'algorithme matriciel de B. ROY", R.I.R.O. (janvier-février 1968).

VINCKE P., (75), "Problèmes multicritères", Cahiers du Centre d'Etudes de Recherche Opérationnelle, (1975).

WARSHALL S., (62), "A theorem on boolean matrices", J. of A.C.M., vol. 9 (1962), p. 11-12.

WEINBLATT H., (72), "A new search algorithm for finding the simple cycles of a finite directed graph", Journal of the Association for Computing Machinery, vol. 19 - n° 1, (January 1972), pp. 43-56.

YEN J.Y., (71), "Finding the K shortest loopless paths in a network", Management Science, vol. 17, n° 11, (1971), 712-716.

YEN J.Y., (75), "Shortest path network problems", (Ed. Prof. Dr W. Eichhorn, et al.), Verlag Anton Hain - Meisenheim Am Glan, Germany, (1975).

PATH ALGEBRA AND ALGORITHMS

M. Gondran

Direction des Etudes et Recherches,
Electricité de France, Paris.

ABSTRACT. The object of the paper is the study of graph problems involving paths or routing.
As a result of the introduction of a very general algebraic structure, most of these problems will be unified into a common presentation. Moreover it will generalize the results of authors having investigated this topic and thus solve a few new problems.

1. PATH ALGEBRA

1.1. Definition of the algebra

The structure $(L, \oplus, *)$ is defined as follows :

- the operation "add" $\oplus$ gives the set L a structure of commutative monoid (closure, commutativity, associativity). Moreover, a neutral element ε is supposed . In case of its absence, it should be added to L.

- The operation "multiply" $*$ gives the set L a monoid structure (closure, associativity). If there is no neutral element e for $*$, it should be added . e will be called the unit.

- The multiplication is right and left distributive for addition and admits ε as an absorbing element ($a * \varepsilon = \varepsilon$ for any $a \in L$).

B. Roy (ed.), Combinatorial Programming: Methods and Applications, 137–148. *All Rights Reserved.*

Such a structure will be denoted "path algebra".

Previous authors had introduced related algebraic structures (Q - semi - ring of ROBERT and FERLAND [14] , distributive lattices of BENZAKEN [2] , A - B - gerbier of PICHAT [13] , C - semi group of PETEANU [12] , algebra of CARRE [3] , binoid of SHIER [17]). With regard to all these, the main generalization is not to postulate that the $\oplus$ operation is idempotent.

This allows to take into account many other problems (especially the K-th shortest path, the η-optimal paths and the network reliabilit problem, cf. GONDRAN [7] , B. ROY [16] and examples 6, 7, 9, 10, 11, in fig. 1).

This path algebra differs from the algebraic structure of ROY [16] , essentially in the fact that the operation $\oplus$ (corresponding to "l'operation d'extraction E") is a closed operation ($a \in L$, $b \in L \Longrightarrow a \oplus b \in L$).

Another generalization consists to introduce the further definitions :

For $a \in L$, $a^{(K)} = e \oplus a \oplus a^2 \oplus \ldots \oplus a^K$

An element a is called p-regular if :

$$(1\text{-}1) \qquad a^{(p)} = a^{(p+1)}$$

For any p-regular element a, it is deduced the existence of $\bar{a}$, quasi-inverse of a , such as :

$$(1\text{-}2) \qquad \bar{a} = \lim_{K \to +\infty} a^{(K)} = a^{(p)} = a^{(p+1)} = \ldots = a^{(p+r)} = \ldots$$

the following equation holds :

$$(1\text{-}3) \qquad \bar{a} = e \oplus a * \bar{a} = e \oplus \bar{a} * a$$

Moreover, considering the equations :

$$(1\text{-}4) \qquad y = a * y \oplus b \quad \text{and} \quad z = z * a \oplus b$$

with a being p-regular, then if $K \geqslant p+1$,

$$(1\text{-}5) \qquad y = a^{(K)} y \oplus \bar{a}\, b \quad \text{and} \quad z = z\, a^{(K)} \oplus b\, \bar{a}$$

where the $*$ sign has been omitted, as usual for the multiplication.

Moreover $y = \bar{a}\, b$ and $z = b\, \bar{a}$ are solutions of (1-4).

In the set L, a preorder relation (symmetry, transitivity) can be defined as follows :

(1-6) $a \geqslant b \Leftrightarrow \exists c \in L : a = b \oplus c$

For this preorder, the equations (1-5) demonstrate that the solutions $\bar{a}\, b$ and $\bar{b}\, a$ are minimal.

Lastly, addition and multiplication are defined for square matrices of order n with elements in L, from operations $\oplus$ and $*$.
The set of matrices M(n,L) thus defined has the same structure as L, with the zero-element :

$$\Sigma = \begin{bmatrix} \varepsilon & \cdots & \varepsilon \\ \vdots & & \vdots \\ \varepsilon & \cdots & \varepsilon \end{bmatrix}.$$

and the unit-element :

$$E = \begin{bmatrix} e & & \varepsilon \\ & \ddots & \\ \varepsilon & & e \end{bmatrix}$$

The operations induced on M(n,L) will also be written $\oplus$ and $*$.

1.2. Properties of the path algebra

Now, the graph G = (X,U) is considered. On any edge (x_i,x_j) an element $l_{ij} \in L$ is associated. Then the incidence matrix $A = (a_{ij})$ of this graph is defined by :

(1-7) $a_{ij} = \begin{cases} l_{ij} & \text{if } (x_i,x_j) \in U \\ \varepsilon & \text{else} \end{cases}$

Then for any path $\mu_{ij} = (x_{i_1}, x_{i_2}, \ldots, x_{i_K})$ with $i_1 = i$ and $i_K = j$, its weight is associated :

(1-8) $w(\mu_{ij}) = l_{i_1 i_2} * l_{i_2 i_3} * \cdots * l_{i_{K-1} i_K}$

Many problems involving path search can be reduced into computing A^K or

(1-9) $A^{(K)} = E \oplus A \oplus \ldots \oplus A^K.$

Solved problems	L	$\oplus$	*	ε	e
1. Connexity	$\{0,1\}$	max	min	0	1
2. Path enumeration	$P(X^*)$	$\cup$	Latin multiply	$\emptyset$	X
3. Multi-criteria problems	$P(\mathbb{R}^p)$	active vectors in the union	active vectors in the Sum	$(+\infty)^p$	$(0)^p$
4. Maximal capacity path	$\mathbb{R}^+ \cup \{+\infty\}$	max	min	0	$+\infty$
5. Shortest path	$\overline{\mathbb{R}} = \mathbb{R} \cup \{+\infty\}$	min	+	$+\infty$	0
6. K-th Shortest path	cone of $\overline{\mathbb{R}}^K$	K smallest terms of two vectors	K smallest terms of sums of couples	$(+\infty)^K$	$(0,+\infty,\ldots+\infty)$
7. n-optimal paths	ordered sequence of elements of $\overline{\mathbb{R}}$ with amplitude η	Sequence of the η-smallest terms of two sequences	Sequence of η-smallest terms of sums of couples	$+\infty$	0
8. Maximal fiability	$\{a \mid 0 \leqslant a \leqslant 1\}$	max	x	0	1
9. Path numbering	$\mathbb{R}$ or $\mathbb{N}$	+	x	0	1
10. Markov chains	$\{a \mid 0 \leqslant a \leqslant 1\}$	+	x	0	1
11. Network fiability	polynomials with Boolean variables	symmetrical difference	x	0	1

Fig. 1

Let $N_{ij}(p)$ be the set of all paths from x_i to x_j, not using more than p times each circuit of the graph ($N_{ij}(0)$ is the set of elementary paths from x_i to x_j). Let N_p be the maximal number of edges for paths $N_{ij}(p)$ ($N_0 = n-1$). Then G is said to be <u>without any p- absorbing circuit</u> if any elementary circuit μ_{ii} has a <u>p- regular weight $w(\mu_{ii})$</u>.

This fundamental theorem holds :

<u>Theorem 1. If G is without any p- absorbing circuit and if either p = 0 , or * is commutative the following equations are satisfied</u> :

(1-10) $a_{ij}^{(Np)} = \sum_{\mu_{ij} \in N_{ij}(p)} w(\mu_{ij})$

(1-11) $\bar{A} = \lim_{K \to +\infty} A^{(K)} = A^{(N_p)} = A^{(N_{p+1})} = \ldots$

(1-12) $\bar{A} = A\bar{A} \oplus E = \bar{A}A \oplus E$

<u>Demonstration</u> . See GONDRAN [7] .

$\bar{A}$ is the relevant matrix in path problems. The next paragraph will show how conventional techniques to solve equation systems will afford efficient algorithms to compute the matrix $\bar{A}$ (or a single line of it).

2. GENERAL ALGORITHMS

When G has no p- absorbing circuit, $\bar{A}$ satisfies the equations (1-12) and searching $\bar{A}$ reduces to solving (1-12). Now it will be seen how conventional methods for linear systems resolution can be adapted to solve routing problems. Conventional algorithms in graph theory appear then as particular cases (cf. CARRE [3]).

Multiplying (1-12) by a matrix B, we get :

(2-1) $Y = AY \oplus B$ and $Z = ZA \oplus B$

where $Y = \bar{A}B$ and $Z = B\bar{A}$

If $B = E$, the solution of (2-1) is the matrix $\overline{A}$; if B is a unit vector, the solutions of (2-1) are respectively a column or a line of $\overline{A}$.

2.1. Iterative methods

The first line of the matrix $\overline{A}$ can be thus computed. It satisfies the equation :

$$Z = Z\,A \oplus B \qquad \text{with } B = (e,\varepsilon,\varepsilon,\ldots,\varepsilon)$$

The generalized JACOBI method states, for $K \geqslant 1$:

$$\text{(2-2)} \qquad \boxed{\begin{aligned} Z_1^{(K+1)} &= \sum_{j=1}^{n} Z_j^{(K)} * a_{j1} \oplus e \\ Z_i^{(K+1)} &= \sum_{j=1}^{n} Z_j^{(K)} * a_{ji} \end{aligned}} \qquad \text{for } i \geqslant 2$$

Starting from initial conditions $Z_1^{(1)} = e$ and $Z_i^{(1)} = a_{1i}$.

Each iteration requires $n^2 \oplus$ operations and $n^2 *$ operations.

For the shortest path problem (example 5), this method is recognized as the BELLMAN algorithm [1] .

Convergence occurs in less than N_p iterations, for the method can be stated, in matrices :

$$\text{(2-3)} \qquad Z^{(K+1)} = Z^{(K)}\,A \oplus B$$

From a certain $Z^{(0)} = (\varepsilon,\varepsilon,\ldots,\varepsilon)$ onwards, we have :

$$\text{(2-4)} \qquad Z^{(K+1)} = Z^{(0)}\,A^{K+1} \oplus B\overline{A} = B\overline{A} \quad \text{for} \quad K \geqslant N_p.$$

The generalized GAUSS-SEIDEL method states for $K \geqslant 1$:

$$(2\text{-}5)\quad \begin{cases} Z_1^{(K+1)} = \left(\sum_{j=2}^{n} Z_j^{(K)} * a_{j1} \oplus e \right) * \overline{a}_{11} \\ Z_i^{(K+1)} = \left(\sum_{j>i} Z_j^{(K)} * a_{ji} \oplus \sum_{j<i} Z_j^{(K+1)} * a_{ji} \right) * \overline{a}_{ii} \end{cases}$$

for $i \geq 2$

Starting from initial conditions $Z_1^{(1)} = \overline{a}_{11}$, $Z_i^{(1)} = \overline{a}_{11} * a_{1i} * \overline{a}_{ii}$

In most cases $a_{ii} = \varepsilon$, therefore $\overline{a}_{ii} = e$ and formula (2-5) are simplified. It can be remarked that $Z^{(1)}$ is given by (2-5) from $Z^{(0)} = (\varepsilon,\varepsilon,\dots,\varepsilon)$.

Each iteration requires n^2 $\oplus$ operations, n^2 $*$ operations and n computings of quasi-inverse.

For the shortest path problem (example 5), the FORD algorighm [6] is thus recognized.

Convergence occurs in less than N_p iterations as a result of the next theorem.

Theorem 2 . The generalized GAUSS-SEIDEL method converges in less than N_p iterations.

Demonstration. See GONDRAN [8] .

2.2. Direct methods

To compute the matrix $\overline{A}$, it is seen that one must have $Y = AY \oplus B$ with $B = E$.

The generalized GAUSS-JORDAN method states for $K \geq 1$:

$$(2\text{-}6)\quad \begin{aligned} a_{K,K}^{[K]} &= \overline{\left(a_{K,K}^{[K-1]}\right)} \\ a_{i,j}^{[K]} &= a_{i,j}^{[K-1]} \oplus a_{i,K}^{[K-1]} * a_{K,K}^{[K]} * a_{K,j}^{[K-1]} \end{aligned}$$

Starting from initial conditions $A^{[0]} = A$

A simplification appears when computing the terms $a_{i,K}^{[K]}$ and $a_{K,j}^{[K]}$, namely for example :

$$a_{i,K}^{[K]} = a_{i,K}^{[K-1]} \oplus a_{i,K}^{[K-1]} * a_{K,K}^{[K]} * a_{K,K}^{[K-1]} = a_{i,K}^{[K-1]}\left(e \oplus a_{K,K}^{[K]} * a_{K,K}^{[K-1]}\right.$$

and according to (1-4) :

$$a_{i,K}^{[K]} = a_{i,K}^{[K-1]} * a_{K,K}^{[K]} \quad \text{for } i \neq K. \tag{2-7}$$

The K-th iteration of the algorithm is then :

$$\boxed{\begin{aligned} a_{K,K}^{[K]} &= \left(\overline{a_{K,K}^{[K-1]}}\right) \\ a_{i,K}^{[K]} &= a_{i,K}^{[K-1]} * a_{K,K}^{[K]} \\ a_{K,j}^{[K]} &= a_{K,K}^{[K]} * a_{K,j}^{[K-1]} \\ a_{i,j}^{[K]} &= a_{i,j}^{[K]} \oplus a_{i,K}^{[K]} * a_{K,j}^{[K-1]} \end{aligned}} \tag{2-8}$$

Each iteration requires $(n-1)^2$ $\oplus$ operations, n^2-1 $*$ operations and one computation of quasi-inverse.

In the case when G has no 0- absorbing circuit (see examples 1, 2, 3, 4, 5, 8, 11), $a_{K,K}^{[K-1]}$ is 0-regular therefore $a_{K,K}^{[K]} = e$ and the number of operation is restricted to $(n-1)^2$.

Convergence occurs with n iterations , as follows from the next theorem.

Theorem 3 . $A^{[n]}$ being computed by the generalized GAUSS JORDAN method is equal to $\overline{A}$.

Demonstration : See GONDRAN [8] .

To compute the matrix $\overline{A}$ requires thus $n(n-1)^2$ $\oplus$ and $*$ operations and n computation of quasi-inverse, with this method.

Many authors have developed particular forms of this algorithm. It was defined by ROY ([15] , 1959) and WARSHALL ([18] , 1962) to determine the transitive closure of a graph (example 1), by FLOYD ([5] , 1962) for the shortest path problem (example 5), by ROBERT and FERLAND ([14] , 1968), CARRE ([3] , 1971) for special algebraic structures, by MÜLLER-MERBACH ([11] , 1969) for the inversion of the Gozinto matrix (example 9), by MINIEKA and SHIER ([10] , 1973) and MINIEKA ([9] , 1974), for the problem of K-th shortest paths (example 6).

The generalized escalator algorithm states for $K \geqslant 2$

(2-9)

$$a^{[K]}_{K,\,K} = \overline{\left(a_{K,\,K} \oplus \sum_{1 \leqslant i,j \leqslant K-1} a_{K,\,i} * a^{[K-1]}_{i,\,j} * a_{j,\,K} \right)}$$

$$a^{[K]}_{i,\,K} = \left(\sum_{j=1}^{K-1} a^{[K-1]}_{i,\,j} * a_{j,\,K} \right) * a^{[K]}_{K,\,K} \qquad 1 \leqslant i \leqslant K-1$$

$$a^{[K]}_{K,\,j} = a^{[K]}_{K,\,K} * \left(\sum_{i=1}^{K-1} a_{K,\,i} * a^{[K-1]}_{i,\,j} \right) \qquad 1 \leqslant j \leqslant K-1$$

$$a^{[K]}_{i,\,j} = a^{[K-1]}_{i,\,j} \oplus \left(\sum_{i=1}^{K-1} a^{[K-1]}_{i,\,1} * a_{1,\,K} \right) * a^{[K]}_{K,\,j} \qquad 1 \leqslant i,\, j \leqslant K-$$

Starting with initial conditions $a^{[1]}_{1,\,1} = \overline{a}_{11}$.

Computation is simpler using, before each iteration, the quantities

$$\text{(2-10)} \qquad \alpha_{i,\,K} = \sum_{j=1}^{[K-1]} a^{[K-1]}_{i,\,j} * a_{j,\,K} \qquad \text{for } i \text{ from } 1 \text{ to } K-1$$

and noticing then that the equation (2-9) become

$$
(2\text{-}11)\quad
\begin{cases}
a^{[K]}_{K,K} = \overline{\left(a_{K,K} \oplus \sum_{i=1}^{K-1} a_{K,i} * \alpha_{i,K} \right)} & \\
a^{[K]}_{i,K} = \alpha_{i,K} * a^{[K]}_{K,K} & 1 \leq i \leq K-1 \\
a^{[K]}_{K,j} = a^{[K]}_{K,K} * \left(\sum_{i=1}^{[K-1]} a_{K,i} * a^{[K-1]}_{i,j} \right) & 1 \leq j \leq K-1 \\
a^{[K]}_{i,j} = a^{[K-1]}_{i,j} \oplus \alpha_{i,K} * a^{[K]}_{K,j} & 1 \leq i,\ j \leq K-1
\end{cases}
$$

The K-th iteration requires $3K^2 - 2K$ $\oplus$ operations, $3K(K-1)$ $*$ operations and one computation of quasi-inverse.

When G has no o- absorbing circuit (see examples 1, 2, 3, 4, 5, 8, 11) $a^{[K]}_{K,K} = e$ and the number of $\oplus$ and $*$ operations is restricted to 3(K-

Convergence is reached with n iterations as a consequence of next theorem :

Theorem 4. $A^{[n]}$ computed by the generalized escalator method is equal to $\overline{A}$.

Demonstration : See GONDRAN [8] .

Computing the matrix $\overline{A}$ requires, with this algorithm, n^3 $\oplus$ and $*$ operations and n computations of quasi-inverse.

The order of magnitude is the same as in GAUSS-JORDAN method. Particular forms of this algorithm have been developed already. First it was defined by DANTZIG ([4] , 1966) for the shortest path problem (example 5), by CARRE ([3] , 1971) for a special a algebraic structure (examples 1, 4, 5, 8), then by MINIEKA and SHIER ([10] , 1973) and MINIEKA ([9] , 1974) for the problem of K-th Shortest paths (example 6).

R E F E R E N C E S

[1] BELLMAN R., "On a routing problem", Quart. Appl. Math., 16 (1958)

[2] BENZAKEN C., "Structures algébriques des cheminements : pseudotreillis, gerbier de carré nul", in Network an Switching Theory, edited by G. BIORCI, Academic Press, 1968, p. 40-47.

[3] CARRE B.A., "An algebra for network routing problems", J. Inst. Maths. Applics, 7 (1971), p. 273-294.

[4] DANTZIG G.B., "All shortest routes in a graph", Proc. I.C.C. Conference on Theory of Graphs, Rome (1966), Gordon and Breach, N.Y., . p. 91-92.

[5] FLOYD R.W., "ALGORITHM 97 : Shortest path", Communication of ACM, Vol. 5 (1962) p. 345.

[6] FORD L.R. and FULKERSON D.R., "Flows in Network", Princeton University Press, 1962.

[7] GONDRAN M., "Algèbre linéaire et cheminement dans un graphe", R.A.I.R.O., 8ième année, V-3, 1974.

[8] GONDRAN M., "Démonstration de la convergence des algorithmes de Gauss-Jordan généralisé et "escalier" généralisé, note EDF à paraître.

[9] MINIEKA E., "On computing Sets of Shortest Paths in a graph", Communications of the ACM, June 1974, V. 17, 6, p. 351-3.

[10] MINIEKA E. and SHIER D.R., "A note on an algebra for the k best routes in a network", J. Inst. Math. Appl. 11, 1973, p. 145-149.

[11] MÜLLER - MERBACH H., "Die Inversion von Gozinto-Matrizen mit einem Graphen-Orientierten Verfahren, Elektroniche Daten Verarbeitung 11, 1969, P. 310-314-

[12] PETEANU V., "An algebra of the optimal path in networks", Mathematica, Vol. 9 (1967), n°2, p. 335-342.

[13] PICHAT E., "Algorithms for finding the maximal elements of a finite universal algebra", Proc. IFIP Congress 1968, EDINBURG, Booklet A, p. 96-101.

[14] ROBERT P. and FERLAND J., "Genéralisation de l'algorithme de WARSHALL", Rev. Française Informatique et R.O. (1968) n° 7, p. 71-85.

[15] ROY B., "Transitivité et connexité", C.R. Acad. Sciences Paris, Tome 249 (1959), p.216.

[16] ROY B., "Chemins et circuits, énumération et optimisation : procédures algébriques", this book.

[17] SHIER D.R., "A decomposition algorithm for optimality problems in tree-structured networks", Discrete Mathematics 6, 1973, p. 175-189

[18] WARSHALL S., "A theorem on boolean Matrices", J. of ACM, vol. 9 (1962), p. 11-12.

HAMILTONIAN CIRCUITS AND THE TRAVELLING SALESMAN PROBLEM

Nicos Christofides

Department of Management Science,
Imperial College, London, Great Britain

ABSTRACT. The problem of finding a hamiltonian circuit in a directed graph is discussed and two algorithms are described and compared. Exact methods for the solution of the travelling salesman problem are given with particular emphasis being placed on the calculation of tight bounds that can be used in a variety of tree-search algorithms. Procedures using the assignment and shortest spanning tree problems to provide such bounds and to direct the tree-search are surveyed.

1. INTRODUCTION

A *graph* G is defined by the doublet (X,A), where X is a set of n *vertices* x_i and A is a set of m directed *arcs* (x_i,x_j). When the arcs do not imply a direction we will refer to them as *links* and refer to the graph as *nondirected*. G can also be defined as the doublet (X,Γ) where Γ is the set of vertex correspondences *i.e.* $\Gamma(x_i) = \{x_j \mid (x_i,x_j) \in A\}$. The *outdegree* $d_o(x_i)$ of a vertex x_i is the number of arcs emanating from x_i, and the *indegree* $d_t(x_i)$ is the number of arcs terminating at x_i. When G is nondirected we will simply use $d(x_i)$ as the number of links incident at vertex x_i. A *path* $(x_{i_1},\cdots,x_{i_q})$ in G is a sequence of q distinct vertices with $(x_{i_p},x_{i_{p+1}}) \in A$ for all p = 1,..., q-1. A *circuit* of G is a path except that $x_{i_q} = x_{i_1}$. A *hamiltonian path* (HP) is a path including every vertex $x_i \in X$, and similarly for a *hamiltonian circuit* (HC). A *spanning tree* of G is a partial graph consisting of the set X of vertices and (n-1) of the links of G chosen so that all vertices are mutually connected by paths using only these links.

B. Roy (ed.), Combinatorial Programming: Methods and Applications, 149–171. *All Rights Reserved.*

In this paper we will be dealing with two questions:
Problem (i) Given a general graph G, find a HC of G, or indicate that no HC exists.
Problem (ii) Given a *complete* graph G whose arcs have arbitrary costs $C = [c_{ij}]$ associated with them, find that HC with the least total cost. The problem of finding the least cost HC is widely known in the literature as the *travelling salesman problem* (TSP) [1,2,15]. It should be noted that if G is not complete, it can be considered as a complete graph with ∞ inserted for the cost of the non-existent arcs.

Solutions to the TSP and its variants have a large number of practical applications in vehicle routing [9], machine scheduling [5,6], network design [3,35], synthesis of sequential machines [17] *etc.* It is quite obvious that problem (i) above is a special case of problem (ii). However, an alternative interpretation can be placed on problem (i) by noting that it is equivalent to the *minimax* TSP, *i.e.* to the problem of finding that HC whose *longest* arc is a minimum. In view of the fact that both problems (i) and (ii) are of some importance we will discuss the two problems separately.

2. HAMILTONIAN CIRCUITS IN A GRAPH

Given a graph G, there exists no easy criterion or algebraic method for deciding whether G contains a HC or not.

The basic theorem on the existence of HC's is due to Posa [29].

Theorem 1 (Pósa)

Let $n \geq 3$ and let the vertices $x_i \in X$ satisfy the conditions:

(a) For $i \leq \frac{n}{2} - 1$, $d(x_i) \geq i + 1$

(b) For $i \geq \frac{n}{2}$, $d(x_i) \geq \frac{n}{2}$

and (c) If n is odd then $d(x_{\frac{n-1}{2}}) \geq \frac{n-1}{2}$,

then G has a HC.

Other theorems expressing sufficient conditions for the existence of HC's have been obtained by Nash-Williams [25] and Ore [26]. The algebraic methods which have appeared in the literature for determining HC's cannot deal with problems of more than ten or twenty vertices since they require large amounts of both computer memory and time [12,14,37]. More successful is the enumerative technique of Roberts and Flores [30,31] which does not have large computer storage requirements but whose time requirement still increases exponentially with the number of vertices in the graph. However, another implicit enumeration method [10,35] has a less than linear dependence of computation time with the number of vertices for most types of graphs, and can therefore be used to find HC's in many very large graphs.

2.1 The enumeration method of Roberts and Flores [30,31]

This method considers a path which is continuously extended until such time as: either a HC is obtained, or it becomes apparent that the path will not lead to a HC. The path is then modified in a systematic way (which will ensure that in the end all possibilities are exhausted), and the search for a HC continues.

The following enumerative scheme which uses the usual backtracking technique was initially suggested by Roberts and Flores [30,31]. The method starts by forming a $k \times n$ matrix $M = [m_{ij}]$ where element m_{ij} is the *ith* vertex (x_q say) for which an arc (x_j, x_q) exists in the graph $G = (X, \Gamma)$. The vertices x_q in the set $\Gamma(x_j)$ can be arbitrarily arranged to form the entries of the *jth* column of the M matrix.

The method now proceeds as follows. An initial vertex (say x_1) is chosen as the starting vertex and forms the first entry of the set S which will store the search path at any one time. The first vertex, (say vertex a) in column x_1 is added to S. Then the first feasible vertex (say vertex b) in column a is added to S, then the first feasible vertex (say vertex c) in column b is added to S and so on, where by "feasible" we mean a vertex which is not already in S. Two possibilities now exist which will prevent any vertex being entered into $S = \{x_1, a, b, c, \ldots, x_{r-1}, x_r\}$ at some stage r. Either:

(1) No vertex in column x_r is feasible.

or (2) The path represented by the sequence of vertices in S is of cardinality $n-1$, *i.e.* it forms a HP.

In case (2) either:

(i) arc (x_r, x_1) exists in G and a HC is therefore found,

or (ii) arc (x_r, x_1) does not exist and no HC can be obtained.

In cases (1) and (2-ii) *backtracking* must occur. Backtracking involves the removal of the last-entered vertex x_r from S to produce the set $S = \{x_1, a, b, c, \ldots, x_{r-1}\}$ and the addition into S the first feasible vertex following vertex x_r in column x_{r-1} of the M matrix. If no such feasible vertex exists a further backtracking step is taken and so on.

2.2 The multi-path method

In the algorithm of Roberts and Flores insufficient notice is taken of the consequences of extending the path being formed, upon the rest of the graph. In general, the formation of a path S_0 by the search *implies* additional paths $S_1, S_2, \ldots$ in other parts of the graph. These implied paths either help to complete a HC more quickly, or point to the fact that no HC exists which contains the path S_0 as a part, in which case backtracking can occur immediately.

This method was originally described by Selby [35] for non-directed graphs and in a somewhat modified form by Christofides [10] for directed ones. The method proceeds as follows.

Suppose that at some stage of the search a path S_0 has been formed and paths $S_1, S_2, \ldots$ are implied. Considering any "middle" vertex of any of these paths (by "middle" here is meant any vertex other than the beginning and end ones), it is obvious that since this vertex is already linked in a path by two arcs, all other arcs to or from such a vertex can be removed from the graph. For any beginning vertex of the above paths all arcs emanating from there (except for the arc linking it to the path) can be removed, and for the end vertex of any of the paths all arcs terminating there (except for the arc linking it to the path) can also be removed. Moreover, except for the case where S_0 is a HP, any existing arcs leading from the end of any path to the beginning vertex of the same path can be removed since such arcs would close non-hamiltonian circuits.

The removal of all these arcs will leave the graph G with many vertices - all the "middle" vertices of the paths - having only one arc terminating at, and one arc emanating from them. All these vertices and the arcs incident on them are removed from G and instead a single arc is introduced for each path from its beginning to its end vertex, the result is called a *reduced graph* $G_k = (X_k, \Gamma_k)$; where k is an index indicating the stage of the search.

Consider now the extension of the path S_0 being formed by the search, by another vertex x_j which is (by itself) a feasible vertex to add to S_0, *i.e.* there is an arc in G_k from the end vertex of S_0 - call this vertex $e(S_0)$ - to vertex x_j. The consequence of adding x_j to S_0 are the following.

Step 1 First remove from G_k all necessary arcs, *i.e.*

(i) All arcs terminating at x_j or emanating from $e(S_0)$ - except arc $(e(S_0),x_j)$.

(ii) Any arc from x_j to the beginning vertex of S_0.

(iii) If x_j happens to be the beginning vertex of another path S_j, remove also any arc from the end vertex of S_j to the beginning vertex of S_0.

Step 2 Let the graph after the arc removals be called $G_k' = (X_k, \Gamma_{k'})$.

- If there exists a vertex x of G_k' which is not the end of any of the paths $S_0, S_1, \ldots$ and which as a result of the arc deletions now has an indegree of unity, then erase all arcs emanating from the vertex v for which $x \in \Gamma_{k'}(v)$, except for arc (v,x).

- If there exists a vertex x of G_k' which is not the beginning of any path and for which as a result of the arc deletions now has an outdegree of unity, then erase all arcs emanating from x except for arc (x,v) - where $v \in \Gamma_{k'}(x)$.

- Update all paths and remove any arcs from the end to the beginning vertices.

Repeat step 2 until no further arcs can be removed.

Step 3 Remove from the final graph G_k' any vertices which have both an indegree and outdegree of unity as mentioned earlier. The result is a new reduced graph G_{k+1} which replaces the previous graph G_k.

If now the addition of vertex x_j to path S_0 causes the indegree or outdegree (or both) of some vertex x at the end of step 2 to become zero, then quite obviously, no HC exists. Vertex x_j is then rejected and another vertex x_j is chosen from the set of vertices $\Gamma_{k'}[e(S_0)]$ as a possible extension of path S_0, until the set $\Gamma_{k'}[e(S_0)]$ is exhausted and backtracking then occurs - (*i.e.* $e(S_0)$ is removed from S_0 and replaced by another vertex, *etc.*). Enough information must be stored about the arcs being removed by steps 1 and 2 at each stage k, so as to be able to reconstruct G_k from G_{k+1} for any k, when the backtracking step occurs.

If (at some stage) at the end of step 2, it is found that only one path is left passing through all the vertices, then the existence of a HC can be immediately checked. If no circuit is found (or if one is found but all are required), backtracking can occur.

If none of the above cases occur, *i.e.* if (at stage k), at the end of step 2, there is more than one path left and all the indegrees and outdegrees are non-zero, no conclusions can yet be drawn. x_j is now added to S_o and another vertex is chosen to extend the new path S_o even further. Steps 1, 2 and 3 are then repeated starting from the new reduced graph.

2.3 Computational results

Roberts and Flores' algorithm and the multi-path method are compared on the basis of the computing times required in order to find a single HC if one exists, or indicate that no such circuit exists. The tests were carried out on randomly generated non-directed graphs with their vertex degrees lying within predefined ranges. A total of about 200 graphs were involved in the tests and the results given are averages. All graphs happened to possess HC's.

Figure 1 shows the computing time required by the Roberts and Flores algorithm plotted against the number of vertices in the graph and where the vertex degrees are in the range 3-5. Three curves are shown in this figure giving the average, maximum, and minimum computing times recorded for different graphs having the same number of vertices. The results indicate that the computing time requirements increase at an exponential rate with the number of vertices.

With the same set of graphs mentioned above, the multi-path algorithm proved much more effective as demonstrated by Fig. 2 showing the computation times required by this algorithm. It is seen from this figure (which is plotted on linear scale), that the time increases *less than linearly* with the number of vertices in the graphs so that very large graphs can be handled by this algorithm.* A further advantage of the method is that there is remarkably little variation in the times taken to solve different graphs of the same size, and therefore one could estimate with reasonable confidence the computational time requirements for various problems. Experiments with graphs whose vertices have degrees in different ranges from the above 3-5 range, have shown that the method is virtually unaffected by the vertex degrees.

---

* This should not be taken to mean that the algorithm is *guaranteed* to terminate in time proportional to n^k for some $k > 0$. Indeed special examples have been constructed which require much larger times to solve than the times shown in Fig. 2. Such counterexamples involve graphs which do not contain HC's [6].

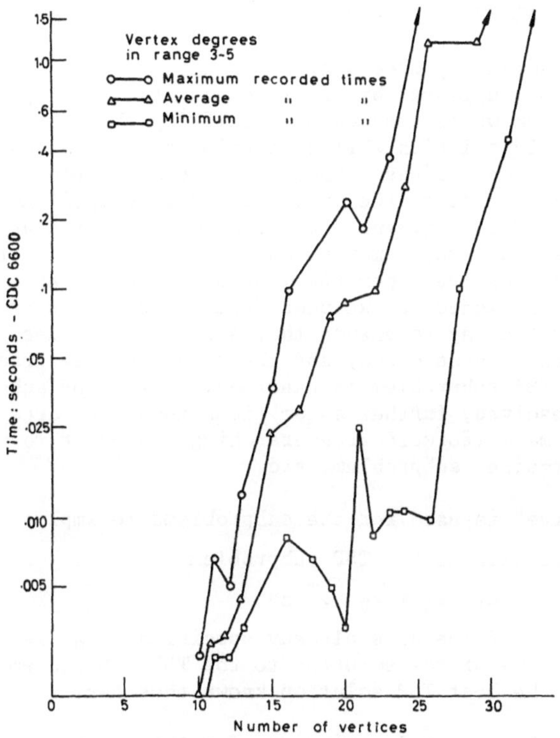

Fig. 1. Computational performance of Roberts and Flores algorithm.

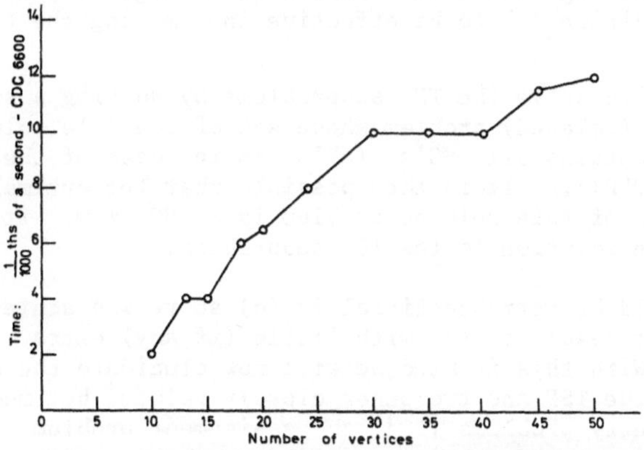

Fig. 2. Computational performance of multipath algorithm.

3. THE TRAVELLING SALESMAN PROBLEM

The TSP can be solved by tree-search (branch and bound) algorithms such as the one suggested by Little *et al.* [23]. Typically, a tree-search algorithm would proceed by specifying that certain arcs must be in the TSP solution whilst certain other arcs must not. This specification defines a *node* of the search tree. With such an *a priori* specification, the original TSP is simplified into a subproblem of smaller dimensions (involving only the arcs which are unspecified) and which may be easier to solve. If the TSP subproblem can be resolved then the *a priori* assumptions made about the arcs to be included or excluded from the solution are changed (in a systematic way to ensure that all possibilities are explicitly or implicitly considered) and the resulting new tree node defining a new TSP subproblem is examined. If a TSP subproblem cannot be resolved, further assumptions about the arcs in the solution are made (forward tree-branching) in order to produce an even smaller-size subproblem, etc.

The word "resolve" is used for the subproblems to imply:

either: (a) The solution of the TSP subproblem

or: (b) Showing that $z_f + z_b \geqslant z^*$ (1)

where z_f is the cost of the arcs already specified, z_b is some lower bound on the value of the solution to the TSP subproblem and z^* is the value of the best TSP solution known thus far.

From the above elementary description of a tree-search it is apparent that two subgoals are desirable for an efficient algorithm for the TSP.

(α) The bound z_b calculated should be as high as possible for condition (1) to be effective in limiting the tree-search,

and (β) Attempt to solve the TSP subproblems by solving a simpler related (relaxed) problem whose set of feasible solutions contains all HC's (HP's in the case of the "open" TSP†). It is then possible that the optimal solution of this relaxed problem is a HC, *i.e.* it is also the solution to the TSP subproblem.

Obviously, it would be very beneficial if (α) above was achieved automatically as a result of (β) with little (if any) extra computational cost. With this in mind we will now elucidate the relationship between the TSP and two other closely related but much simpler graph theory problems [10], the assignment problem (AP)

---

* The "open" TSP is the problem of finding the shortest HP of a graph.

and the shortest spanning tree (SST) problem.

Let us define G(TSP), G(SST) and G(AP) to be the partial graphs of G on n vertices and including the arcs (or links) which are in the optimal solutions of the TSP, SST and AP respectively.

Graph G(TSP) is: (i) connected and (ii) has vertex degrees of value 2. Graph G(SST) has property (i) but not necessarily property (ii) - (even if the two vertices of the SST which must, by necessity, have degrees of 1 are ignored). Graph G(AP) has property (ii) but not necessarily property (i). Thus, the AP and SST are problems which are relaxed TSP's - (the SST corresponding to the "open" problem) - and have solutions whose properties are complementary with respect to the properties of the TSP solution. Hence the SST and AP could be used to perform both the above-mentioned functions (α) and (β) in a tree-search algorithm.

4. THE TSP AND THE SST

Because of the slightly more direct relationship between the "open" TSP and the SST, we will begin by considering this problem first and postpone till the end of the section the discussion of the few changes needed to deal with the closed (ordinary) TSP.

Given a spanning tree $T = (X,A_T)$ of a graph G and denoting the degrees of the vertices with respect to T as $d^T(x_i)$ we can define the closeness ε_T of this tree to a HP as

$$\varepsilon_T = \sum_{d^T(x_i) > 2} \{d^T(x_i) - 2\} \tag{2}$$

The above definition gives $\varepsilon_T = 0$ for a HP and it is assumed that the larger the value of ε_T the greater is the departure of the tree T from a HP.

Two problems will now be considered as follows.

Problem (a) : Shortest HP

Find the SST $T^* \equiv (X,A^*)$ of the graph G so that the degree of no vertex exceeds 2.

Problem (b) : Shortest HP with specified end vertices

Given two vertices x_1 and x_2 $(x_1,x_2 \in X)$, find the SST $T^*_{1,2} \equiv (X,A_{1,2})$, so that the degree of no vertex exceeds 2 and the degree of vertices x_1 and x_2 is one.

The implication in the problems stated above, that a tree T all of whose vertices have degrees less than or equal to 2 is in fact a HP needs justification. Thus, since T is a tree, the degree of no vertex can be zero and hence $d^T(x_i) = 1$ or 2 for all i. Let q of the vertices have degree 1 and n-q vertices have degree 2. The number of links in the tree is given by

$$m_T = \frac{1}{2} \sum_{i=1}^{n} d^T(x_i) \tag{3}$$

since in the summation every link is counted twice, once for each of its end vertices.

Thus equation (3) becomes

$$m_T = \frac{1}{2}[q + 2(n-q)] = n - \frac{q}{2}$$

Since the number of links in a tree is n-1, q = 2 and hence exactly two vertices have degree 1 and (n-2) vertices degree 2 *i.e.* T is a HP.

Theorem 2 [7]

Let $C = [c_{ij}]$ be the link-cost matrix of the original graph G and k be a large positive number greater than the cost of any HP. Then the solution to Problem (a) with the link-cost matrix C' where:

$$\left.\begin{aligned} c'_{j1} &= c_{j1} + k \\ c'_{1j} &= c_{1j} + k \\ c'_{2j} &= c_{2j} + k \\ c'_{j2} &= c_{j2} + k \end{aligned}\right\} \quad (\text{for all } x_j \neq x_1 \text{ or } x_2),$$

$$c'_{ij} = c_{ij} + 2k \qquad (\text{for } x_i \text{ and } x_j = x_1 \text{ or } x_2)$$

$$c'_{ij} = c_{ij} \qquad (\text{for all } x_i, x_j \neq x_1 \text{ or } x_2)$$

is the solution to Problem (b) with the original cost matrix.

Theorem 3 [7]

To the set X of vertices of the graph G add two more vertices, say x_1 and x_2, to form the new set $X' = X \cup \{x_1, x_2\}$. To the set A of links of G add the two sets of links

$$S_1 = \bigcup_{j=1}^{n} \{(x_1, x_j)\} \quad \text{and} \quad S_2 = \bigcup_{j=1}^{n} \{(x_2, x_j)\}$$

to produce the new set $A' = A \cup S_1 \cup S_2$. Set the costs of links $(x_1, x_j) = a$ and $(x_2, x_j) = b$ for all $j=1, \ldots, n$, where a and b are any two constants.

The solution of Problem (b) for graph $G' = (X', A')$ with end vertices x_1 and x_2 is then the solution of Problem (a) for graph G.

4.1 The vertex penalty algorithm for SST transformations

The spirit of this algorithm is similar to that used in the proof of Theorem 2 above [7], *i.e.* to transform the cost matrix C in such a way so that various categories of trees are penalized differently, but at the same time the relative costs of all trees within a category remain unchanged. The objective is to separate the various categories and make the category of HP's the most attractive (least penalized) so that the application of the SST algorithm will automatically produce the shortest HP.

Theorem 4 [7]

If the cost matrix C is transformed to a matrix C' so that

$$c'_{ij} = c_{ij} + p(i) + p(j) \quad \text{for all } i,j = 1, \ldots, n \tag{4}$$

where $p(k)$ is an n-dimensional vector of real positive or negative constants, then the relative costs under matrix C' of all HP's having specified end vertices remain unchanged.

A. Solution of problem (b). An algorithm to find the shortest HP with specified end-vertices (Problem (b)) and which is based on Theorem 4 will now be explained with the aid of an example. The solution of Problem (a) is then implied by Theorem 3.

Example

Consider a completely connected graph G of 10 vertices whose cost matrix C_0 is shown in Table 1 and suppose that we want the shortest HP whose end vertices are 8 and 9.

Table 1. Cost matrix of the example.

	1	2	3	4	5	6	7	8	9	10
1	0	28	31	28	22	36	50	67	40	74
2	28	0	31	40	41	64	74	80	63	101
3	31	31	0	14	53	53	53	50	42	83
4	28	40	14	0	50	41	39	41	28	69
5	22	41	53	50	0	40	61	86	53	78
6	36	64	53	41	40	0	24	58	22	39
7	50	74	53	39	61	24	0	37	11	30
8	67	80	50	41	86	58	37	0	36	60
9	40	63	42	28	53	22	11	36	0	41
10	74	101	83	69	78	39	30	60	41	0

In accordance with Theorem 2, we add a large number k (say 1,000) to rows and columns 8 and 9 of the matrix of Table 1 and we will call the resulting cost matrix C.

We now proceed as follows:

Find the SST of G. If this tree is a HP, the problem is solved. However, in this example the SST is not a HP and is shown in Fig. 3(a). The degree of vertices 1 and 7 is 4 instead of 2 as a HP demands - we could therefore "penalize" these vertices in accordance with the spirit of Theorem 4. Suppose we arbitrarily choose a small step size (say 5 units) so that all penalties are in multiples of this. Thus if we decide to penalize only the vertices which have degrees greater than 2, we will put

$$p(i) = 5(d^T(x_i) - 2) \qquad (5)$$

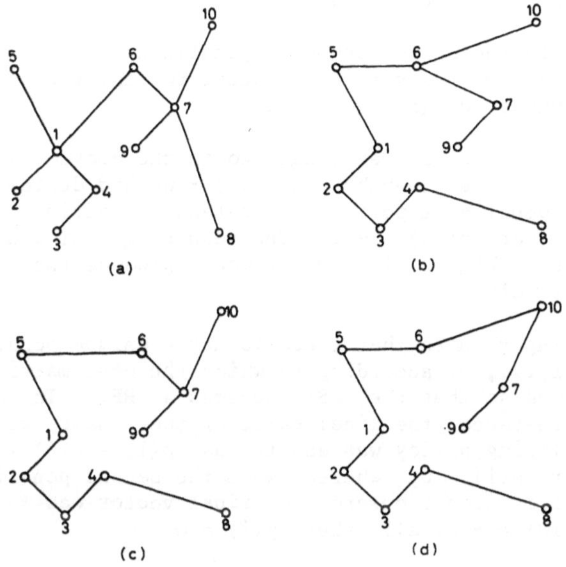

Fig. 3. The SST's during the vertex penalty iterations.

Note, however, that this method of penalizing vertices is arbitrary and other computationally superior alternatives exist [4,10,18,19].

According to equation (5), the penalties on vertices 1 and 7 become p(1) = p(7) = 10, all other p(i) being 0. We now calculate the new cost matrix according to equation (4) and solve for the SST. The result is shown in Fig. 3(b) and it is seen that this tree is much closer to a HP, having $\varepsilon = 1$ instead of $\varepsilon = 4$ as in the previous case.

In exactly the same way, we continue by penalizing vertex 6 and set p(6) = 5. (One should note that this new penalty is added to the previous cost matrix and not to the original matrix C.) Thus the total penalty is now p(1) = p(7) = 10, p(6) = 5 and all other p(i) = 0. The resulting SST is shown in Fig. 3(c) having an $\varepsilon = 1$ which is the same as that for the previous SST. We now penalize vertex 7, setting p(7) = 5, and the resulting SST reverts to that shown in Fig. 3(b). We continue by penalizing vertex 6 once more, setting p(6) = 5, and again solve for the SST. The result is shown in Fig. 3(d) from which it is noted that this is now a HP and hence, according to Theorem 4, this is the shortest HP. The cost of this path under the original cost matrix C_0 is 258 units.

An alternative to the above method of penalizing is to place negative penalties only on the vertices (except for the two specified end vertices) whose $d^{T'}(x_i) = 1 < 2$.

As an example, suppose that at stage two in the above calculation - when the SST was given by Fig. 3(b) - we had decided to adopt the second penalizing policy and instead of setting $p(6) = 5$ we were to set $p(10) = -5$. The resulting SST would then become as shown in Fig. 3(d), *i.e.* it would produce the shortest HP immediately.

It is interesting to note that there is not a unique penalty vector $p(i)$, $i = 1,\ldots, n$, according to which the cost matrix C must be transformed so that the SST becomes a HP. In the above example, for instance, the final value of the penalty vector when the first penalizing policy was adopted as $p(1) = p(6) = 10$, $p(7) = 15$, all other $p(i) = 0$; whereas when the second penalizing policy was adopted from step 2 onward, the final vector was $p(1) = (7) = 10$, $p(10) = -10$, all other $p(i) = 0$.

4.2 Convergence of the vertex-penalty method

The vertex-penalty method described above was developed simultaneously by Christofides [7] and in a somewhat different form by Held and Karp [18], who also showed that the method is not always convergent. Nevertheless the method is important for two reasons. Firstly, it converges in the majority of cases [10].

Secondly, suppose the iterations are stopped at a time when the SST under the modified matrix is T', the vertex penalties $p(i)$, $(i = 1,2,\ldots,n)$ and the vertex degrees $d^{T'}(x_i)$; and consider the problem when the shortest HP with end vertices x_1 and x_2 is required. The cost of T' under the modified cost matrix is:

$$\overline{F}_{T'} = F_{T'} + \sum_{i\neq 1,2} p(i)\, d^{T'}(x_i) + p(1) + p(2)$$

where $F_{T'}$ is the cost of T' evaluated under the initial cost matrix.

If H is the shortest HP of the graph, then the cost of H under the modified matrix is:

$$\overline{F}_H = F_H + 2 \sum_{i\neq 1,2} p(i) + p(1) + p(2).$$

Since $\overline{F}_{T'} < \overline{F}_H$ by definition, the difference:

$$f(\underline{p}) \equiv \overline{F}_H - \overline{F}_{T'} = F_H - \left[F_{T'} + \sum_{i\neq 1,2} p(i)(d^{T'}(x_i) - 2) \right] \quad (6)$$

is a measure of how near the tree T' is to the shortest HP, $f(\underline{p})$ being 0 when $T' = H$.

The quantity $f(\underline{p})$ can be considered as a function of the penalty vector $\underline{p} = (p_i | i=1,\ldots,n)$. Held and Karp gave two methods of finding the penalties $\underline{p}^*$ which minimise $f(\underline{p})$, one based on a column-generation technique and the other being a steepest descent method. An alternative and slightly more general sequential approach based on heuristically guided search was recently used successfully by Camerini *et al.* [4]. In addition to these methods there are graph theoretic methods of calculating penalties [10], which are effective in minizing $f(\underline{p})$. When the vertex-penalty method converges we will have the minimum value $f(\underline{p}^*) = 0$ since $T' \to H$ and $d^{T'}(x_i) = 2$ for all $i \neq 1,2$. On the other hand it was mentioned earlier that the method is not always convergent in which case the minimum value $f(\underline{p}^*)$ of $f(\underline{p})$ is not zero but some positive number. In this case it is quite apparent that the quantity:

$$F_{T'} + \sum_{i\neq 1,2} p^*(i)\ (d^{T'}(x_i) - 2) \quad (7)$$

is a lower bound on the value of the shortest HP. In this latter case, the bound derived is very tight and could be used with great effect [4,19] in a tree-search algorithm. TSP's involving 100 or more vertices have been solved optimally in this way [4].

4.3 The "closed" TSP

We dealt initially with the "open" TSP because of the more direct relation of the "open" problem with the SST. On the other hand, only a very minor modification is needed to deal with the "closed" TSP. Held and Karp [18], for example, introduce the notion of a shortest 1-tree of G, this being defined as a SST of the subgraph of G with vertex 1 removed, plus the two shortest links from vertex 1 to two other vertices of the tree. Obviously, the same relationship exists between the shortest 1-tree and the "closed" TSP as between the SST and the "open" problem. The vertex-penalty method discussed earlier on in the present section can, therefore, be used with virtually no change to solve the "closed" TSP as well.

5. THE TSP AND AP

The AP for a graph with a general cost matrix $C = [c_{ij}]$ can be stated as follows:

Let ξ_{ij} be an $n \times n$ matrix of 0-1 valued variables so that $\xi_{ij} = 1$ if vertex x_i is "assigned" to vertex x_j and $\xi_{ij} = 0$ if x_i is not assigned to x_j. In the TSP we could use a similar scheme where $\xi_{ij} = 1$ would mean that the salesman travels from x_i to x_j directly and $\xi_{ij} = 0$ would mean that he does not. For this last problem we can start by setting all c_{ii} $(i = 1,\ldots, n)$ to ∞ thus eliminating nonsensical solutions with $\xi_{ii} = 1$.

The AP now becomes:

Find 0-1 variables ξ_{ij} so as to minimise:

$$z = \sum_{i=1}^{n} \sum_{j=1}^{n} c_{ij} \xi_{ij} \tag{8}$$

$$\text{subject to} \qquad \sum_{i} \xi_{ij} = \sum_{j} \xi_{ij} = 1 \tag{9}$$

(for all i and $j = 1,2,\ldots, n$)

and $\xi_{ij} = 0$ or 1. (10)

Equation (9) simply ensures that the solution is cyclic, *i.e.* one arc enters and one leaves every vertex.

Equations (8) to (10) together with the additional constraints:

$$\sum_{i \in Q} \sum_{j \in \overline{Q}} \xi_{ij} \geqslant 1 \qquad \forall \quad Q \subset N \equiv \{1,\ldots,n\} \text{ and } \overline{Q} = N - Q \tag{11}$$

(which obviously eliminate the possibility of more than one unconnected circuit in the solution) can also be used to represent the TSP.

5.1 A tree-search algorithm for circuit elimination

Let the solution of the AP with a cost matrix $[c_{ij}]$ (and $c_{ii} = \infty$, $\forall i$), be composed of a number of circuits. What is now needed is to eliminate this solution together with as many other solutions as possible without eliminating the solution to the TSP under the same cost matrix. Since the TSP solution is a HC we will attempt to eliminate any solutions which correspond to more than one circuit.

A. <u>A simple branching rule</u>. In general, let the solution to the AP contain the (non-hamiltonian) circuit $(x_1,x_2,\ldots,x_k, x_1)$ with cardinality k. This circuit (and all solutions containing it), can be removed from further consideration by insisting that at least one of the arcs (x_1,x_2), (x_2,x_3) ... (x_k,x_1) must not be in the solution. This can be done quite simply by subdividing the original problem P_0 with the cost matrix $[c_{ij}]$, into k subproblems $P_1,P_2,\ldots, P_k$. In problem P_1 $c(x_1,x_2)$ is set to ∞ (all other c_{ij} remaining unchanged), in P_2 $c(x_2,x_3) = \infty$, *etc.* and for problem P_k $c(x_k,x_1) = \infty$. Obviously any solution to problem P_0 not containing the circuit $(x_1,x_2, \ldots, x_k,x_1)$ is a solution to at least one of the problems $P_1,\ldots, P_k$ and hence the optimal TSP solution is the solution to one or more of these subproblems. These subproblems can now be solved as AP's and if the solution to any one subproblem still contains more than one circuit further branching can continue by partitioning this subproblem further in exactly the same way as mentioned above. Obviously, the value of the AP solutions can be used as bounds to the cost of the corresponding TSP in order to limit the search.

B. <u>A disjoint branching rule</u>. All that is required for a valid branching from a problem P_0 to subproblems P_1, P_2, ... is that every feasible solution of P_0 (except the ones being eliminated) should be a solution of at least one subproblem [1,2]. However, an obviously desirable characteristic for a branching method to possess, is for the subproblems created to be disjoint as far as the feasible solutions of P_0 are concerned, *i.e.* that every feasible solution of P_0 should be a solution to one and only one of these subproblems.

The previously described branching rule was based on the fact that a circuit such as $(x_1,x_2,\ldots, x_k,x_1)$ could be removed by excluding one of its arcs. This, however, does not lead to branching into mutually exclusive subproblems.

A different branching rule which removes a circuit $(x_1, x_2, \ldots, x_k)$ but produces disjoint subproblems is as follows [2].

For problem P_1 set $c(x_1,x_2) = \infty$
" " P_2 set $c(x_1,x_2) = -M$ and $c(x_2,x_3) = \infty$
" " P_3 set $c(x_1,x_2) = c(x_2,x_3) = -M$ and $c(x_3,x_4) = \infty$
$\vdots$
For problem P_k set $c(x_1,x_2) = c(x_2,x_3) = \ldots = c(x_{k-1},x_k) = -M$

and $c(x_k,x_1) = \infty$

where $-M$ is a large negative number to ensure that the arc whose cost is $-M$ is in the optimal solution.

With this branching rule the subproblems are certainly disjoint since for any two subproblems there is at least one arc excluded from the solution in one, and which is definitely included in the solution in the other subproblem. It is also easy to see that no feasible solution of P_0 is lost, since any solution of P_0 has some sequence of arcs leading from x_1, such as (x_1,x_α), (x_α,x_β) *etc.* and these must coincide in the first r arcs with the arcs of the path $(x_1,x_2,x_3,\ldots,x_k)$ for some value of $r = 0, 1,\ldots, k$; $r = 0$ corresponding to the case where there is no coincidence at all, $r = 1$ to the case where $x_\alpha = x_2$ but $x_\beta \neq x_3$ *etc.*

C. Another branching rule. Both of the previous two branching rules, eliminated (at each branching) all solutions containing a given circuit such as $(x_1,x_2,\ldots, x_k,x_1)$. However, not only must this circuit not exist in a TSP solution, but, obviously, there must be at least one arc leading from the set of vertices $S = \{x_1, \ldots, x_k\}$ to the set of vertices $\overline{S} = X - S$, as expressed by equation (11). In fact the existence of an arc from S to $\overline{S}$ not only guarantees that solutions containing the circuit based on S are eliminated, but also that solutions in which the subset of vertices in S are joined to form several circuits (instead of just one) are also removed. Thus, a branching rule, based on the insistence that some arc from S to $\overline{S}$ must exist could be expected to be uniformly better than the previous two branching rules [2].

Since an arc from S to $\overline{S}$ must start from some vertex in S, a problem could be split up into k subproblems P_1, P_2, $\ldots$, P_k where for subproblem P_i we would insist that the initial vertex of the arc is $x_i \in S$ and the final vertex is some vertex in $\overline{S}$. This can be done by setting $c(x_i,x_j) = \infty \,\forall\, x_j \in S$ and leaving all other costs unchanged. In the solution of the resulting AP we would then certainly have the arc from x_i leading into $\overline{S}$ since all other alternatives have had their costs set to ∞.

The performance of the above tree-search algorithm, with circuit elimination done according to the branching rule C, was investigated by Bellmore and Malone [2]. At any one stage branching from a node was continued by choosing to eliminate the lowest cardinality circuit in the solution of the AP corresponding to that node. TSP's with random asymmetric cost matrices could be solved in T seconds on the IBM 7094 II, where

$$T \simeq .55 \times 10^{-4} \times n^{3.46}$$

n being the number of vertices in the problem. (The other two branching rules were shown to be inferior, especially in problems where the graph formed clusters with arcs between vertices in the same cluster having small costs and arcs between vertices in different clusters having large costs.)

In symmetrical cost TSP's, the above algorithm does not perform very well because solution of AP's usually consists of large numbers of circuits of cardinality 2. However, in these cases the AP's could be replaced by matching problems [2], which like AP's can also be solved efficiently. This completely eliminates all circuits involving 2 vertices from the subproblem solutions, although it is now likely that many circuits of cardinality 3 would appear. The performance of the algorithm becomes even worse in cases where the TSP is defined on a graph which does not contain a HC of finite cost.

5.2 A tighter bound from the AP

In the tree-search algorithm of the last section, the lower bound to the cost of the TSP solution at a tree node was assumed to be the value of the solution to the corresponding AP. The purpose of the present section is to describe a lower bound which can be calculated from the solution to the AP with little extra effort, and which is considerably tighter than the previously used bound. Let the solution to the AP contain a number of circuits as shown for example in Fig. 4(a). Let the *ith* of these circuits be called $S_{1,i}$ and let their number be n_1. (We will use the same symbol $S_{1,i}$ to represent also the set of vertices in circuit i.)

A *contraction* is defined as a replacement of a circuit by a single vertex, thus forming a contracted graph containing n_1 vertices $S_{1,i}$ $(i = 1,2,\ldots, n_1)$. The cost matrix

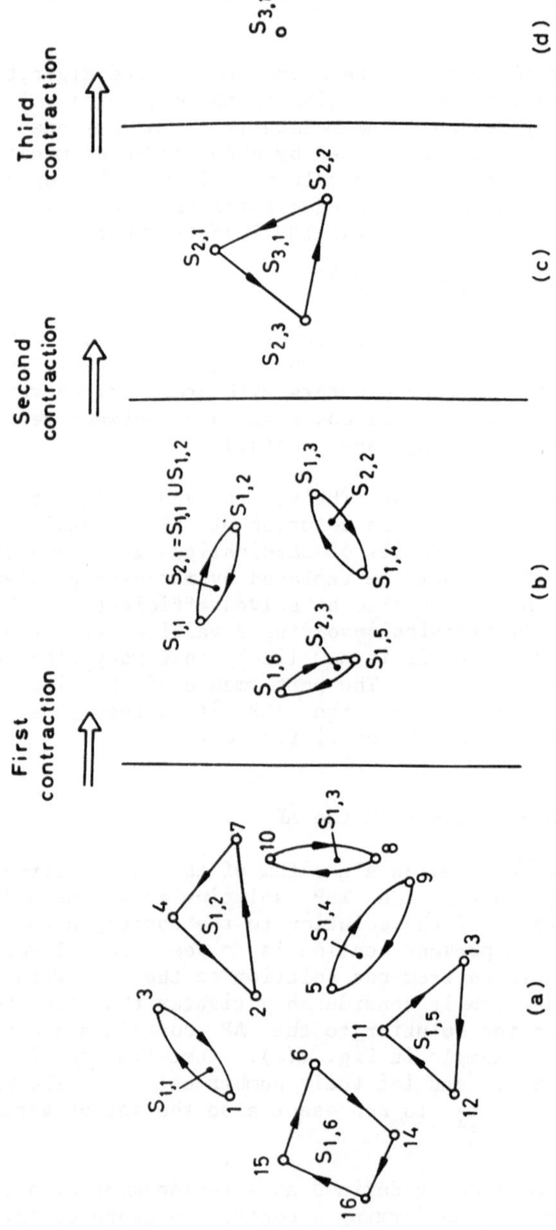

Fig. 4. The contraction process.

$C_1 \equiv [c_1(S_{1,i}, S_{1,j})]$ of the contracted graph is taken as:

$$c_1(S_{1,i}, S_{1,j}) = \min_{\substack{k_i \in S_{1,i} \\ k_j \in S_{1,j}}} [f_1(k_i, k_j)] \tag{12}$$

where $F_1 = [f_1(k_i,k_j)]$ is the resulting relative cost matrix at the end of the solution to the AP by (say) the hungarian method.

Now, a second solution to the AP of this contracted problem under the matrix C_1 may still produce circuits having the previous circuits as vertices. Figure 4(b) shows one possible formation of the new circuits $S_{2,i}$ $(i = 1,2,\ldots,n_2)$ where n_2 is their total number, $(n_2 = 3$ in Fig. 4(b)). These circuits may again be contracted into vertices to form a new problem where the new cost matrix $C_2 \equiv [c_2(S_{2,i},S_{2,j})]$ is calculated from an equation similar to equation (12), *i.e.*

$$c_2(S_{2,i}, S_{2,j}) = \min_{\substack{k_i \in S_{2,i} \\ k_j \in S_{2,j}}} [f_2(k_i, k_j)] \tag{13}$$

where the various S_2 are the union of all the sets S_1 forming the particular circuit, and where $F_2 = [f_2(k_i,k_j)]$ is the relative cost matrix at the end of the second solution to the AP.

A solution to the AP of the new doubly contracted graph may still produce circuits and the iterative process of solution-contraction can be continued until the problem is reduced to a single vertex.

Compression is defined as the transformation of a matrix which does not satisfy the triangularity condition of metric space into one that does. Thus, to compress a matrix M what is necessary is to replace every element m_{ij} for which

$$m_{ij} > m_{ik} + m_{kj} \quad \text{(for some k)}$$

by the value of $\min_k [m_{ik} + m_{kj}]$, and to continue this replacement until all $m_{ij} \leq m_{ik} + m_{kj}$ for any k.

Theorem 5

The sum of the values of the solutions to the AP's obtained during the "solution-contraction-compression" process (up to the stage when the contracted problem becomes a single vertex) is a valid lower bound to the TSP.

6. REFERENCES

1. M. Bellmore and G.L. Nemhauser, *Ops. Res.* 16, 538, 1968.
2. M. Bellmore and J.C. Malone, *Ops. Res.* 19, 278, 1971.
3. R.M. Burstall, Tree-searching methods with an application to a network design problem, in: *Machine Intelligence*, ed. by Collins and Michie, 1, Oliver and Boyd, London, 1967.
4. P.M. Camerini, L. Fratta and F. Maffioli, The travelling salesman problem: heuristically guided search and modified gradient techniques (to appear).
5. J.M. Charlton and C.C. Death, *Ops. Res.* 18, 689, 1970.
6. N. Christofides, *The Computer Jl.* 16, 263, 1973.
7. N. Christofides, *Jl. of SIAM - (Appl. Match.)* 19, 689, 1970.
8. N. Christofides, *Ops. Res.* 20, 1044, 1972.
9. N. Christofides and S. Eilon, *Opl. Res. Quart.* 20, 309, 1969.
10. N. Christofides, *Graph Theory - An Algorithmic Approach*, Academic Press, New York, 1974.
11. N. Christofides and S. Eilon, *Opl. Res. Quart.* 23, 511, 1972.
12. G.H. Danielson, *IEEE Trans.* CT-15, 294, 1968.
13. N. Deo and S.L. Hakimi, The shortest generalised hamiltonian tree, *Proc. 3rd Allerton Conference on Circuit and Systems Theory*, University of Illinois, Urbana, p.879, 1965.
14. V. Dhawan, *Hamiltonian circuits and related problems in graph theory*, M.Sc. Report, Imperial College, London, 1969.
15. S. Eilon, C.D.T. Watson-Gandy and N. Christofides, *Distribution Management: Mathematical Modelling and Practical Analysis*, Griffin, London, 1971.
16. P.C. Gilmore and R.E. Gomory, *Ops. Res.* 12, 655, 1964.
17. D.R. Haring, *Sequential-circuit Synthesis*, MIT Press, Research Monograph 31, Cambridge, Massachusetts, 1966.
18. M. Held and R.M. Karp, *Ops. Res.* 18, 1138, 1970.
19. M. Held and R.M. Karp, *Math. Prog.* 1, 6, 1971.
20. P. Krolak, W. Felts and G. Marble, *Comm. of ACM* 14, 327, 1971.
21. E.L. Lawler, *Math. Prog.* 1, 267, 1971.
22. S. Lin, *Bell. Syst. Tech. Jl.* 44, 2245, 1965.
23. J.D.C. Little, K.G. Murty, D.W. Sweeney and C. Karel, *Ops. Res.* 11, 979, 1963.
24. F. Maffioli, *The Travelling Salesman Problem and its Implications*, Report, Istituto di Elettrotecnica ed Elettronica, Politecnico di Milano, 1973.
25. C. St. J.A. Nash-Williams, On hamiltonian circuits in finite graphs, *Proc. American Mathematical Soc.* 17, 466, 1966.

26. O. Ore, *Theory of Graphs*, American Mathematical Society, New York, 1962.
27. V.A. Pevepeliche and E.X. Gimadi, *Diskret Analyz.* (in Russian) 15, 57, 1969.
28. I. Pohl, *Artificial Intelligence* 1, 193, 1970.
29. L. Pósa, *Magyar Tnd. Akad. Mat. Kutató Int. Közl* 7, 225, 1962.
30. S.M. Roberts and B. Flores, *Man. Sci.* 13, 269, 1967.
31. S.M. Roberts and B. Flores, *Comm. of ACM* 9, 690, 1966.
32. B. Roy, *Recherche des circuits élémentaires et des circuits hamiltoniens dans un graphe quelconque*, Mimeographe, Soc. de Math. Appl., Paris, 1959.
33. B. Roy, *Algèbre moderne et théorie des graphes*, Vol. 1 (1969), Vol. 2 (1970), Dunod, Paris.
34. M.I. Rubinshtein, *Automatica i Telemekanika* 9, 126, 1971.
35. G.R. Selby, *The use of topological methods in computer-aided circuit layout*, Ph.D. Thesis, London University, 1970.
36. M.M. Syslo, *Math. Prog.* 4, 347, 1973.
37. S.S. Yau, *IEEE Trans.* CT-14, 79, 1967.

THE PERIPATETIC SALESMAN AND SOME RELATED UNSOLVED PROBLEMS

Jakob Krarup

Spadille, Inc. &
Institute of Datalogy, University of Copenhagen, Denmark

ABSTRACT. Some generalizations of the traveling salesman problem are suggested, leading to problems in which we seek to minimize the summed weight of two or more line-disjoint hamiltonian cycles. A number of seemingly open questions extending the concept of hamiltonian graphs are raised. Finally, pursuing the Held-Karp approach for solving symmetric traveling salesman problems, an extension of the minimum spanning tree problem is briefly discussed.

1. INTRODUCTION

Whenever a paper is submitted for publication in a respected OR-journal, the referees are urged to structure their judgment by answering specific questions such as: Does it detail methods and report results? Is adequate credit given to other contributors in the field and are references sufficiently complete? Will it be of interest to a significant group of OR-workers, either now or in the future?

In the present case, the answers would undoubtedly be negative except - hopefully - to the third question. The reason is that the problems to be presented here evolved only a few weeks before the Versailles-meeting took place. Thus, the presentation was not even on the regular schedule but merely an impulsive act. In addition, the main objectives for the presentation were rather selfish: a number of problems were posed to the audience in order to obtain useful references and suggestions for appropriate solution methods. This article is therefore confined to a series of seemingly open questions; no methods are discussed, no results are reported on and no credit is given to other contributors.

B. Roy (ed.), Combinatorial Programming: Methods and Applications, 173–178.

2. THE PERIPATETIC SALESMAN PROBLEM

A quadratic assignment-like problem arose recently in connection with a real-world problem on how to move some 30 governmental institutions from Stockholm to a number of different Swedish cities. The problem is characterized by certain side constraints and by the presence of so-called fixed points such that the distance matrix and the communication matrix are both of the magnitude 70 by 70. But a more essential feature in this context is the sparsity of the communication matrix and the structure of its non-zero elements. An extensive description of the problem and its background can be found in [7].

As is well known, a quadratic assignment problem (QAP) is equivalent to a traveling salesman problem (TSP) provided that any of the two matrices defining the QAP is a cyclic permutation matrix. Since highly effective algorithms exist for the solution of the latter for problems of modest size (i.e. up to some 100 cities), one might perhaps devise an approach for solving certain classes of structured QAP's by generalizing and exploiting the above-mentioned relationship.

The first step ahead leads to the following extension of TSP: Given a graph G with a certain *weight* associated with each edge, and let $r \geq 1$ be an integer-valued parameter. Determine a subgraph $S_r(G) \subseteq G$ of minimum weight such that $S_r(G)$ is the union of r line-disjoint hamiltonian cycles.

Obviously, for r = 1, the problem is TSP itself. For r > 1, two different names have been proposed. Peter M. Pruzan, a close friend of mine who unfortunately was unable to attend the meeting, drew my attention to the adjective *peripatetic*. Jack Edmonds, on the other hand, spoke in favor of *moonlighting* which in U.S. vernacular denotes somebody having two jobs, one by day and the other by moonlight. "Moonlighting" is perhaps appropriate for r=2; for the general case, peripatetic is hereafter preferred and the problem is accordingly abbreviated by PSP.

3. HAMILTONIAN NUMBERS AND PERFECT r-HAMILTONIAN GRAPHS

A number of new concepts and questions related to PSP almost suggest themselves.

We may define the *hamiltonian number* $h(G)$ of a graph G as the maximum number of line-disjoint hamiltonian cycles of G. Or. for the sake of brevity, G is said to be *r-hamiltonian* if h(G) = r.

Some obvious observations:

$$h(K_p) \leq \left[\frac{p-1}{2} \right] \tag{1}$$

$$h(K_{m,n}) = \begin{cases} 0 \text{ for } m \neq n \\ [\frac{m}{2}], \text{ otherwise} \end{cases} \qquad (2)$$

where [ ] denotes the integral part.

We may also define G to be *perfect r-hamiltonian* if G itself is the union of r hamiltonian cycles.

If sign of equality holds in (1) which most likely is true, then

K_p is perfect $(\frac{p-1}{2})$-hamiltonian for p odd

And, of course, $K_{m,m}$ is perfect $(\frac{m}{2})$-hamiltonian for m even

According to F. Harary [5], no elegant characterization of hamiltonian graphs (1-hamiltonian in our terminology) exists, although several necessary and sufficient conditions are known.

Now, besides the theorem of Posa [8], how do we in general characterize r-hamiltonian graphs, perhaps in terms of line-connectivity or forbidden subgraphs? And perfect r-hamiltonian graphs for $r > 1$? What is the maximum number of lines a graph with p points can have without being r-hamiltonian? Etc., etc.

By means of perfect r-hamiltonian graphs, the PSP may be stated in a somewhat different form:

Determine a perfect r-hamiltonian subgraph $S_r(G) \subseteq G$ of minimum weight (and decompose $S_r(G)$ into r line-disjoint hamiltonian cycles if we for some reason want the individual cycles explicitly listed).

4. PSP's WITH *r* = 2

A heuristic approach for obtaining near-optimal solutions to PSP's with r=2 might be the following two-step procedure:

a) Determine $S_1(G)$ and define $G' = G - S_1(G)$ (i.e. G' is derived from G by deleting all edges of the hamiltonian cycle $S_1(G)$)

b) Determine $S_1(G')$ and take $S_1(G) \cup S_1(G')$ as an approximation of $S_2(G)$

It can easily be demonstrated that $S_2(G)$ is not necessarily equal to the union of $S_1(G)$ and $S_1(G')$.

A graph G with nine points is shown in Fig. 1. The weights of the edges are as indicated; a single edge is seen to be of weight α.

For any positive α, $S_1(G)$ is uniquely determined as the subgraph in Fig. 2 of weight $w(S_1(G)) = 9$.

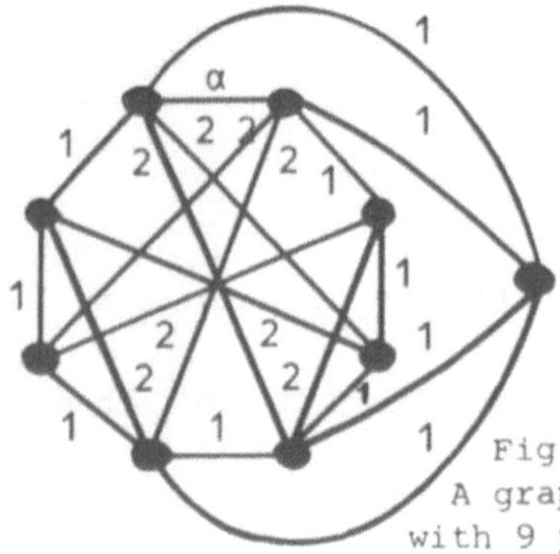

Fig. 1
A graph G
with 9 points

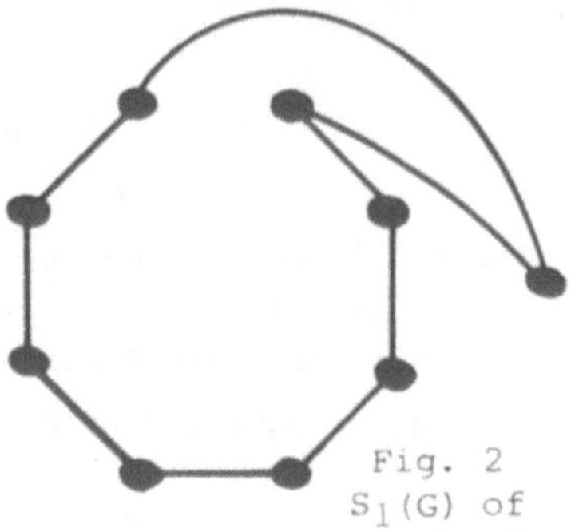

Fig. 2
$S_1(G)$ of
weight 9

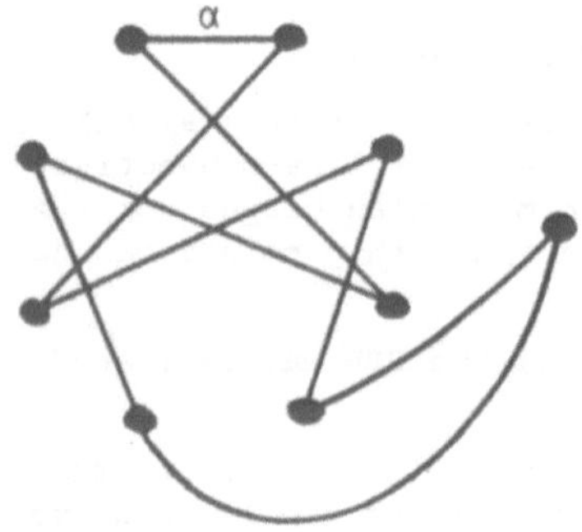

Fig. 3
$S_1(G')$ of weight $14+\alpha$

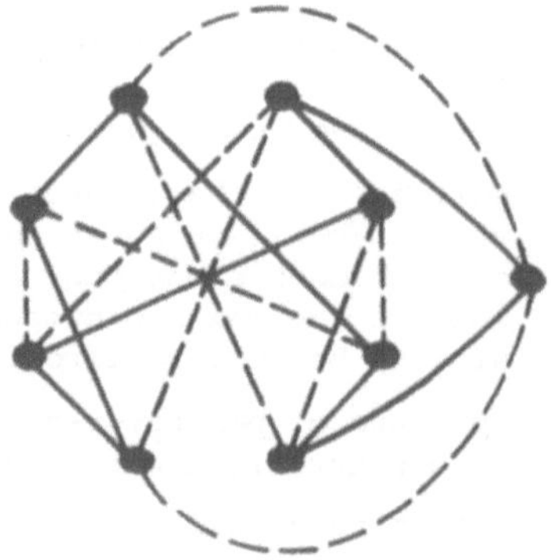

Fig. 4
For $\alpha > 3$: $S_2(G)$ of
weight $14+12 = 26$

Upon deletion of $S_1(G)$ from G, $S_1(G - S_1(G)) = S_1(G')$ is found as the subgraph in Fig. 3 with $w(S_1(G')) = 14+\alpha$ (more optimal solutions exist but the edge of weight α has to be included in all cases; without that edge, G' would not be hamiltonian). Finally, $S_2(G)$ is approximated by $S_1(G) \cup S_1(G')$ of weight $9+14+\alpha = 23+\alpha$.

However, the total weight of the two line-disjoint hamiltonian cycles in Fig. 4 appears to be $14 + 12 = 26 < 23 + \alpha$ for $\alpha > 3$.

Thus, in general

$$w(S_2(G)) \leq w(\, S_1(G) \cup S_1(G')\,)$$

The example shows furthermore, that $S_1(G)$ is not necessarily a subset of $S_2(G)$.

5. MINIMUM SPANNING TREES

The Held-Karp approach for solving symmetric TSP's [6] as well as an improved version [4] were both based on an intimate relationship between the TSP and minimum spanning trees.

Pursuing those ideas, efficient algorithms for solving PSP's might be based on an extension of the concept of minimum spanning trees. This gives rise to the following subproblem: Determine a subgraph $T_r(G) \subseteq G$ of minimum weight such that $T_r(G)$ is the union of r line-disjoint spanning trees.

By introducing t(G) as the maximum number of line-disjoint spanning trees of G, a new sequence of questions concerning the characterization of graphs with a specified value of $t(G) > 1$ emerges.

6. DISCUSSION

Christofides: Related to a problem as to the design of a communication network, the solution to a PSP (r=2) has been suggested as an approximation [3].

Edmonds: In terms of matroid partitioning, it has been proved that the subproblem of determining $T_r(G)$ is solvable by the greedy algorithm, see [1] and [2].

Padberg: The concept of factorization might prove to be useful in determining whether a given graph can be decomposed into line-disjoint spanning subgraphs possessing a prescribed property (see Ch. 9 in [5]).

Unidentified voice: It has been proved that sign of equality holds in (1).

7. SUGGESTIONS FOR FUTURE RESEARCH

Due to a publishing deadline, I was given less than 2½ weeks after the Versailles-meeting to produce these pages. The time has not permitted me to judge the usefulness of the very few references which were given by the above-mentioned participants and thus to shed more light on the different problems.

However, it seems appropriate to cite a few lines of a letter, just received from F. Harary: "... all questions which you have asked me are open and have not been studied".

This statement of his is my conclusion as to "suggestions for future research".

8. ACKNOWLEDGMENTS

Thanks are due to P.M. Pruzan and J. Edmonds for having enriched my English vocabulary by two adjectives. Furthermore to N. Christofides for allotting me half an hour of his talking time. Finally, I am indebted to F. Harary for a prompt communication of his points of view and to B. Roy, editor of this book, for his kind permission to include these non-scheduled pages.

REFERENCES

[1] Edmonds, J., "Matroid Partition", in G.B. Dantzig and A.F. Veinott, Jr. (eds.) *Mathematics of the Decision Sciences*, American Mathematical Society, Providence, Rhode Island, (1968)

[2] Edmonds, J., "Matroids and the Greedy Algorithm", *Mathematical Programming* 1 (1971)

[3] Frank, H. and I.T. Frisch, "*Communication, Transmission and Transportation Networks*", Addison-Wesley (1971)

[4] Hansen, K.H. and J. Krarup, "Improvements of the Held-Karp Algorithm for the Symmetric Traveling-Salesman Problem", *Mathematical Programming* 7 (1974)

[5] Harary, F.,"*Graph Theory*", Addison-Wesley (1969)

[6] Held, M. and R.M. Karp, "The Traveling-Salesman Problem and Minimum Spanning Trees", *Mathematical Programming* 1 (1971)

[7] Persson, C. "*Kontaktarbete och framtida lokaliseringsförändringar*" Meddelanden från Lunds Universitets Geografiska Institution, Avhandlingar LXXI, CWK Gleerup/Lund (1974)

[8] Pósa, L., "A Theorem concerning Hamiltonian Lines", *Magyar Tud. Alad. Mat. Kutato Int. Kozl.* 7 (1962)

SOME RESULTS ON THE CONVEX HULL OF THE HAMILTONIAN CYCLES OF SYMETRIC COMPLETE GRAPHS

J.F. Maurras

Département "Méthodes d'optimisation", Direction des Etudes et Recherches d'Electricité de France

ABSTRACT. We give a characterisation of certain facets of the convex hull of Hamiltonian cycles a complete symetric graph in terms of facets in a strictly smaller graph, whenever possible. This result yields some interesting corollaries.

In order to talk about the convex hull of the Hamiltonian cycles we must define a function f of E when G = (V,E), $E \xrightarrow{f} [0,1]$ such that for every Hamiltonian cycle (H.C. in short) γ, $\gamma \subset E$,

$$i \in E,\ i \in \gamma,\ f(i) = 1$$
$$i \in E,\ i \notin \gamma,\ f(i) = 0$$

G is symetric, then $(i,j) \in E$, $(i,j) = (j,i)$

$\forall A \subset V$, $A \neq V, \omega(A) = \{(i,j),\ i \in A,\ j \in (V-A)\}$

a_{ij} is a letter indiced by the edge (i,j).

Let G = (V,E) be the complete graph

$\forall F \subset E, V(F) = \{x \in V,\ \exists e \in F,\ e = (x,y)\}$

$\forall X \subset V, E(X) = \{e \in E,\ e = (x,y),\ x \text{ and } y \in X)\}$

We already know that this convex hull is contained in ;

$$\forall j \in V, \quad \sum_{i \in \omega(j)} x_{ij} = 2 \qquad (j)$$

First, we want to prove the following :

B. Roy (ed.), Combinatorial Programming: Methods and Applications, 179–190.

Prop o : *The Hamiltonian cycles of* G *spans this linear variety* [12] .

PROOF : Suppose that opposite is true, $\exists$ a proper subvariety of this one defining by all the equations (j) containing all the H.C. of G. Then $\exists$ an equation (t) independent of equations (j) satisfied by all the H.C.

$$(t),\ \alpha_{ij}\ x_{ij} = \beta\ ,\ \alpha_{ij} \text{ not all equal to zero.}$$

We are going to transform (t) by adding to it some linear combinations of (j).

First adding :
$$\begin{cases} 1/2\ (\alpha_{23} - \alpha_{12} - \alpha_{13})\ x(1) \\ 1/2\ (\alpha_{13} - \alpha_{12} - \alpha_{23})\ x(2) \\ 1/2\ (\alpha_{12} - \alpha_{13} - \alpha_{23})\ x(3) \end{cases}$$

$$\text{where (j) is } \sum_{i \in \omega(j)} x_{ij} = 2$$

We have (t') with $\alpha_{12} = \alpha'_{23} = \alpha'_{13} = 0$

Subtracting then from (t') $\alpha'_{ij}\ x(i), \forall\ i \in V, i \neq 1,2,3$

We have then (t") with $\alpha''_{1i} = 0\ \forall\, i \in V,\ \alpha''_{23} = 0$

Consider now two H.C. passing through (i,1), (1,2), (2,3) and (i,2), (2,1), (1,3); and using between i and 3 the same Hamiltonian chain denoted (3, ,,, i), we know that there exist always at least one in any complete graph with at least 4 vertices.

Then $\alpha''_{1i} + \alpha''_{12} + \alpha''_{23} = \alpha''_{12} + \alpha''_{21} + \alpha''_{12} \Longrightarrow \alpha''_{i2} = 0\ \forall i$

Similarly we have $\alpha''_{i3} = 0\ \forall i$.

Using the same argument over replacing 1,2,3 by 1,2,i, we arrive at the contradiction that is $\alpha_{ij} = 0, \forall\ (ij) \in E$, and prove the result.

Q.E.D.

We shall now establish a characterisation for certain facets of the convex hull of the H.C.

By facet we mean a supporting hyperplane H of this convex hull such that the variety defined by $\{(j)\} \cap H,\ j \in V$ is spanned by its H.C.

Let first defined certain H of the form :

$$H = \{x, \sum_{(i,j)\in E'} x_{ij} \doteq p, E' \subset E)\}$$

Let P be the convex hull of the H.C. in G.

Then p is such that $\forall x \in P, \sum_{(i,j)\in E'} x_{ij} \leq p, (o)$

Let tell ($\underline{o}$) : $\sum_{(i,j)\in E'} x_{ij} = p$

Let $C \subset E$ be a maximal clique of G in E' connected to the rest of E' by at most 2 vertices, and such that $|V(C)| \geq 4$

We have then Prop 1

(o) is a facet of the convex hull of the H.C. *of* G *iff* $\sum_{(i,j)\in E_1'} x_{ij} \leq p-1$ *is a facet of the convex hull of the* H.C. *of* G_1 *with* $G_1 = (V-c, E(V-c))$, $c \in V(C)$, *with* E_1' *derived from* E', *by replacing* C *by* C(V(C)-c).

We are going first to give some intermediate results.

In the following let a,b be the two vertices of $V(C) \cap V(E'-C)$ when $|V(C) \cap V(E'-C)| = 2$.

Lemma 1

Let γ *be a* H.C. *satisfying* ($\underline{o}$) , *let* $q = |\gamma \cap C|$ *then* $q \geq |V(C)| - 3$.

PROOF : In order to have $q < |V(C)| - 3$, the number of connected components of $\gamma \cap C$ must be great or equal 4, using the fact that the cyclomatic number of C is equal to 0, suppose that q is 4. We shall construct in this case one H.C. of G having one edge more in E' that contradict (o). In the most difficult case for the proof (see figure) and without any loss in generality, we can suppose that de and gh are connected by the chains (d,,,,e) and (g,,,h) when the graph has enough vertices.

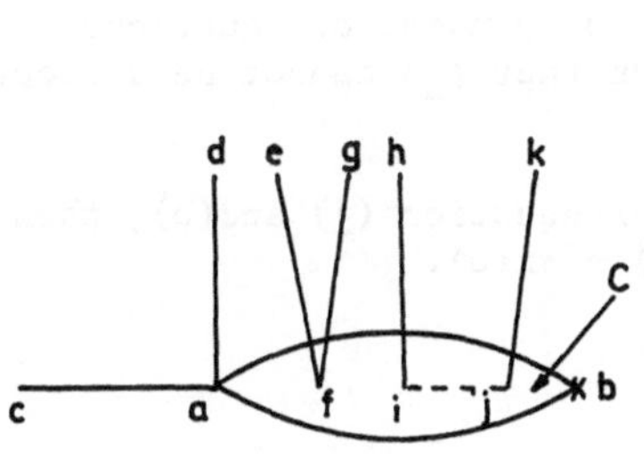

Between c and k, we have the chains (see figure in order to know which edges or chains belong or not to C) : (c,a), (a,d), (d,,,,,e), (e,f), (f,g), (g,,,,h), (h,i), (i,,,,j), (j,k) and (c,a), (a,j), (j,,,,i), (i,f), (f,d), (d,,,,e), (e,g), (g,,,,h), (h,k).

The second one contain one more edge at least ((a,j) + (i,f) - (a,d)) in E' than the first one.

Q.E.D.

Lemma 2

Among the H.C. *satisfying* (o) , *there exist a non empty set passing through one edge of* C *of the type* (a,i) *with* $a \in V(E'-c) \cap V(C)$, $i \in (V(C) - \{a\} - \{b\})$.

PROOF : Either the proposition is verified or (Lemma 1) we are necessarly in the case where $|\gamma \cap C| = |V(C)| - 3$ (3 connected composants (see figure). The chains (c,a), (a,d), (d,,,,e), (e,h), (h,,,,,i), (i,f) and (c,a), (a,i), (i,,,,,h), (h,d), (d,,,,,e), (e,f) contain the same number of edges in E', otherwise the second one will have one edge more, and then the second will not satisfied(o), and we have the same contradiction as in the previous proof.

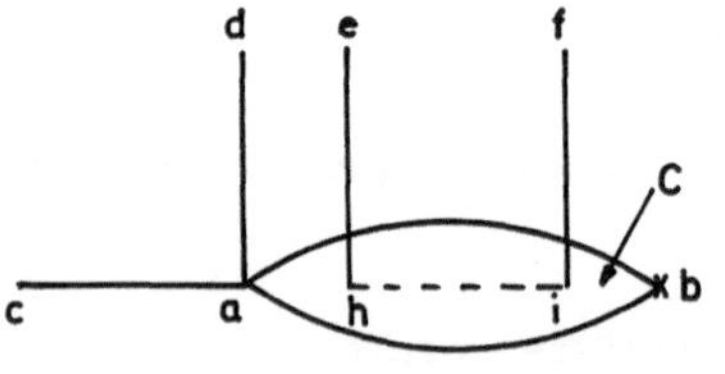

Q.E.D.

Lemma 3

Let $c \in V(C)$, *when (o) is a facet of* P *for each* (c,i), $(c,i) \notin E'$ *there exist some* H.C. *of* G *satisfying* (o) *and containing* (c,i).

PROOF : If it is not true $\exists K \subset V, |K| \neq 0$ st .. all the H.C. verifying (o) verify $\sum_{j \in K} x_{cj} = 0$ (u) too.

If we can show that this equation is independent of equations (j) and (o) , then we shall have shown that (o) cannot be a facet of P.

Suppose that (u) is not independent of equation (j) and(o), then $\exists \lambda_j$ and π such that (u) = $\sum_{j \in V} \lambda_j \, x(j) + \pi x(o)$.

If we identify term by term, we get :

(1) $\lambda_c + \lambda_j = 1 \quad j \in K$

(2) $\lambda_i + \lambda_j = 0 \quad (i,j) \notin E', \; i \in V(C), \; j \in K$

(3) $\lambda_i + \lambda_j + \pi = 0,\ (i,j) \in E'$

Using 3 equations of type (3) for $i,j \in V(C)$ we have $\lambda_i = -\frac{\pi}{2}, i \in V(C)$

then (1) $\Longrightarrow$ $\lambda_j = 1 + \frac{\pi}{2},\ j \in K$

then (2) $\Longrightarrow$ $\lambda_j = \frac{\pi}{2}\ j \notin K,\ j \notin V(C)$

Using these value of λ defined for each vertex of G we shall show that E' will have some special form.

We shall have 3 cases $|V(C) \cap V(E' - C)| = 0,1,2$

1°) $|V(C) \cap V(E' - C)| = 0$

Suppose that $\exists\,(i,j),\ (i,j) \notin E',\ (i,j) \notin C,\ i \in K,\ j \notin K$

Then $\lambda_i + \lambda_j = 0 = 1 + \frac{\pi}{2} + \frac{\pi}{2} \Longrightarrow \pi = -1$

Then $\lambda_j = +\frac{1}{2}\ j \in K$

$\lambda_j = -\frac{1}{2}\ j \in V(C)$

$\lambda_j = \frac{1}{2}\ j \in (V - K - V(C))$

Then $\forall (i,j),\ i,j \in (V - K - V(C))$ by (3) $(i,j) \in E'$, hence E' is of the form of 2 disjoint cliques (C, C', C' = E(V-K-V(C)), and then it is some H.C. h aving V(C) - 1 edges in C and V(C') - 1 edges in C' and passing through each edge, particularly (c,j) with $c \in V(C)$, $j \in K$ which is a contradiction.

2°) $|V(C) \cap V(E' - C)| = 1$

Using a similar way of proof we arrive at two cliques, that are adjacent by one single vertex.

3°) $|V(C) \cap V(E' - C)| = 2$

Then we arrive at two cliques adjacent by two vertex.

Q.E.D.

<u>Lemma 4</u>

Among the H.C. *of* G *satisfying* ($\underline{o}$) *in the case where* $V(C) \cap V(E' - C) = \{a,b\}$ *there exist at least one containing a Hamiltonian chain of* C *starting at* a *or* b *and containing the Hamiltonian chain of* C : (b,,,a), (a,c), and (c,i) *with* $c \in V(C)$, $i \notin V(C)$.

In order to prove this Lemma we must remarked that if it was not true, then all the H.C. of G will satisfied the following equation

$$(v) \quad \sum_{(i,j) \in C} x_{ij} + \sum_{(i,j) \notin E',\ i \in \{V(C)-V(E'-C)\}} x_{ij} = |V(C)| - 1$$

In fact we must remarked that if a H.C. have the pictured form with a chain between j and k for instance we can construct one other H.C. having the propertie described in the statement of the Lemma.

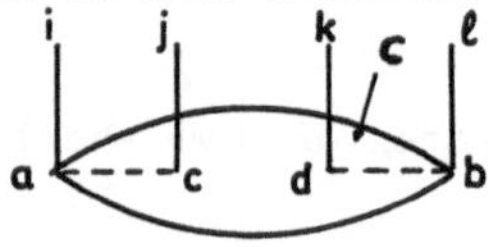

In the other case using Lemmas 1 and 2 we have the 3 types of pictures that all satisfy (v).

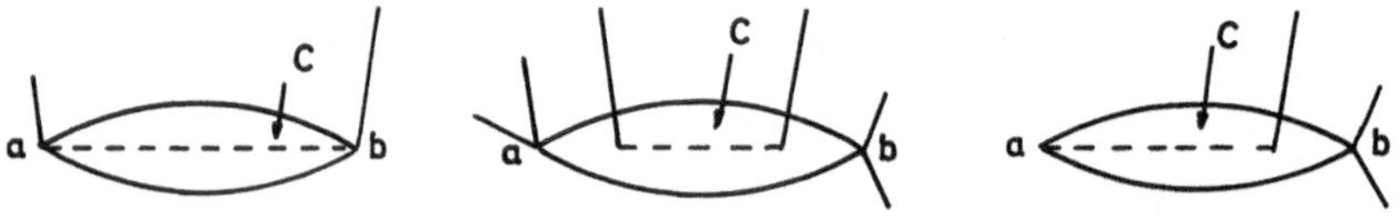

Then suppose that (v) is dependent of (j), (O), as in previous proof,

$\exists \lambda_j, \pi$ such that

$\forall i, j \in C \ \lambda_i + \lambda_j + \pi = 1 \Longrightarrow \lambda_i = \frac{1-\pi}{2}$

$\forall i, j, (i,j) \in E', i \in (V(C) - V(E'-C)) \Longrightarrow \lambda_i + \lambda_j = 1 \Longrightarrow \lambda_j = \frac{1+\pi}{2}$

then for (a,j), $(a,j) \notin E'$, $j \in (C)$ $\frac{1-\pi}{2} + \frac{1+\pi}{2} = 0$ which is a contradiction.

Remark

The remark used at the beginning of the proof allows us to said that it is a H.C. of G containing a chain of C containing all the vertices of C except b and this for the same reason.

In order to prove Prop 1 we shall describe the process that we shall use.

Suppose that the variety

$$\begin{cases} (j) & \sum_{i \in \omega(j)} x_{ij} = 2 \\ (\underline{\underline{o}}) & \sum_{(i,j) \in E'} x_{ij} = p \end{cases}$$

is not spanned by the H.C. of G satisfying $(\underline{\underline{o}})$

Then $\exists$ a proper subvariety containing all the H.C. satisfying ($\underline{\underline{o}}$)

$\exists$ (t) : $\sum_{(i,j)\in E} \alpha_{ij}\, x_{ij} = \beta$ verified by all the H.C. verifying ($\underline{\underline{o}}$) independent of $\{(j)\}$ and ($\underline{\underline{o}}$).

Subtracting some linear combination of (j) to (t) we can always posed $\alpha_{ci} = \alpha_{ad} = 0$ for any given $a,c,d, \in V$, $\forall i \in V$ (see the beginning of the proof of Prop o).

Let now defined

$$G_1 = G(V-c,\ E(V-c)),\quad E_1 = E(V-c)$$
$$E_1' = E'(V-c)$$
$$(o_1),\qquad \sum_{(i,j)\in E_1'} x_{ij} \leqslant p-1$$
$$(t_1),\qquad \sum_{(i,j)\in E_1} \alpha_{ij}\, x_{ij} = \beta$$
$$(j_1),\qquad \sum_{i\in\omega(j_1)} x_{ij_1} = 2,\ j_1 \in (V-c)$$

Remark

Using Lemmas each H.C. of G_1 satisfying ($\underline{\underline{o}}_1$) can be attached with at least one of these of G satisfying ($\underline{\underline{o}}$).

Such H.C. of G_1 either contains (a,d) or does not contain (a,d). In the first case it will be put into correspondence with the H.C. of G that contains (a,c) and (c,d) and the same chain between a and d. In the second case it will be put into correspondence with the H.C. of G that contain (d,c) and (c,i) and not (d,i) (that is contain in the H.C. of G) and the same chains between a,i and d.

Moreover in each if the two steps of the following proof we determine the value of each $\alpha_{ei}, \alpha_{ei} = 0$ with $e \in V(C)$, $e \notin V(C) \cap V(E'-C)$ then with this correspondence each one of the H.C. satisfying ($\underline{\underline{o}}_1$) will satisfy (t_1) too.

Let now consider two cases.

1°) $|V(C)| \geqslant 5$

Let $\{a,b\} = (V(C) \cap (E-C))$ if $|V(C) \cap V(E-C)| = 2$

Let c,d,e, be 3 others vertices of C.

Then by the remark of Lemma 4 and Lemma 3, it is a H.C. of G containing a chain (a,,,,e) or (b,,,,e), having 2 edges in E(c,d,e) and passing through each one of the edges (c,i).

Assuming that $\alpha_{ci} = \alpha_{de} = 0$ we can use for each i, $i \in V(C)$ the propertie of this triangle in order to determine the value of α_{di}. (eg : the chain (e,c), (c,d), (d,i) and (e,d), (d,c), (c,i)) $\alpha_{di} = 0, \forall i \in V(C)$.

Similarly using Lemma 4 we can do the same into C (using the remark of Lemma 4 too).

Then $\alpha_{di} = 0$ and conversely $\alpha_{ei} = 0$

Suppose that in G_1,(t_1) is dependent of (j_1) and $(\underline{\underline{o}}_1)$ then $\exists \lambda_j, \pi$ such that $(t_1) = \Sigma \lambda_j x(j_1) + \pi x(\underline{\underline{o}}_1)$

$\alpha_{de} = 0 = \lambda_d + \lambda_e + \pi$

$\alpha_{di} = 0 = \lambda_d + \lambda_i \quad \forall i \in V(C)$

$\alpha_{ei} = 0 = \lambda_e = \lambda_i$

then $\lambda_i = -\frac{\pi}{2} \; \forall\, i \in V(C)$, $\lambda_i = \frac{\pi}{2} \forall i \notin V(C)$

With the same λ_i and $\lambda_c = -\frac{\pi}{2}$ we have in $G_{ci} = 0 \, \forall i$

then if (t_1) is dependent (t) will be dependent

it (t_1) is independent (t) must be independent, if not (t_1) was dependent and conversely.

2°) $|V(C)| = 4$, $V(C) = a,b,c,d$, $V(C) \cap V(E-C) = \{a,b\}$

Let $\alpha_{ci} = \alpha_{ad} = 0$

Assuming by Lemma 4 and its remark that it is one H.C. γ such that $((a,d), (d,c), (c,b)) \subset \gamma$ then $\alpha_{db} = 0$.

Assuming by Lemma 4 that it is one containing ((a,d), (d,b), (b,c), (c,i)) then $\alpha_{di} = 0$, then using ((a,b), (b,c), (c,d), (d,i)), $\alpha_{ab} = 0$ then by Lemma 4, α_{bi} or $\alpha_{ai} = 0$ for the same reason.

Then we can complete the proof in the same form as the previous one. Q.E.D.

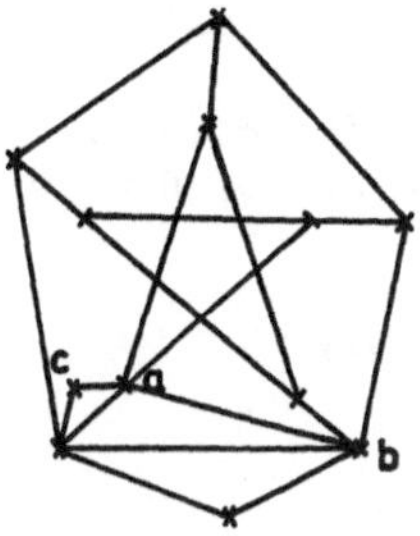

In order to be more clear let show with this example that we cannot always have a better result.

Let this graph be E',

we have obviously $\sum_{(i,j)\in E'} \lambda_{ij} \leqslant 11$ then (a,b) cannot belong to a H.C. γ such that $|\gamma \cap E'| = 11$ and we cannot applied the reducing scheme, because we have not a correspondence between the H.C. of $G_1 = G((V-c), E(V-c))$ and this one of G.

In fact we have one H.C. γ_1 in G_1 such that $(a,b) \in \gamma$ and $|\gamma_1 \cap E_1'| = 10$ but in G we have not such one γ with $(a,b)\ \gamma$ and $|\gamma \cap E'| = 11$

Q.E.D.

COROLLARY 1

$\forall G, |X| \geqslant 5$ (o); $\sum_{(i,j)\in C} x_{ij} \leqslant |X(C)| - 1$ *with* $|X(C)| = |X| - 2$, *then (o) is a facet of the convex hull of* H.C. *of* G.

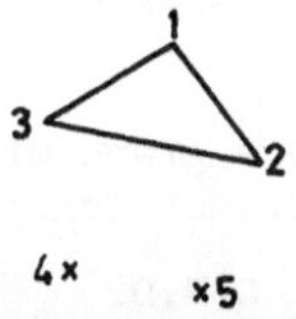

	12	13	14	15	23	24	25	34	35	45
1	1	1					1	1		1
2	1	1				1			1	1
3	1			1	1			1		1
4	1		1		1				1	1
5		1		1	1	1				1
6		1	1		1		1			1

All what we need to verify that in the complete graph with five vertices, there are five independent H.C. having exactly two arcs in a given triangle.

This will be done easily by checking that the matrix the columns of which are (14,15,24,25,34) and the rows of which are (1,2,3,4,5) is non singular.

Q.E.D.

COROLLARY 2

$\forall G |X| \geqslant 5$ (o), $\sum_{(i,j)\in C} x_{ij} \leqslant |X(C)| - 1$, $3 \leqslant |X(C)| < |X| - 2$ *then (o) is a facet of the convex hull of the* H.C. *of* G.

PROOF : As previously, we can replace C by a triangle; we can then reduce X - X(C) as in the proof of P_1, as long as :

$|X| - |X(C)| \geqslant 3$ we use the same argument and apply the previous results.

Q.E.D.

COROLLARY 3

For the complete graph, the set of H.C. *containing* (a,b), *has one dimension* N - 1 *if* N *is the dimension of the set of* H.C. *of* G *with :* G = (X.E), $|X| \geqslant 4$.

PROOF : Let E' = E - (a,b) these cycles satisfy

$$\sum_{(i,j)\in E'} x_{ij} = n - 1 \text{ with } X = n.$$

Using the same argument as in part 1 of the proof of P_1, it is sufficient to verify that in the complete graph with four vertices there are two independent H.C. containing the arc (a,b).

Q.E.D.

COROLLARY 4

The set of H.C. *of a given complete graph, such that* $|X| \geqslant 5$ *which do not contain a given edge, has a dimension* N - 1, *where* N *is defined as in corollary 3.*

Let E' = E - (a,b) we have $\sum_{(i,j)\in E'} x_{ij} = |X|$

We can use the same argument as in part 1 of the proof of P_1 until $|X| \geqslant 6$.

It is sufficient to verify that in the complete graph with five vertices, there are exactly 5 independent H.C. not containing (a,b).

Q.E.D.

COROLLARY 5

Let G = (X,E) *be any complete graph with* $|X| \geqslant 10$, *let* E' *be any partial graph of* G *with* $|X(E')| = |X|$ *isomorph to the petersen graph obtained by replacing by one edge one of his cliques having only two common vertices with the rest of* E', *then*

$$(1) \quad \sum_{(i,j)\in E'} x_{ij} \leqslant |X| - 1$$

is a facet of the convex hull of the H.C. *of* G.

PROOF : If $|X| > 11$, then using P_1 it is sufficient to prove the property for $|X| = 11$, E' is represented on the figure to the left.

Using the same reducing scheme that

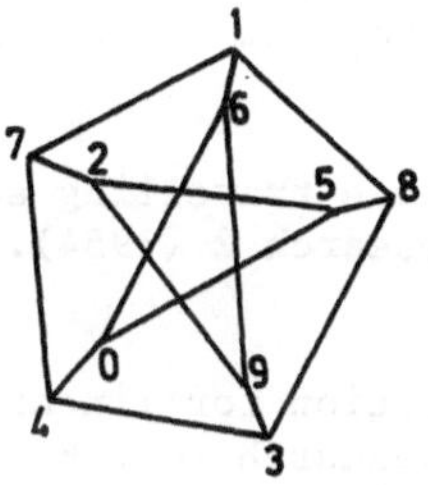

in the proof of P_1, we can say that if

(2) $\mathop{}_{i,j\ E'} x_{ij} \leqslant 9$ is a facet, when E' is the petersen graph and G the complete graph with 10 vertices, then (1) is also a facet, otherwise we can not say anything.

(2) is a facet assuming that the 7 following H.C. are linearly independent and contain 9 edges of the petersen graph.

(2,7),(4,7),(3,8),(5,8),(3,9),(6,9),(4,0),(5,0),(1,6),(1,2)

(1,7),(4,7),(3,8),(5,8),(3,9),(6,9),(4,0),(6,0),(2,5),(1,2)

(1,7),(4,7),(3,8),(5,8),(2,9),(6,9),(5,0),(6,0),(3,4),(1,2)

(2,7),(4,7),(1,8),(5,8),(3,9),(6,9),(5,0),(6,0),(3,4),(1,2)

(2,7),(4,7),(3,8),(5,8),(2,9),(3,9),(5,0),(6,0),(1,6),(1,4)

(1,7),(2,7),(3,8),(5,8),(2,9),(6,9),(5,0),(6,0),(3,4),(1,4)

(2,7),(4,7),(1,8),(3,8),(3,9),(6,9),(5,0),(6,0),(2,5),(1,4)

We can add to these H.C. 28 obviously linearly independent H.C. having 9 edges in the petersen graph they are those passing through each one of the edges not belonging the petersen graph, different from (1,2), (1,4), we have then 35 L.I. H.C. that span this linear variety.

Q.E.D.

BIBLIOGRAPHY

[1] C. BERGE "Graphes et Hypergraphes" (Dunod, Paris 1971 .

[2] P. CAMION "Problèmes de flots et tensions dans un graphe" (ENSTA 1972).

[3] P. CAMION J.F. MAURRAS "Polyèdres à sommets entiers dans le cube unité"(soumis à publication).

[4] V. CHVATAL "Edmonds' polytopes and weakly hamiltonien graphs" (Mathematical Programming Vol. n° 1 1973 pp. 29-40).

[5] G.B. DANTZIG, R. FULKERSON, S. JOHNSON "Solution of a large-scale travelling salesman problem" - Operation Research 2 (1954). pp 393-410.

[6] G.B. DANTZIG, P. WOLFE "Principles of decomposition for linear programs" - Operation Research Vol. 8 1960. pp. 101-111.

[7] J. EDMONDS "Matroids and the greedy algorithm" (Lecture, Princeton University 1967 and mathematical programming 1 (1971) pp. 127-136).

[8] J. EDMONDS "Submodular function, Matroids and certain polyedra (Combinatorial Structure and their Applications, Calgary Alberta June 1969, G.B. Science Publisher pp. 69-87).

[9] B. GRUNBAUM "Convex Polytopes" (Wiley - New York 1967).

[10] M. HELD, R.M. KARP "The travelling-salesman problem and minimum spanning trees" (Operation Research 18 - 1970 pp. 1138-1162).

[11] J.B. KRUSKAL "On the shortest spanning subtree of a graph" (Proceedings of America Mathematical Society 7, 1956).

[12] M. GROTSCHEL, M. PADBERG "Linear characterization on travelling salesman problem" Report n° 7316 June 1974 Institut für Okonometric and Operation Research - Universität

[13] E.L. LAWLER "Polynomial-bounded and (apparently) non polynomial-bounded matroid computations".

[14] J.F. MAURRAS "Une utilisation de la méthode de Dantzig et Wolfe - Le problème du voyageur de commerce" note EDF HR 0379/3 du 19/4/73.

FINDING MINIMUM SPANNING TREES WITH A FIXED NUMBER OF LINKS AT A NODE

Fred Glover * and Darwin Klingman **

*University of Colorado, Boulder, Colorado 80302; **University of Texas, Austin, Texas 78712

ABSTRACT. This paper addresses a variant of the minimum spanning tree problem in which a given node is required to have a fixed number of incident edges. We show that this problem, which is combinatorially a level of complexity beyond the ordinary minimum spanning tree problem, can be solved by a highly efficient "quasi-greedy" algorithm. Applications include a tele-communication linking problem and a new relaxation strategy for the traveling salesman problem via appropriately defined order-constrained one-trees.

1. INTRODUCTION

The minimum weight spanning tree problem has enjoyed a good deal of notoriety ever since Kruskal first provided a greedy algorithm for solving it [12]. Interest in the problem at least in the beginning, appeared to center primarily around the novelty that something with a nontrivial statement could be solved by an "almost trivial" procedure. Philosophically, this was both intriguing and unsettling, and other manifestations and generalizations of greedy algorithms were sought [1, 13]. A broad characterization of such methods in the context of matroid theory was accomplished by Edmonds [3], who coined the term "greedy algorithm."

With rare exception (e.g., [4]), the precise form assumed by a greedy algorithm is usually one of the first possibilities that springs to mind, and the validity of such an approach can typically be established without notable effort. The early applications seemed for some time to have little practical significance and little relevance outside their immediate contexts. Recently, however, things have changed. Practical applications in such diverse

B. Roy (ed.), Combinatorial Programming: Methods and Applications, 191–201.

areas as least cost electrical wiring, minimum cost connecting communication and transportation networks and minimum stress networks have found their way into the literature and textbooks (see, e.g., [10a, 11, 15]). A variation of the minimum spanning tree problem, called the minimum "1-tree" problem was shown by Held and Karp [8,9] to be extremely useful as a relaxation of the traveling salesman problem. In addition, Dijkstra [1] Kershenbaum and Van Slyke [11] have shown that there is more to the implementation of greedy algorithms than previously suspected, and have developed rather ingenious procedures for organizing and updating the information used by a greedy algorithm to improve its efficiency.

Throughout all this flurry of activity, an extremely important relative of the minimum spanning tree problem has surprisingly been neglected: that of determining a minimum weight spanning tree subject to the additional restriction that a given node be constrained to a specified order (i.e., have a fixed number of incident edges). Such a problem is directly relevant in the traveling salesman context, where nodes are constrained to order 2. The problem also arises, with perhaps greater practical immediacy, in a telecommunications setting. Here the objective is to find the minimum cost way of setting up transmission cables to connect users in various cities to a common computer installation. The "order constraint" derives from the requirement that the immediate links to the computer facility must be at least of a certain number, in order to accommodate the fact that too few links will be unable to support the anticipated transmission load. (The requirement that a node be constrained to "at least" or "at most" a certain order can be handled as a simple variant of constraining it to be exactly of that order.)

In view of the foregoing remarks, the purpose of this paper is to address the following problem:

P(K) - Find a minimum weight spanning tree with node 0 constrained to order K.

Here, as customary, we implicitly have reference to an underlying graph of nodes and edges, and the weight of a subgraph (hence a spanning tree) is defined to be the sum of the weights of the edges in that subgraph. Node 0 may of course represent any selected node in the graph, and K is assumed to be a positive number for which a spanning tree with exactly K edges incident to node 0 exists. (Otherwise, the solution of P(K) will determine the nonexistence of such a tree.)

Our principal results for characterizing optimal spanning trees with a constrained order at node 0 consist of a "primal theorem" and a "dual theorem". The former gives a method for constructing an optimal tree beginning with any tree that already satisfies the order requirement at node 0, and the latter gives a method for constructing an optimal tree beginning with any tree that already satisfies problem P(K), of order K + 1, or K - 1 at node 0 (as desired).

The dual theorem is in fact a characterization of a "quasi-greedy" algorithm, for it makes the very best move from the category available to it, not by "putting things into a bucket" (in Edmond's terminology) but by trading things between two buckets.

We also provide special labeling procedures that enable the primal and dual methods to be applied by means of "modified pivot steps" analogous to the basis exchange steps employed in specialized linear programming procedures for solving minimum cost flow network problems. The "modified pivot steps", of course, do not involve the use of a specialized linear programming algorithm, since the problem under consideration is combinatorial and has no LP network equivalent; however, the amount of calculation of these modified pivot steps is in fact on the same order as--or somewhat better than--that of an LP basis exchange in a network. Further in the dual case each step immediately gives an optimal spanning tree of the next higher or lower order at node 0, thereby producing an algorithm of considerable efficiency. In the concluding section we discuss how this "quasi-greedy" algorithm can be similarly applied to the constrained minimum one-tree problem enhancing the significance of this method for the traveling salesman problem.

2. NOTATION AND RESULTS

To lay the groundwork for the primal and dual theorems for constructing optimal ordered-constrained trees we introduce the following definitions and notational conventions. T and T' will denote distinct spanning trees, defined on a common graph. We also allow T and T' to represent the sets of edges for these trees, writing for example, $e \in T - T'$ to indicate that e is an edge in T but not in T'.

The unique edge-simple path in T connecting the endpoints of an edge e will be denoted T(e) (and likewise will interchangeably be used to represent the set of edges for this path). For two edges e, e' such that $e \in T$ and $e' \notin T$, we will call the process of adding e' to T and deleting e from T an <u>admissible exchange</u> (relative to T) if the result is also a spanning tree. Thus, in particular, such an exchange is admissible if and only if $e \in T(e')$.

Using these definitions, we will first state a theorem of [7] concerning the existence of a special "matching" of edges from T and T' that is particularly useful for establishing the main results of this paper. (Due to its subordinate role in the present setting, we state it as a lemma.)

Lemma 1.

For any two distinct spanning trees T and T', there is a way of pairing the edges of T - T' with those of T' - T (in a one-one matching) so that every pair gives an admissible exchange relative to T.

The proof of this result in [7] gives a constructive procedure for producing a pairing that satisfies the stated conditions. Such a construction will not concern us here, but we require an additional preliminary (and somewhat nonintuitive) result to complete the foundation for our principal theorems.

Lemma 2.

Assume that e_0, $e \in T$, e_0', $e' \notin T$ and e_0 and e_0' are incident to the same node. Further assume that at least one of the pairs e, e' and e_0, e'_0 does not give an admissible exchange relative to T(by deleting the first member of the pair and adding the second). Then e_0, e' and e, e_0' both yield an admissible exchange relative to T if and only if the addition of e' and e_0' and the deletion of e_0 and e result in a spanning tree (hence, if and only if the pairs e_0, e' and e, e_0' yield successively admissible exchanges, executed in either order).

Proof:

For the "only if" part, assume $e_0 \in T(e')$ and $e \in T(e')$. Swapping e' and e_0 gives a tree T' in which e_0' and e still give an admissible exchange unless $T'(e'_0) \neq T(e'_0)$, which occurs only if $e_0 \in T(e_0')$, implying e_0 can exchange admissibly with e_0'. By assumption it follows that $e \notin T(e')$ (else e and e' could exchange admissibly). Thus $e \in T(e_0') - T(e')$, and it follows that the edge simple path $T(e') \cup \{e'\} \cup T(e_0') - (T(e') - T(e_0'))$ in fact contains e and is $T'(e_0')$. Thus the second exchange is admissible in T', proving that a tree results. (A similar argument leads to the same conclusion by considering the swaps in reverse order.) For the "if" part of the lemma, assume that $T \cup \{e_0', e'\} - \{e_0, e\}$ is a tree. By lemma 1 there is some way of pairing the edges, e_0', e' with the edges e_0, e so that every pair gives an admissible exchange relative to T. If e_0' cannot be paired with e_0 or if e' cannot be paired with e, this leaves the two pairings, e, e_0' and e_0, e' by default. The equivalence of the statement that these two pairings give successively admissible swaps when executed in either order follows immediately from the foregoing.

For the statement of the following "primal" theorem, we call an admissible exchange <u>improving</u> if the resulting tree has a smaller weight than the original (hence if the weight of the added edge is less than the weight of the deleted edge). We also follow the convention that an edge is incident to node 0 if and only if it is subscripted with a "0".

Theorem 1 (Primal Approach)

A spanning tree T with order K at node 0 is optimal for problem P(K) if and only if

(1). There are no improving admissible exchanges involving a pair e, e', where $e \in T$, $e' \notin T$ (and neither edge is incident to node 0);

(2). There are no improving admissible exchanges involving a pair e_0, e_0', where $e_0 \in T$, $e_0' \notin T$ (and both edges are incident to node 0);

(3). There are no two exchanges, both admissible relative to T, involving a pair e_0, e' and a pair e, e_0', such that $e_0, e \in T$, $e_0', e' \notin T$, which together yield a net improvement--i.e., for which the sum of the weights of e_0' and e' are less than the sum of the weights of e_0 and e. (In particular, this says that coupling the "best admissible pair" of the form e_0, e' with the "best admissible pair" of the form e_0', e does not yield a net improvement, disregarding whether the exchanges can actually be carried out in sequence.)

Proof:

First we prove the "only if" part of the theorem. Clearly if there are any improving exchanges of the type indicated in (1) or (2), then T is nonoptimal. If there are no such exchanges but there exists a pair of exchanges such as described in (3), then we may assume that either e_0, e_0' or e, e' cannot give an admissible exchange, else at least one would be improving, contrary to assumption. But then by Lemma 2 the two exchanges of (3) can in fact be carried out sequentially, again establishing that T is nonoptimal. To prove the "if" part of the theorem, suppose that (1), (2) and (3) hold, but that there exists a spanning tree T' which is feasible for P(K) and has a smaller weight than T. By Lemma 1 we can match the edges of T - T' with those of T' - T so that each pair gives an admissible exchange in T. Since node 0 has the same order in both T and T', it follows that these admissible exchanges consist exactly of the types indicated in (1) and (2) together with the two types of exchanges indicated in (3), where the number of each of these two latter types is equal. Since the weight of T' is less than that of T, and since no admissible e, e' and no admissible e_0, e_0' exchanges are improving, it follows that the sum of weights of all the admissible exchanges of the e, e_0' and the e_0, e' type must be negative (adding the weights of the edges in T' and subtracting those of the edges in T). But then the sum of the weights of some admissible e, e_0' exchange and some admissible e_0, e' exchange (in particular, the "best" of each type) must be negative, contrary to the assumptions of (3). The contradiction establishes the theorem.

By means of the foregoing theorem we can now state and prove the two forms of the "dual" theorem for order-constrained spanning trees (expressed as Theorem 2 and its corollary), which show how to obtain optimal solutions for P(K+1) and P(K-1) from an optimal solution for P(K).

Theorem 2 (Dual Approach-increasing order):

Assume T is optimal for P(K) and T' is obtained from T by applying a single admissible exchange involving the edges e_0', e where $e \in T$, $e_0' \notin T$ (e_0' is incident to node 0 and e is not incident to node 0), and the weight of e_0' less the weight of e is minimum over all admissible exchanges of the specified type. Then T' is optimal for P(K+1).

Proof:

We will show that T' satisfies the optimality conditions of Theorem 1. First, we show that (1) holds. We may restrict attention to admissible exchanges of the form e_1, e_1' in T' that were not available in T. Such an exchange yields a tree $T'' = T \cup \{e_0', e_1'\} - \{e, e_1\}$ and by Lemma 2 e_0', e_1 and e_1', e must both give admissible exchanges in T. But the first of these is no better than e_0', e and the second is a nonimproving move, and hence T" is not better than T'. Next we establish condition (2). The admissible exchange of the form indicated in (2) applied to T', gives a tree $T'' = T \cup \{e_0', e_0''\} - \{e, e_0\}$ where $e_0 \in T'$ hence $e_0 \in T$ (disregarding $e_0 = e_0'$ which reduces to a tree already known to be no better than T') and $e_0'' \notin T'$ hence $e_0'' \notin T$. By Lemma 2, and the fact that e_0, e_0'', cannot give an admissible exchange in T, both e_0', e_0 and e_0'', e must give admissible exchanges in T. But the first is nonimproving and the second no better than e_0', e, and hence T' again cannot be improved. Finally, we show that (3) holds. A double exchange involving e_0'', e_1 and e'_1, e_0^* which yields a net improvement must be capable of being executed in sequence, applying Lemma 2 and the fact that conditions (1) and (2) have been established for T'. Here e_1, $e_0^* \in T'$ hence $\in T$, and e_0'', $e_1' \notin T'$ hence $\notin T$, disregarding $e_0^* = e_0'$ and $e = e'_1$, both of which reduce to earlier cases.

Thus we have a tree $T'' = T \cup \{e_0', e_0'', e_1'\} - \{e, e_1, e_0^*\}$ where the latter set of edges is from T and the former is not.

Applying Lemma 1, these two sets of edges may be matched in some way so that all resulting pairs give admissible exchanges in T. We shall examine the relevant "possible" matchings to determine their implications for T". First the pairing $\{e_0^*, e_1'\}$, $\{e_1, e_0''\}$, $\{e_0', e\}$ is not possible, because if the first two pairs had been admissible (i.e., given rise to admissible exchanges) in T they would have implied the nonoptimality of T'. Similarly $\{e_0^*, e_0''\}$, $\{e_1, e_1'\}$, $\{e_0', e\}$ is impossible, because at least one of the first two pairs must be improving by the assumed improvement of T" over T', and the admissibility of such a pair in T violates its presumed optimality. This leaves the following cases: $\{e_0'', e\}$, $\{e_1, e_0'\}$, $\{e_0^*, e_1'\}$; $\{e_0'', e\}$, $\{e_1, e_1'\}$, $\{e_0^*, e_0'\}$; $\{e_0'', e_1\}$, $\{e_1', e\}$, $\{e_0^*, e_0'\}$; $\{e_0'', e_1\}$, $\{e_1', e\}$, $\{e_0^*, e_0'\}$. All of these may be ruled out because in each case the last two pairs are nonimproving (due to the optimality of T) and the first pair gives a tree no better than T'. This contradicts the postulated improvement of T" over T' and completes the proof.

From this theorem we may infer the following "inverse" result.

<u>Corollary</u> (Dual Approach-decreasing order): Assume T is optimal for P(K) and T' is obtained from T by applying a single admissible exchange involving the edges e_0, e', where $e_0 \in T$, $e' \notin T$ (e_0 is incident to node 0 and e' is not), and the weight of e' less the weight of e_0 is minimum over all admissible exchanges of the specified type. Then T' is optimal for P(K-1).

Proof:

The corollary follows by essentially the same reasoning used to establish Theorem 2.

In Theorem 2 and its corollary, the absence of an admissible exchange that increases or decreases the number of edges incident to node 0 of course implies the nonexistence of a spanning tree of the resulting order at this node. (This is a direct consequence of the stated results and the use of "infinite weight" edges to represent those not contained in the graph.)

We now show how to take advantage of these theorems in an efficient manner.

3. LABELING PROCEDURES

The identification of an admissible exchange that is the "best" of all admissible exchanges in its category, which is required by both Theorem 2 and its corollary (and also, indirectly by Theorem 1) appears at first glance to involve the computation of "exchange values" over a potentially vast number of partial chains. We will show in this section how to apply labeling procedures (different, but comparably efficient, in each of the three cases) that succeed in generating all such relevant values, with an amount of computation essentially no greater than that of evaluating updated objective function coefficients for nonbasic variables in specialized linear programming approaches to ordinary network problems. (We refer here to "streamlined" basis evaluation procedures such as those of [5,6,14].) In addition, we show how to apply the foregoing primal and dual results iteratively by means of correspondingly refined updating steps that impose minimal amounts of recalculation (likewise, comparable in efficiency to the approaches of [5,6]).

In all of the labeling procedures, it is assumed that the current spanning tree T is recorded as an arborescence with Johnson's "triple label" scheme [10], with the root at node 0. As customary, a node r will be called an <u>immediate successor</u> of node q if there is an edge in T incident on nodes q and r and if the unique path in the arborescence from r to the root contains node q. A node r will be called a <u>successor</u> of node q if the unique path from r to the root contains node q.

Labeling Rule For The Dual Approach - decreasing order

1. Assign a label $t_q = r$ to each successor q of an immediate successor r of node 0. To each immediate successor node r of node 0 also assign a label of $t_r = r$. Assign node 0 a label of 0.

2. For each edge $(i,j) \notin T$ whose node labels are not the same and for which neither i nor j is node 0, set

$$\Theta_{ij} = w_{ij} - \max(w_{0t_i}, w_{0t_j})$$

where w_{ph} denotes the weight on edge (p,h). Set $\Theta_{ij} = \infty$ for all other edges.

3. To determine the e_0, e' exchange of the corollary to Theorem 2: let $\Theta_{rs} = \min_{(i,j)} \Theta_{ij}$. If Θ_{rs} is finite, then edge (r,s) = e', and e_0 is the edge associated with max (w_{0t_i}, w_{0t_j}) in step 2. If Θ_{rs} is infinite, no spanning tree of the desired order exists.

The validity of the foregoing procedure follows from the corollary to Theorem 2 and the fact that e_0, e' gives an admissible exchange if and only if $e_0 \in T(e')$.

The above procedure is clearly quite easy to implement. Additionally, the labels used in the procedure can easily be updated. Specifically, suppose an optimal spanning tree T for P(K) is known and an optimal spanning tree T' for P(K-R) (where R<K) is desired. The above procedure can be successively used without completely re-labeling the nodes for each intermediate spanning tree. This is readily accomplished by using the API method [5] to update the rooted tree pointers (predecessor, successor, and brother indexes) and using the following observations to update the node labels.

Deleting edge e_0 splits T into two disjoint trees. One of these trees (say T_0) contains the root (node 0) and the other tree (say T_1) does not. (Note that all the node labels of T_1 are the same.) The addition of edge e' = (r,s) reconnects these trees. When T_1 is re-attached to T_0 via edge (r,s) then all node labels of T_0 are still correct and all node labels of T_1 should be changed to t_r^0 if $r \in T_0$ or t_s is $s \in T_0$.

Labeling Rule For The Dual Approach - increasing order

1. Assign a label $w_r = 0$ to each immediate successor r of node 0, and assign node 0 a label of 0. To each immediate successor r of a node t whose node label has been set, assign a label $w_r = \max (w_t, w_{tr})$, where w_{tr} is the weight on edge (t,r).

2. To determine the e, e_0' exchange of Theorem 2:
For each edge $(0,j) \notin T$, set $\Theta_{0j} = w_{0j} - w_j$ and let $\Theta_{0q} = \min_{(0,j) \notin T} \Theta_{0j}$.

Then edge $(0,q) = e_0'$ and e is the edge in $T(e'_0)$ whose weight is equal to w_q. (If this edge is not unique pick any such edge that is not incident to node 0).

The validity of this procedure follows directly from Theorem 2. As in the case of decreasing node order, the procedure is quite easy to implement and the labels can be updated with minimal effort. In particular, suppose an optimal spanning tree T for P(K) is known and an optimal spanning tree T' for P(K+R) is desired. Then the node labels can be easily updated using the observations similar to those made earlier. Deleting edge e splits the minimum spanning tree into two disjoint trees. As before, one of the trees (say T_0) contains the root (node 0) and the other tree (say T_1) does not. The addition of edge e'_0 re-connects these trees. When T_1 is re-attached to T_0 via edge $e'_0 = (0,q)$ then all node labels of T_0 are still correct and thus only tree node labels of T_1 need to be updated. The updating of the node labels in T_1 occurs by setting $w_q = 0$ and assigning a node label w_r to each immediate successor r of each node $t \in T_1$ (whose node label has been set) equal to $w_r = \max (w_t, w_{tr})$.

4. ORDER-CONSTRAINED ONE-TREES AND MATROID EXTENSIONS

By rough analogy to the characterization of a one-tree in

[8] we can define an order-constrained one-tree to be a subgraph which as a spanning tree with order at most k at node 0 when node 1 is deleted, and in which node 1 has exactly two incident edges. For k equal to two the minimum order-constrained one-tree problem (defined in the natural manner) is easily established to be a relaxation of the traveling salesman problem. Also an optimal solution to this problem results simply by solving the ordinary minimum spanning tree problem with node 1 deleted, then solving P(2) utilizing the quasi-greedy algorithm of the corollary to theorem 2 if node 0 has an order exceeding two, and finally re-introducing node 1 together with its two incident edges of least weight. Thus the results of this paper provide the basis for a new relaxation strategy for solving the traveling salesman problem. Moreover, as might be expected, these results have direct analogs of greater generality in the context of matroids. These considerations are treated in [7a].

REFERENCES

1. E.W. Dijkstra, "A Note on Two Problems in Connexion with Graphs, Numerische Mathematik 1, 269-271, 1959.
2. Jack Edmonds, "Optimum Branchings," Journal of Research of the National Bureau of Standards 71B, 233-240, 1967.
3. Jack Edmonds, "Matroids and the Greedy Algorithm," Mathematical Programming 1, 2, 127-136, November 1971.
4. Fred Glover, "Maximum Matching in a Convex Bipartite Graph," Naval Research Logistics Quarterly 15, 3, 313-316, September 1967.
5. Fred Glover, D. Karney, and D. Klingman, "Augmented Predecessor Index Method for Locating Stepping Stone Paths and Assigning Dual Prices in Distribution Problems," Transportation Science 6, 171-180, 1972.
6. Fred Glover, D. Karney, D. Klingman, and A. Napier, "A Computational Study on Start Procedures, Basis Change Criteria, and Solution Algorithms for Transportation Problems," Management Science 20, 5, 793-814, 1974.
7. Fred Glover, and D. Klingman, "A Note on Admissible Exchange in Spanning Trees," MSRS 74-3, University of Colorado, April 1974.

7a. Fred Glover, and D. Klingman, "Minimum Order-Constrained One-Trees and The Traveling Salesman Problem." To appear.

8. M. Held, and R.M. Karp, "The Traveling Salesman Problem and Minimum Spanning Trees," Operations Research 18, 6, 1138-1162, November-December 1970.
9. M. Held and R.M. Karp, "The Traveling Salesman Problem and Minimum Spanning Trees: Part II," Mathematical Programming 1, 1, 6-25, October 1971.
10. Ellis Johnson, "Networks and Basic Solutions," Operations Research 14, 4, 619-623, 1966.

10a. F.S. Hillier, and G.J. Lieberman, Introduction to Operations Research, San Francisco, California: Holden-Day, Inc., 1967.

11. J. Kershenbaum, and R. Van Slyke, "Computing Minimum Trees Efficiently," Proc. ACM Annual Conference, 518, 1972.

12. J.B. Kruskal, Jr., "On the Shortest Spanning Subtree of Graphs and the Traveling Salesman Problem," Proc. Am. Math. Soc. 7, 48-50, 1956.

13. P. Rosenstiehl, "L'Arbre Minimum d'un Graphe," Proc. Int'l. Symposium on the Theory of Graphs in Rome 1966, Dunod/Gordon-Breach, 1967.

14. V. Srinivasan, and G.L. Thompson, "Accelerated Algorithms for Labeling and Relabeling of Trees with Application for Distribution Problems," Journal of the Association for Computing Machinery 19, 4, 712-726, October 1972.

15. H.M. Wagner, Principles of Operations Research, Prentice-Hall, Englewood Cliffs, N.J., 1969.

P A R T I I I

SET PARTITIONING, COVERING AND PACKING

SET PARTITIONING

Egon Balas* and Manfred W. Padberg**

*Carnegie-Mellon University
**New York University

INTRODUCTION

1. BACKGROUND

1.1. Set Partitioning and Its Uses
1.2. Set Packing and Set Covering
1.3. Edge Matching and Covering, Node Packing and Covering
1.4. Node Packing, Set Packing, Clique Covering

2. THEORY

2.1. Facets of the Set Packing Polytope
2.2. Facets of Relaxed Polytopes: Cuts from Disjunctions
2.3. Adjacent Vertices of the Set Partitioning and Set Packing Polytopes

3. ALGORITHMS

3.1. Implicit Enumeration
3.2. Simplex-Based Cutting Plane Methods
3.3. A Column Generating Algorithm
3.4. A Symmetric Subgradient Cutting Plane Method
3.5. Set Partitioning Via Node Covering

REFERENCES

APPENDIX: A BIBLIOGRAPHY OF APPLICATIONS

B. Roy (ed.), Combinatorial Programming: Methods and Applications, 205–258. *All Rights Reserved.*

INTRODUCTION

This paper discusses the set partitioning or equality-constrained set covering problem. It is a survey of theoretical results and solution methods for this problem, and while we have tried not to omit anything important, we have no claim to completeness. Critical comments pointing out possible omissions or misstatements will be welcome.

Part 1 gives some background material. It starts by discussing the uses of the set partitioning model; then it introduces the concepts to be used throughout the paper, and connects our problem to its close and distant relatives which play or may play a role in dealing with it: set packing and set covering, edge matching and edge covering, node packing and node covering, clique covering. The crucial equivalence between set packing/partitioning and node packing problems is introduced.

Part 2 deals with structural properties of the set packing and set partitioning polytopes. First we describe the facial structure of the set packing polytope to the extent that it is known. Families of facets generated by certain types of subgraphs (cliques, odd holes, etc.) are characterized, and necessary and sufficient conditions are discussed for all basic solutions to the set partitioning linear program to be integer. Since many of the facets are computationally expensive to generate, other, easily computable inequalities (cutting planes) are then derived from the disjunctive conditions of the set partitioning problem, which are facets of some relaxation of the set partitioning polytope. Finally, we characterize adjacency relations between vertices of the set partitioning and set packing polytopes, on these polytopes as well as on their linear programming relaxations. The basic property that every edge of the set partitioning (set packing) polytope is also an edge of the linear programming relaxation of the latter, is viewed in the context of the need for appropriate criteria to identify such edges that meet a given vertex. All this theory is relatively new, a product of the last five years. Proofs are in general omitted, but sources are referenced in each case.

Part 3 focuses on algorithms. We first discuss the two main types that are by now well established, implicit enumeration and (traditional) cutting planes. While in the first category several specialized algorithms have been developed, of which we discuss the ones that to our knowledge have been tested and found successful, algorithms in the second category are basically nonspecialized. Nevertheless, since cutting planes are known to be relatively efficient on set partitioning problems, we discuss some features of the algorithms and codes in this class. For both of these approaches, we briefly review the published computational experience. Next we discuss three recently developed approaches which are either untested or tested to a very limited extent, but which are based on new ideas that seem to hold some promise. The first one is a column generating procedure, based on the adjacency properties discussed in Part 2. It uses a modified all-integer version of the primal simplex algorithm, and generates composite columns corresponding to edges of the feasible set which connect a given integer vertex to a better one. The second approach uses a new symmetric subgradient method to solve the set partitioning linear program, in an attempt to eliminate the difficulties involved in solving these large, very constrained and very degenerate linear programs by the simplex method, and generates cutting planes of a novel type. Finally, the third one deals with the set partitioning problem via an equivalent weighted node covering problem, which it solves by a hybrid cutting plane-branch and bound algorithm, in which the main subroutine (generating cutting planes and a sequence of "improving" dual-feasible solutions) is again accomplished without recourse to the simplex method, by a labeling procedure requiring a number of steps bounded by the number of nodes times the number of edges.

We assume some familiarity on the part of the reader with the basic concepts of graph theory. For background reading in this field, the reader is referred to Berge [1970], Harary [1969], Roy [1969, 1970]. For background in the general areas of linear and integer programming, we recommend Dantzig [1963] for the former and Garfinkel and Nemhauser [1972] for the latter.

1. BACKGROUND

1.1. Set Partitioning and its Uses

Among all special structures in integer programming, there are three which have the most wide-spread applications: set partitioning, set covering and the traveling salesman (or minimum length hamiltonian cycle) problem; and if we were to rank the three, set partitioning would probably be number one.

The (weighted) set partitioning (or equality-constrained set covering) problem is

$$\text{(SPP)} \qquad \min \{cx \mid Ax = e,\ x_j = 0 \text{ or } 1,\ \forall\, j \in N\}$$

where A is an m $\times$ n matrix of zeroes and ones, c is an arbitrary n-vector, e = (1,...,1) is an m-vector, and $N = \{1,\dots,n\}$. Its name comes from the following interpretation: if the rows of A are associated with the elements of the set $M = \{1,\dots,m\}$ and each column a_j of A with the subset M_j of those $i \in M$ such that $a_{ij} = 1$, then (SPP) is the problem of finding a minimum-weight family of subsets M_j, $j \in N$, which is a partition of M, each subset M_j being weighted with c_j.

A partial list of applications described in the literature includes: railroad crew scheduling, truck deliveries, airline crew scheduling, tanker routing, information retrieval, switching circuit design, stock cutting, assembly line balancing, capital equipment decisions, location of offshore drilling platforms, some other facility location problems, political districting, etc. A special bibliography on applications is attached to the paper.

A great variety of scheduling problems can be formulated as follows.

Given

(i) a finite set M;

(ii) a constraint set defining a family F of "acceptable" subsets of M; and

(iii) a cost (real number) associated with each member of F;

find a minimum-cost collection of members of F which is a partition of M.

The usefulness and wide applicability of the set partitioning model follows from the simple observation that in most cases a problem of the above form can be solved to a satisfactory degree of approximation by the following two-stage procedure:

Stage 1. Using (ii), generate explicitly a subset $\bar{F} \subset F$, such that the probability of an optimal solution being contained in $\bar{F}$ is sufficiently high.

Stage 2. Replace the constraint set (ii) by a list of the members of $\bar{F}$ and solve the resulting (SPP).

The most widely used application to date of the set partitioning model seems to be the airline crew scheduling problem, in which M corresponds to the set of flight legs (from city A to city B, at time t) to be covered during a planning period (usually a few days), while each subset M_j stands for a possible tour (sequence of flight legs with the same initial and terminal point) for a crew. In order to be acceptable, a tour must satisfy certain regulations. To set up the problem, one starts with a given set of (usually several hundred) flight legs, and one generates by computer a set of (usually several thousand) acceptable tours, with their respective costs. This produces A (of density usually $\leq .05$) and $c > 0$, after which one attempts to solve the set partitioning problem. If the attempt is successful, the solution yields a minimum-cost collection of acceptable tours such that each flight leg is included in exactly one tour of the collection.

Airline crew scheduling problems with 300-500 constraints and 2,500-4,000 variables are sometimes solved (to optimality); but often much smaller problems (with several hundred variables) defy solution within reasonable time limits.

1.2. Set Packing and Set Covering

The set partitioning problem (SPP) has two seemingly close relatives, the set packing problem

(SP) $\quad \max \{c'x \mid Ax \leq e,\ x_j = 0 \text{ or } 1,\ \forall\, j \in N\}$

and the set covering problem

(SC) $\quad \min \{c''x \mid Ax \geq e,\ x_j = 0 \text{ or } 1,\ \forall\, j \in N\}$,

where A, e and N are defined as in (SPP), while c' and c'' are arbitrary n-vectors.

At a closer look, however, it turns out that (SC) is a much more distant relative than (SP). Intuitively, one can guess this from the fact that (SP), like (SPP), is a "tightly constrained" problem (each constraint requires at most one, or exactly one, of many variables to be 1), whereas (SC) is a "loosely constrained" problem (at least one of many variables is required to be 1). More precisely, the relationship is as follows.

(SPP) can be brought to the form (SC) by writing

$$\min \{cx + \theta ey \mid Ax - y = e,\ y \geq 0,\ x_j = 0 \text{ or } 1,\ j \in N\}$$

and then, using $y = Ax - e$,

$$\min \{-\theta m + c'x \mid Ax \geq e,\ x_j = 0 \text{ or } 1,\ j \in N\},$$

with $c' = \theta eA + c$. For sufficiently large θ (e.g., $\theta > \sum_{j \in N} c_j$), this problem has the same set of optimal solutions as (SPP) whenever the latter is feasible (see Lemke, Salkin and Spielberg, [1971]). The converse, however, is not true, i.e., (SC) cannot be brought to the form (SPP).

On the other hand, (SP) is a special case of (SPP); and conversely, (SPP) can be restated as

$$\max \{\theta m + c''x \mid Ax \leq e,\ x_j = 0 \text{ or } 1,\ j \in N\},$$

with $c'' = \theta eA - c$; and again, for θ sufficiently large, this problem has the same set of optimal solutions as (SPP), whenever the latter is feasible.

The equivalence of (SP) and (SPP) is crucial to some of the results to be discussed.

Next we turn to a family of four interrelated problems defined on an undirected graph, two of which are special cases of (SP).

1.3. Edge Matching and Covering, Node Packing and Covering

Let $G = (N,E)$ be a finite undirected graph with $n = |N|$ nodes and $q = |E|$ edges. Let A_G be the $n \times q$ node-edge incidence matrix of G, e_n and e_q the n-vector and q-vector respectively, whose components are all 1.

An <u>edge matching</u> in G is a subset E' of edges such that every node of G is incident with at most one edge in E'. If every node of G is incident with exactly one edge in E', then E' is a perfect matching. An edge cover (a covering of nodes by edges) in G is a subset E'' of edges such that every node of G is incident with at least one edge in E''. The edge matching problem, or the problem of finding a maximum-cardinality edge matching in G, is then

$$\text{(EM)} \qquad \max \{e_q y \mid A_G y \leq e_n , \; y_i = 0 \text{ or } 1, \; i = 1,\ldots,q\}$$

while the edge covering problem, or the problem of finding a minimum-cardinality edge cover in G, is

$$\text{(EC)} \qquad \min \{e_q y \mid A_G y \geq e_n, \; y_i = 0 \text{ or } 1, \; i = 1,\ldots,q\} .$$

A node packing (vertex packing) in G is a subset N' of nodes such that every edge of G is incident with at most one node in N'. A node cover (covering of edges by nodes) in G is a subset N'' of nodes such that every edge of G is incident with at least one node in N''. The node packing problem, or the problem of finding a maximum-cardinality node packing (internally stable node set, independent node set) in G, is then

$$\text{(NP)} \qquad \max \{e_n x \mid A_G^T x \leq e_q, \; x_j = 0 \text{ or } 1, \; j = 1,\ldots,n\}$$

while the node covering problem, or the problem of finding a minimum cardinality node cover in G, is

$$\text{(NC)} \qquad \min \{e_n x \mid A_G^T x \geq e_q, \; x_j = 0 \text{ or } 1, \; j = 1,\ldots,n\}.$$

If α_0, β_0, α_1 and β_1 is the cardinality of a maximum node packing, minimum node cover, maximum edge matching and minimum edge cover in G respectively, then these four numbers are connected by the following simple formula:

Theorem 1.3.1. (Gallai [1959]). For any nontrivial connected graph G with n nodes,

$$\alpha_0 + \beta_0 = n = \alpha_1 + \beta_1 .$$

A maximum edge matching and a minimum edge cover are easily obtained from each other; and the same is true of a maximum node packing and a minimum node cover.

Clearly, (EM) and (NP) are special cases of (SP). The problem of finding a perfect edge matching, obtained from (EM) by replacing the inequality with equality, is on the other hand a special case of (SPP).

When G is bipartite, A_G is totally unimodular and the four integer programs listed above can be replaced by the associated linear programs.

In the general case, Edmonds [1965] has characterized the facets of the edge matching polytope (the convex hull of feasible integer solutions), and given an algorithm of complexity $O(n^3)$ for solving (EM) or its weighted version (in which e_q is replaced by an arbitrary integer vector), based on the above characterization and Berge's [1958] theorem of alternating chains.

The second pair of problems is more difficult. Balinski [1967] has obtained a characterization of maximum node packings in terms of alternating subgraphs, but no polynomially bounded algorithm is known for the solution of this problem. More recently, several classes of facets of the node packing polytope have been characterized (see Padberg [1971], 1973]; Nemhauser and Trotter [1973], Trotter [1974]).

1.4. Node Packing, Set Packing, Clique Covering

Denote by a_j the j-th column of the matrix A of (SP). The intersection graph $G_A = (N,E)$ of A has one node for every column of A, and one edge for every pair of nonorthogonal columns of A [i.e., $(i,j) \in E$ if and only if $a_i a_j \geq 1$]. Let A_G be the node-edge incidence matrix of G_A, and denote by (NP) the weighted node packing problem whose weights c_j are the same for each node as those of (SP), i.e.,

$$\text{(NP)} \qquad \max \{cx \mid A_G^T x \leq e_q,\ x_j = 0 \text{ or } 1,\ j = 1,\dots,n\}.$$

Remark 1.4.1. (Padberg [1971]) x is a feasible (optimal) solution to (SP) if and only if it is a feasible (optimal) solution to (NP).

Thus, one way of solving set packing (and set partitioning) problems, is to solve the associated node packing problem. Obviously, A_G^T has a more special structure than A (exactly two ones per column). Note, however, that while the two integer programs are equivalent, the two associated linear programs are not:

Remark 1.4.2. $\max \{cx \mid Ax \leq e_m,\ x \geq 0\} \leq \max \{cx \mid A_G^T x \leq e_q,\ x \geq 0\}$

It can easily be seen that the linear program associated with (SP) is more tightly constrained and that, apart from very special situations (e.g., when G is bipartite), the above relation holds with strict inequality.

A clique in G is a maximal complete subgraph. A clique covering of the edges of G is a set K of cliques such that each edge of G belongs to the edge set of some clique in K.

Remark 1.4.3. (Padberg [1973]). Let K be a clique covering of the edges of G, and let A_K be the incidence matrix of the cliques in K (rows of A_K) versus the nodes of G (columns of A_K). Then (SP) is equivalent to (has the same set of feasible and optimal solutions respectively, as) the set packing problem obtained from (SP) by replacing A with A_K.

Thus, many (seemingly different) set packing problems are equivalent to the same (unique) node packing problem (NP).

A clique covering of the nodes of G is a set K' of cliques such that each node of G belongs to the node set of some clique in K'.

The clique matrix A_C of G is the incidence matrix of the set C of all cliques in G (rows of A_C) versus the nodes of G (columns of A_C). In view of the last remark, the unweighted node packing problem is equivalent to

$$(SP_C) \qquad \max \{e_n x \mid A_C x \leq e_C,\ x_j = 0 \text{ or } 1,\ j = 1,\ldots,n\}\ ,$$

where $e_C = (1,\ldots,1)$ is dimensioned compatibly with A_C.

Consider now the problem of finding a minimum-cardinality clique covering of the nodes of G:

$$(KC) \qquad \min \{e_C y \mid A_C^T y \geq e_n,\ y_i = 0 \text{ or } 1,\ i = 1,\ldots,|C|\}\ .$$

If $\alpha_o(G)$ is the value of an optimal solution to (SP_C), i.e., the cardinality of a maximum independent node set in G, and $\omega_0(G)$ the value of an optimal solution to (KC), i.e., the cardinality of a minimum clique covering of the nodes of G, then $\alpha_o(G) \leq \omega_0(G)$, since the linear programs associated with the two problems are dual to each other. Further, $\alpha_o(G) = \omega_0(G)$ if and only if both linear programs have integral optimal solutions.

The subgraph of $G = (N,E)$ induced by a subset N' of the nodes of G, is $G' = (N',E')$, where $(i,j) \in E' \iff i \in N', j \in N', (i,j) \in E$. The complement $\bar{G}$ of a graph $G = (N,\bar{E})$, is the graph $\bar{G} = (N,\bar{E})$, where $(i,j) \in \bar{E} \iff (i,j) \notin E$. A chordless cycle C in G is a cycle each of whose nodes is adjacent to exactly two other nodes of C. A cycle is called odd or even according to whether it is of odd or even length. A cycle of length 3 is obviously chordless, and is a clique. A chordless cycle of length greater than 3 is called a hole, its complement an anti-hole.

A graph $G = (N,E)$ such that $\alpha_o(G') = \omega_o(G')$ for all induced subgraphs G' of G is called perfect. The perfect graph theorem, conjectured by Berge [1961] and proved by Lovász [1972] (see also Fulkerson [1971], [1973]) asserts that G is perfect if and only if its complement $\bar{G}$ is perfect. Further, it is known that G is perfect if and only if all vertices of the polytope

$$P = \{x \in R^n | A_C x \leq e_C , x \geq 0\}$$

are integral (Chvátal [1972]). Finally, the strong perfect graph conjecture (Berge [1970]) asserts that G is perfect if and only if it contains no odd holes or anti-holes.

An alternative way of looking at arbitrary zero-one matrices is via the theory of hypergraphs (see Berge [1970]). A hypergraph is a pair $H = (N, \mathcal{E})$, where N is a set of elements called nodes, and $\mathcal{E}$ is a family of nonempty subsets of N, called edges. The incidence matrix $A = (a_{ij})$ of the hypergraph H has a column for every node and a row for every edge of H, with $a_{ij} = 1$ if node j is contained in edge i, $a_{ij} = 0$ otherwise. Every 0-1 matrix which has no zero rows or zero columns is the incidence matrix of some hypergraph. Thus (SP) and (SPP) can be formulated in terms of hypergraphs (see Berge [1970]; Lovász [1972]).

2. THEORY

2.1. Facets of the Set Packing Polytope

Throughout this paper, we assume that A has no zero rows or columns. Then the constraint sets of the linear programs associated with (SP) and (SPP) are bounded.

Let

$$P = \{x \in R^n | Ax \leq e, x \geq 0\}$$

where A is the coefficient matrix of (SP), and let P_I be the set packing polytope, i.e., the convex hull of points satisfying the constraints of (SP):

$$P_I = \text{conv} \{x \in P | x \text{ integer}\} .$$

We first note that dim P = dim P_I = n. A <u>facet</u>, or (n-1)-dimensional face, of P_I, is a set $P_I \cap \{x \in R^n | \pi x = \pi_o\}$ such that $\pi x \leq \pi_o$, $\forall$ x $\in P_I$, and $\pi x = \pi_o$ for exactly n affinely independent points x $\in P_I$. As customary in the literature, an inequality $\pi x \leq \pi_o$ defining a facet will itself be called a facet. It is easily seen that each inequality $x_j \geq 0$, j$\in$N, is a (trivial) facet of P_I. From the non-negativity of A it follows easily that every facet $\pi x \leq \pi_o$ of P_I that is different from the above trivial facets satisfies $\pi_j \geq 0$ for j$\in$N and $\pi_o > 0$. We first examine the conditions under which some of the constraints Ax $\leq$ e themselves are facets of P_I. As before, G_A denotes the intersection graph of A. The next theorem is from Padberg [1973]; but it also follows from Theorem 8 of Fulkerson [1971].

<u>Theorem 2.1.1.</u> The inequality

$$\sum_{j\in K} x_j \leq 1$$

where K$\subseteq$N, is a facet of P_I if and only if K is the node set of a clique in G_A.

As a direct consequence, the polytope

$$P_C = \{x \in R^n | A_C x \leq e_C \ , \ x \geq 0\}$$

where A_C is, as before, the clique matrix of G_A, satisfies $P_I \subseteq P_C \subseteq P$. In general, P_C is different from P_I as well as from P. There is, however, a large class of matrices A for which the three polytopes P, P_C and P_I <u>coincide</u>, i.e., P = P_C = P_I. Zero-one matrices with this property are called <u>perfect</u> and can be characterized in terms of certain "forbidden" submatrices.

Let A' be a m x k zero-one matrix, with m $\geq$ k. A' is said to have the <u>property</u> $\pi_{\beta,k}$ if the following conditions are met:

(i) A' contains a k x k nonsingular submatrix A_1' whose row and column sums are all equal to β.

(ii) Each row of A' which is not a row of A_1', either is componentwise equal to some row of A_1', or has row sum strictly less than β.

<u>Theorem 2.1.2.</u> (Padberg [1974]). The following two conditions are equivalent for an arbitrary m x n zero-one matrix A:

(i) A is perfect, i.e., $P = P_C = P_I$.

(ii) For $\beta \geq 2$ and $3 \leq k \leq n$, A does not contain any $m \times k$ submatrix A' having the property $\pi_{\beta,k}$.

Perfect matrices are closely related to perfect graphs (Berge [1970]), and normal hypergraphs (Lovász [1972]). They properly subsume nonnegative totally unimodular matrices, as well as balanced matrices (Berge [1972]). As mentioned in section 1.4, the clique-matrices of perfect graphs are all perfect.

Whenever $P_C \neq P$, a facet of P_I of the type characterized by Theorem 2.1.1 is absent from the constraint set defining P. Facets of P_I of that type are easy to detect. In general, however, more complicated types of inequalities are needed in order to characterize P_I. A second class of facets of P_I is obtainable from the odd holes and odd anti-holes of G_A. Part (i) of the next theorem is from Padberg [1973], part (ii) is from Nemhauser and Trotter [1974].

Theorem 2.1.3. For any $S \subseteq N$, let

$T(S) = \{j \in N-S \mid a_k a_j \geq 1 \text{ for some } k \in S\}$.

If S defines either (i) an odd hole, or (ii) an odd anti-hole, in G_A, then there exist integers β_j satisfying $0 \leq \beta_j \leq s$ for $j \in T(S)$ such that

$$\sum_{j \in S} x_j + \sum_{j \in T(S)} \beta_j x_j \leq s$$

is a facet of P_I with $s = 1/2\,(|S| - 1)$ in case (i) and $s = 2$ in case (ii).

Theorem 2.1.3 defines a two-step procedure for generating facets of P_I. In step 1, a subset $S \subseteq N$ is found such that the subgraph G' of G induced by S is an odd hole or anti-hole. If P_I' is the set packing polytope defined on G' (in the same way as P_I is defined on G), then

$$\sum_{j \in S} x_j \leq s$$

is a facet of P_I', with $s = 1/2\,(|S| - 1)$ if G' is an odd hole, and $s = 2$ if G' is an odd anti-hole.

In step 2, a facet of P_I is obtained by "lifting" the above facet of P_I' into the space of P_I, i.e., by calculating the coefficients β_j for $j \in T(S)$.

This two-step procedure can be generalized to obtain facets of P_I from facets of any lower-dimensional set packing polytope P_I' defined on some induced subgraph G' of G:

<u>Theorem 2.1.4</u>. (Nemhauser and Trotter [1974]). Let P_I' be the set packing polytope defined on the subgraph G' of G induced by $S \subset N$. If

$$\sum_{j \in S} \alpha_j x_j \leq s$$

is a facet of P_I', then there exist integers β_j, $0 \leq \beta_j \leq s$, such that

$$\sum_{j \in S} \alpha_j x_j + \sum_{j \in N-S} \beta_j x_j \leq s$$

is a facet of P_I.

Padberg's procedure for calculating the coefficients β_j requires the solution of a sequence of set packing problems (one for each β_j) of a special type in the variables $j \in S \cup S'$, where S' is the set of those $j \in N-S$ for which β_j has already been computed. The sequence in which the coefficients β_j are computed does matter, and different sequences may give rise to different facets. Obviously, these facets of P_I are computationally much more expensive than those of Theorem 2.1.1.

Generalizations of this class of facets to other than set packing and set partitioning polytopes are given in Padberg [1973b], Nemhauser and Trotter [1974], Balas [1973], Hammer, Johnson and Peled [1973], Wolsey [1973].

The facets of Theorems 2.1.1 and 2.1.3 were obtained from cliques and odd holes or anti-holes, all of which share the property of being <u>regular</u> graphs (i.e., graphs whose nodes have all the same degree). It turns out that the facet producing property of these graphs generalizes to a larger class of regular graphs.

A web, denoted $W_{(n,k)}$ (Trotter [1974]) is a graph $G = (N,E)$ such that $|N| = n \geq 3$ and for all $i,j \in N$,

$$(i,j) \in E \iff j = i + k, i + k + 1, \ldots, i + n - k$$

(where sums are taken modulo n), with $1 \leq k \leq [n/2]$. The web $W_{(n,k)}$ is regular of degree $n - 2k + 1$, and has exactly n maximum node packings of size k. The complement $\bar{W}_{(n,k)}$ of a web $W_{(n,k)}$ is regular of degree $2(k - 1)$ and has exactly n maximum cliques of size k.

Theorem 2.1.5. (Trotter [1974]). Let G' be the subgraph of G induced by $S \subseteq N$, let $s = |S|$, and let P_I' be the set packing polytope defined on G'.

(i) If G' is a web, $G' = W_{(s,k)}$, the inequality

$$\sum_{j \in S} x_j \leq k$$

is a facet of P_I' if and only if s and k are relatively prime.

(ii) If G' is the complement of a web, $G' = \bar{W}_{(s,k)}$, with s and k relatively prime, then

$$\sum_{j \in S} x_j \leq [s/k]$$

is a facet of P_I'.

Facets of P_I can then be obtained from the above facets of P_I' by using Padberg's procedure for calculating the coefficients β_j, $j \in N-S$.

The facets described in the above theorems do not fully characterize P_I, i.e., do not exhaust the family of facets of P_I. To illustrate this, consider the graph G of Fig. 1, whose clique-matrix is

$$A = \begin{pmatrix} 1 & 0 & 0 & 0 & 0 & 0 & 1 & 0 & 0 & 0 \\ 1 & 1 & 0 & 0 & 0 & 0 & 0 & 0 & 0 & 0 \\ 0 & 1 & 1 & 0 & 0 & 0 & 0 & 1 & 0 & 0 \\ 0 & 0 & 1 & 1 & 0 & 0 & 0 & 0 & 0 & 0 \\ 0 & 0 & 0 & 1 & 1 & 0 & 0 & 0 & 0 & 1 \\ 0 & 0 & 0 & 0 & 1 & 1 & 0 & 0 & 0 & 0 \\ 0 & 0 & 0 & 0 & 0 & 1 & 1 & 0 & 0 & 0 \\ 0 & 0 & 0 & 0 & 0 & 0 & 0 & 1 & 1 & 0 \\ 0 & 0 & 0 & 0 & 0 & 0 & 0 & 0 & 1 & 1 \end{pmatrix}$$

G:

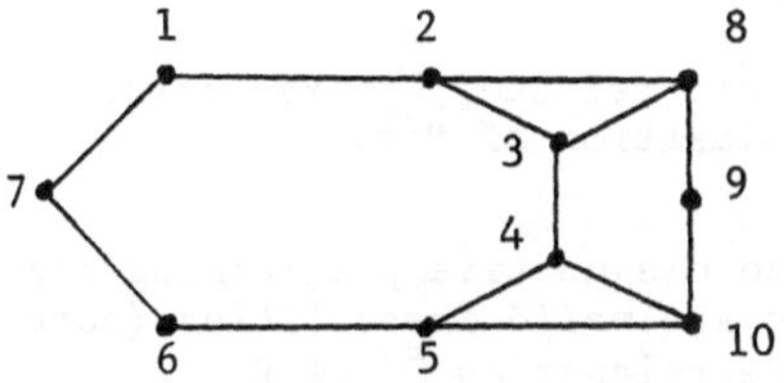

Figure 1

There are two facets of the associated P_I, given by $\sum_{j=1}^{7} x_j \leq 3$ and $x_3 + x_4 + x_8 + x_9 + x_{10} \leq 2$ that are obtained from an application of Theorem 2.1.3. The inequality $\sum_{j=1}^{10} x_j \leq 4$, however, is a facet of P_I that is not obtainable from an odd hole or anti-hole; nor is it obtainable from a web or its complement. Instead, this inequality is related to the concept of a hypo-matchable graph, introduced by Pulleyblank and Edmonds [1973] in the context of the matching polytope. Chvátal [1972] has obtained some results concerning the conditions under which facets obtained from cliques and odd holes fully characterize P_I.

Since not all facets of P_I are of a known form, and the facets whose form is known seem to be, with the exception of those of Theorem 2.1.1, computationally rather expensive, for practical purposes one has to look for cutting planes which, though they are not facets of P_I, have other desirable properties. In the next section we introduce some valid inequalities which are facets of polytopes obtained from the set partitioning polytope by relaxing some of the constraints of (SPP). While these cutting planes are weaker than the facets of P_I, they are easy to compute and have some other desirable properties.

2.2. Facets of Relaxed Polytopes: Cuts from Disjunctions

Let $\bar{P}$ be the feasible set of the linear program associated with (SPP),

i.e., $\bar{P} = \{x \in R^n | Ax = e, x \geq 0\}$,

and let

$$\bar{P}_I = \text{conv } \{x \in \bar{P} | x \text{ integer}\}$$

be the set partitioning polytope.

If some constraints of $\bar{P}$ are relaxed, the resulting polytope $\bar{P}'(\bar{P}_I')$ will be called a relaxation of $\bar{P}(\bar{P}_I)$.

In this section we use the disjunctive programming approach of Balas [1974a, 1974b] to generate valid inequalities (cutting planes) which are facets of some relaxation $\bar{P}_I'$ of $\bar{P}_I$.

By disjunctive programming we mean linear programming with disjunctive constraints. Integer programs (pure or mixed) and a host of other nonconvex programming problems can be stated as linear programs with logical conditions, and the latter can always be expressed as a disjunction between sets of linear inequalities. Special cases of this class of problems have been examined by several authors in the past (see Glover and Klingman [1972, 1973], Owen [1973], Zwart [1972]). However, a theoretical study of the general disjunctive programming problem has only recently been undertaken (see Balas [1974a, 1974b], Jeroslow [1974]).

Not only can integer programs be formulated as disjunctive programs, but for special structures, like (SPP) and (SP), as well as other combinatorial problems, such a formulation offers definite advantages. Cutting planes can be obtained which are computationally cheap, and have the important feature of displaying coefficients of different signs, unlike the traditional cuts; a property which tends to mitigate the tendency towards dual degeneracy, common to cutting plane algorithms (for background on the latter, see Garfinkel and Nemhauser [1972]).

The disjunctive normal form of a disjunctive program is

(DP) $\min \{cx | x \in F\}$

where

$$F = \{x \in R^n | \bigvee_{h \in Q} (A^h x \geq b^h , x \geq 0)\}$$

and where each A^h is an $m_h \times n$ matrix, each b^h is an m_h-vector, while " $\vee$" stands for "or," i.e., at least one of the $|Q|$ systems $A^h x \geq b^h$, $x \geq 0$, must hold. It is usually convenient to express the problem in the nonbasic variables associated with an optimal solution to the linear program; for in that case one can view the inequalities $\alpha x \geq \alpha_o$ implied by the constraints of F as potential cutting planes, which cut off the current solution $x = 0$ if and only if $\alpha_o > 0$.

Let Q* be the set of those $h \epsilon Q$ such that

$$\{x \epsilon R^n | A^h x \geq b^h , x \geq 0\} \neq \emptyset.$$

Theorem 2.2.1. (Balas [1974b]).

(i) $\alpha x \geq \alpha_o$ is a valid inequality for (DP) (i.e., is satisfied by all $x \epsilon F$) if and only if there exist vectors $\theta^h \epsilon R^{m_h}$, $h \epsilon Q^*$, such that

$$\alpha \geq \theta^h A^h , \alpha_o \leq \theta^h b^h , \theta^h \geq 0 , h \epsilon Q^* .$$

Further, if conv F is closed and full dimensional, then (ii) and (iii) holds:

(ii) If $\alpha_o \neq 0$, $\alpha x \geq \alpha_o$ is a facet of conv F if and only if $\alpha \neq 0$ is a vertex of

$$F^{\#} = \left\{ y \epsilon R^n \;\middle|\; \begin{array}{l} y \geq \theta^h A^h \\ \theta^h b^h \geq \alpha_o \\ \theta^h \geq 0 , \forall h \epsilon Q^* \end{array} \right\}$$

(iii) If $\alpha x \geq 0$ is a facet of conv F, then $\alpha \neq 0$ is an extreme direction vector of $F^{\#}$.

Remark 2.2.1. If some of the inequalities of F are replaced by equalities, Theorem 2.2.1 holds without the nonnegativity constraint on the corresponding components of the vector θ.

The vertices of the set $F^{\#}$, which define the facets of conv F, can be obtained by solving a linear program. When Q is large, this may be hopeless, though the linear program is strongly structured. However, by relaxing part of the constraints of (SPP) and retaining only a convenient subset, one can take advantage of the structure imposed by the latter so as to solve the resulting linear program trivially.

For instance, let the linear program associated with (SPP) have an optimal solution of the form

$$x_i = a_{io} + \sum_{j\epsilon J} a_{ij}(-t_j) \ , \ i\epsilon I \cup J$$

where I and J are the basic and nonbasic index sets respectively (i.e., for $i\epsilon J$, $a_{io} = 0$ and $a_{ij} = 0$ for $i \neq j$, $a_{ij} = -1$ for $i = j$), and let

$$\sum_{j\epsilon Q} x_j = 1$$

be one of the constraints of (SPP), such that $\{i\epsilon Q | 0 < a_{io} < 1\} \neq \emptyset$. Let $Q = \{1,\ldots,q\}$. Note that this equality is satisfied by the current solution, so it cannot be used as a cut. However, the logical condition that it expresses, namely that exactly one of the variables x_j, $j\epsilon Q$, must be one, and all the others zero, i.e.,

$$\bigvee_{i\epsilon Q} (x_i = 1 \ , \ \sum_{h\epsilon Q-\{i\}} x_h = 0)$$

is stronger than the above linear equality without the 0-1 constraints on the variables, and can be used to generate a cut.

Let $\sigma = (\sigma_i)$ be a q-vector, where $q = |Q|$, such that $0 \leq \sigma_i \leq 1$, $\forall \ i\epsilon Q$. If the numbers σ_i, $1-\sigma_i$ are used to take convex combinations of the two equations within each member of the above disjunction, the latter becomes

$$\bigvee_{i\epsilon Q} [(1-\sigma_i)x_i + \sigma_i(\sum_{h\epsilon Q-\{i\}} x_h) = 1-\sigma_i]$$

Consider now the family of relaxations of $\bar{P}_I$ whose members are of the form conv $F(\sigma)$, for some $\sigma \ \epsilon \ R^q$ such that $0 \leq \sigma_i \leq 1$, $i\epsilon Q$, where

$$F(\sigma) = \left\{ t\epsilon R^n \ \middle| \ \begin{array}{l} x_i = a_{io} + \sum_{j\epsilon J} a_{ij}(-t_j), \ i\epsilon I \cap Q \\ t_j \geq 0 \ , \ j\epsilon J \\ \bigvee_{i\epsilon Q} [(1-\sigma_i)x_i - \sigma_i\left(\sum_{h\epsilon Q-\{i\}} x_h\right) = 1 - \sigma_i] \end{array} \right\}$$

The family of cuts defined in the next theorem is from Balas [1974a]. The fact that it represents the family of those facets of conv $F(\sigma)$ which cut off the current solution follows from Theorem 4.5 of Balas [1974b].

Theorem 2.2.2. For every $\sigma \in R^q$ such that $0 \leq \sigma_i \leq 1$, $\forall$ $i \in Q$, the unique facet of conv $F(\sigma)$ which cuts off the solution $t_j = 0$, $j \in J$, is

$$\sum_{j \in J} \alpha_j(\sigma) t_j \geq 1$$

where

$$\alpha_j(\sigma) = \max_{i \in Q} (\sigma_i \sum_{h \in Q} a_{hj} - a_{ij})(1 - a_{io})^{-1}, \quad j \in J.$$

These cuts are computationally not expensive, and one has some freedom in choosing the parameters σ_i so as to make the cut stronger in one direction or another. A very convenient choice of the parameters, which makes the cut particularly easy to compute, is $\sigma_i = (1 - a_{io})$, $\forall$ $i \in Q$, which yields

$$\alpha_j = \sum_{h \in Q} a_{hj} - \min_{i \in Q} a_{ij}(1 - a_{io})^{-1}.$$

Note that this cut is likely to have many negative entries, since the coefficients a_{hj} of the current simplex tableau are of arbitrary signs.

The next theorem gives two additional cuts (see Balas [1974a]) which can be shown to be facets of appropriate relaxations of $\bar{P}_I$.

Theorem 2.2.3. Let $Q' = \{i \in Q | 0 < a_{io} < 1\}$. For the definitions (i) and (ii) of the coefficients α_j, $j \in J$,

$$\sum_{j \in J} \alpha_j t_j \geq 1$$

is a valid inequality for (DP):

(i) $$\alpha_j = \max_{i \in Q_2'} \frac{a_{ij}}{a_{io}}$$

where Q_2' is any subset of size 2 of Q';

$$\text{(ii) } \alpha_j = \begin{cases} \frac{1}{|Q'|} \sum_{i\epsilon Q'} \frac{a_{ij}}{a_{io}} & \text{, if } j\epsilon J \cap Q \text{ or } a_{ij} \geq 0,\ \forall\ i\epsilon Q \\ \frac{1}{|Q'|} \left[\sum_{i\epsilon Q'} \frac{a_{ij}}{a_{io}} - \min_{i\epsilon Q'} \frac{a_{ij}}{a_{io}(1-a_{io})} \right] & \text{, if } j\epsilon J \sim Q \text{ and } a_{ij} < 0 \text{ for some } i\epsilon Q. \end{cases}$$

The cuts defined by (i) are the easiest to compute among those of the last two theorems, and one has complete freedom in choosing two rows of Q'. It is reasonable to choose a pair of rows with the largest number of columns having negative entries in both rows; this yields a cut $\sum_{j\epsilon J} \alpha_j t_j \geq 1$ with exactly that number of negative α_j.

As to the cut defined by (ii), its coefficients are obtained, roughly speaking, by taking averages of the coefficients a_{ij}/a_{io}, $i\epsilon Q'$, of each column. Since the coefficients a_{ij}/a_{io} have arbitrary signs, the larger the set Q', the more likely it is that the coefficients α_j will be small in comparison with the right hand side of 1, i.e., that the cut will be strong.

The use of cutting planes in solving set partitioning problems is discussed in Part 3.

2.3. Adjacent Vertices of the Set Partitioning and Set Packing Polytopes

Integer programmers have often been puzzled by the frequency of the occurrence of integer solutions among the basic solutions to the linear program associated with (SPP), which we will call (LSPP). This is one of the features which makes (SPP) relatively easily accessible to cutting plane methods: a few cuts applied to a fractional tableau, even very large, often (though not always) yield an integer solution. The results to be discussed below throw some light on this phenomenon.

On the other hand, the linear program associated with (SPP) is often difficult to handle, because of the large size, massive degeneracy, and the lack of any specialized technique to take advantage of the structure at hand. Thus, solving the linear program usually becomes the bottleneck of cutting plane algorithms

Therefore, it is potentially of great practical interest to know that, due to certain adjacency properties of the vertices of $\bar{P}$ and $\bar{P}_I$, the set partitioning problem can in principle be solved by a modified version of the simplex method, generating only integer solutions and not using any cutting planes. More precisely, the following is true, where two bases of (LSPP) are called adjacent if they differ by only one column, i.e., can be obtained from each other by one pivot.

Theorem 2.3.1. (Balas and Padberg [1972a]). Let x^1 be a feasible integer (but not optimal) solution to (LSPP) associated with the basis B_1. If x^2 is an optimal solution to (SPP), then there exists a sequence of adjacent bases $B_{10}, B_{11}, B_{12}, \ldots, B_{1p}$, such that $B_{10} = B_1$, $B_{1p} = B_2$ is a basis asociated with x^2, and

(i) the basic solutions $x^{1i} = B_{1i}^{-1}e$, $i = 0, 1, \ldots, p$, are all feasible and integer,

(ii) $cx^{10} \geq cx^{11} \geq \ldots \geq cx^{1p}$; and

(iii) $p = |J_1 \cap Q_2|$, where J_1 is the index set of nonbasic variables associated with B_1, while $Q_2 = \{j \in N | x_j^2 = 1\}$.

Statement (iii) of the above theorem proves the famous Hirsch conjecture (see Dantzig [1963], p. 168) for the special class of linear programs discussed here if it is restricted to integer solutions only, since clearly $p \leq m$.

Two vertices of a polytope are adjacent if they lie on an edge, i.e., are contained in a one-dimensional face, of the polytope. Theorem 2.3.1 implies that, given a basic feasible integer solution x^1 to (LSPP), there is a better integer solution if and only if there is one which is a vertex of $\bar{P}$, the feasible polytope of (LSPP), adjacent to x^1. The difficulty lies in identifying such adjacent vertices. Since set partitioning problems tend to be highly degenerate, there are many bases associated with the same solution; and there is a very large number of vertices of (LSPP) adjacent to a given vertex. Furthermore, lexicographic or similar techniques are of no avail in coping with degeneracy, since the sequence of pivots required to reach an adjacent vertex may include pivots on a negative entry in a degenerate row (i.e., a row with $a_{io} = 0$). What is needed therefore, is a detailed knowledge of adjacency relations among integer vertices of $\bar{P}$.

Next we give a constructive characterization of such adjacency relations, based on Balas and Padberg [1972b], which makes it possible to generate all edges of $\bar{P}$ connecting a given integer vertex to integer adjacent vertices.

We start out with a general characterization of an integer vertex of $\bar{P}$ in terms of any other integer vertex, and an associated basis.

Given a basic feasible integer solution x^1 to (LSPP), with associated basis B_1 and (basic and nonbasic) index sets $I_1 = \{1,\ldots,m\}$, J_1, $(I_1 \cup J_1 = N)$, we will denote $\bar{a}_j = B_1^{-1} a_j$, $\bar{a}^j = \begin{pmatrix} \bar{a}_j \\ -e_j \end{pmatrix}$, where e_j is the (n-m)-dimensional unit vector with 1 in position j, and

$$Q_1 = \{j \in N | x_j^1 = 1\} \quad , \quad \bar{Q}_1 = N - Q_1 \ .$$

Theorem 2.3.2. (Balas and Padberg [1972b]). Let x^1 be a basic feasible integer solution to (LSPP). Then x^2 is a basic feasible integer solution to (LSPP) if and only if there exists $Q \subseteq J_1$ such that

$$(1) \quad \sum_{j \in Q} \bar{a}_{kj} = \begin{cases} 0 \text{ or } 1 & k \in Q_1 \\ 0 \text{ or } -1 & k \in I_1 \cap \bar{Q}_1 \end{cases}$$

and

$$x_j^2 = \begin{cases} 1 & j \in Q_2 = Q \cup S \\ 0 & \text{otherwise} \end{cases}$$

where

$$S = \{k \in Q_1 | \sum_{j \in Q} \bar{a}_{kj} = 0\} \cup \{k \in I_1 \cap \bar{Q}_1 | \sum_{j \in Q} \bar{a}_{kj} = -1\}.$$

When this condition holds, then

$$x^2 = x^1 - \sum_{j \in Q} \bar{a}^j \ .$$

The next theorem characterizes adjacent integer vertices of $\bar{P}$. From the last part of Theorem 2.3.2, it follows that x^2 is an integer vertex adjacent to x^1 on $\bar{P}$ if and only if

$$\Lambda = \{x \in R^n | x = x^1 - (\sum_{j \in Q} \bar{a}^j)\lambda, \ 0 \leq \lambda \leq 1\}$$

is an edge (1-dimensional face) of $\bar{P}$ which is also an edge of $\bar{P}_I$. The necessary and sufficient condition for this to be true is given in terms of a certain property of the set of columns indexed by Q.

Given a basic feasible integer solution x^1, with J_1 defined as above, a set $Q \subset J_1$ which satisfies (1) is called <u>decomposable</u>, if it can be partitioned into two subsets Q* and Q**, such that (1) remains true when Q is replaced by Q* and Q** respectively. This concept of decomposability is used in the next theorem to characterize pairs of adjacent integer vertices of $\bar{P}$ in terms of a basis associated with one member of the pair. While this characterization can be used directly to generate the integer vertices adjacent to a given vertex from any simplex tableau associated with the latter, it is desirable to also have an equivalent characterization in terms of the matrix A, without reference to a specific basis. This requires a concept analogous to decomposability, defined in terms of the columns of A.

For any $S \subset N$, $T \subset N$, such that

$$(2) \qquad \sum_{j \in S} a_j = \sum_{j \in T} a_j \leq e ,$$

we say that (S,T) is <u>pairwise decomposable</u> if there exists a pair (S′,T′) of proper nonempty subsets $S' \subset S$, $T' \subset T$ such that (2) remains true when S and T are replaced by S′ and T′ respectively.

The central result of the next theorem is the equivalence of statements (i) and (iii), established by Balas and Padberg [1972b]. This constitutes the key to a procedure for generating integer vertices adjacent to a given integer vertex, and also implies the equivalence between (i) and (ii), obtained earlier by Trubin [1969]. The result on the equivalence of (iii) and (iv) is due to Padberg and Rao [1973].

<u>Theorem 2.3.3</u>. Let x and y be any two vertices of $\bar{P}_I$, and for z = x,y let

$$Q(z) = \{j \in N | z_j = 1\} , \bar{Q}(z) = \{j \in N | z_j = 0\}.$$

Further, let J(x) be the nonbasic index set for some (arbitrarily chosen) basis associated with x. Then the following four statements are equivalent:

(i) x and y are adjacent on $\bar{P}$

(ii) x and y are adjacent on $\bar{P}_I$

(iii) $Q(y) \cap J(x)$ is not decomposable

(iv) $[Q(x) \cap \overline{Q(y)}, \overline{Q(x)} \cap Q(y)]$ is not pairwise decomposable.

It is known that all vertices of the feasible set (convex hull of feasible 0-1 points) of a 0-1 program are vertices of the associated linear programming polytope. The equivalence of (i) and (ii) above puts (SPP) into the class of 0-1 programs having the much stronger geometric property, that all edges of the feasible set (convex hull of feasible 0-1 points) are edges of the associated linear programming polytope.

For the set packing polytope P_I, which is a special case of $\bar{P}_I$, a necessary and sufficient condition for the adjacency of two vertices (on P_I only) was given independently, in graph-theoretical terms, by Chvátal [1972]:

Theorem 2.3.4. Let x and y be two vertices of P_I and let G' be the subgraph of (the intersection graph) G_A induced by the node set

$$[Q(x) \cap \overline{Q(y)}] \cup [\overline{Q(x)} \cap Q(y)].$$

Then x and y are adjacent on P_I if and only if G' is connected.

This last theorem is closely related to an earlier result on weighted node packings, due to Balinski. Given any node packing S, define an alternating subgraph $H(S) = (N',E')$ of G_A relative to S to be a bipartite graph whose edges only connect nodes in S to nodes in N-S, and such that if $i \in N'$, $j \in N-N'$, and $(i,j) \in E$, then $j \notin S$. Define an augmenting subgraph to be an alternating subgraph such that the weight-sum of the nodes in $N'-S$ exceeds that of the nodes in S. Let the weight of a node packing be the weight-sum of its nodes. Then Balinski's result can be stated in terms of the node packing polytope as follows.

Theorem 2.3.5. (Balinski [1967]). A vertex x of P_I is of maximum weight if and only if G_A admits no connected augmenting subgraph relative to Q(x).

In other words, the graphs G' of Chvátal's Theorem 2.3.4 are precisely the connected alternating subgraphs defined above. Note however, that Balinski's and Chvátal's results only concern the adjacency of vertices of P_I; they are not concerned with adjacency on the associated linear programming polytope P.

Returning now to the more general case of the set partitioning polytope $\bar{P}_I$, Theorem 2.3.3 above implies a necessary and sufficient condition for two vertices of the set partitioning polytope $\bar{P}_I$ to be <u>non-adjacent</u>. This condition leads to an interesting geometric characterization of $\bar{P}_I$. For an arbitrary polyhedron P, a <u>path</u> between two vertices x and y of P is a sequence of vertices $x^1, x^2, \ldots, x^k$ with $x^1 = x$, $x^k = y$, such that every pair of vertices x^i, x^{i+1}, $i = 1,\ldots,k-1$, is connected by an edge of P, the length of the path being k-1. The <u>edge-distance</u> d(x,y) between x and y is then defined as the length of a shortest path on P between x and y. The diameter $\delta(P)$ of P is the longest edge-distance between any pair of vertices of P, i.e., $\delta(P) = \max_{x,y \in \text{vert } P} d(x,y)$. If we require the matrix A in the definition of $\bar{P}_I$ not to have identical columns, we then have

<u>Theorem 2.3.6</u>. (Balas and Padberg [1972b]).

$$\delta(\bar{P}_I) \leq \left[\frac{z^*}{2}\right] \leq \left[\frac{m}{2q}\right]$$

where $q = \min_{j \in N} \sum_{i=1}^{m} a_{ij}$, and $z^* = \max \left\{ \sum_{j=1}^{n} x_j \,|\, x \in \bar{P}_I \right\}$.

In fact, the upper bound on the diameter of $\bar{P}_I$ provided by the above theorem is a best possible one, that is actually attained if $A = (A_G, I)$ in the definition of $\bar{P}_I$, where A_G is the $m \times \binom{m}{2}$ node-edge incidence matrix of a complete graph with m nodes, and I is the identity of order m.

A further geometric property is contained in the following theorem, which has some interesting algorithmic implications:

<u>Theorem 2.3.7</u>. (Balas and Padberg [1972b]). Let x^1 be a non-optimal vertex of $\bar{P}_I$, let x^{1i}, $i = 1,\ldots,k$, be those vertices of $\bar{P}_I$ adjacent to x^1, and such that $cx^{1i} < cx^1$, $i = 1,\ldots,k$. Then the convex polyhedral cone

$$C = \{x \in R^n | x = x^1 + \sum_{i=1}^{k} \lambda_i (x^{1i} - x^1),\ \lambda_i \geq 0,\ i = 1,\ldots,k\}$$

contains an optimal vertex of $\bar{P}_I$.

The property stated in Theorem 2.3.7 is not true for arbitrary integer programs, as shown by the trivial counter-example of Fig. 2.3.1. In this example, $cx^1 > cx^2 > cx^3$, and the cone C (here just a halfline) clearly does not contain the unique optimal point x^3.

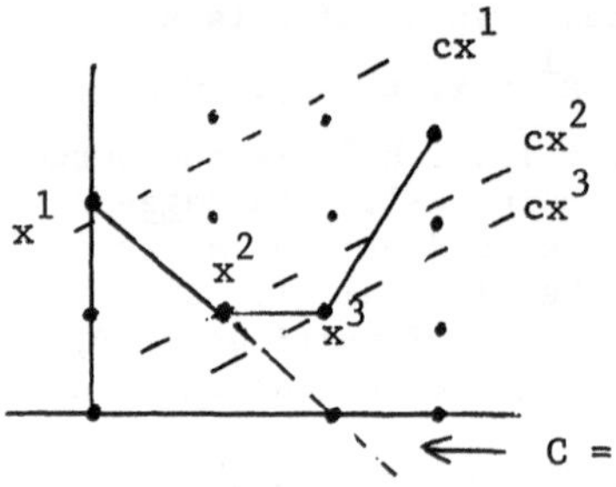

Figure 2.3.1.

Since the set packing polytope P_I is a special case of the set partitioning polytope $\bar{P}_I$, all the results of this section stated for (SPP), are also valid for (SP). Furthermore, the main results, including Theorems 2.3.2, 2.3.3 without (i), and 2.3.7, can be generalized to arbitrary 0-1 programs (see Balas and Padberg [1973]).

3. ALGORITHMS

Before discussing any particular algorithm, it should be mentioned that problem size can often be substantially reduced, by using one or more of the rules listed below, prior to applying any solution method.

Let M and N be the row and column index sets of A; let a^i be the i-th row, and a_j the j-th column, of A.

The following three "reduction" rules are well known and easy to implement.

1. If for some $i \in M$ and $k \in N$, $a_{ik} = 1$, $a_{ij} = 0$, $\forall\, j \in N - \{k\}$, then one can

   (a) set $x_k = 1$ and remove column k

   (b) remove all columns $j \in N-\{k\}$ such that $a_k a_j \geq 1$

   (c) remove all rows $h \in M$ such that $a_{hk} = 1$.

2. If for some $i,k \in M$, $a^i \leq a^k$, then one can

(a) remove row k

(b) remove all columns $j \in M$ such that $a_{ij} = 0$, $a_{kj} = 1$.

3. If for some $k \in N$ and some subset $N' \subset N$, $\sum_{j \in N'} a_j = a_k$ and $\sum_{j \in N'} c_j \leq c_k$, one can remove column k.

Less well known, and somewhat more expensive to implement, is the following rule.

4. For each $i \in M$, let $N_i = \{j \in N | a_{ij} = 1\}$. Then any column a_k such that

$$a_k a_j \geq 1 \quad , \quad \forall\, j \in N_i \quad \text{for some } i \in M,$$

can be removed.

3.1. Implicit Enumeration

Several specialized versions of the implicit enumeration approach of Balas [1964, 1965] (see also Glover [1965], Geoffrion [1967]) have been proposed for the set partitioning problem and implemented. The ones that seem to have been successful include Pierce [1968], Garfinkel and Nemhauser [1969], Pierce and Lasky [1970], Marsten [1974].

The first two of these algorithms are very similar, and we will discuss the Garfinkel-Nemhauser version. The solution space is systematically searched by generating partial solutions (assigning 0-1 values to variables taken one at a time) and exploring the logical implications of these value assignments. The special structure simplifies the logical tests and lends them great power. Like the general implicit enumeration procedures, these algorithms are additive, i.e., require no divisions and therefore pose no numerical stability problems. Furthermore, since in this case all constraint coefficients are binary, they can be stored and manipulated as bits. Also, the use of the logical "and" and logical "or" statements permits the efficient execution of many of the required operations.

To start with, the matrix A is brought by row and column permutations to the staircase form shown in Fig. 3.1.1.

In other words, the columns of A are partitioned into t nonempty subsets ("blocks") B_j, $j = 1,\ldots,t$, such that block B_j satisfies $a_{ik} = 1$ for all $k \in B_j$ and $a_{ik} = 0$ for $k \in \bigcup_{\ell=j+1}^{t} B_\ell$ for some row i of the matrix A. The rows of A are then ordered so that the row defining block B_j becomes the j-row for

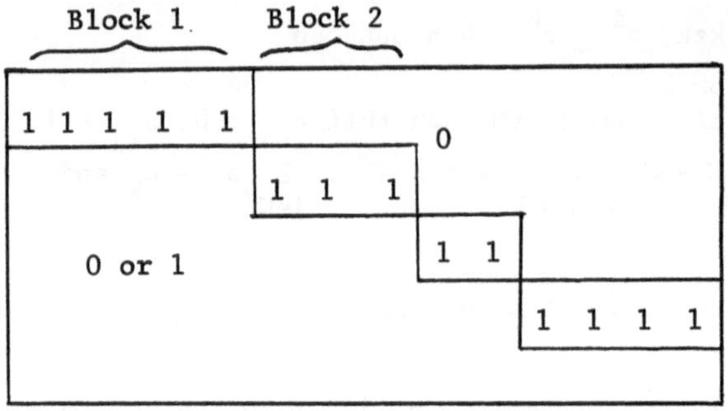

Fig. 3.1.1.

$j = 1,\ldots,t$. If $t < m$, empty blocks B_j are defined for $j = t+1,\ldots,m$. Within each block the columns are ordered by some heuristic criterion: according to increasing costs (Garfinkel-Nemhauser), or increasing costs per number of rows covered (i.e., increasing $c_j / \sum_{i=1}^{m} a_{ij}$) (Pierce), or increasing reduced costs, obtained by solving (LSPP) (Pierce and Lasky, Heurgon).

Denote by S (the index set of) a partial solution, by S^+ its subset of variables fixed at 1, by z its value, and by R the set of rows (constraints) satisfied by S. Further, let $\bar{z}$ be the value of the best solution found so far (if any).

Then the algorithm proceeds as follows.

Step 1. (Initialization): Set up the initial tableau, let $S = \emptyset$, $R = \emptyset$ and $\bar{z} = \infty$. Go to Step 2.

Step 2. (Choose next block): Let $r = \min\{i \mid i \notin R\}$. Set a marker at the top (lowest cost element) of block r. Go to Step 3.

Step 3. (Test for augmenting variable): Beginning at the marked position in block r, examine all columns of A in block r in order. If a column j is found such that $a_{ij} = 0$, $\forall\, i \in R$, and $z + c_j < \bar{z}$, go to Step 4. If a column j is reached such that $z + c_j \geq \bar{z}$, or if block r is exhausted, go to Step 5.

Step 4. (Test for a new solution): Redefine S^+ to be $S^+ \cup \{j\}$, R to be $R \cup \{i \mid a_{ij} = 1\}$ and z to be $z + c_j$. If $R = \{1,\ldots,m\}$, a better solution has been found, which is recorded, and $\bar{z}$ is updated. Go to Step 5. Otherwise, go to Step 2.

<u>Step 5</u>. (Backtrack): If $S^+ = \emptyset$ (i.e., block 1 has been exhausted), terminate with the best solution found (if any). Otherwise, let k be the last index included in S^+. Redefine S^+ to be $S^+ - \{k\}$. Let B_r be the (unique) block to which column a_k belongs. Put a marker at the next column in block r, remove the previous marker in block r, and go to Step 3.

As one would expect, this algorithm performs better on high density than on low density problems (where density means the number of nonzero entries of A divided by m·n). Computational results reported by Garfinkel and Nemhauser include the solution of 4 problems with 26-100 constraints and 385-1790 variables, and a density of 0.16-0.25, in 25-900 seconds of IBM 7094 time; but a fifth problem (37 x 1790, 0.25) could not be solved in 15 minutes. Comparable results are reported by Pierce.

One of the means of enhancing the efficiency of implicit enumeration is to calculate for each partial solution a lower bound on the cost of its completion. This can be done, for instance, by solving the linear program in the free variables, as done by Geoffrion [1969] for general 0-1 programs, by Lemke, Salkin and Spielberg [1971] in the context of an algorithm primarily designed for set covering problems, or by Michaud [1972] in his implicit enumeration algorithm for the (SPP). Pierce, and Pierce and Lasky, avoid solving a linear program for each partial solution, by solving instead, or finding a lower bound on the value of, a knapsack problem obtained by adding up all the constraints. Ming-Te Lu [1970] weights the constraints before adding them up. A stronger bound, which brought a considerable improvement in computing time, was obtained by Christophides and Korman [1973] by solving an auxiliary problem via dynamic programming techniques. While this was achieved in the context of a set covering algorithm, the bound applies to set partitioning problems as well.

Another important improvement was obtained, first by Pierce and Lasky, then also by others (see Gondran and Laurière [1974], Heurgon [1972]), by replacing the cost vector c with the reduced cost vector $c-c^B B^{-1}A$ of an optimal simplex tableau for (LSPP). This is permissible, since $(c-c^B B^{-1}A)x = cx-c^B B^{-1}e$ for any feasible x, i.e., the value of the reduced cost function differs from that of the original cost function by a constant, for any feasible solution. This requires of course the solution of (LSPP) prior to implicit enumeration, which for large problems is quite a high price to pay for hopefully speeding up the subsequent enumeration. But the gain seems to be worth the price, for Pierce and Lasky have solved by implicit enumeration, without making any other use of the linear program except for solving it once to obtain an optimal reduced cost vector, 7 out of 10 problems with 15-60 constraints and 1200-3500 variables in 15-300 seconds of CPU time on an IBM 360/67. But their code could not solve the remaining 3 problems within 9, 23, and 23 minutes respectively. A cheaper way of improving the cost structure (see Gondran and Laurière [1974]) is the following. Choose any row a^i of A, and replace c by $c - c_{j_i} a^i$, where $c_{j_i} = \min \{c_j | a_{ij} = 1\}$. Then choose another row and repeat the procedure. Since no row can yield an improvement twice, it is sufficient to consider each row once. The legitimacy of the procedure follows from the same argument as that of replacing the initial costs by the reduced costs of the linear program.

An implicit enumeration algorithm based on a different enumerative scheme, which can be viewed as a specialization of the one proposed for general 0-1 programming by Graves and Whinston [1968], was developed by Marsten [1974]. The columns of A are partitioned into blocks, just like in the above procedure, but the enumeration is based on assigning rows to blocks. If $M_i = \{k \in N | a_{ik} = 1\}$ and $M_{ij} = M_i \cap B_j$, where i is the index of any row and j that of any block, then assigning row i to block j amounts to assigning the value 1 to the <u>sum</u> of variables x_k, $k \in M_{ij}$, rather than to a single variable. The logical implications of such value assignments are then explored in the usual manner. This enumerative scheme gives rise to a different search tree, whose number of nodes usually has a smaller bound than the number of nodes in a usual search tree. This does not necessarily have anything to do with the number of nodes actually generated in the two cases, and at this moment no convincing evidence is available in favor of one search tree or another. Marsten also solves (LSPP) first and uses the reduced costs instead of the original ones. He reports the solution on an IBM 360/91 of four large problems, of size 90 x 303, 63 x 1641, 111 x 4826 and 200 x 2362, in 40.64, 168.76, 479.77 and 418.86 seconds, respectively (excluding the time required to bring A to the proper format). Marsten's code seems to perform better than the Garfinkel-Nemhauser code on low density problems, while the latter has the lead for higher densities. Unfortunately, however, it is not clear to what extent these differences can be ascribed to the different search trees used, since the two codes have a good number of other differences. A limited comparative study of the two search strategies, undertaken by Nemhauser, Trotter and Nauss [1972], indicates better performance for the usual type of search tree.

One important fact that has emerged from Marsten's experience, and confirms earlier computational experience by Martin and others, is the difficulty of solving the linear programs associated with large set covering problems. The reasons for this were already mentioned and will be taken up again later.

3.2. Simplex-Based Cutting Plane Methods

As mentioned earlier, the properties of the set partitioning polytope discussed in section 2.3 produce a high frequency of integer solutions among the basic solutions of (LSPP). This makes (SPP) relatively easily accessible via cutting plane methods. Martin [1969] reports in his, unfortunately unpublished, talk, the solution of several large set partitioning (airline crew scheduling) problems with 300-500 constraints and 1500-4000 variables, by the use of Gomory's [1963a] cutting planes, generated in a special way described in Martin [1963]. In spite of the large size of the problems involved, the number of cuts used was reportedly less than 10 in all but one of the cases (when it was 16). However, other problems, in some cases with less than 300 variables, could not be solved within reasonable time limits.

In a recent study on solving (SPP) by cutting plane methods, Délorme [1974] describes a computer code implementing a version of Gomory's [1963a] algorithm, and reports on his computational experience with several fairly large set partitioning problems, used in the scheduling of crews for the Paris bus lines (see Heurgon [1972] on the treatment of some of the same problems by implicit enumeration). The problems are of a special type, namely (SPP) with two additional constraints, one of which is an upper bound on a positively weighted sum of all the variables, while the other one is $ex = k$, $e = (1,\dots,1)$, i.e., a constraint that fixes the cardinality of a feasible partition. These two constraints drastically reduce the feasible set, and thus make the problem easier than a general (SPP).

The cuts are generated from the row with largest fractional constant term. After each pivot, a new cut is generated (unlike in Gomory's algorithm) until the solution (though not necessarily the whole tableau) becomes integer, which rarely seems to take more than 3-4 cuts. Once integer, however, the solution is not necessarily primal feasible, and in the process of reoptimization, integrality may be lost again. The main data of the study are summarized in Tableau 3.3.1.

1	2	3	4	5	6	7	8	9
No.	m X n	cuts in sequence	cuts total	time in post opt	pivots in post opt	basis det	Z_{LP}	Z_{INT}
1	111 X 2186	4	6	2'32"	59	4	3320	3327
2	77 X 969	4	7	46"	27	122	3240	3271
3	78 X 693	4	5	35"	66	12	2942	2945
4	91 X 1019	3	3	28"	42	4	3161	3162
5	51 X 913	3	3	15"	49	3	450	479
6	88 X 953	1	1	2"	1	68	3305	3316
7	58 X 405	4	5	23"	35	24	2870	2930
8	185 X 1043	1	1	12"	5	3	3061	3080

Tableau 3.3.1

Tableau data: 1, problem number; 2, constraints times variables; 3, maximum no. of cuts in one sequence; 4, total no. of cuts; 5, time spent on postoptimization; 6, no. of pivots in postoptimization; 7, basis determinant at LP optimum; 8, optimal LP value; 9, optimal integer value.

Densities are not shown, but judging from the above data, they must have been very low. The time and number of pivots used to solve the LP are given only for the first two problems, and they are 8'42" and 577 pivots for problem 1, 2'51" and 343 pivots for problem 2.

The procedure of generating sequences of cuts (one cut after each pivot) is compared with the usual one of reestablishing primal feasibility after the addition of each cut. It is found that the number of cuts required is about the same in the two cases, whereas the number of pivots required is considerably higher in the second case. Also, the first procedure is compared with the one which "consolidates" the sequence of cuts into a single cut as recommended by Martin [1963] (see also Gondran [1973]), and found superior to the latter. A number of questions of general interest for solving large linear programs are discussed. But the above 8 problems all seem to have been easily solved, and failure of solving larger or denser problems, as well as the reasons for such failure, are not reported, except for a mention of the fact that sometimes the program had to be stopped because it had generated 12 cuts in a sequence (the threshold parameter) without making the solution integer. The program has reportedly been compared with the version of the Garfinkel-Nemhauser algorithm described by Heurgon [1972] and found to be able to solve a larger number of problems, in shorter average times; but no factual basis is given for this statement in terms of the problems on which the comparisons were made, their size and density, and the actual differences in performance. An evaluation of the effect of the two extra constraints was not attempted, and no information is given on the performance of the code on "pure" set partitioning problems (i.e., without the two extra constraints). Nevertheless, the study contains much useful information.

Another simplex-based cutting plane method that was tested on (SPP) is Gomory's [1963b] all-integer algorithm. In a computational study undertaken by Salkin and Koncal [1973], this algorithm was applied, basically unchanged, to the set partitioning and set covering problems. A set of 13 problems with 30 constraints and 30-90 variables, having unit costs and density of 0.07, were solved on a Univac 1108 in less than 3 seconds each. The average number of cuts generated per problem was 22, with a maximum of 45, and the average number of pivots was 131. These performances are quite good. The code failed to solve any of a set of 8 larger problems with about 400-900 variables, within the time limit of 2 minutes. But apparently the time limit was set too low, since the maximum number of pivots performed on any of the problems was 3m (where m is the number of constraints) which is about the number of pivots it usually takes to solve a linear program; and we cannot reasonably expect to be able to solve integer programs by the same number of pivots as one needs to solve the corresponding linear program.

The cutting plane methods discussed above have three characteristics in common: they are all based on the simplex method (primal and dual, or only dual) they all use the traditional cutting planes introduced by Gomory, and they are all general-purpose algorithms which take little if any advantage of problem structure. The fact that, in spite of this last feature, they perform reasonably well on (SPP), shows that the cutting plane approach holds great promise for this class of problems. One possible direction of improvement seems to be at hand in the form of cutting planes derived from the special structure of (SPP). These cuts, discussed in part 2, have not yet been computationally tested. What they might be able to accomplish, is to substantially reduce the number of cuts needed. While this could render solvable those problems which were not solved by the above procedures because they required too many cuts, it cannot of course affect the effort required to solve the linear program itself, and the latter is currently the main bottleneck in solving large (SPP)'s. In this respect, two directions of improvement seem to be open: specializations of the simplex method which use the structure of (LSPP), and non-simplex-type methods for solving (LSPP). One development in the first of these directions is discussed in the next section (though not in a cutting plane context); and another one, in the second direction, is discussed in section 3.4.

While the methods discussed in this and the previous section have achieved a certain maturity in the sense of having been implemented and tested by different persons in different versions, the approaches discussed in the next three sections are new and have only been tested to a very limited extent.

3.3. A Column Generating Algorithm

Next we discuss a column generating primal simplex algorithm for (SPP), which produces a sequence of integer solutions that converges on an optimal one. The algorithm is based on the characterization of adjacency relations among vertices of $\bar{P}_I$ described in section 2.3. This is a modified version of the algorithm by Balas and Padberg [1972b], discussed in Balas, Gerritsen and Padberg [1974]. The algorithm performs non-degenerate primal simplex pivots on +1 entries as long as this is possible. When this cannot be continued, degenerate pivots are performed on positive or negative entries, as long as they decrease total dual infeasibility. (In the present context, a pivot in row i is called degenerate if $a_{io} = 0$, nondegenerate if $a_{io} > 0$.) When neither type of pivoting can be continued, a column generating procedure is used to produce a composite column defining an edge of $\bar{P}_I$ which connects the current vertex of $\bar{P}_I$ to a better one, or to establish the absence of any better vertex. This procedure differs from the one described in Balas and Padberg [1972b], mainly in that it is performed entirely on the original A matrix instead of the current simplex tableau, and thus it is all-binary (see Balas, Gerritsen and Padberg [1974]). The idea of allowing for degenerate pivots or -1 entries is due to Andrew, Hoffman and Krabek [1968], who implemented it and obtained remarkably good computational results in the sense of being able to get to, or close to, the integer optimum fairly often. Experience has shown, however, that it pays to go further and allow for degenerate pivots on any nonzero entry (i.e., to give up the integrality of the tableau, though not that of the solution) as long as improvements can be obtained according to some reasonable criterion.

We start by describing the binary column generating procedure, then imbed it into the rest of the algorithm.

Let $\bar{x}$ denote a feasible integer solution to (LSPP) with basis B, and reduced cost vector $\bar{c} = c - c^B B^{-1} A$, and let $Q = \{j \in N | \bar{x}_j = 1\}$. Let T designate initially the binary tableau consisting of those columns a_h of A such that $h \in S = N-Q$. Each composite column is of the form $a_j = \sum_{h \in Q_j} a_h$, where the index j represents the set Q_j. For the original columns, $Q_j = \{j\}$. T and S always refer to the current tableau, T' and S' to the next one.

<u>BCGP</u> (Binary Column Generating Procedure):

0. Initialization: $S = N-Q$, $T = \{a_j\}_{j \in S}$.
1. If $\bar{c}_j \geq 0$, $\forall j \in S$, stop: the current tableau is optimal. Otherwise go to 2.
2. Choose $t \in S$ such that $\bar{c}_t = \min_{j \in S} \bar{c}_j$. Define $R(t) = \{j \in Q | a_j a_t \geq 1\}$ and let $a(t) = \sum_{j \in R(t)} a_j$. If $a_t = a(t)$, stop: an improving adjacent vertex x^* is given by $x^*_j = 1$ for all $j \in (Q-R(t)) \cup \{t\}$, $x^*_j = 0$ otherwise. If $a_t \neq a(t)$, let $C(t) = \{j \in S | a_j a(t) \geq 1, a_j a_t = 0\}$ and go to 3.

3. Find all $N' \subseteq C(t)$ such that

(i) $a_t + \sum_{j \in N'} a_j \geq a(t)$

(ii) $a_j a_k = 0, \forall\, j,k \in N'$

(iii) $\bar{c}_t + \sum_{j \in N'} \bar{c}_j + z(t,N') < 0,$

where $z(t,N')$ is a lower bound on the value of an optimal solution to the problem obtained by setting $x_k = 1, \forall\, k \in \{t\} \cup N'$.

(iv) $Q_t \cup \left(\bigcup_{j \in N'} Q_j \right)$ cannot be partitioned into Q_h, $h = j_1, \ldots, j_p$, with $j_i \in S$, $j_i \neq t$, for $i = 1, \ldots, p$.

3a. If there exists no $N' \subseteq C(t)$ satisfying (i)-(iv), remove a_t permanently from the tableau; set $S' = S - \{t\}$, $T' = T - \{a_t\}$, and go to 4.

3b. If there exists $N' \subseteq C(t)$ satisfying (i)-(iv), such that (i) holds with equality, and $z(t,N') = 0$, stop: pivoting into the basis the composite column

$$a_{j_*} = \sum_{j \in Q_{j_*}} \bar{a}_j ,$$

where $Q_{j_*} = \{t\} \cup N'$, or each of the columns $\bar{a}_j$, $j \in Q_{j_*}$, yields an integer solution x^*, with $x^*_j = 1$, $\forall\, j \in [Q-R(t)] \cup Q_{j_*}$, $x^*_j = 0$ otherwise, which is adjacent to and better than $\bar{x}$.

3c. Otherwise, adjoin a new column to T and a composite index to S for every (t,N') satisfying (i)-(iv) but not satisfying (i) with equality; discard column a_t and index t; call the resulting tableau T' and index set S', and go to 4.

4. Define T' and S' to be the current tableau T and index set S, respectively, and go to 1.

We now turn to the execution of Step 3 of BCGP. First, we notice that a crude lower bound $z(t,N')$ for test (iii) can be obtained as follows. Let

$$Z = \{j \in S \mid j \notin \{t\} \cup N',\ a_j(a_t + \sum_{h \in N'} a_h) = 0,\ \bar{c}_j < 0\} .$$

Then $z(t,N') = \sum_{j \in Z} \bar{c}_j$ is a usable bound.

Further, finding the sets $N' \subseteq C(t)$ which satisfy (i)-(iv) involves solving an auxiliary set partitioning problem defined on a submatrix of A. To be more specific, let A_R^C be the submatrix of A with column set $C = C(t)$ and row set $R = \{i \in \{1,\ldots,m\} \mid a_i(t) = 1,\ a_{it} = 0\}$. Then identifying the sets $N' \subseteq C(t)$ which satisfy (i)-(iv) amounts to finding those solutions to

$$\text{(APP)} \quad \begin{aligned} A_R^C \eta &= e_r \\ \eta_j &= 0 \text{ or } 1,\ j = 1,\ldots,|C| \end{aligned}$$

that satisfy the additional tests to qualify for a feasible improving solution to (SPP), where $e_r = (1,\ldots,1)$ has $r = |R|$ components. This is best done by a modified implicit enumeration procedure which includes in its tests those conditions (ii)-(iv) not present in (APP).

Having discussed the column generating procedure, we can now state the algorithm in its entirety.

1. NPIP (Nondegenerate primal integer pivot) Apply the primal simplex method to (LSPP) as long as you can pivot on +1 in a nondegenerate row. Whenever this becomes impossible, let $\bar{x}$ be the current (integer) solution, B the associated basis, and $\bar{c} = c - c^B B^{-1} A$. If $\bar{c} \geq 0$, stop: $\bar{x}$ is optimal. Otherwise go to 2.

2. DP (Degenerate pivot) Let $N_o = \{j \in N \mid \bar{c}_j < 0\}$, and $c_o = \sum_{j \in N_o} \bar{c}_j$. If there exists $\bar{a}_{ij} \neq 0$ in a degenerate row (i.e., $\bar{x}_i = 0$), such that
   (i) pivoting on $\bar{a}_{ij}$ replaces $\bar{c}$, N_o, and c_o by $\bar{c}'$, N_o' and c_o' respectively;
   (ii) $c_o' < c_o$

   then pivot on $\bar{a}_{ij}$. If $\bar{c}' \geq 0$, stop: the solution $\bar{x}'$ obtained from the pivot is optimal. Otherwise go to 1. If no such $\bar{a}_{ij}$ exists, go to 3.

3. BCGP (Binary column generating procedure). This was described above. It either shows the current solution to be optimal, or yields an index set $Q_{j_*} = \{t\} \cup N'$. In the latter case, go to 4.

4. BP (Block pivot) Pivot into the basis each a_j, $j \in Q_{j_*}$, and go to 1.

The version of the algorithm described here was not yet tested. An earlier version, tested on a set of problems with unit cuts, 30 rows and 40-90 columns, density 0.07, showed behavior somewhat similar to implicit enumeration, which is not surprising. Thus, finding a good (often optimal) solution usually takes a small fraction of the time required to prove optimality. The importance of step 2 emerged clearly, in that its inclusion or exclusion has affected computing times by a factor of about 4.

3.4. A Symmetric Subgradient Cutting Plane Method

In Section 3.2 we have mentioned that in solving large set partitioning problems by cutting plane techniques, the main bottleneck is the handling of the linear program (LSPP). This, and the special structure of (LSPP), suggests the idea of trying to solve the latter by other methods than the (primal or dual) simplex algorithm. One such experiment currently under way (see Balas and Samuelsson [1974b]) uses some of the cutting planes discussed in part 2 of this paper, while solving the linear program by a subgradient method of the general type used by Held and Karp [1971] for the traveling salesman problem and discussed by Held, Wolfe and Crowder [1974]. The subgradient approach used here (see Samuelsson [1974]) differs from that of the above mentioned authors in that it works simultaneously with the primal and the dual, which makes it possible to achieve faster convergence. Among the positive features of this approach, we mention a high degree of numerical stability, low memory requirements and an ability to use data in compactly stored form. Next we briefly outline the procedure.

First (SPP) is restated as (SP), a set packing problem, via the cost transformation mentioned in Section 1.2. Since it is essential to keep the costs as low as possible, a tight bound is derived for the transformation parameter θ. Let

(P) $\max \{cx \mid Ax \leq b,\ x \geq 0\}$

be the linear program associated with (SP), possibly amended with some cutting planes; and

(D) $\min \{yb \mid yA \geq c,\ y \geq 0\}$

its dual. Let A be $q \times n$. The constraints of (SP) imply $x \leq e$, where $e = (1,\dots,1)$ is a n-vector, but the procedure requires upper bounds on the dual variables too. Whenever c and A are non-negative,

$$\bar{y}_i = \max_{j \in N | a_{ij} > 0} (c_j / a_{ij})$$

is easily seen to be a valid upper bound on y_i, $\forall\, i$. The rows of A corresponding to the coefficient matrix of (SP) are by definition non-negative, and the cutting planes to be generated can be shown to have only non-negative coefficients when expressed in the structural variables x_j, $j \in N$. Thus the above bounds on the dual variables are valid.

The pair of dual linear programs can now be restated as

$$(P') \qquad \max_{0 \leq x \leq e} z(x)$$

and

$$(D') \qquad \min_{0 \leq y \leq \bar{y}} w(y)$$

where z(x) and w(y) are defined by

$$L_P(x) \qquad z(x) = \min_{0 \leq \eta \leq \bar{y}} \{\eta(b - Ax) + cx\}$$

and

$$L_D(y) \qquad w(y) = \max_{0 \leq \xi \leq e} \{(c - yA)\xi + yb\}$$

respectively.

For any given $x \in R^n$ and $y \in R^q$ all optimal solutions $\eta^*(x)$, $\xi^*(y)$ to the pair of linear programs $L_P(x)$, $L_D(y)$ satisfy

$$\eta_i^*(x) = \begin{cases} 0 & \text{if } a^i x < b_i \\ 0 \text{ or } \bar{y}_i & \text{if } a^i x = b_i \\ \bar{y}_i & \text{if } a^i x > b_i \end{cases}$$

and

$$\xi_i^*(y) = \begin{cases} 0 & \text{if } ya_j > c_j \\ 0 \text{ or } 1 & \text{if } ya_j = c_j \\ 1 & \text{if } ya_j < j \end{cases}$$

where a^i and a_j are the i-th row and j-th column of A, respectively. Clearly, $\eta^*(x)$ and $\xi^*(y)$ are trivially easy to compute for any given x and y.

Consider now the problem

$$\text{(PD)} \qquad \min_{\substack{0 \le x \le e \\ 0 \le y \le \bar{y}}} \quad v(x,y) = w(y) - z(x)$$

This problem is amenable to subgradient optimization; and unlike other formulations, it has the advantage of a known optimal value, 0, which helps choosing an appropriate step length.

At any point $(\hat{x},\hat{y})$, each pair of optimal solutions $\eta^* = \eta^*(\hat{x})$, $\xi^* = \xi^*(\hat{y})$, to $L_P(\hat{x})$ and $L_D(\hat{y})$ respectively, defines a subgradient $(s_x, s_y) \in R^n \times R^q$ of $v(x,y)$, given by

$$(s_x, s_y) = (\eta^* A - c,\ b - A\xi^*),$$

which is again trivially easy to compute; and the convex hull of these subgradients for all optimal η^*, ξ^*, is

$$\partial\, v(x,y) = \operatorname{conv} \bigcup_{\eta^*,\xi^*} (\eta^* A - c,\ b - A\xi^*),$$

the subdifferential of $v(x,y)$ at the point $(\hat{x},\hat{y})$.

For any point $(x,y) \in R^n \times R^q$, let $P_F(x,y)$ denote the projection of (x,y) on the set

$$F = \{(x,y) \in R^n \times R^q \mid 0 \le x \le e,\ 0 \le y \le \bar{y}\}.$$

Projecting a point $(x,y) \notin F$ on F consists of simply replacing those components of (x,y), which exceed one of their bounds, with the respective bound, while leaving the other components unchanged.

The procedure can now be summarized as follows:

0. (Initialize). Let A be the coefficient matrix of (SPP), and b = e. Define F by computing the upper bounds $\bar{y}_i$ for

each component of y. Start with any $(x^0, y^0) \epsilon F$, set $i = 0$, and go to 1.

1. Compute $v(x^i, y^i)$. If $v(x^i, y^i) < \epsilon$, where $\epsilon > 0$ is a given parameter, define $N_0 = \{j \epsilon N | y^i a_j = c_j\}$ and go to 3. Otherwise go to 2.

2. Compute a subgradient $(s_x^i, x_y^i) \epsilon \partial v(x^i, y^i)$ and set

$$(x^{i+1}, y^{i+1}) = P_F[(x^i, y^i) - t^i(s_x^i, s_y^i)]$$

where the step-length t^i is given by

$$t^i = \lambda \frac{v(x^i, y^i)}{\|s_x^i\|^2 + \|s_y^i\|^2}$$

for some λ, $0 < \lambda < 2$, and where $\|s\|$ is the Euclidean norm of s. Set $i \leftarrow i + 1$ and go to 1.

3. Search N_0 for a subset N_0' such that

$$\sum_{j \epsilon N_0'} a_j \leq b$$

and equality holds for the rows of (SPP) (i.e., those of the starting problem, as opposed to those corresponding to cuts). If such N_0' **exists**, stop: x^* given by $x_j^* = 1$, $j \epsilon N_0'$, $x_j^* = 0$ otherwise, is an optimal solution to (SPP). Otherwise go to 4.

4. Generate a set of cuts, expressed in the structural variables as

$$Dx \leq d$$

where $D = (d_{ij}) \geq 0$, $d > 0$.

Redefine (PD) and F by replacing A and b with

$$\begin{pmatrix} A \\ D \end{pmatrix} \quad \text{and} \quad \begin{pmatrix} b \\ d \end{pmatrix}$$

respectively, and setting

$$\bar{y}_h = \max_{j \epsilon N | d_{hj} > 0} (c_j / d_{hj})$$

for each new component of $\bar{y}$. Define the new components of y^i to be $y_h^i = \bar{y}_h$ for each new constraint h, and go to 1.

If all the cuts were present in the tableau at the start, the rate of convergence of the above procedure would be geometrical, as it is known to be in the case of the general class of algorithms to which it belongs. Since they are not, the actual convergence rate will, of course, depend on the number of cuts that have to be introduced. Convergence seems to depend crucially on the step length t^i. The value $\lambda = 1$ appears to give most of the time the best performance, though sometimes switching from $\lambda = 1$ to $\lambda = 1/2$ at some stage in the process improves the convergence.

The main advantage of the symmetric procedure over the asymmetric subgradient method discussed in Held, Wolfe and Crowder [1974] lies in the fact that the latter requires an estimate of the optimal objective function value for a proper choice of the step length. Experience shows that when the estimate is replaced by the actual value of the optimum, convergence is very fast. In the symmetric procedure such an estimate is not needed, since the function that one minimizes is known to have 0 as its optimal value. To compare the two procedures, an adaptation of the asymmetric method described by Held, Wolfe and Crowder [1974] to (LSPP) was implemented, with three different estimates of the optimal objective function value, namely the true optimum, an overestimation of 20%, and one of 50%. Both the symmetric and the asymmetric procedures were run on 6 set partitioning linear programs, with 30 constraints, 70-90 variables, and density 0.07 (problems 9-14 of Salkin and Koncal [1973]). When the exact optimum was assumed known in the one-sided procedure, the two methods performed about equally. When the estimate was 20% off, for 4 of the 6 problems the one-sided procedure required between 1.3 and 2.1 times the number of iterations needed for the symmetric procedure, while for the remaining 2 problems it converged to the wrong value. When the estimate was 50% off, the asymmetric procedure converged to the right value for only one of the 6 problems. The average number of iterations required with the symmetric procedure to reach a value of v(x,y) less than 1.0 was between 133 and 759, with an average of 299. The computational effort involved in an iteration of this procedure can be estimated (very roughly) to be about m times less than for a usual revised simplex iteration, where m is the number of constraints. These initial tests are of course insufficient to draw any conclusion, but they certainly suggest that the method may hold good promise.

3.5. Set Partitioning Via Node Covering

As discussed in Section 1.4, a set packing problem (SP) with coefficient matrix A is equivalent to the weighted node packing problem defined on the intersection graph G_A of A, where the weights are the same as in (SP). On the other hand, the weighted node packing problem is equivalent to the weighted node covering problem, since the complement of any node packing is a node covering; and if the node packing is of maximum weight, its complement must certainly be of minimum weight. Thus, one way of solving set packing and set partitioning problems is via solving the corresponding (weighted) node packing or node covering problems.

In this section we discuss one such method (see Balas and Samuelsson [1973, 1974a]). We first discuss the procedure for the unweighted node covering problem, then its extension to the weighted case.

The unweighted node covering problem can be stated as

$$\text{(NC)} \qquad \min \{e_n x \mid A^T x \geq e_q \ , \ x_j = 0 \text{ or } 1, \ j \in N\}$$

where $N = \{1,\ldots,n\}$, A is the $n \times q$ node-edge incidence matrix of a graph $G = (N,E)$, T means transpose, and e_n, e_q are vectors of ones of appropriate dimensions.

A minimum partial cover $\tilde{N}$ is a subset of nodes which is a minimum cover in the subgraph obtained from G by removing all edges not incident with $\tilde{N}$. For the purposes of this section, a clique will be defined as a set of pairwise adjacent nodes (i.e., a set of nodes inducing a complete subgraph; but the set does not have to be maximal, and the term refers to the node set instead of the subgraph itself).

The algorithm starts with a minimum partial cover and uses a labeling procedure to increase the number of edges that are covered. This procedure ends after at most $n(q + 1)$ steps. If all edges are covered, the solution is optimal. Otherwise the problem is partitioned, i.e., G is replaced by two proper subgraphs, and the procedure is applied to the latter.

The key concept behind the labeling procedure is that of a dual node-clique set. If K is the set of all cliques (in the above sense) in G, then $(\tilde{N},\tilde{K})$, where $\tilde{N} \subset N$, $\tilde{K} \subset K$, is defined to be a dual node-clique set if

(i) the cliques of $\tilde{K}$ are pairwise node-disjoint
(ii) each node in $\tilde{N}$ belongs to some clique in $\tilde{K}$
(iii) each clique in $\tilde{K}$ contains exactly one node not in $\tilde{N}$.

It can be shown that if $(\tilde{N},\tilde{K})$ is a dual node-clique set, then $\tilde{N}$ is a minimum partial cover, which defines a dual-feasible solution to the linear program obtained from (NC) by removing the integrality requirement and adding a constraint of the form

$$\sum_{j\in Q} x_j \geq |Q|-1$$

for each clique in G. (When the cliques are maximal, this constraint is a facet - the complement of the corresponding clique-facet for the node packing or set packing problem, discussed in Section 2.1.)

These properties are used in the algorithm to perform implicitly, via a clique-labeling procedure, what in fact amounts to sequences of pivots in an all integer dual cutting plane method, where the cuts are the above inequalities. Dual feasibility is preserved by the fact that the partial covers generated by the labeling procedure are all associated with dual node-clique sets, i.e., are all minimal. A statement of the algorithm follows.

0. <u>Finding an initial solution</u>. Any edge matching (set of disjoint 2-cliques) can be used to generate an associated minimal partial node cover (and dual node-clique set). The larger the size of the edge-matching, the better the starting solution. A heuristic is used to find rapidly a good matching.

   Let $(\tilde{N},\tilde{K})$ be the current dual node-clique set ($\tilde{K}$ is the set of <u>labeled</u> cliques).

1. <u>Improving the solution (Labeling Procedure)</u>.

   Scan E for edges not covered by $\tilde{N}$, and for each such edge (i,j), attempt to perform one of the following steps in order:

   (a) (First labeling step). If neither i nor j belongs to a labeled clique (i.e., a clique in $\tilde{K}$), label the 2-clique $\{i,j\}$, and put into $\tilde{N}$ either i or j, whichever covers more new edges.
   (b) (Reassignment step). If either i or j can replace in $\tilde{N}$ one of the members of the labeled clique to which it belongs without uncovering an edge, make the switch to cover (i,j).
   (c) (Second labeling step). Find a largest unlabeled clique Q_* containing i and j, if it exists, such that

   $|Q_*| \geq 3$ and

(i) if any $h \in Q_*$ belongs to some $Q \in \tilde{K}$, then $Q \subset Q_*$ or Q is a 2-clique;
(ii) Q_* contains a labeled clique or a node $j \in \tilde{N}$.

If found, then

(α) label (put into $\tilde{K}$) Q_*, and "unlabel" (remove from $\tilde{K}$) all labeled cliques contained in Q_* and labeled 2-cliques incident with Q_*;

(β) put into $\tilde{N}$ all but one of the nodes in Q_*, and remove from $\tilde{N}$ all nodes not in Q_*, belonging to labeled 2-cliques incident with Q_*.

If, when no more applications of (a), (b), (c) are possible, the current $\tilde{N}$ is a cover, then it is optimal (for its subproblem). Otherwise go to 2.

2. Partitioning (Branching and Bounding).

Choose $i_* \in \tilde{N}$ having a maximum number of adjacent nodes not in $\tilde{N}$, and partition the feasible set by

$$(x_{i_*} = 1) \bigvee [x_{i_*} = 0 \text{ and } x_j = 1, \forall_j : (i_*, j) \in E]$$

This gives rise to two subproblems, whose associated graphs are the subgraphs of G induced by the node sets $N - \{i_*\}$, and $N - [\{i_*\} \cup \{j \in N | (i_*, j) \in E\}]$ respectively. For each of the two subgraphs, a dual node-clique set can be obtained from the dual node-clique set of the parent graph, by local modifications only.

Calculate a lower bound on the value of each subproblem (the cardinality of the minimal partial cover $\tilde{N}$ defined by the new dual node-clique set is one such bound; solving a structured linear program yields another, often stronger bound).

Select a subproblem and go to 1.

A first version of a computer code implementing the above algorithm was tested on 9 problems with 50 nodes and 64-329 edges, that were randomly generated by Trotter [1973] for testing his implicit enumeration algorithm for the same problem. For 6 of the 9 problems (the sparser ones), the number of partitions required was between 1 and 7; while for the remaining 3 problems (the denser ones), it was between 81 and 102. The results for the sparser problems are very encouraging, but of course testing on much larger problems is needed before any conclusions can be drawn.

The algorithm for the weighted node covering problem (Balas and Samuelsson [1974a]) is very similar in spirit to the one just described above. It is based on the equivalence of the weighted problem to an unweighted problem on an associated graph. If the weighted problem, with positive integral weight-vector c, is defined on a graph $G = (N,E)$, the node set of the associated graph $G(c) = [N(c),E(c)]$ contains c_i copies $i_1,\ldots,i_{c_i}$ of each node $i \in N$, i.e.,

$$N(c) = \bigcup_{i \in N} N_i \ ,$$

where $N_i = \{i_1,\ldots,i_{c_i}\}$, while the edge set of G(c) contains an edge for each pair of nodes i_k, j_ℓ in N(c) that are copies of nodes $i,j \in N$ connected by an edge of E; i.e.,

$$E(c) = \{(i_k,j_\ell) \mid (i,j) \in E\} \ .$$

It can then be shown that the weighted node covering problem on G is equivalent to the unweighted node covering problem on G(c), in the sense that for each optimal solution to one, there is an optimal solution with the same value to the other. This would make it possible to apply the algorithm discussed above to the unweighted problem defined on G(c), but the latter problem is unwieldy, and one can do better. Indeed, the steps of the above algorithm on G(c) can be carried out implicitly by a labeling procedure that operates only on the original graph G. This is accomplished via the concept of a <u>weighted dual node-clique set</u> in G, defined to be a pair $(\hat{N},\hat{K}) \subseteq (N,K)$ (where K, as before, is the set of all cliques in G, while $\hat{K}$ is a subset of labeled cliques), with an associated positive weight-vector w, such that

(i) $\hat{N}$ contains exactly one node i_Q of each labeled clique $Q \in \hat{K}$ ($i_{Q_1} = i_{Q_2}$ not excluded);

(ii) w has exactly one component for each $Q \in \hat{K}$ and

$$\sum_{Q \in \hat{K} \mid i \in Q} w(Q) \leq c_i, \ \forall \ i \in N \ .$$

These weighted dual node-clique sets can be shown to have properties similar to their unweighted counterparts. In particular, one can associate with each set a solution x to the linear programming relaxation of the weighted (NC), for which there exists an easily computable function f(x) such that if f(x) = 0 then x is integer and optimal. This makes it possible to transform a given weighted dual node-clique set into a "better" one with the same properties (i) and (ii), by a labeling procedure on G. Like in the unweighted case, this procedure terminates in a polynomially bounded number of steps, after which, if the terminating solution is not optimal, the problem is partitioned. Strong bounds on the resulting subproblems can be obtained via a procedure proposed by Samuelsson [1974a] which uses Lagrangean duality together with a relaxation of (NC) to a network flow problem. Computational experience with the weighted version of the node covering algorithm is not yet available.

REFERENCES

Andrew, G., Hoffman, Th. and Krabek, Ch. [1968]: "On the Generalized Set Covering Problem." CDC, Data Centers Division, Minneapolis.

Balas, E. [1964]: "Un algorithme additif pour la résolution des programmes linéaires a variables bivalentes." Comptes Rendus de l'Académie des Sciences, Paris, 258, 3817-3820.

Balas, E. [1965]: "An Additive Algorithm for Solving Linear Programs With Zero-One Variables." Operations Research, 13, 517-546.

Balas, E. [1973]: "Facets of the Knapsack Polytope." MSRR No. 323, Carnegie-Mellon University, September. Forthcoming in Mathematical Programming.

Balas, E. [1974a]: "Intersection Cuts from Disjunctive Constraints." MSRR No. 330, Carnegie-Mellon University, February.

Balas, E. [1974b]: "Disjunctive Programming: Properties of the Convex Hull of Feasible Points." MSRR No. 348, Carnegie-Mellon University, July.

Balas, E., Gerritsen, R. and Padberg, M. W. [1974]: "An All-Binary Column Generating Algorithm for Set Partitioning." Paper presented at the ORSA-TIMS meeting in Boston, April.

Balas, E. and Padberg, M. W. [1972a]: "On the Set Covering Problem." Operations Research, 20, 1152-1161.

Balas, E. and Padberg, M. W. [1972b]: "On the Set Covering Problem, II. An Algorithm for Set Partitioning." MSRR No. 295, Carnegie-Mellon University, May-November. Forthcoming in Operations Research.

Balas, E. and Padberg, M. W. [1973]: "Adjacent Vertices of the Convex Hull of Feasible 0-1 Points." MSRR No. 298, Carnegie-Mellon University, November-April.

Balas, E. and Samuelsson, H. [1973]: "Finding a Minimum Node Cover in an Arbitrary Graph." MSRR No. 325, Carnegie-Mellon University, November.

Balas, E. and Samuelsson, H. [1974a]: "Finding a Minimum Node Cover in an Arbitrary Graph. II: The Weighted Case." MSRR No. 336, Carnegie-Mellon University, April.

Balas, E. and Samuelsson, H. [1974b]: "A Symmetric Subgradient Cutting Plane Method for Set Partitioning." W.P. 5-74-75 Carnegie-Mellon University, August.

Balinski, M. L. [1970]: "On Maximum Matching, Minimum Covering and Their Connections," in Kuhn, H. W. (ed.), Proceedings of the Princeton Symposium on Mathematical Programming, Princeton University Press.

Berge, C. [1957]: "Two Theorems in Graph Theory." Proc. Nat. Acad. of Sciences, USA, 43, 842-844.

Berge, C. [1970]: Graphes et Hypergraphes, Dunod (English translation North Holland, 1973).

Berge, C. [1972]: "Balanced Matrices." Mathematical Programming, 2, 19-31.

Christofides, N. and Korman, S. [1973]: "A Computational Survey of Methods for the Set Covering Problem." Report No. 73/2, Imperial College of Science and Technology, April.

Chvátal, V. [1972]: "On Certain Polytopes Associated with Graphs." CRM-238, Universite de Montreal, October. Forthcoming in the Journal of Combinatorial Theory.

Dantzig, G. B. [1963]: Linear Programming and Extensions. Princeton University Press.

Délorme, J. [1974]: "Contribution à la résolution du problème de recouvrement: méthodes de trancatures." Thèse de Docteur Ingénieur, Université Paris VI.

Edmonds, J. [1965]: "Maximum Matching and a Polyhedron with 0, 1 Vertices." Journal of Research of the National Bureau of Standards, 69B, 125-130.

Fréhel, J. [1974]: Problèmes de partition: algorithme du simplexe, expériences numériques." Forthcoming in R.A.I.R.O.

Fulkerson, D. R. [1971]: "Blocking and Anti-Blocking Pairs of Polyhedra." Mathematical Programming, 1, 168-194.

Fulkerson, D. R. [1973]: "On the Perfect Graph Theorem," in Hu, T. C. and Robinson, S. M. (ed.), Mathematical Programming, Academic Press.

Gallai, T. [1958]: "Über Extreme Punkt-und Kantenmengen." Ann. Univ. Sci Budapest, Eötvös, Sect. Math., 2, 133-138.

Garfinkel, R. S. and Nemhauser, G. L. [1969]: "The Set Partitioning Problem: Set Covering with Equality Constraints." Operations Research, 17, 848-856.

Garfinkel, R. S. and Nemhauser, G. L. [1972]: Integer Programming, Wiley.

Geoffrion, A. M. [1967]: "Integer Programming by Implicit Enumeration and Balas' Method," SIAM Review, 7, 178-190.

Glover, F. [1965]: "A Multiphase Dual Algorithm for the Zero-One Integer Programming Problem." Operations Research, 13, 94-120.

Glover, F. and Klingman, D. [1973a]: "The Generalized Lattice Point Problem." Operations Research, 21, 141-156.

Glover, F. and Klingman, D. [1973b]: "Improved Convexity Cuts for Lattice Point Problems." CS133, University of Texas, April.

Gomory, R. E. [1963a]: "An Algorithm for Integer Solutions to Linear Programs," in Graves, R. L. and Wolfe, Ph. (ed.), Recent Advances in Mathematical Programming, McGraw-Hill.

Gomory, R. E. [1963b]: "All-Integer Integer Programming Algorithm," in Muth, J. F. and Thompson, G. L. (ed.), Industrial Scheduling, Addison-Wesley.

Gondran, M. [1973]: "Un outil pour la programmation en nombres entiers: la méthode des congruences décroissantes." RAIRO, 3, 35-54.

Gondran, M. and Laurière, J. L. [1974]: "Un algorithme pour le problème de partitionnement." RAIRO, 8, 27-70.

Graves, G. W. and Whinston, A. B. [1968]: "A New Approach to Discrete Mathematical Programming." Management Science, 15, 177-190.

Hammer, P. L., Johnson, E. L. and Peled, U. N. [1973]: "Facets of Regular 0-1 Polytopes." CQRR 73-19, University of Waterloo, October.

Harary, F. [1969]: Graph Theory, Addison-Wesley.

Held, M. and Karp, R. M. [1971]: "The Traveling-Salesman Problem and Minimum Spanning Trees: Part II." Mathematical Programming, 1, 6-25.

Held, M., Wolfe, P., and Crowder, H. D. [1974]: "Validation of Subgradient Optimization." Mathematical Programming, 6, 62-88.

Heurgon, E. [1972]: "Un problème de recouvrement exact: l'habillage des horaires d'une ligne d'autobus." RAIRO, 6.

Jeroslow, R. G. [1974]: "Principles of Cutting Plane Theory: Part I." Carnegie-Mellon University, February.

Lemke, C. E., Salkin, H. M. and Spielberg, K.[1971]: "Set Covering by Single Branch Enumeration with Linear Programming Subproblems." Operations Research, 19, 998-1022.

Lovász, L. [1972]: "Normal Hypergraphs and the Perfect Graph Conjecture." Discrete Mathematics, 2, 253-267.

Marsten, R. E. [1974]: "An Algorithm for Large Set Partitioning Problems." Management Science, 20, 779-787.

Martin, G. T. [1963]: "An Accelerated Euclidean Algorithm for Integer Programming," in Graves, R. L. and Wolfe, Ph. (ed.), Recent Advances in Mathematical Programming, Wiley.

Martin, G. T. [1969]: "Gomory Plus Ten." Paper presented at the ORSA Meeting in Miami, November.

Michaud, P. [1972]: "Exact Implicit Enumeration Method for Solving the Set Partitioning Problem." IBM Journal of Research and Development, 16, 573-578.

Ming-Te Lu [1970]: "A Computerized Airline Crew Scheduling System." Ph.D. Thesis, University of Minnesota.

Nemhauser, G. L. and Trotter, L. E. [1974]: "Properties of Vertex Packing and Independence System Polyhedra." Mathematical Programming, 6, 48-61.

Nemhauser, G. L., Trotter, L. E. and Nauss, R. M. [1972]: "Set Partitioning and Chain Decomposition." Technical Report No. 161, Cornell University.

Owen, G. [1973]: "Cutting Planes for Programs with Disjunctive Constraints." Journal of Optimization Theory and Applications, 11, 49-55.

Padberg, M. W. [1971]: "Essays in Integer Programming." Ph.D. Thesis, Carnegie-Mellon University, May.

Padberg, M. W. [1973a]: "On the Facial Structure of Set Packing Polyhedra." Mathematical Programming, 5, 199-215.

Padberg, M. W. [1973b]: "A Note on Zero-One Programming." Research Report CQRR 73-5, University of Waterloo, March.

Padberg, M. W. [1974]: "Perfect Zero-One Matrices." Mathematical Programming, 6, 180-196.

Padberg, M. W. and Rao, M. W. [1973]: "The Travelling Salesman Problem and a Class of Polyhedra of Diameter Two." IIM Preprint No. I/73-5, International Institute of Management, Berlin. Forthcoming in Mathematical Programming.

Pierce, J. F. [1968]: "Application of Combinatorial Programming to a Class of All Zero-One Integer Programming Problems. Management Science, 15, 191-209.

Pierce, J. F. and Lasky, J. S. [1973]: "Improved Combinatorial Programming Algorithms for a Class of All Zero-One Integer Programming Problems." Management Science, 19, 528-543.

Roy, B. [1969]: Algèbre moderne et Théorie des Graphes, I, Dunod.

Roy, B. [1970]: Algèbre moderne et Théorie des Graphes, II, Dunod.

Salkin, H. M. and Koncal, R. D. [1973]: "Set Covering by an All Integer Algorithm: Computational Experience." ACM Journal, 20, 189-193.

Samuelsson, H. [1974a]: "Integer Programming Duality for Set Packing-Partitioning Problems." MSRR No. 337, Carnegie-Mellon University, March.

Samuelsson, H. [1974b]: "A Symmetric Ascent Method for Finitely Regularizable Linear Programs." W.P. 6-74-75, Carnegie-Mellon University, August.

Thiriez, H. M. [1971]: "The Set Covering Problem: A Group Theoretic Approach," RAIRO, 5, 83-104.

Trotter, L. E. [1973]: "Solution Characteristics and Algorithms for the Vertex Packing Problem." Technical Report No. 168, Operations Research, Cornell University.

Trotter, L. E. [1974]: "A Class of Facet Producing Graphs for Vertex Packing Polyhedra." Technical Report No. 78, Yale University, February.

Trubin, V. A. [1969]: "On a Method of Solution of Integer Linear Programming Problems of a Special Kind." Soviet Math. Dokl., 10, 1544-1596.

Wolsey, L. [1973]: "Faces for Linear Inequalities in Zero-One Variables." CORE Discussion Paper No. 7338, November.

Zwart, P. B. [1972]: "Intersection Cuts for Separable Programming." Sch. of Eng. Appl. Sci., Washington University, St. Louis, Missouri, January.

APPENDIX
A BIBLIOGRAPHY OF APPLICATIONS

This bibliography lists articles, research reports and a few books on applications of the set partitioning (and in some cases, the set covering) model, by area of applications, in chronological order within each area.

Crew Scheduling (Airline, Railroad, etc.)

1. A. Charnes and M. H. Miller, "A Model for the Optimal Programming of Railway Freight Train Movements," Man. Sci. 3, 74-92, 1956.
2. J. F. McCloskey and F. Hanssmann, "An Analysis of Stewardess Requirements and Scheduling for a Major Airline," Naval Res. Log. Quart. 4, 183-192, 1957.
3. G. H. E. Evers, "Relevant Factors Around Crew - Utilization," AGIFORS Symposium, KLM, 1956.
4. F. Stieger, "Optimization of Swiss Air's Crew Scheduling by an Integer Linear Programming Model," Swiss Air O.R. SDK 3.3.911, 1965.
5. T. K. Kolner, "Some Highlights of a Scheduling Matrix Generator System," AGIFORS Symposium, 1966.
6. M. Niederer, "Optimization of Swissair's Crew Scheduling by Heuristic Methods Using Integer Linear Programming Models," AGIFORS Symposium, September 1966.
7. J. Agard, "Monthly Assignment of Stewards," Air France, AGIFORS Symposium, Killarney, 1966.
8. J. P. Arabeyre, "Methods of Crew Scheduling," AGIFORS, Air France, 1966.
9. J. A. Moreland, "Scheduling of Airline Flight Crews," M.S. Thesis, M.I.T., 1966.
10. J. Agard, J. P. Arabeyre and J. Vautier, "Génération automatique de rotations d'équipages," RIRO I-6, 107-117, 1967.
11. F. Steiger and M. Niederer, "Scheduling Air Crews by Integer Programming," Presented at IFIPS Congress, Edinburgh, 1968.

12. H. M. Thiriez, "Implicit Enumeration Applied to the Crew Scheduling Algorithm," Department of Aeronautics, MIT, 1968.
13. J. P. Arabeyre, J. Fearnley, F. Steiger and W. Teather, "The Air Crew Scheduling Problem: A Survey," Trans. Sci. 3, 140-163, 1969.
14. H. Thiriez, "Airline Crew Scheduling - A Group Theoretic Approach," Ph.D. Dissertation, MIT, October 1969.
15. M. Spitzer, "Solution to the Crew Scheduling Problem," AGIFORS Symposium, October 1961.

Airline Fleet Scheduling

16. A. Levin, "Fleet Routing and Scheduling Problems for Air Transportation Systems," Ph.D. Dissertation, MIT, January 1969.

Truck Delivery

17. G. B. Dantzig and J. H. Ramser, "The Truck Dispatching Problem," Man. Sci. 6, 80-91, 1959.
18. M. L. Balinski and R. E. Quandt, "On an Integer Program for a Delivery Problem," Opns. Res. 12, 300-304, 1964.
19. G. Clarke and S. W. Wright, "Scheduling of Vehicles from a Central Depot to a Number of Delivery Points," Opns. Res. 12, 4, 568-581, 1964.
20. J. F. Pierce, "Application of Combinatorial Programming to a Class of All Zero One Integer Programming Problems," Man. Sci. 15, 191-209, 1968.

Stock Cutting

21. J. F. Pierce, "Pattern Sequencing and Matching in Stock Cutting Operations," Tappi 53, 4, 668-678, April 1970.

Line and Capacity Balancing

22. M. E. Salveson, "The Assembly Line Balancing Problem," Jour. of Indus. Eng. 6, 3, 18-25, 1955.
23. D. R. Freeman and J. V. Jucker, "The Line Balancing Problem," Journal of Industrial Engineering 18, 361-364, 1967.
24. H. Steinmann and R. Schwinn, "Computational Experience with a Zero-One Programming Problem," Opns. Res., 17, 5, 917-920, 1969.

Facility Location

25. C. Revelle, D. Marks and J. C. Liebman, "An Analysis of Private and Public Sector Location Models," Man. Sci. 16, 12, 692-707, 1970.

26. C. Toregas, R. Swain, C. Revelle and L. Bergman, "The Location of Emergency Service Facilities," Opns. Res. 19, 1363-1373, 1971.

Capital Investment

27. J. R. Valenta, "Capital Equipment Decisions: A Model for Optimal Systems Interfacing," M.S. Thesis, MIT, June 1969.

Switching Current Design and Symbolic Logic

28. W. V. Quine, "A Way to Simplify Truth Functions," Am. Math. Mon. 62, 627-631, 1955.
29. E. J. McCluskey, Jr., "Minimization of Boolean Functions," Bell System Tech Journal 35, 1412-1444, 1956.
30. S. R. Petrick, "A Direct Determination of the Redundant Forms of a Boolean Function from the Set of Prime Implicants," AFCRC-TR-56-110, Air Force Cambridge Research Center, 1956.
31. J. P. Roth, "Algebraic Topological Methods for the Synthesis of Switching Systems - I," Trans. Amer. Math. Soc. 88, 301-326, 1958.
32. M. C. Paul and S. H. Unger, "Minimizing the Number of States in Incompletely Specified Sequential Functions," IRE Trans. on Electronic Computers, Ec-8, 356-367, 1959.
33. I. B. Phyne and E. J. McCluskey, Jr., "An Essay on Prime Implicant Tables," SIAM J. 9, 604-631, 1961.
34. A. Cobham, R. Fridshal and J. H. North, "An Application of Linear Programming to the Minimization of Boolean Functions," Res. Rep. RC-472, IBM, 1961.
35. ______________, "A Statistical Study of the Minimization of Boolean Functions Using Integer Programming," Res. Rep. R.C.-756, IBM, 1962.
36. A. Cobham and J. H. North, "Extensions of the Integer Programming Approach to the Minimization of Boolean Functions," Res. Rep. R.C.-915, IBM, 1963.
37. J. G. Root, "An Application of Symbolic Logic to a Selection Problem," Opns. Res. 12, 4, 519-526, 1964.
38. M. L. Balinski, "Integer Programming: Methods, Uses, Computation," Man. Sci. 12, 3, 253-313, 1965.
39. J. F. Gimpel, "A Reduction Technique for Prime Implicant Tables," IEEE Trans. on Electronic Computers, EC-14, 535-541, 1965.

Information Retrieval

40. R. H. Day, "On Optimal Extracting from a Multiple File Data Storage System: An Application of Integer Programming," Opns. Res. 13, 3, 482-494, 1965.

Marketing

41. R. J. Shanker, R. E. Turner and A. A. Zoltners: "Integrating the Criteria for Sales Force Allocation: A Set-Partitioning Approach," Working paper #48-72-3, GSIA, CMU, December 1972.

Political Districting

42. R. S. Garfinkel, "Optimal Political Districting," Ph.D. Dissertation, The Johns Hopkins University, 1968.
43. W. H. Wagner, "An Application of Integer Programming to Legislative Redistricting," Presented at the 34th National Meeting of ORSA, 1968.
44. R. S. Garfinkel and G. L. Nemhauser, "Optimal Political Districting by Implicit Enumeration Techniques," Man. Sci. 16, B495-B508, 1970.

AN ALGORITHM FOR LARGE SET PARTITIONING PROBLEMS

Roy E. Marsten

Sloan School of Management M.I.T.
Cambridge, Massachusetts, U.S.A.

ABSTRACT. An algorithm is presented for the special integer linear program known as the set partitioning problem. This problem has a binary coefficient matrix, binary variables, and unit right-hand-side. Furthermore, all of its constraints are equations. In spite of its very special form, the set partitioning problem has many practical interpretations. The algorithm is of the branch and bound type. A special class of finite mappings is enumerated rather the customary set of binary solution vectors. Linear programming is used to obtain bounds on the minimal cost of the subproblems that arise. Computational results are reported for several large problems.

1. INTRODUCTION

The integer linear program of the special form:

$$\text{(PP)} \quad \text{minimize} \sum_{j=1}^{n} c_j y_j$$

$$\text{subject to} \sum_{j=1}^{n} a_{ij} y_j = 1 \text{ for } i = 1, \ldots ,m$$

$$y_j = 0 \text{ or } 1 \text{ for } j = 1, \ldots ,n$$

where $a_{ij} = 0$ or 1 for all i, j and $c_j \geq 0$ for all j, is known as the <u>set partitioning problem</u>. It is a special case of the well-known set covering problem which has inequality ($\geq$) rather than equality constraints. The name "set partitioning problem" comes from the following interpretation. Think of each column of $A = (a_{ij})$ as a subset A_j of the index set $I = \{1, \ldots , i, \ldots ,m\}$ where

B. Roy (ed.), Combinatorial Programming: Methods and Applications, 259–267.

$i \varepsilon A_j$ if and only if $a_{ij} = 1$. The problem is then to select a set of columns which gives a minimal cost partition of I. An excellent survey of applications of covering and partitioning problems is given by Garfinkel and Nemhuser [1].

In most of the remainder of this paper it will be more convenient to discuss problem (PP) in terms of sets and partitions than in terms of constraints and variables. Let us begin by giving the set theoretic statement of the problem. Let $I = \{1, \ldots, m\}$ be the row index set and $J = \{1, \ldots, n\}$ be the column index set. Then

(1.1) $$A_j \equiv \{i \varepsilon I | a_{ij} = 1\} \quad \text{for } j \varepsilon J$$

is the subset of I containing exactly those rows covered by column j. A subset $J^1 \subseteq J$ is called a covering of I if

(1.2) $$\bigcup_{j \varepsilon J^1} A_j = I.$$

Any covering of I is a partition of I if the corresponding sets are mutually disjoint:

(1.3) $$j, k \varepsilon J^1 \quad \text{and } j \neq k \text{ implies } A_j \cap A_k = \emptyset$$

Let F denote all those partitions of I that can be obtained from the columns of the matrix A,

(1.4) $$F = \{J^1 \subseteq J | J^1 \text{ satisfies (1.2) and (1.3)}\}.$$

Then problem (PP) can be stated as:

(PP) Choose $J^1 \varepsilon F$ so as to minimize $\sum_{j \varepsilon J^1} c_j$

The algorithm developed below will perform an implicit enumeration of the set F.

2. METHOD OF SOLUTION

To describe a branch and bound algorithm it suffices to show how the set of feasible solutions is separated and how the lower bounds on the value of the objective function are computed. A general framework for such descriptions can be found in [3]. Accordingly, the separation principle and the bounding procedure will be described in this section. First, however, the constraint matrix will be placed in a special form which facilitates both the presentation and the implementation of the algorithm.

2.1 Ordering the matrix

To begin, the constraint matrix $A = (a_{ij})$ will be placed in the "staircase form" first suggested by Pierce [5]. Let the ordering of the rows be fixed and define B_t as the set of all those columns which have their first one in row t. This set will be referred to as block t. B_t is defined for t = 1, ... ,m but may be empty for some of these values. Note that no member of F can contain more than one column from any block. This is because any two columns in block t share a one in row t.

Within each block, the columns can now be placed in lexicographic order. This is equivalent to regarding the columns as binary numbers and placing them in increasing numerical order. Table 1 presents a matrix ordered in this manner. If the columns of A are numbered after the ordering is performed, then there are indices $n_0, n_1, \ldots ,n_m$ such that

$$B_t \equiv \{j\varepsilon J | n_{t-1} + 1 \leq j \leq n_t\} \quad (2.1)$$

for t = 1, ... ,m where $n_0 = 0$ and $n_m = n$. If B_t is empty, then $n_{t-1} = n_t$. In the example we have $n_1 = 5$, $n_2 = 8$, $n_3 = 10$, and $n_4 = 10$. For this matrix there are exactly five feasible solutions.

$$F = \{(1,8), (2,7), (4,10), (5,9), (1,6,9)\}. \quad (2.2)$$

2.2 Separating the feasible solutions

The set F could be separated into mutually exclusive and exhaustive subsets in the following way. For any given row i, decide which column is to cover row i. There is a subset of F corresponding to each possible choice. This is the basic decision involved in the algorithms of Pierce [5] and Pierce and Lasky [6] and of Garfinkel and Nemhauser [2].

TABLE 1
Sample Matrix After Ordering

		COLUMN									
		1	2	3	4	5	6	7	8	9	10
	1	1	1	1	1	1	0	0	0	0	0
ROW	2	0	0	0	1	1	1	1	1	0	0
	3	0	0	1	0	0	0	1	1	1	1
	4	0	1	1	0	1	1	0	1	0	1

However, since the columns are grouped together in blocks and no member of F can contain more than one column from any block, we could just as well associate a whole block with row i rather than a single column. Assigning row i to block t restricts attention to the members of F which cover row i with some column from block t. This is the method of separation to be used here.

Suppose that rows 1, ... ,r are assigned to blocks g(1), ... , g(r) respectively. Let F^g denote all those elements of F in which row i is covered by some column from block g(i) for i = 1, ... ,r. Let $g^{-1}(t)$ denote the set of rows that have been assigned to block t for t = 1, ... ,m. Then it is easy to see that column $j \in B_t$ can not belong to any member of F^g unless

$$(2.3) \qquad A_j \cap \{1, \ldots, r\} = g^{-1}(t).$$

This condition means that column j must cover every row already assigned to block t, and must not cover any row already assigned to some other block.

The partial assignment g therefore eliminates some of the columns of each block from further consideration. Define

$$(2.4) \qquad B_t^g \equiv \{j \in B_t | A_j \text{ satisfies (2.3)}\}.$$

These are the columns of B_t that may belong to members of F^g. Note that if r = m, then B_t^g is either empty or a singleton. Define

$$(2.5) \qquad LHB_t^g \equiv \min \{j \in B_t | A_j \text{ satisfies (2.3)}\}$$

$$(2.6) \qquad RHB_t^g \equiv \max \{j \in B_t | A_j \text{ satisfies (2.3)}\}$$

where the names are chosen to suggest left and right hand boundaries, respectively. Thus

$$(2.7) \qquad B_t^g = \{j \in B_t | LHB_t^g \leq j \leq RHB_t^g\}.$$

In the implementation of the algorithm each block has left and right hand boundaries which are adjusted as g changes so that (2.7) is always satisfied. This adjustment process is very simple because of the lexicographic ordering of each B_t. In the example of Table 1, suppose that g(1) = 1, g(2) = 2, and g(3) = 2. Then the boundaries are as in Table 2.

Now let T^g denote the set of permissible choices for g(r + 1) when $0 \leq r < m$. It follwos immediately from the staircase form of A that

$$(2.8) \qquad g(r+1) \in \{1, \ldots, r+1\}.$$

Consider the choice of g(r + 1) = t where $t \leq r$. There are two cases:

Case 1. If $g(t) \neq t$, then B_t^g is empty and row (r + 1) cannot be assigned to block t.

Case 2. If g(t) = t, then there are three sub-cases:

A. No column of B_t^g has a one in row (r + 1). Then row (r + 1) cannot be assigned to block t.
B. At least one column of B_t^g has a one in row (r + 1). Then row (r + 1) may be assigned to block t.
C. The set B_t^g is non-empty and every column in it has a one in row (r + 1). Then row (r + 1) must be assigned to block t.

If two or more choices of $t \leq r$ satisfy Case 2C, then it is impossible to assign row (r + 1) and we set $T^g = \emptyset$. If exactly one $t^* \leq r$ satisfies Case 2C, then we set $T^g = \{t^*\}$. Otherwise, we put into T^g every $t \leq r$ which satisfies Case 2B, and also (r + 1) if B_{r+1} is nonempty. Note that $T^g = \emptyset$ if every $t \leq r$ falls in Case 1 or 2A and $B_{r+1} = \emptyset$

TABLE 2
Boundary Positions for Sample Matrix and Given g

	LHB	RHB
B_1	1	2
B_2	7	8
B_3	10	9

TABLE 3
Complete Enumeration for the Sample Matrix

node	pred	i	g(i)	soln
1	0	1	1	
2	1	2	1	
3	2	3	3	
4	3	4	1	(5, 9)
5	3	4	3	(4, 10)
6	1	2	2	
7	6	3	1	
8	6	3	2	
9	8	4	1	(2, 7)
10	8	4	2	(1, 8)
11	6	3	3	
12	11	4	2	(1, 6, 9)

Table 3 represents the tree generated by a complete enumeration for the sample problem of Table 1. This tree has 13 nodes, the root node having the label zero. There is a row in this table for each node, permitting reconstruction of the tree itself. The columns headed "i" and "g(i)" refer to the branch which connects this node to its predecessor. For each terminal node corresponding to a solution, the solution is given in the last column. Note that Table 2 givens the boundary positions that obtain at node 8.

This completes the discussion of the separation principle. For a more detailed discussion the reader may consult [4].

2.3 Computing the lower bounds

The set F^g defined above is the set of feasible solutions of the restricted version of (PP):

$$(PP^g) \qquad \text{minimize } \textstyle\sum_{j\varepsilon J_a^g} c_j y_j$$

$$\text{subject to } \textstyle\sum_{j\varepsilon J_a^g} a_{ij} y_j = 1 \text{ for } i \varepsilon I$$

$$y_j = 0 \text{ or } 1 \text{ for } j \varepsilon J_a^g$$

where

$$(2.9) \qquad J_a^g \equiv \bigcup_{t=1}^{m} B_t^g$$

is the set of all available columns, given g. Let (LP^g) denote the linear program obtained by dropping the integrality condition and requiring only $y_j \geq 0$. A lower bound on the minimal value of (PP^g) is given by the value of (LP^g). Let y^g be an optimal solution of (LP^g) and let

$$(2.10) \qquad J_b^g = \text{the set of columns that are basic in } y^g.$$

Now consider h such that

$$(2.11) \qquad h(i) = \begin{cases} g(i) & \text{for } i = 1, \ldots ,r \\ t & \text{for } i = r + 1 \end{cases}$$

for any $t \varepsilon T^g$. Then $J_a^h \subseteq J_a^g$ and therefore y^g is a dual feasible solution of (LP^h). If

$$(2.12) \qquad J_b^g \subseteq J_a^h$$

then y^g is in fact an optimal solution of (LP^h). If (2.12) is not satisfied, then

$$(2.13) \qquad (J - J_a^h) \cap J_b^g = \{j_1, \ldots ,j_k\} \neq \emptyset.$$

That is, some of the columns which are basic under g are not available under h. In this case we can compute a lower bound on the increase in the objective function of (LP^g) caused by imposing the additional constraint

(2.14) $y_{j_1} + \ldots + y_{j_k} = 0.$

This lower bound, denoted PENALTY (h), is just the amount by which the objective function would increase in one dual pivot. If (2.12) is satisfied, then PENALTY (h) = 0. In either case we have a lower bound on the value of (LP^h) which can be computed directly from the optimal tableau for (LP^g). Using v(LP) to denote the value of (LP), define

(2.15) BOUND (h) $\equiv$ v(LP^g) + PENALTY (h).

The algorithm computes BOUND (h) for every $t \in T^g$ (see (2.11)). The set T^g is then sorted into increasing order according to BOUND so that the extension of g with the lowest BOUND is tried first.

2.4 The algorithm

The special results obtained above can now be brought together in a branch-and-bound algorithm for (PP). Let $\emptyset$ denote the null set or null function, as appropriate.

Step 0. Set i = 0, g = $\emptyset$, BOUND ($\emptyset$) = 0, $T^\emptyset = \{1\}$ and V = + ∞.
Step 1. If (LP^g) is infeasible, go to Step 10.
Step 2. If v(LP^g) $\geq$ V, go to Step 10.
Step 3. If the optimal solution of (LP^g) is integer, go to Step 9.
Step 4. If i = m, go to Step 9.
Step 5. Set i = i + 1.
Step 6. If $T^g = \emptyset$, go to Step 13.
Step 7. Compute BOUND for each $t \in T^g$ and sort T^g into increasing order according to the BOUND's
Step 8. Set $T_i = T^g$, go to Step 11.
Step 9. Record the solution. Set V = min {V,v(LP^g)}.
Step 10. If $T_i = \emptyset$, go to Step 13.
Step 11. Let t* = the first element in T_i. Set g(i) = t* and $T_i = T_i - \{t^*\}$.
Step 12. If BOUND (g) $\geq$ V, go to Step 10. Otherwise go to Step 1.
Step 13. If i = 0, STOP
Step 14. Set i = i - 1 and go to Step 10.

3. COMPUTATIONAL EXPERIENCE

TABLE 4

Results for Pure Set Partitioning Problems (360/91)

ID	m	n	t(lp)	piv(lp)	cost(lp)	t(e)	piv(e)	cost(e)	rmax	nsol	d %
CS1	90	303	8.53	128	42,719.50	32.11	19	42,855.00	56	1	7
CS2	63	1,641	84.50	326	60,902.50	84.26	201	60,990.00	12	2	11
CS3	111	4,826	314.93	455	217,351.00	164.84	122	217,687.00	19	3	5
CS4	200	2,362	418.86	612	81,730.00	0.00	0	81,730.00	0	1	1 1/2
CS5	419	21,585	>3 hrs.	?	>119,800	?	?	?	?	?	2

The results for pure set partitioning problems are presented in Table 4. The following symbols are used for the column headings.

ID - problem identifier
m - the number of rows (partitioning constraints)
n - the number of columns (binary variables).
t(1p) - the time, in seconds, required to solve the initial linear program.
piv(1p) - the number of (dual) pivots required to solve the initial linear program.
cost(1p) - the optimal cost for the initial linear program.
t(e) - the additional time, in seconds, required to perform the enumeration. That is, to find and verify the optimal integer solution.
piv(e) - the number of (dual) pivots required for reoptimization during the enumeration phase.
cost(e) - the cost of the optimal integer solution.
rmax - the maximum depth of the search, i.e. the maximum number of rows assigned at any one time.
nsol - the number of integer solutions found.
d - the density of the coefficient matrix.

Time spent on basis reinversion is included in t(1p) and t(e). The pivots performed during these reinversions are not counted in piv(1p) or piv(e). All of the times quoted in Table 1 are for the UCLA IBM 360/91.

REFERENCES

1. Garfinkel, R.S. and Nemhauser, G.L., "Optimal Set Covering: A Survey", in A. Geoffrion (ed.), Perspectives on Optimization.

2. _____AND_____, "The Set Partitioning Problem: Set Covering with Equality Constraints," Operations Research, 17, 5, 848-856, September-October, 1969.

3. Geoffrion, A.M. and Marsten, R.E., "Integer Programming Algorithms: A Framework and State-of-the-Art Survey", Management Science, 18, 9, 465-491, 1972.

4. Marsten, R.E., An Implicit Enumeration Algorithm for the Set Partitioning Problem with Side Constraints, Ph.D. Dissertation, University of California, Los Angeles, October, 1971.

5. Pierce, J.F., "Application of Combinatorial Programming to a Class of All-Zero-One Integer Programming Problems," Management Science, 15, 191-209, 1968.

6. _____ AND Lasky, J.A., "Improved Combinatorial Programming Algorithms for a Class of All-Zero-One Integer Programming Problems," Management Science, 19, 528-543, 1973.

LE PROBLEME DE PARTITION SOUS CONTRAINTE

J. Fréhel

SEMA, Direction Scientifique

1. Introduction

Les problèmes de tournées de véhicules et de rotations d'équipages se formalisent aisément sous forme d'un problème de partition de la forme :

$$\text{Min } c.x = \sum_{1}^{n} c_j x_j$$

$$\text{avec} \quad \sum_{j=1}^{n} a_{ij} x_j = 1 \qquad \forall i = 1, 2, \ldots, m$$

$$\text{et} \quad x_j \in \{0, 1\} \qquad \forall j = 1, 2, \ldots, n$$

où les a_{ij} valent 0 ou 1. C'est maintenant un résultat classique que l'algorithme du simplexe s'applique à la résolution de ce problème (cf. [2], [4], [5]).

Malheureusement la modélisation des problèmes de rotation d'équipages et de tournées de véhicules introduit en général une ou plusieurs contraintes additionnelles qui ne sont pas du type $\Sigma\, l_j x_j = 1$ avec $l_j \in \{0, 1\}$ pour tout j.

En particulier, le nombre total des rotations ou tournées sélectionnées peut être soit majoré, soit minoré, soit fixé à l'avance. Cela se traduit par l'addition d'une contrainte de type :

$$\sum_{j=J}^{j=n} x_j \; \begin{matrix} \geq \\ = \\ \leq \end{matrix} \; N.$$

B. Roy (ed.), Combinatorial Programming: Methods and Applications, 269–274.

Un autre type de contrainte qui peut être rencontré est de la forme : $\sum_{j \in J} x_j \leq N_j$ où J est un sous-ensemble de $\{1, 2, \ldots, n\}$. Une telle contrainte signifie que l'on désire obtenir une solution ne contenant pas plus de N rotations de la classe définie par J. J sera par exemple les rotations qui ont plus de p tronçons ou les rotations qui comportent un nombre d'heures de vol trop élevé.

Le but de cet article est de montrer que ces contraintes additionnelles peuvent être introduites dans un algorithme du simplexe du type décrit dans [2], [4] ou [5].

On trouvera par ailleurs dans [1] un exemple concret d'habillage d'horaires dans lequel une contrainte $\sum_1^n x_j = N$ est inévitable.

2. Introduction d'une contrainte $\sum_1^n x_j = N$

Rappelons tout d'abord le résultat essentiel qui permet d'adapter sur un plan théorique la méthode du simplexe au problème de partition.

Proposition 2.1 : Soit B' et B" deux bases entières du problème de partition où B" eest une base optimale et $c_{B'} x_{B'} \geq c_{B''} x_{B''}$. Alors il existe une séquence de bases entières adjacentes :

$$B' = B_1, B_2, \ldots, B_p = B'' \text{ telle que :}$$

$$c_{B'} x_{B'} \geq c_{B_2} x_{B_2} \geq \cdots \geq c_{B_p} x_{B_p} = c_{B''} x_{B''}.$$

Preuve : On trouvera la démonstration de ce résultat dans [2], [4] ou [5].

Introduisons alors le problème perturbé $P(\lambda)$

$$\text{Min } \sum_1^n c_j x_j + \lambda \sum_1^n x_j = \sum_1^n c'_j x_j$$

$$\text{avec } \sum_1^n a_{ij} x_j = 1 \qquad \forall i = 1, 2, \ldots, m$$

$$\text{et } x_j \in \{0, 1\} \qquad \forall j = 1, 2, \ldots, n.$$

Proposition 2.2 : Si λ est positif assez grand, alors la solution optimale du problème perturbé est une solution qui a un nombre minimum de variables égales à + 1 et est une solution de coût minimal (au sens des coûts initiaux c_j) parmi ces solutions de longueur minimale.

Preuve : Cette proposition est un corollaire immédiat de la théorie classique de la pénalisation.

Proposition 2.3 : Soit deux bases B' et B'' de même longueur $|x_{B'}| = |x_{B''}| = N$ et soit $B' = B_1, B_2, \ldots, B_p = B''$ une séquence de bases adjacentes telles que :

$$c'_{B_1} x_{B_1} \geq c'_{B_2} x_{B_2} \geq \ldots \geq c'_{B_p} x_{B_p}.$$

Alors, si λ est assez grand, on a :

$$|x_{B_1}| = |x_{B_2}| = |x_{B_3}| = |x_{B_p}| = N.$$

Preuve : Si λ est assez grand, toute solution comportant moins de N variables égales à 1 est moins coûteuse que toute solution comportant au moins N variables égales à 1. En conséquence, $x_{B_i} \geq N \quad i = 1, 2, \ldots, p.$

Soit $k \in \{2, 3, \ldots, p\}$. Si λ est assez grand, on aura pour les mêmes raisons : $|x_{B_{k-1}}| \geqq |x_{B_h}|$, ce qui achève la démonstration.

Proposition 2.4 : Soit deux bases entières B', B'' de longueurs $|x_{B'}| = |x_{B''}|$ de longueur minimale parmi les solutions entières telles que $c_{B'} x_{B'} \geq c_{B''} x_{B''}$.

Alors il existe une séquence de bases entières adjacentes

$$B' = B_1, B_2, \ldots, B_p = B''$$

telles que :

$$|x_{B_1}| = |x_{B_2}| = \ldots = |x_{B_p}|.$$

Preuve : On a $c'_j = c_j + \lambda$. Donc $c'_{B'} x_{B'} = c_{B_1} x_{B_1} + \lambda |x_{B_1}|$.

Par application du théorème 2.3, il existe une séquence de bases adjacentes entières $B_1, B_2, \ldots, B_p$ telle que :

$$c'_{B_1} x_{B_1} \geq \ldots \geq c'_{B_p} x_{B_p}$$

soit :

$$c_{B_1} x_{B_1} + \lambda |x_{B_1}| \geq \ldots \geq c_{B_p} x_{B_p} + \lambda |x_{B_p}|.$$

Si λ est assez grand, on a nécessairement :

$|x_{B_1}| = |x_{B_2}| = \ldots = |x_{B_p}|$ sinon la séquence d'inégalités ne pourrait être satisfaite ; on a donc :

$$c_{B_1} x_{B_1} \geq c_{B_2} x_{B_2} \geq \ldots \geq c_{B_p} x_{B_p}.$$

Ces deux propositions vont nous permettre de résoudre le problème de partition sous contrainte :

$$\text{Min} \sum_1^n c_j x_j$$

$$\sum_1^n a_{ij} x_j = 1 \quad \forall i = 1, 2, \ldots, m$$

$$\sum x_j = N \text{ minimum}$$

$$x_j \in \{0, 1\} \quad \forall j = 1, 2, \ldots, n.$$

Il suffit d'appliquer tout d'abord un algorithme du simplexe au problème de partition sous contrainte avec comme fonction économique $\sum_1^n x_j$. Lorsque l'on aura obtenu une solution de coût minimum, on poursuivra l'algorithme avec la fonction économique initiale $\sum_1^n c_j x_j$ en ne tolérant que les pivotages qui maintiennent les longueurs des solutions constantes.

Si N n'est pas le nombre minimum de variables égales à 1 et si le problème contraint à une solution, alors il existera une valeur de λ, λ_N telle que la solution optimale du problème perturbé soit de longueur N. On choisira une valeur initiale de λ

égale à 0 par exemple et l'on ajustera cette valeur de λ jusqu'à ce que la solution optimale du problème perturbé ait la longueur voulue.

3. Introduction d'autres types de contraintes

3.1 Un autre type de contrainte très semblable est :

$$\sum_J x_j = N_J \quad \text{où} \quad J \subset \{1, 2, \ldots, n\}.$$

Il est clair que les raisonnements faits pour les cas précédents sont immédiatement applicables.

3.2 Contrainte de la forme $\sum_J x_j \leq N_J$

On commencera par perturber le problème initial avec une fonction additive $\lambda \sum_J x_j$. Si l'on prend λ assez grand et s'il existe des solutions de longueur relative à J inférieure ou égale à N_J, on trouvera une telle solution au bout d'un nombre fini d'itérations.

A partir de cette solution optimale pour un λ, on relachera progressivement la perturbation λ jusqu'à ce que $\sum_J x_j$ dépasse la longueur N_J maximum.

3.3 Contrainte de la forme $\sum_J x_j \geq N_J$

En changeant le signe de λ, on pourra utiliser la même procédure que dans 3.2.

3.4 Contrainte générale $\sum_{j=1}^{j=n} l_j x_j = L$

On considèrera le problème perturbé :

$$\text{Min} \sum c_j x_j + \lambda \sum l_j x_j$$

$$\text{avec} \quad \sum a_{ij} x_j = 1 \qquad \forall i = 1, 2, \ldots, m$$

$$x_j \in \{0, 1\} \qquad \forall j = 1, 2, \ldots, n.$$

On pourra développer sur cette nouvelle contrainte les mêmes arguments de perturbation que pour la recherche de solutions de longueur fixée.

REFERENCES

[1] HEURBON, E. - "Un problème de recouvrement : l'habillage des horaires dans une ligne d'autobus".
R.I.R.O., 6e année, V-1, 1972, p. 13-29.

[2] BALAS, E. ; PADBERG, M. - "On the set covering problem".
Management Sciences, Research Report n° 197, February 1970, Carnegie-Mellon University, Published in Operations Research, 20, n° 6, 1972.

[3] BALAS, E. ; PADBERG, M. - "On the set covering problem II - An algorithm".
Management Sciences, Research Report n° 295, May-November 1972.

[4] FREHEL, J. - "Sur quelques propriétés du problème de partitionnement".
SEMA (Metra International), Direction Scientifique, Note de Travail n° 179, décembre 1972.

[5] FREHEL, J. - "Problèmes de partition : algorithme du simplexe, expériences numériques".
En publication Revue Verte de l'A.F.C.E.T., R.I.R.O.

CHARACTERISATIONS OF TOTALLY UNIMODULAR, BALANCED AND PERFECT MATRICES

Manfred W. Padberg

New York University

Introduction

We consider combinatorial programming problems of the form (IP): $\max\{cx | Ax \leq e, x_j = 0 \text{ or } 1, \forall_j\}$, where A is a mxn matrix of zeroes and ones, e is a column vector of m ones and c is an arbitrary (non-negative) vector of n reals. This class of problems is known as the set packing problem, see e.g. [1]. It is closely related to the set partitioning problem (SPP) and to the set covering problem. In the former case, the inequality constraints $Ax \leq e$ of (IP) are replaced by equality constraints $Ax=e$, whereas in the latter case one requires the constraints to hold with reversed inequality, i.e. $Ax \geq e$. With respect to the set partitioning problem (SPP), it can be shown, that by appropriately modifying the objective function, the problem (SPP) can always be transformed into the form (IP) above. This is, however, not true in general if the set covering problem is considered. It is true, however, if the matrix A has at most two +1 entries per row, i.e. if the set covering problem assumes the special form of a node-covering problem in a (finite undirected) graph. As has been noted in [2], some of the structural properties of set partitioning and set packing problems do not carry over to the (general) set covering problem.

In this paper, we give an overview of necessary and sufficient conditions which ensure that the <u>relaxed</u> linear programming problem (LP): $\max\{cx | Ax \leq e, x_j \geq 0, \forall_j\}$ associated with (IP) always has an <u>integer</u> (zero-one) solution <u>irrespective</u> of what linear form cx is maximized. The best-known sufficient condition for this to be true is that the matrix A be <u>totally unimodular</u> [14]. A further sufficient condition which generalizes the notion of total uni-

B. Roy (ed.), Combinatorial Programming: Methods and Applications, 275–284.

modularity is that the matrix A be balanced (5). Alluding to the notion of a perfect graph due to C. Berge (3), we have termed in (20) matrices A with the above property perfect and derived a complete, i.e. a necessary and sufficient, characterization of perfect zero-one matrices in terms of forbidden submatrices. In this paper we discuss in detail the relationship between totally unimodular, balanced and perfect matrices. We discuss some implications for the Strong Perfect Graph Conjecture due to C. Berge (3) and in an appendix give a new proof for the characterization of balanced matrices.

TOTALLY UNIMODULAR, BALANCED AND PERFECT ZERO-ONE MATRICES

For any mxn matrix A of integers and vector b of m integers let P(A,b) and $P_I(A,b)$ denote the polytopes

$$P(A,b) = \{x \epsilon R^n | Ax \leq b, x \geq 0\}, \quad P_I(A,b) = \text{conv}\{x \epsilon P(A,b) | x \text{ integer}\},$$

i.e. $P_I(A,b)$ is the convex hull of integer points in P(A,b). It is well-known from linear programming theory, that P(A,b) and $P_I(A,b)$ coincide if and only if the linear program $\max\{cx | x \epsilon P(A,b)\}$ produces an integral solution for every vector c of n integers. (We can assume without loss of generality that the polytope P(A,b) and, hence, $P_I(A,b)$ is bounded, so that the maximum is actually attained). Whenever P(A,b) and $P_I(A,b)$ coincide, i.e. $P(A,b) = P_I(A,b)$, the integer linear programming problem $\max\{cx | x \epsilon P_I(A,b)\}$ can thus be solved by solving the associated linear programming problem $\max\{cx | x \epsilon P(A,b)\}$ for which - at least empirically - efficient solutions procedures exist. Since integer linear programming problems are as of today in general not yet satisfactorily solvable, it appears to be of prime interest to know under what conditions on the matrix A and vector b the linear programming problem will produce an integral solution; or expressed alternatively: to know what makes integer programming problems so hard to solve.

As is well-known, in case of net work flow problems and related optimizations on directed graphs, see (13), the solutions always turn out integer. The reason for this nice property is that the associated matrix A in such problems is totally unimodular, i.e. the determinant of every square submatrix of A equals 0 or ± 1. By Cramer's rule, this property implies that all vertices of P(A,b) are integral, no matter what vector b of m integers is used. This is the easy part of the Theorem of Hoffmann and Kruskal (17), which states the reverse statement is true also. (For a proof, see (10), also (14)):

Theorem 1 (Hoffmann and Kruskal, 1956): Let A be any mxn matrix of integers and b any vector of m integers. Then the following two statements are equivalent:

(i) A is totally unimodular.
(ii) $P(A,b) = P_I(A,b)$ for all integer m-vectors b.

Whereas Theorem 1 provides a characterization of a totally unimodular matrix A by means of two geometric objects in R^n, one is naturally led to investigating those square submatrices of A that produce determinants whose values are different from the "permitted" values of 0 and ± 1, thus rendering the matrix A not totally unimodular. Such an algebraic characterization of totally unimodular matrices was obtained by Camion (6):

Definition 2 (Camion, 1965): A matrix A of size kxk with coefficient a_{ij} equal to 0 or ± 1 is called eulerian if

(i) $\sum_{i=1}^{k} a_{ij} \equiv 0 \bmod 2$ for j=1,...,k and (ii) $\sum_{j=1}^{k} a_{ij} \equiv 0 \bmod 2$ for i=1,...,k.

With this definition, Camion then proved the following theorem:

Theorem 3 (Camion, 1965): Let A be any mxn matrix with coefficients a_{ij} equal to 0 or ± 1. Then the following two statements are equivalent:

(i) A is totally unimodular.
(ii) A does not contain any nonsingular eulerian submatrix.

Moreover, Camion has provided a further, topological characterization of totally unimodular matrices by means of eulerian graphs: If one associates to a matrix A with coefficients a_{ij} equal to 0 or ± 1 a bi-partite graph G(A) by defining a node for every row and for every column of A and an edge (i,j) connecting node i to node j if $a_{ij} \neq 0$, then eulerian submatrices of A are in one-to-one correspondence to (vertex-induced) eulerian subgraphs of G(A). Defining a_{ij} to be the length of the edge (i,j) in G(A) and for any eulerian subgraph G' of G(A) $\ell(G')$ to be the length of an euler cycle in G', a characterization of totally unimodular matrices is contained in the following theorem which we quote from (16):

Theorem 4 (Camion, 1965): Let A be any mxn matrix with coefficients a_{ij} equal to 0 or ± 1 and G(A) denote the graph associated to A as above. Then the following two statements are equivalent:

(i) A is totally unimodular.
(ii) For every eulerian subgraph G' of G(A) we have $\ell(G') \equiv 0 \bmod 4$.

Theorem 4 provides an easy way to check the nonsingularity of a kxk eulerian matrix A: A is nonsingular if and only if $\sum_{i=1}^{k} \sum_{j=1}^{k} a_{ij} \not\equiv 0 \bmod 4$. Whereas the above characterizations of totally unimodular matrices are necessary and sufficient and do not provide per se a computationally easy way to check the total unimodularity of a given matrix, they allow to deduce for various special cases more readily verified sufficient conditions, see e.g. (16). For other necessary and sufficient conditions, see (7), (9), (15), (23). The important conclusion to be derived from Theorem 1 and 3 is that, for any matrix A having 0, $\pm$ 1 coefficient, $P(A,b) \neq P_I(A,b)$ for some integer vector b if and only if A contains a nonsingular eulerian submatrix. In fact, if A itself is eulerian and nonsingular, we immediately know an integer b with that property. For, let A be of size kxk and $e^T = (1,\ldots,1)$ be the vector with k components equal to 1, then we can choose $b = \frac{1}{2} Ae$. (More generally, for matrices A that are almost totally unimodular in the sense that A is not, but every proper submatrices of A is totally unimodular, it is possible to determine the set of integer vectors b for which $P(A,b) \neq P_I(A,b)$).

Whereas the concept of a totally unimodular matrix A has been appropriate in characterizing polytopes P(A,b) with the property that $P(A,b) = P_I(A,b)$ no matter what the right-hand side vector b, we will turn now to the case of a given right-hand vector b. More specifically, we will turn now to the case where A is any mxn matrix of zeroes and ones and b is the vector of m components equal to 1. We observe, however, that, due to the periodicity property of integer linear programs we have $P(A,b) = P_I(A,b)$ for some integer matrix A and integer vector b if and only if $P(A,tb) = P_I(A,tb)$ for all integer scalars t, $t \neq 0$. (Proof: Cramer's rule). Consequently, the above case is more general than may appear to be the case at first.

From the requirement that part (ii) of Theorem 1 holds for all integer m-vectors b, we have immediately the following equivalent formulation of part (ii) of Theorem 1:

(ii') $P(A',b') = P_I(A',b')$ for all submatrices A' and (compatibly dimensioned) integer vectors b'.

One can therefore in an attempt to generalize the notion of total unimodularity for zero-one matrices use (ii') as the starting point for the definition of a larger class of matrices by requesting that (ii') holds for all vectors b' with components equal to 1 rather than for arbitrary integer vectors b'. This is in fact the concept underlying the notion of a balanced matrix as introduced by C. Berge (5):

Definition 5 (Berge, 1971): Let A be any zero-one matrix. A is called balanced if $P(A',e') = P_I(A',e')$ for all submatrices A' of A and all (compatibly dimensioned) vectors e' with all components equal to 1.

An algebraic characterization of balanced matrices in terms of forbidden submatrices is implicit in the paper by C. Berge (5), but to our knowledge has been formulated explicitly by Hoffmann and Oppenheim (17a). In the appendix to this paper we will give a different proof relying on Theorem 10 below to the following:

Theorem 6 (Berge, 1971): Let A be any mxn matrix of zeroes and ones. Then the following two statements are equivalent:

(i) A is balanced.
(ii) A does not contain any odd submatrix with row sums and column sums equal to two.

A topological characterization of balanced matrices can be obtained as follows: Denote by G(A) the (intersection) graph which can be associated to every zero-one matrix A in the following natural way: G(A) has a node for every column a_j of A and an edge connecting node i to node j if $a_i a_j \geq 1$, i.e. if columns i and j have at least one +1 entry in common. Every submatrix of A defines a (edge-induced) partial subgraph of G(A). Let $\mathcal{G}$ be the collection of all partial subgraphs of G(A) that correspond to some submatrix of A. Then A is balanced if and only if $\mathcal{G}$ does not contain any cycle of odd length greater than or equal to 3 having no chord. A somewhat different graphical characterization is given in C. Berge (4), using the notion of a hypergraph, see also (18). In fact, C. Berge (5) has used the characterization of balanced matrices in terms of hypergraphs as the starting point for the definition of a balanced matrix.

Whereas in the case of balanced matrices one considers all submatrices A' of a mxn zero-one matrix A, the next step of the analysis considers only submatrices A' of A that are of size mxk, where $1 \leq k \leq n$, i.e. we do no longer request that $P(A',e') = P_I(A',e')$ for all submatrices A' of A, rather we want $P(A',e) = P_I(A',e)$ to hold for all mxk submatrices A' of A. On account of the non-negativity of A, every vertex of $P(A',e)$ where A' is a mxk submatrix of the mxn matrix A is basically seen to be a vertex of $P(A,e)$. Consequently, we are led to the following:

Definition 7 (Padberg, 1973): Let A be any zero-one matrix. A is called perfect if $P(A,e) = P_I(A,e)$.

The motivation to call matrices with the property of Definition 7 perfect, rests with the following connection to the concept of a perfect graph due to C. Berge (3): Given a finite undirected graph $G = (V,E)$, denote by $\alpha(G)$ the maximum cardinality of a stable (independent) node set in G, by $\Theta(G)$ the minimal number of cliques that cover G, by $\gamma(G)$ the chromatic number of G, and by $w(G)$ the maximal cardinality of a clique in G. (A clique is a maximal complete subgraph of G). A graph G is called γ-perfect if $\gamma(G') = w(G')$ for every induced subgraph G' of G; G is called α-perfect if $\alpha(G') = \Theta(G')$ for every induced subgraph G' of G. A graph is perfect if it is both α-perfect and γ-perfect.

Let A denote now the clique-matrix of a graph G, i.e. every row of A corresponds to a clique of G and vice versa, every clique furnishes a row of A. Basing on recent results by Lovasz [19,18], Chvatal [8] has proven the following theorem, see also Fulkerson [12,11]:

Theorem 8 (Chvatal, 1973): Given any finite undirected graph G and its associated mxn clique-matrix A the following two conditions are equivalent:

(i) Every vertex of P(A,e) is integral, i.e. $P(A,e) = P_I(A,e)$.
(ii) G is perfect.

In order to obtain an algebraic characterization of perfect matrices in terms of forbidden submatrices one needs the following.

Definition 9 (Padberg, 1973): Let A be a zero-one matrix of size mxn, $m \geq n$. A is said to have property $\Pi_{\beta,n}$ if the following conditions are met:

(i) A contains a nxn nonsingular submatrix A, whose row and column sums are all equal to β.

(ii) If a^T is a row of A with row sum equal to β and a^T is not contained in the submatrix A, defined under (i), then there exists a row b^T in A such that componentwise a=b.

(iii) All other rows of A have row sums strictly less than β.

Obviously, if a given zero-one matrix A contains a mxk submatrix A' having the property $\Pi_{\beta,k}$ for some $\beta \geq 2$, then $P(A,e) \neq P_I(A,e)$. This is the easy part of the following theorem which states that the reverse is also correct:

Theorem 10 (Padberg, 1973): Let A be any zero-one matrix of size mxn. The following two conditions are equivalent:

(i) A is perfect.
(ii) For $\beta \geq 2$ and $3 \leq k \leq n$, A does not contain any mxk submatrix having the property $\Pi_{\beta,k}$.

Using the notion of a clique-matrix to mean that A is the clique-matrix of its associated (intersection) graph G(A), condition (ii) can be sharpened as follows:

(ii') A is a clique-matrix and A does not contain any mxk submatrix having the property $\Pi_{\beta,k}$ for $5\leq k\leq n$ and $2\leq\beta\leq\left(\frac{1}{2}(k-1)\right)$.

The main vehicle in proving Theorem 10 is the consideration of critically imperfect matrices A, i.e. matrices A that are themselves not perfect, but perfect upon deletion of any single column of A, see [20] and also [21]. Thus the main difficulty in proving Theorem 10 consists in showing that a mxn zero-one matrix that is critically imperfect has the property described in Definition 9.

A topological characterization of a perfect zero-one matrix A in terms of forbidden subgraphs of the associated (intersection) graph G(A) is not known to date, but would - in view of Theorem 8 - follow from a proof of the Strong Perfect Graph Conjecture due to C. Berge [3]: In fact, in view of this conjecture we have formulated in [21] the following stronger form of Theorem 10 as a conjecture:

Conjecture 11 (Padberg, 1973): Let A be any mxn matrix of zeroes and ones. Then the following two conditions are equivalent:

(i) A is perfect.

(ii) A does not contain any mxk submatrix A' having property $\Pi_{\beta,k}$ for any k satisfying $3\leq k\leq n$ and $\beta=2$, $\left(\frac{k}{2}\right)$, and $k-1$.

Some support for Conjecture 11 (and thereby for the Strong Perfect Graph Conjecture) can be inferred from the following. Denote by C_s the nxn circulant having exactly s one entries in each row and column. More specifically, for $1\leq j\leq n$ let $c_{jj}=\ldots=c_{j,j+s-1}=1$, $c_{j,k}=0$ otherwise, where the indices are taken modulo n. Different from the above, let us term a zero-matrix A critically imperfect if its associated (intersection) graph G(A) is critically imperfect, i.e. G(A) is not perfect, but every proper induced subgraph of G(A) is perfect. We then have the following result:

Proposition 12: Let C_s be the nxn circulant having exactly s one entries in each row and column. Furthermore, let n be such that $\frac{n-1}{s}=t$ is a natural number, $s\leq t$ and C_s is arranged as above. Then C_s is critically imperfect if and only if $n\geq 5$ is odd and $s=2$, i.e. C_s is the incidence matrix of an odd cycle of length $2t+1$ without chords.

Proof: The sufficiency of the condition is immediate. To prove the necessity, we have to show that the graph G associated with C_s cannot be critically imperfect if $3 \leq s \leq (\frac{n}{2}) - 1$. To prove this statement, all that is needed is to exhibit in G a cycle of odd length strictly less than n and without chords. This, however, is readily achieved by construction. More precisely, we distinguish three cases :

(1) $s=3$, $t=3$. By inspection, we find two 5-cycles, (1,3,5,7,1) and (2,4,6,8,10,2).

(2) $s=3$, $t \geq 4$. A cycle without chords of length $2t-1$ is given by the node set N_o where
$N_o = \{1,2,s+1,s+2,\ldots,3t-11,3t-10,3t-8,3t-6,3t-4,3t-2,3t,1\}$.

(3) $t \geq s \geq 4$. We find again a cycle without chords of length $2t-1$ given by the node set N_1 where
$N_1 = \{1,2,s+1,s+2,\ldots,ts+1-3s,ts+2-3s,ts+1-2s,ts-s,ts+3-s,1\}$.

The rationale for considering the specific assumptions made in the proposition follows from a characterization of clique-matrices of critically imperfect graphs, see (20).

Finally, to relate the notion of a perfect zero-one matrix to totally unimodular matrix we mention that given any natural number k there exists a perfect matrix having a minor with a determinent ± k, see (20). This indicates why a characterization of perfect matrices is appropriate in terms of forbidden sub-matrices rather than forbidden determinantal values as was the case for totally unimodular matrices.

Appendix

To prove Theorem 6, we note that the implication (i)$\Rightarrow$(ii) is obvious; hence we will have to prove that (ii)$\Rightarrow$(i) or equivalently, that any matrix that is not balanced contains an odd submatrix with row sums and column sums equal to two. Suppose that A is of size mxn and that A is not balanced. We can assume without loss of generality that every proper submatrix of A is balanced. Consequently, since $P(A,e) \neq p_I(A,e)$, it follows from Theorem 10, that A is nonsingular and $e^T A^I = \beta e^T$, $Ae = \beta e$ with an integer β satisfying $2 \leq \beta \leq (\frac{n-1}{2})$. Consider the polytope $D(A,e) = \{y \varepsilon R^n | y^T A \geq e^T, y \geq 0\}$. The vertex $\bar{y}^T = \frac{1}{\beta} e^T$ of $D(A,e)$ has exactly n adjacent vertices satisfying $y^T e \geq ((n-z)/(\beta-1))$ with equality, see (22), where $z = \max\{e^T x | x \varepsilon P_I(\bar{A},e)\}$ satisfies $z\beta = n-1$. By construction, every vertex $\hat{y}$ of $D(A,e) \cap \{y \varepsilon R^n | y^T e \geq ((n-z)\ (\beta-1))$ satisfies $\hat{y}_j = 0$ for some $j \varepsilon \{1,\ldots,n\}$. But requiring $y_j = 0$ in the problem $\min\{y^T e | y^T A \geq e^T, y \geq 0\}$ corresponds to "dropping" the j-th constraint in the (primal) problem: $\max\{e^T x | Ax \leq e, x \geq 0\}$. Consequently, $z+1 \leq ((n-z)/(\beta-1))$ and hence $\beta \leq 2$.

References

(1) Balas, E. and M.W. Padberg: Lectures on Set Packing and Set Partitioning, this volume.

(2) Balas, R. and M.W. Padberg: "On the Set Covering Problem II: An Algorithm for Set Partitioning", to appear in Operations Research, (1974).

(3) Berge, C.: Graphes et Hypergraphes, Dunod, Paris 1970.

(4) Berge, C.: Introduction à la Théorie des Hypergraphes, Lectures notes, Université de Montréal, Summer 1971.

(5) Berge, C.: Balanced Matrices, Mathematical Programming, Vol. 2 (1972), pp. 19-31.

(6) Camion, P.: "Characterization of Totally Unimodular Matrices", Proc. Am. Math. Soc., 16, 1068-1073, (1965).

(7) Chandrasekaran, R.: "Total Unimodularity of Matrices", SIAM J., 17, 1032-34, (1969).

(8) Chvàtal, V.: On certain Polytopes Associated with Graphs, Centre de Recherches Mathématiques, Université de Montréal, CRM-238, October 1972.

(9) Commoner, F.G.: "A Sufficient Condition for a Matrix to be Totally Unimodular", Networks, 3, 351-365, (1973).

(10) Dantzig, G.B. and A.F. Veinott: "Integral Extreme Points", SIAM Review, 10, pp. 371-372, (1968).

(11) Fulkerson, D.R.:"Blocking and Antiblocking Pairs of Polyhedra", Mathematical Programming, Vol. 1 (1971), pp. 168-194.

(12) Fulkerson, D.R.: "On the Perfect Graph Theorem", in: Mathematical Programming, Eds. T.C. Hu and S.M. Robinson, Academic Press, New York, 1973.

(13) Ford, L.R. and D.R. Fulkerson: Flows in Networks, Princeton University Press, Princeton, N.J., 1962.

(14) Garfinkel, R. and G. Nemhauser: Integer Programming, John Wiley and Sons, 1972.

(15) Ghouila-Houri, A.: "Caractérisation des matrices totalement unimodulaires", C.R. Acad. Sc. Paris, 254, 1192, (1962).

(16) Gondran, M.: "Matrices totalement unimodulaires", E.D.F. Bulletin, Séries C, No. 1, 55-74 (1973).

(17) Hoffman, A.J. and J.B. Kruskal: "Integral Boundary Points of Convex Polyhedra", in H.W. Kuhn and A.W. Tucker (eds): Linear Inequalities and Related Systems, Annals of Mathematics Studies, No. 38, Princeton, N.J., 1956.

(17a) Hoffman, A.J.: "On Combinatorical Problems and Linear Inequalities", IBM Watson Research Center, Yorktown Heights, N.Y. (paper presented at the 8th International Symposium on Mathematical Programming at Stanford, August 1973).

(18) Lovàsz, L.: "Normal Hypergraphs and the Perfect Graph Conjecture", Discrete Mathematics, Vol. 2 (1972), pp. 253-268.

(19) Lovàsz, L.: "A Characterization of Perfect Graphs", Journal of Combinatorial Theory, (B), Vol. 13 (1972), pp. 95-98.

(20) Padberg, M.W.: "Perfect Zero-One Matrices", Mathematical Programming, 6, 180-196 (1974).

(21) Padberg, M.W.: "Perfect Zero-One Matrices -II", in Proceedings in Operations Research, 3, Physica-Verlag, Würzburg-Wien (1974), pp. 75-83.

(22) Padberg, M.W.: "A Note on the Adjacent Vertices Cut", IIM Preprint No. I/72-9, International Institute of Management, Berlin (1972).

(23) Padberg, M.W.: "A Note on the Total Unomodularity of Matrices", Forthcoming.

SOME WELL-SOLVED PROBLEMS IN COMBINATORIAL OPTIMIZATION

Jack Edmonds

Department of Combinatorics and Optimization
University of Waterloo, Waterloo, Ontario

One form of the <u>integer l.p. problem</u> is to

(1) find integers $x = (x_j : j \in J)$ such that

(2) $x \geq 0$, $Ax \leq b$, and

(3) cx is maximum,

where $A = (a_{ij} : i \in I, j \in J)$, $b = (b_i : i \in I)$, and $c = (c_j : j \in J)$ are given integers. Usually some condition holds on A, b, and c which makes it obvious that there is a finite algorithm -- let us say that

(4) $x \leq d$ for every x of (2).

The amount of work in applying a straightforward "enumerative algorithm" to instances of problem (1)-(4) tends to grow as $k \cdot \pi\{d_j + 1 : j \in J\}$ where k is a linear function of the total number of bits used to express A, b, and c. (The memory required tends to grow only as k). Assuming $A \geq 0$, the amount of work in applying a "dynamic programming algorithm" to instances of the problem tends to grow something like $k(\pi\{b_i + 1 : i \in I\})^2$.

There are refinements of these methods which with good luck are sometimes not so bad for large $|J|$ and $|I|$. But for moderately large $|J|$ and $|I|$, all known general methods tend often to work almost as terribly as the above functions suggest.

B. Roy (ed.), Combinatorial Programming: Methods and Applications, 285–301.

About sixteen years ago the integer l.p. problem came to be regarded as "solved" by the discovery of "cutting plane methods". It became popular to "solve" other combinatorial problems by reducing them to integer l.p.'s.

These cutting plane methods make sophisticated use of the simplex method. Their description makes an impressive sequel to the methods of linear programming which we have come to know and love. They were proved to be finite, which is not obvious, in a manner similar to proving that the simplex method is finite. The simplex method had worked so well for many years that no one felt compelled to investigate the existence of good upper bounds on the efficiency of the simplex method. Cutting plane methods were, and still are, often presumed to work similarly to the simplex method. It is not obvious that they tend to work as terribly as the obvious algorithms. While they were receiving academic homage, enumerative-type methods were ridiculed as uninteresting and obviously inefficient.

Though the main criterion for the academic appreciation of integer l.p. methods still seems to be theoretical sophistication and unobvious inefficiency, practitioners have learned that relatively uninteresting and obviously not very good methods tend to work better than the cutting plane algorithms. IBM, the home of cutting plane algorithms, does not include one in its commercial integer-programming software package.

Versions of "branch-and-bound", i.e. "truncated enumeration", and dynamic programming, all characterized by the fact that they do not appear to substantially improve on the aforementioned functions as upper bounds on the amount of work they require, have been for some years now, the main type of method described at combinatorial optimization symposia, and I presume the main type of method actually used for the exact solution of combinatorial optimization problems. Probably the most used and most practical methods for combinatorial optimization are "heuristics" which settle for sub-optimum answers.

About 12 years ago, prompted by skepticism toward prevailing knowledge and by an innocent optimism toward what I might do, I began looking for a really good algorithm, one provably better than the obvious, for the integer l.p. problem or at least for some combinatorial optimization problem.

I conjectured that there do not exist "good algorithms" for various combinatorial problems -- for example, the integer l.p. problem where A, b, and c are 0, 1 valued, "good" being a euphemism for the modest requirement that some polynomial in $|I|$ and $|J|$ be an upper bound on the amount of work required by any application of the algorithm. As far as I know the question had never before been asked. It seemed obvious to me that the question is as meaningful as "algorithms" and as important as any in mathematics, but whenever asked it I got blank stares or frowns. Anyway, I did not come up with any ideas for answering it negatively, and it seemed more likely that I might answer it positively, at least for some interesting special cases.

(5) The b-matching problem is the integer l.p. problem (1)-(4) where each column of A contains two ones and the rest zeroes. In other words, A is the incidence matrix of a graph G. The rows $i \in I$ correspond to the nodes of G and the columns $j \in J$ correspond to the edges of G. Edge j meets node i when $a_{ij} = 1$.

In graphic terminology, the b-matching problem is:

(6) Given a graph G with node-set I and edge-set J, given integers $b_i \geq 0$, $i \in I$, and given numbers c_j, $j \in J$, find integers $x_j \geq 0$ such that

(7) For each node $i \in I$, $\Sigma\{x_j :$ edge j meets node $i\} \leq b_i$ and such that $\Sigma\{c_j x_j : j \in J\}$ is maximum.

(8) There is an algorithm, called the blossom method, for solving the b-matching problem (5) such that the amount of work in applying the algorithm to any instance of (5) is at most $k|J| \cdot |I|^2 \{b_i : i \in I\}$, where k is a linear function of the number of bits in c.

The description of the algorithm, and a listing of the PL1 computer program of it, called BLOSSOM II, distributed to members of the present Symposium, is too long to include here. They will appear soon as part of a book called <u>Optimum Matching Theory</u>, by W. Pulleyblank and myself [11].

Ellis Johnson and I developed a generalized blossom algorithm some time ago to directly solve, just as efficiently, certain generalizations of (5) -- in particular, with $\geq$ and $=$ as well as $\leq$, with an additional constraint of the form $x \leq d$, and with any matrix A of integers such that, for each $j \in J$, $\Sigma\{|a_{ij}|: i \in I\} \leq 2$. [6] This generalized form includes for example all the standard integer network flow problems. A Fortran program, called Blossom I, of this generalized blossom algorithem was written by Scott Lockhart [6].

The more general form of problem treated directly by Blossom I is also called the b-matching problem because it can be efficiently initialized to the more special form for input to Blossom II by using the same kind of tricks which initialize any optimum network flow problem to a Hitchcock transportation problem. Blossom II deliberatly sacrifices direct versatility, relying on initialization of input if necessary, for the sake of relative simplicity. In either version, the algorithm is rather complicated. Each code, Blossom I and Blossom II, solves any admissible input, with hundreds of variables, very quickly -- always.

I will describe here a main theorem proved by the algorithm, and discuss its significance.

An integer-solution of (2) for the case (5) is called a b-matching in the graph G. Let P(G,b) denote the convex hull of the set H(G,b) b-matching in G.

Let $Q \equiv \{S \subseteq I: b(S) = \Sigma\{b_i: i \in S\}$ is odd, and $|S| \geq 3\}$. Let $q_S \equiv (b(S)-1)/2$. Let $\gamma(S)$ denote the set of edges j which have both ends in S, and let $\delta(i)$ denote the set edges which meet node i.

(9) Theorem. P(G,b) is the set of solutions of (7) and

(10) $\forall S \in Q,\ \Sigma\{x_j: j \in \gamma(S)\} \leq q_S$.

This theorem is equivalent to the following

(11) Theorem. For any real-valued $c=(c_j: j \in J)$, $\max\{cx: x \in H(G,b)\} = \min \Sigma\{y_i: i \in I\} + \Sigma\{q_S y_S: S \in Q\}$

(12) where for $i \in I$ $y_i \geq 0$, for $\delta \in Q$ $y_S \geq 0$ and,

for every edge $j \in J$, $\Sigma\{y_i: i \in I, j \in \delta(i)\}$

$$+ \Sigma\{y_S: S \in Q, j \in \gamma(S)\} \geq c_j$$

(13) and where at most $|J|$ of the numbers y_i, y_s are non-zero.

To derive (11) from (9), observe that (9) implies $\max\{cx: x \in H(G,b)\} = \max\{cx: x$, satisfying $x \geq 0$, (7), and (10). The latter is a linear program, and the min expressed in (11) is the dual linear pgoram, so the two are equal by the l.p. duality theorem. The restriction (13) expressed on the number of non-zero dual variables may be specified in the statement of the l.p. duality theorem for any pair of dual l.p.'s. It is not usually specified, and it is not important for a usual l.p. where the number of dual variables is moderate. However in (11) where the number of dual variables tends to be astronomical the restriction that at most $|J|$ be non-zero is extremely important. (See below the discussion of the algorithmic value of (11).)

To derive (9) from (11), observe that saying polyhedron P is the convex hull of finite set $H(G,b)$ is the same thing as saying P is bounded, $H(G,b) = P$, and $v(P) \subseteq H(G,b)$, where $v(P)$ denotes the set of vertices of P; and observe further that x^0 is vertex of P if and only if there is some c such that cx is maximized over P only by x^0. Let $P'(G,b)$ denote the polyhedron of $x \geq 0$, (7), and (10). Clearly $P'(G,b)$ is bounded. It can easily be shown that $H(G,b) \subseteq P'(G,b)$. To prove $v(P'(G,b)) \subseteq H(G,b)$, let $x^0 \in v(P'(G,b))$. Let c be such that cx is maximized over $P'(G,b)$ only by x^0. Suppose $x^1 \in H(G,b)$ maximizes cx over $H(G,b)$. Theorem (11) says such that cx^1 equals a certain minimum which, by the (weak) l.p. duality theorem, is greater than or equal to $\max\{cx: x \in P'(G,b)$. Thus x^1 maximizes cx over $P'(G,b)$. Thus $x^0 = x^1$. (Notice that to derive (9) from (11) we use only very easy propositions from linear programming theory).

In view of (9), one could get an algorithm for the b-matching problem simply by applying the simplex algorithm to $x \geq 0$, (7), (10), but I would advise against this -- not only because the linear system is astronomical in size for a moderate size graph -- but because the linear system is (necessarily) so astronomically degenerate.

For us, (9) is simply a nice way of saying (11). Theorem (11) is direct consequence of the algorithm, and enormously important to the success of the algorithm. Simply from the elementary fact that $H(G,b) \subseteq P'(G,b)$ and from the weak l.p. duality theorem it is obvious that for any $x \in H(G,b)$ and for any y satisfying (12), we have $cx \leq qy$. The blossom algorithm does stop within (8) and it does not stop until it obtains an $x^0 \in H(G,b)$ and a y such that $cx = qy$. When this happens we know that it is alright to stop since x^0 is certainly optimum, and (11) is proved. (The algorithm passes through a number tentative b-matchings x and vectors y. The tentative y, and its relationship to the tentative $x \in H(G,b)$, must evolve in a very specially structured way -- many vectors y satisfying (12), even with only $|J|$ non-zeroes, are combinatorial messy and would never arise in the algorithm.)

(14) Theorem (11) certainly does not make it clear that there is a good algorithm for the b-matching problem. However, the theorem provides a very necessary ingredient for a good algorithm which we lack for other integer l.p. problems -- that is, a good universal criterion for recognizing that a b-matching is optimum, i.e., "a good characterization" for optimum b-matchings.

(15) Suppose a master has slaves which he can make work as long and hard as necessary using any finite algorithm to find an optimum b-matching x^0 and to find also y as described in (11). They bring the x^0 and the y to the master. Then using (11), the master has a good algorithm, relative to the size of G and b, for verifying, without trusting his slaves the least bit, that the x^0 which they bring him is indeed optimum. This is what we mean by a "good characterization" of optimum b-matchings. Suppose for some instance of the integer l.p. problem (1) of a different kind, the master has his slaves find and bring him an optimum solution x. What else can he require them to bring him so that he can easily be sure that the x is optimum?

Actually, in order for (11), to be a good characterization of optimum b-matchings, we should further restrict y in order to be sure that y is not expressed using so many bits that it is difficult to do the arithmetic of (11).

(16) Where c is integers, we can in fact require that the y be half-integers.

For any instance of (1)-(4), we know that there is some system $A'x \leq b'$, $x \geq 0$, whose solution-set is the convex hull of the set H of integer solutions to (2). And we have the theorem:

(17) $\max\{cx: x \in H\} = \min\{yb': y \geq 0, yA' \leq c_j\}$ at most $|J|$ components of y are non-zero.

Whether this is a good characterization of optimum x depends not on how large the system $A'x \leq b'$ is, and depends not on the number of superfluous inequalities of $A'x \leq b'$. It does depend on having a good description of a $A'x \leq b'$ -- that is, on having a good algorithm, relative to the size of $Ax \leq b$, for recognizing when any given inequality $a^0 x \leq b_0$ is a member of the system $A'x \leq b'$. The system may in fact be easier to describe when, as in the case of the matching problem, many superfluous inequalities are included.

It follows from the finiteness of cutting plane algorithms that for the integer l.p. problem, (1)-(4), that a system $A'x \leq b'$, $x \geq 0$, can be generated starting with $Ax \leq b$, $x \geq 0$, by successively deriving new valid inequalities as follows:

(18) Take a non-negative linear combination of known valid inequalities, either previously derived or from $Ax \leq b$, to obtain an inequality $a^0 x \leq b_0$. Then obtain valid inequality $a^1 x \leq b$, from $a^0 x \leq b_0$ by $a^1_j = [a^0_j]$ and $b_1 \geq [b_0]$, where $[b_0]$ means the greatest integer not greater than b_0. (See [3].)

What is nice about the inequalities (10) for the b-matching polyhedron is that each is obtainable from (7) by only one application of (18). A system $A'x \leq b'$ is said to be of height h, and width k, with respect to (2) if each member of $A'x \leq b'$ can be derived from (2) by at most h applications of (18) and each number which arises in that derivation has at most k bits. If for some class C of instances of (2), we have for each member of C, a system $A'x \leq b'$ of length h and length k, where h and k are some nice functions, say polynomial functions, of the size of the member of

E and a non-empty family $F \subseteq 2^E$ of so-called <u>independent</u> subsets of E such that $R \subseteq S \in F$ $R \in F$. For any $S \subseteq E$, an <u>M-basis</u> B of S is a maximal (not necessarily largest) independent subset of S, i.e. $S \supseteq B \in F$, and $B \cup \{j\} \notin F$ for any $j \in S-B$. For any $S \subseteq E$, the <u>M-rank</u>, $r_M(S)$, of S is $\max\{|B|: S \supseteq B \in F\}$.

For $S \subseteq E$, let $x^S = (x_j^S: j \in E)$ where $x_j^S = 1$ if $j \in S$ and $x_j^S = 0$ if $j \notin S$. For any independence system $M=(E,F)$, let $H_M = \{x^S: S \in F\}$. Clearly the 1-matching problem is loco problem (19) where $H = H_M$ for a certain independence system M determined by graph G.

A <u>matroid</u> $M=(E,F)$ is an independence system such that, for any $S \subseteq E$, every M-basis of S has cardinality equal to $r_M(S)$. (Thus, we essentially define matroids as those independence systems for which a certain very simple algorithm solves a certain optimization problem.)

I will leave for your pleasure and ingenuity the simple puzzle of devising an abstract algorithm for

(21) the loco problem (19), $H=H_M$, whenever M is a matroid. (In my earlier days of suggesting such homework, it provided publications for needy authors).

One of the better known propositions of mathematics is that the family F of the linearly independent subsets of a set E of vectors, say, the set E of column vectors of a matrix A, is a matroid (called <u>the</u> matroid of matrix A). A set $H=H_M$, where M is the matroid of a matrix A, is well-described by A, using some varient of the Gaussian elimination algorithm, to recognize independence. This Gauss elimination algorithm together with your abstract algorithm for (21), is a good algorithm for finding a linear independent subset $J \subseteq E$ columns in A such that $\Sigma\{c_j: j \in J\}$ is maximum

One can easily find counterexamples to the proposition that, for any independence system M,

(22) the convex hull of H_M is $P_M \equiv \{x \in R^E: x \geq 0;\ \forall S \subseteq E,\ \Sigma\{x_j: j \in S\} \leq r_M(S)\}$. (Describe a facet-inequality of the convex hull of H_M, for some M, where non-zero coefficients are not all equal.)

C , then we would have, by using $A'x \le b'$ in (17), a good characterization of max cx over integer solutions x of (2), where (2) is any member of C.

If there do not exist functions h and k, and a system $A'x \le b'$ for each member of C, as described, then I would surmise that there does not exist a good algorithm for (1)-(4) for each member (2) of C, because there cannot be a good algorithm without a good characterization, and I cannot imagine a good characterization for these optima which is not equivalent to a theorem of the form (17) with an $A'x \le b'$ as described.

Chvatal [3] has shown that for problem (1) where b is all ones and where A is the transpose of the incidence matrix of a graph, it is not possible to take h to be a constant.

The matching problem is essentially the only kind of integer l.p. problem for which a good algorithm, or even a good characterization of optimum solutions, is known. However there is one other kind of combinatorial optimization problem for which similar success has been obtained. These we call <u>matroid optimization</u> problems.

A problem of the form

(19) maximize cx over $x \in H$ where H is some (well-described) set of vectors in R^J , we call a <u>loco</u> problem. "Loco" is short for "linear objective combinatorial optimization". By "well-described" we mean that we have a good algorithm which, for each instance of H and for any $x \in R^J$, determines whether or not $x \in H$. One can imagine well-described sets H which are not well-described as the integer valued solution of a system of linear inequalities.

One can imagine sets H which, though perhaps not well-described, satisfy certain abstract properties, and these properties enable us to describe an "abstract" algorithm for the loco problem (19) such that the primitive operation of the algorithm is to determine for a given x whether or not $x \in H$. The goodness of a concrete realization of the abstract algorithm will depend in part on the goodness of an algorithm for the primitive operation.

An <u>independence system</u> M = (E,F) is a finite set

Theorem (9) implies that the proposition is true where M is the system of 1-matchings in a graph G.

The proposition is also true whenever M is a matroid. By the same argument used to relate (9) and (11), the proposition for matroids is equivalent to:

(23) Theorem. For any matroid $M=(E,F)$, and any $c=(c_j: j\in E)\in R^J$, $\max\{cx: x\in H_M\}$ = the minimum of $r\cdot y \equiv \Sigma\{r_M(S)y_S: S\subseteq E\}$ where

(24) $y=(y_S: S\subseteq E)$ satisfies $y\geq 0$, and for every $j\in E$, $\Sigma\{y_S: j\in S\subseteq E\} \geq c_j$.

One way to prove (23) for matroids, and to prove at the same time that your abstract algorithm for (21) is valid, is to describe a "dual" abstract algorithm which produces a vector y of (24) such that $cx=r\cdot y$ where x is the output of your "primal" algorithm [7]. One can prove at the same time that

(25) $r\cdot y$ can always be minimized by a y of (24) such that the only non-zero components of y correspond to the members of a nested sequence, $S_1\supseteq S_2\supseteq\ldots$, of subsets of E.

(26) For any matroid M, the P_M of (22) is called a <u>matroid polytope</u>, or the polytope of M. Since P_M is the convex hull of H_M, and since H_M consists entirely of 0, 1-valued vectors, H_M is precisely $v(P_M)$, the set of vertices P_M.

In view of the great variety of matroids and their elusiveness in many ways, I still find the following result slightly incredible.

(27) Theorem. Let P_i, $i = 1$ and 2, be the polytopes of any two matroids $M_i=(E,F_i)$ defined on the same set E. Then $v(P_1\cap P_2) = v(P_1)\cap v(P_2)$.

The analogous statement for the polytopes of three matroids is not true. $v(P_1\cap P_2\cap P_3)$ will generally include many messy non-integer valued vertices as well as $v(P_1)\cap v(P_2)\cap v(P_3)$.

The min-max version of (27) is

(28) Theorem. For any $c=(c_j: j\in E)\in R^J$,

$\max\{\Sigma\{c_j: i\in J\}: J\in F_1\cap F_2\} = \min\Sigma\{r_1(S)y_S^1+r_2(S)y_S^2: S\subseteq E\}$

where, for every $S\subseteq E$ and $i=1$ and 2, $y_S^i\geq 0$ and for every $j\in E$, $\Sigma\{y_S^1+y_S^2: j\in S\}\geq c_j$ and where at most $|E|$ of the numbers y_S^i are non-zero. ($r_i(S)$ denotes the M_i-rank of S.)

The relation can be further strengthened by:

(29) When the numbers c_j are all integers, the numbers y_S^i may be restricted to integers.

This is a characterization of optimum weight sets J independent in both M_1 and M_2 which is clearly as good as the algorithms one has for recognizing for any $K\subseteq E$ whether or not $K\in F_i$. Theorem (28)-(29) may be proved by a good algorithm which finds an appropriate J and y. [8]

Using the fact that rank is sub-additive, and nondecreasing, i.e., $r_i(A)\leq r_i(A\cup B)\leq r_i(A)+r_i(B)$, it follows immediately from (29) and (20) that, if the c_j's are all ones then the numbers y_S^i may be restricted to being zeroes and ones such that, for each i, there is at most one S such that $y_S^i=1$. Thus, we have

(30) <u>Theorem</u>. $\max\{|J|: J\in F_1\cap F_2\}$

$$= \min\{r_1(S_1)+r_2(S_2): S_1\cup S_2=E\}.$$

There are a number of interesting applications of (28)-(30).

Let $\underline{M}=\{M_i=(E,F_i): i\in I\}$ be a collection of matroids, not necessarily distinct. A set $K\subseteq E$ is called <u>$\underline{M}$-partitionable</u> if it can be partitioned into sets J_i, $i\in I$, such that $J_i\in F_i$. The problem is to

(31) Find a largest $\underline{M}$-partitonable subset of E.

It can be solved by considering the following two matroids: $M_1=(I\times E, F_1)$ where $F_1=\{S\subseteq I\times E: \forall i\in I, \{j\in E: (i,j)\in S\}\in F_i\}$. $M_2=(I\times E,F_2)$ where $F_2=\{S\subseteq I\times E: \forall j\in E, |\{i\in I: (i,j)\in S\}|\leq 1\}$.

Clearly $J=\{(i,j): j\in J'_i\}\in F_1\cap F_2$ if and only if $J_i=\{j\in E: (i,j)\in J\}$, $i\in I$, is a collection of disjoint subsets of E such that $J_i\in F_i$, and clearly $|J|=|\cup\{J_i: i\in I\}|$. Thus we can solve problem (31) by solving the problem of (30), $\max\{|J|: J\in F_1\cap F_2\}$.

Conversely for any two matroids $M_1=(E,F_1)$ and $M_2=(E,F_2)$, one can solve problem (30) by solving a certain instance of problem (31). To obtain the initialization procedure for this, we describe the dual of a matroid.

(32) Theorem [9]. For any matroid $M=(E,F)$, $M^*=(E,F^*=\{S\subseteq E: E-S$ contains an M-basis of $E\})$ is a matroid, called the <u>dual</u> of M.

(33) If we have a good algorithm for recognizing when any set $S\subseteq E$ is M-independent (i.e., $S\in F$) then we certainly have a good algorithm for recognizing when a set is M^*-independent.

For any matroids $M_1=(E,F_1)$ and $M_2=(E,F_2)$, let $\underline{M}=\{M_1,M_2^*\}$. Find a largest $\underline{M}$-partitionable set K. Then find an M_2^*-basis B of K. It is easy to show that $J=K-B$ is a largest set such that $J\in F_1\cap F_2$. A direct algorithm for (31) is described in [9].

Here is another application of (30) developed by W.H. Cunningham in [2]. Suppose we have a homogeneous linear system $Ax=0$. The column-index set of matrix A is E.

(34) For specified $R_1\subseteq E$ and $R_2\subseteq E-R_1$, we wish to find a partition of E into $E_1\geq R_1$ and $E_2\geq R_2$, and a linear system $A^0x=0$, equivalent to $Ax=0$, such that the cardinality of the set, say K, of rows of A^0 which have non-zeroes in both an E_1-column and an E_2-column is minimized.

An advantage of the system $A^0x=0$ is that by introducing $|K|$ new variables, say x_j, $j\in K$, we can easily obtain from $A^0x=0$ two new systems, $A'x_1=0$ in the variables $x_1=(x_j: j\in E_1\cup K)$ and $A^2x_2=0$ in the variables $x_2=(x_j: j\in E_2\cup K)$, such that $x^0=(x_j^0: j\in E)$

is a solution of $Ax=0$ if and only if there exists values $(x_j^0\colon j\in K)$ such that $x_1^0=(x_j^0\colon j\in E_1\cup K)$ is a solution of $A^1x_1=0$ and $x_2^0=(x_j^0\colon j\in E_2\cup K)$ is a solution of $A^2x_2=0$. Thus, for sufficiently small K, we have a certain kind of decomposition of $Ax=0$ into two linear systems which each involve fewer variables than $Ax=0$. (The decomposition is well-known for $|K|=0$.)

To solve problem (34), we must describe the minors of a matroid $M=(E,F)$.

(35) For any $S\subseteq E$, $(S,\{J\colon J\subseteq S,\ J\in F\})$ is a matroid, called the <u>submatroid</u> of M obtained by <u>deleting</u> $E-S$.

(36) For any $S\subseteq E$, $(S,\{J\colon J\subseteq S,\ J\cup B\in F$ for some M-basis B of $E-S\})$ is a matroid, called the <u>contraction</u> of M obtained by <u>contracting</u> $E-S$.

A matroid obtained from M by deleting some of its elements and contracting some others of its elements is called a <u>minor</u> of M. Remark (33) applies to minors of M as well as to the dual of M. Some more interesting homework is: if M is the matroid of matrix A, and M' is a specified minor of M, how can we obtain a matrix A' whose matroid is M'?

We can solve problem (34) as follows: Let M be the matroid of A. Let M_1 be the minor of M obtained by contracting R_1 and deleting R_2. Let M_2 be the minor of M obtained by contracting R_2 and deleting R_1. Apply to M_1 and M_2 the algorithm of theorem (30) to find a partition of $E-(R_1\cup R_2)$ into sets S_1 and S_2 such that $r_1(S_1)+r_2(S_2)$ is minimum. Let $E_1=R_1\cup S_1$ and $E_2=R_2\cup S_2$. Knowing E_1 and E_2, it is easy to perform row operations on matrix A to obtain a matrix A^0.

Here is another application of (29). Let G be a directed graph having edge-set E and node-set V. Let $v_0\in V$. A <u>spanning</u> <u>directed</u> <u>tree</u> of G <u>rooted</u> at v_0, or what I am accustomed to call a <u>branching</u> of G <u>rooted</u> at v_0, is a spanning tree T of G such that for every $v\in V-\{v_0\}$, there is exactly one edge of T directed toward v.

(37) The problem is: given G, given a collection $(v_i: i\in I)$ of nodes of G, not necessarily distinct, and given a cost $c_j\in R$ for each $j\in E$, find (if one exists) a collection $\underline{T}=(T_i: i\in I)$ of branchings T_i of G, rooted respectively at v_i, such that they are edge-wise disjoint and such that their total cost, $\Sigma\{c_j: j \text{ in some } T_i\}$, is minimum.

(38) Assuming a $\underline{T}$ exists, a set $B\subseteq E$ can be partitioned into the edge-sets of the branchings T_i of a $\underline{T}$ if and only if B is both an M_1-basis of E and an M_2-basis of E where $M_1=(E,F_1=\{J\subseteq E: J$ partitionable into the edge-sets of $|I|$ forests in $G\})$ and $M_2=(E,F_2=\{J\subseteq E: \forall v\in V$, at most $|\{i\in I: v_i\neq v\}|$ members of J are directed toward $v\})$.

It is rather obvious that M_2 is matroid; M_1 is a matroid because $\underline{M}$-partionable sets as previously defined form a matroid, and because the edge-sets of forests in G are the independent sets of a matroid M_G (called <u>the</u> matroid of G).

Subtracting each c_j from a very large constant to get c_j', a set $B\subseteq E$ is both an M_1-basis and M_2-basis of E such that $\Sigma\{c_j: j\in B\}$ is minimum if and only if B is an optimum solution of $\max\{\Sigma\{c_j': j\in J\}: J\in F_1\cap F_2\}$. Hence we can solve (37) as an instance of (28).

The "only if" part of (38) is obvious but the "if" part is not at all obvious. It is a corollary of the following very special theorem [10]:

(39) For any directed graph G and any collection $(v_i: i\in I)$ of nodes in G, there exists a collection $(T_i: i\in I)$ of edge-disjoint branchings in G, rooted respectively at v_i, if and only if there is no proper subset S of nodes of G such that $|\{i: v_i\in S\}|$ is greater than the number of edges of G directed away from a node in S and directed toward a node in $V-S$.

This theorem is a good characterization of the existence of a $(T_i: i\in I)$. The proof in [10] is an algorithm which either finds a $(T_i: i\in I)$ or finds an S. However, I was unable to prove that the algorithm is a good one. (A computer program of it by Scott Vanstone [ ] seems to work extremely well.) Thus I was faced with the possibility of having a good characterization with no good algorithm. (The l.p. duality theorem provides another such possibility). To make matters even more frustrating, the good algorithm for (28) provides a good algorithm for finding the edge-set B of a $(T_i: i \in I)$ whenever there is one -- in fact for finding an optimum edge-set B. So all that was lacking was a good algorithm for partitioning the edges of a known B into branchings T_i, known to exist.

Recently both Lovasz [13] and Tarjan [14] provided a good algorithm to go with (39). (I admit that the only aspect of this achievement which really pleases me is the two men who did it.)

The classical prototype for both (28) and (11), and their accompanying algorithms, is the Konig-Egervary theory and algorithms for the optimum assignment problem.

(40) Konig-Egervary Theorem. For any bipartite graph G, with node-set $V = V_1 \cup V_2$ and edge-set E such that each $j \in E$ meets one node in V_1 and one node in V_2, and any $c = (c_j: j \in E) \in R^E$, $\max\{\Sigma\{c_j: j \in J\}: J \subseteq E$ such that no node $v \in V$ is met by more than one edge of $J\} = \min \Sigma\{y_v: i \in V\}$ where $y = (y_v: v \in V\}$ satisfies $\forall v \in V,\ y_v \geq 0$ and $\forall j \in E,\ \Sigma\{y_v: j \in \delta(v)\} \geq c_j$.

In other words, where A is the incidence matrix of G, and where b is all ones,
$\max\{cx:$ integer $x \geq 0,\ Ax \leq b\} = \min\{yb: y \geq 0,\ yA \geq c\}$

(41) Where c is all integers, the y may be restricted to all integers.

Where $M_i = \{E, F_i = \{J \subseteq E:$ no node $v \in V_i$ is met by more than one edge of $J\}$, $i \in 1$ and 2, theorem (40)-(41) is a corollary of (28)-(29).

Let $G = (V,E)$ be any graph. For each node $v \in V$, let $M_v = (\delta(v), F_v)$ be a matroid defined on the set $\delta(v)$ of edges which meet v. Consider the problem,

(42) for given $c=(c_j: j\in E)\in R^J$,
$\max\{\Sigma\{c_j: j\in J\}: J\subseteq E$ such that $\forall v\in V$, $J\cap\delta(v)\in F_v\}$.

(43) When G is bipartite, as in (40), the problem is solved by the matroid intersection theory where $M_i=(E,F_i=\{J\subseteq V: \forall v\in V_i, J\cap\delta(v)\in F_v\}$, i=1 and 2.

(44) Whether or not G is bipartite, the problem is solved by the b-matching theory for the special matroids,
$M_v=(\delta(v), F_v=\{J\subseteq\delta(v): |J| \le b_v\})$.

($b = (b_v: v\in V)$ as may be regarded as all ones, though it is not necessary in order for the statements to be correct.)

The intersection of cases (43) and (44) of problem (42) is the subject of the Konig-Egervary theory. T. Jenkyns in [12] investigates the difficulties of generalizing the methods of (43) and (44) to problem (42).

REFERENCES

1. Aroaz, J. Polyhedral Neopolarities, Thesis, Univ. of Waterloo, 1974.
2. Cunningham, W., A Combinatorial Decomposition Theory, Thesis, University of Waterloo, 1974.
3. Chvatal, V., Edmonds Polyedra and a Hierarchy of Combinatorial Problems.
4. Giles, R., and Edmonds, J., Supermodular Functions and Combinatorial Polyhedra, Report, University of Waterloo.
5. Edmonds, J., Maximum Matching and Polyhedron with 0, 1 Vertices
6. ___________, Johnson, E., Lockhart, S., Blossom I, A computer code for the Matching Problem.
7. ___________, Submodular functions, Matroids, and Certain Polyhedra, Comb. Structures and their applic.
8. ___________, Matroid Intersection, Report, University of Waterloo
9. ___________, Matroid Partition, Mathematics of the decision sciences, G.B. Dantzig and A.F. Veinott editors.
10. ___________, Edge-disjoint branchings, Combinatorial Algorithms, R. Rustin (ed.), Algorithmics Press, New York, 1972.

11. __________ and Pulleyblank, W., Optimum Matching Theory, to appear, Johns Hopkins Press.
12. Jenkyns, T., Matchoids: A Generalization of Matchings and Matroids, Thesis, University of Waterloo, 1974.
13. Lovasz, L., "On Two Theorems in Graph Theory", to appear.
14. Tarjan, R., "A Good Algorithm for Edge-Disjoint Branchings", to appear.
15. Pulleyblank, W., The Faces of Matching Polyhedra, Thesis, University of Waterloo, 1974

P A R T I V

OTHER COMBINATORIAL PROGRAMMING TOPICS

HOW TO COLOR A GRAPH

D. de Werra

Département de Mathematiques
Ecole Polytechnique Fédérale de Lausanne (Switzerland)

1. INTRODUCTION AND SUMMARY

This paper attempts to give a short survey of graph coloring problems. The first two sections deal with edge colorings and node colorings of graphs. In section 4 some generalizations to hypergraph coloring are described. Finally section 5 is devoted to the problem of balancing the colorings. For notations and definitions we follow C. Berge [4]. The multigraphs considered here have no loops.

2. EDGE COLORING

A <u>k-coloring</u> of the edges of a multigraph $G = (X,U)$ is a partition of its edges into k subsets $U_1, U_2, \ldots, U_k$; u_i will denote the cardinality of U_i and $u_i(x)$ the number of edges in U_i which are adjacent to node x. Of particular interest are the k-colorings such that $u_i(x) \leq 1$ for each node x and each color i (<u>usual</u> k-colorings). The <u>chromatic index</u> $q(G)$ of G is the smallest k for which G has a usual k-coloring.

Several generalizations of usual k-colorings have been given.

B. Roy (ed.), Combinatorial Programming: Methods and Applications, 305–325. *All Rights Reserved.*

Let $(U_1, U_2, \dots, U_k)$ be a k-coloring of the edges of a multigraph G ; for each node x we define

$$e(x) = \max_{i,j} |u_i(x) - u_j(x)|$$

If $e(x) \leq 1$ for each node x of G , then the k-coloring is said to be <u>equitable</u>. Clearly a usual-k-coloring is equitable.

<u>Proposition 2.1</u> [15] : A connected multigraph G has an equitable bicoloring if and only if G is not an odd cycle. If G is an odd cycle there exists an edge bicoloring (U_1, U_2) such that $u_1(x_0) - u_2(x_0) = 2$ for an arbitrary node x_0 and $u_1(x) = u_2(x)$ for any $x \neq x_0$.

<u>Proof</u> : A) If G is an odd cycle, then for any equitable bicoloring we must have $u_1(x) = u_2(x)$ for each x . This is impossible since the number of edges is odd. However starting from x_0 and coloring the edges of the cycle alternately with colors 1 and 2 we get the above mentioned bicoloring.

B) If G is an even cycle, the same procedure gives an equitable bicoloring. If G is not a cycle, by introducing fictitious edges joining pairs of nodes with odd degree in G (and possibly a fictitious node on one fictitious edge) we get an even cycle C . Any equitable bicoloring of C defines an equitable bicoloring of G .

By successive applications of this result we obtain :

<u>Theorem 2.1</u> : Let $G = (X,U)$ be a multigraph and S a subset of nodes such that each elementary odd cycle of G has at least one node in S . Then for each $k \geq 2$ there exists a k-coloring of the edges of G such that $e(x) \leq 1$ for each

node x in $X-S$.

Proof : Let $(U_1,\dots, U_k)$ be a k-coloring of G . Assume there is a node y_0 in $X-S$ with $e(y_0) = u_a(y_0) - u_b(y_0) \geq 2$ and let C be the connected component containing y_0 of $G_{ab} = (X,U_a \cup U_b)$. A new bicoloring (U'_a, U'_b) of G_{ab} is obtained by recoloring C as follows : if it is not an odd cycle, we determine an equitable bicoloring of C . Otherwise there is a node $z \neq y_0$ with $z \in C \cap S$. We recolor C in such a way that $u'_a(z) = u'_b(z) + 2$ and $u'_a(x) = u'_b(x)$ for each node $x \neq z$ in C .

Let $U'_i = U_i$ $(i \neq a,b)$. Clearly the k-coloring $(U'_1,\dots, U'_k)$ satifies $e'(x) \leq e(x)$ for each node x in $X-S$. For y_0 the number of pairs p,q with $u'_p(y_0) - u'_q(y_0) = e(y_0)$ has decreased by at least 1 since $|u'_a(y_0) - u'_b(y_0)| \leq 1$. If $e'(y_0) > 1$ we may repeat this procedure. So we will obtain a k-coloring $(\overline{U}_1,\dots, \overline{U}_k)$ with $\overline{e}(x) \leq e(x)$ for every node x in $X-S$ and $\overline{e}(y_0) \leq 1$.

The result is finally obtained by iterating this process as long as $e(y) > 1$ for some node y in $X-S$. End of proof.

We may in fact slightly improve the above result as follows: it can be shown that by using a similar recoloring procedure we may construct a k-coloring $(U_1,\dots, U_k)$ satisfying $e(x) \leq 1$ for each node x in $X-S$ and $e(x) \leq 2$ for each node x in S.

As a consequence of theorem 2.1 we have :

Theorem 2.2 [15] : For each $k \geq 2$ a bipartite multigraph G has an equitable k-coloring.

Corollary 2.2.1 : For a bipartite multigraph G $q(G) =$

$\max_x d(x)$.

Here $d(x)$ is the degree of node x . If we define a covering in G as a subset U' of edges with $u'(x) \geq 1$ for each x , we have :

Corollary 2.2.2 : For a bipartite multigraph G $c(G) = \min_x d(x)$.

$c(G)$ is the largest k for which there exists a partition of U into k coverings (covering index).

A k-coloring $(U_1, U_2, \ldots, U_k)$ is good if for each color i and each node x we have $u_i(x) \leq 1$ whenever $d(x) \leq k$ and $u_i(x) \geq 1$ otherwise. The number $k(x)$ of colors appearing at any node x satisfies : $k(x) = |\{i | u_i(x) \geq 1\}| = \min(k, d(x))$. Any equitable k-coloring is good, but the coverse is not true.

Proposition 2.2 [7] : A connected multigraph G has a good bicoloring if and only if G is not an elementary odd cycle.

Proof : Clearly an elementary odd cycle has no good bicoloring. If G is a non elementary odd cycle, the procedure of proposition 2.1 (when choosing a node x_0 with $d(x_0) \geq 4$) will give a good bicoloring.

Using this proposition J.C. Fournier has proved :

Theorem 2.3 [7] : For each $k \geq 2$ a simple graph G has a k-coloring such that for each node x $k(x) = d(x)$ if $d(x) < k$ and $k(x) \geq k-1$ if $d(x) \geq k$.

Corollary 2.3.1 (Vizing's theorem) [13] : For a simple graph G , $q(G) \leq \max_x d(x) + 1$.

In fact a similar proof gives Vizing's theorem for multigraphs: $q(G) \leq \max d(x) + p$ where p is the maximum number of parallel edges joining any 2 nodes.

We finally mention a few results which are related to the notions of edge coloring and orientation. Here $d^+(x)$ (resp. $d^-(x)$) is the number of arcs in a graph $G = (X,U)$ with initial (resp. terminal) endpoint x.

Let now $u_i^+(x)$ (resp. $u_i^-(x)$) denote the number of arcs in $U_i \subset U$ whose initial (resp. terminal) endpoint is x. For each node x we define $e^+(x)$ and $e^-(x)$ as

$$e^+(x) = \max_{i,j} |u_i^+(x) - u_j^+(x)|$$

$$e^-(x) = \max_{i,j} |u_i^-(x) - u_j^-(x)|$$

Then we have the following consequence of theorem 2.2 :

<u>Theorem 2.4</u> : For each integer $k \geq 2$ there exists a k-coloring $(U_1, \ldots, U_k)$ of the arcs of a graph G such that $e^+(x) \leq 1$ and $e^-(x) \leq 1$ for each node x.

This result is simply obtained by replacing each node x of G by 2 nodes x' and x'' and each arc (x,y) by an edge (x',y''). Any equitable k-coloring of the edges of the bipartite multigraph thus obtained defines a k-coloring of the arcs of G with $e^+(x) \leq 1$ and $e^-(x) \leq 1$ for each node x.

Using the same idea we may formulate a sufficient condition for a multigraph G to have an equitable k-coloring :

If the edges of a multigraph G may be oriented in such a way that for each node x either $d^+(x) \equiv 0 \pmod{k}$ or $d^-(x) \equiv 0 \pmod{k}$ holds, then there exists an equitable k-coloring of the edges of G.

For a good k-coloring the condition on the orientation would become :

$$\max\,(d^+(x), d^-(x)) \geq \min\,(k, d(x)) \quad \text{for each node } x .$$

Remark : The bicolorings (U_1,U_2) in Propositions 2.1 and 2.2 may always be chosen such that $|u_1-u_2| \leq 1$. This results from the coloring procedure whenever G is a cycle. If G is not a cycle, we may insert a fictitious node on each fictitious edge; clearly any bicoloring of the even cycle C' thus obtained defines an equitable bicoloring of G with $|u_1-u_2| \leq 1$. The problem of balancing the cardinalities will be discussed in section 5 .

3. NODE COLORING

In this section all graphs will be simple. A usual k-coloring of the nodes of $G = (X,U)$ is a partition $(S_1,S_2,\ldots,S_k)$ of X into k stable sets. The chromatic number $\gamma(G)$ is the smallest k for which G has a usual k-coloring. No formula has been found yet for the chromatic number of an arbitrary graph. Thus most of the results in this area are bounds for $\gamma(G)$.

$G = (X,U)$ is k-critical if $\gamma(G) = k$ and if for each node x the subgraph G' generated by $X - \{x\}$ satisfies $\gamma(G') < \gamma(G)$. Every graph G with $\gamma(G) = k$ contains a k-critical subgraph. We will need the following :

Proposition 3.1 [4] : A k-critical graph $G = (X,U)$ cannot be disconnected by removing $p \leq k-2$ edges.

Proof : This result is straightforward for $k \leq 3$; we assume that $k \geq 4$ and that there exists a cut $C = (A,\bar{A})$ of G with $p \leq k-2$ edges. $\gamma(G_A) \leq k-1$ and $\gamma(G_{\bar{A}}) \leq k-1$. There is at least one edge of C with both nodes of the same color (otherwise $\gamma(G) < k$) . Let $x_1,x_2,\ldots,x_r$ be the nodes of A which are adjacent to some edge of C . If all neighbours of x_1 in $\bar{A}$ have not the same color as x_1 , we do nothing. Otherwise we permute the k-1 colors in G_A in such a way that x_1 has a color different from those of its neighbours in $\bar{A}$ (this is possible since x_1

has at most k-2 such neighbours). Next if x_2 has some neighbour in $\bar{A}$ with the same color, we permute in A the k-2 colors different from that of x_1 in such a way that x_2 is colored differently from its neighbours in $\bar{A}$ (x_2 has at most k-3 neighbours in $\bar{A}$) . Continuing like this we get a usual (k-1)-coloring of G . This contradicts $\gamma(G) = k$.

The <u>edge-connectivity</u> e(G) of a simple graph G with at least 2 nodes is the minimum number of edges in any cut $(A,\bar{A})$ of G . The <u>strength</u> s(G) is the maximum edge-connectivity of its subgraphs.

The following bound for $\gamma(G)$ was given by D.W. Matula :

<u>Theorem 3.1</u> [10] : For any simple graph G $\gamma(G) \leq s(G) + 1$.

<u>Proof</u> : Let $k = \gamma(G)$ and let G' be a k-critical subgraph of G ; each cut C of G' has at least k-1 edges from Proposition 3.1 ; hence $e(G') \geq k-1 = \gamma(G) - 1$. So $\gamma(G) \leq 1 + s(G)$.

Furthermore since $e(G') \leq \min_x d_{G'}(x)$ in any subgraph G (here $d_{G'}(x)$ is the degree of node x in subgraph G') , we obtain a result of Szekeres and Wilf :

<u>Corollary 3.1.1</u> [12] : For any simple graph G

$$\gamma(G) \leq 1 + \max_{G'=(X',U')} \min_{x \in X'} d_{G'}(x)$$

(The maximum is taken over all subgraphs G' of G) .

We are about to describe algorithms for coloring the nodes of a graph. We need some more definitions. An ordered partition $P = (C_1, C_2, \ldots, C_p)$ of the edges of a simple graph $G = (X,U)$ is a <u>slicing</u> of G if C_1 is a cut of G and C_i is a cut of $\bar{G}_i = (X, U-C_1-\ldots-C_{i-1})$ for $i = 2,\ldots,p$. P is a <u>marrow slicing</u> if each C_i is a minimum cut of some connected component of $\bar{G}_i$.

The <u>width</u> $w(P)$ of P is defined as $\max_i |C_i|$ where C_i is a cut of P.

<u>Proposition 3.2</u> [10] : For any simple graph G with at least one edge $\min_P w(P) = s(G)$.

<u>Proof</u> : Let G^* be a subgraph of G (with at least 2 nodes) such that $e(G^*) = s(G)$. In any slicing P there is a first cut C_i which separates G^* ; this C_i contains a cut of G^*, so $w(P) \geq |C_i| \geq s(G)$. So $\min w(P) \geq s(G)$. On the other hand if $\overline{P} = (C_1,\ldots,C_p)$ is a narrow slicing of G with $w(\overline{P}) = |C_i|$, then the subgraph $\overline{G}_i$ cut by C_i satisfies $e(\overline{G}_i) = w(\overline{P})$. Hence $\min w(P) \leq s(G)$.

An algorithm for coloring the nodes of G with at most $s(G) + 1$ colors would be the following :

a) determine a narrow slicing $P = (C_1,C_2,\ldots,C_p)$ of G ; a minimum cut in a graph might be obtained with network flow techniques for instance.

b) all nodes in $\overline{G}_{p+1} = (X,U-C_1-\ldots-C_p)$ get color 1 since this graph has no edges. At most $1+s(G)$ colors have been used.

c) if $\overline{G}_i = (X,U-C_1-\ldots-C_{i-1})$ has been colored with at most $1+s(G)$ colors, then $\overline{G}_{i-1}$ may be colored with $k \leq 1+s(G)$ colors by using the recoloring procedure described in Proposition 3.1. (Recall that $|C_i| \leq s(G)$).

d) At the end we get a usual k-coloring of G with $k \leq 1+s(G)$.

A much simpler algorithm can be used if one is satisfied with the bound of Corollary 3.1.1 . A <u>star slicing</u> P^* of $G = (X,U)$ is a slicing where each cut $C_i = (A,\overline{A})$ consists of adjacent edges, i.e. $|A| = 1$. A star slicing decomposes G into isolated nodes by eliminating (isolating) a single node at each step. A star slicing P^* is <u>minimum</u> if the node eliminated by each cut has minimum degree in the remaining subgraph.

Proposition 3.3 [10] : For any minimum star slicing P^* of G , $w(P^*) = \max_{G'=(X',U')} \min_{x \in X'} \{d_{G'}(x) \mid G' \text{ subgraph of } G\}$

Proof : Let $w(P^*) = |C_i|$ and let $G^* = (X^*,U^*)$ be the subgraph cut by C_i ; then $w(P^*) = \min_x d_{G^*}(x)$. Furthermore the first node removed from any subgraph G' by P^* has degree at most $w(P^*)$.

The algorithm we are going to describe belongs to the class of sequential node coloring algorithms (Matula et al. [11]) :

Let $x_1,x_2,\ldots,x_n$ be an ordering of the nodes of G ; define X_i as $\{x_1,x_2,\ldots,x_i\}$ and $G(i)$ as the subgraph generated by X_i $(i=1,\ldots,n)$.

a) x_1 gets color 1 , so $G(1)$ is colored with one color.

b) if $G(i-1)$ has been colored with p colors, then x_i gets color q , where q is the smallest positive integer not assigned to neighbours of x_i in $G(i)$. Now $G(i)$ is colored with p or $p+1$ colors.

c) This is repeated until all nodes of G are colored.

With this algorithm the number k of colors used satisfies $k \leq 1 + \max_{i \leq n} d_{G(i)}(x_i)$.

Let $x_n,x_{n-1},\ldots,x_2,x_1$ be the nodes of G successively eliminated by a minimum star slicing of G . Then if we color sequentially the nodes $x_1,x_2,\ldots,x_n$ we use at most $1+w(P^*)$ colors since $\max_{i \leq n} d_{G(i)}(x_i) = w(P^*)$. From Proposition 3.3 this is the bound of Corollary 3.1.1 .

If the nodes are ordered according to the non increasing degrees in the sequential algorithm, a k-coloring is obtained with $k \leq \max_{i \leq n} \min (i,1+d(x_i))$. (Welsh and Powell [14]) .

Finally we give a proof of Brooks theorem based on sequential colorings and apparently due to L. Lovász. In the proof we will use the following property which is easily established :

Proposition 3.4 : Let $G = (X,U)$ be a simple connected graph without articulation node and with maximum degree $h \geq 3$; if G is not a complete graph, then there exists a triple of nodes $(\bar{x},a,b)$ such that

a) $(\bar{x},a)$, $(\bar{x},b) \in U$, $(a,b) \notin U$

b) $\{a,b\}$ is not an articulation set .

Proof : Let C be a cycle (without chord) in G ; let $x_1,\ldots,x_r$ be the nodes of C . Consider successively the triples of consecutive nodes in C ; if there is one triple satisfying a) and b) we are done. Otherwise G consists of blocks $B_1,B_2,\ldots,B_r$ (a block is a maximal subgraph without articulation node) such that $B_1 \ni (x_r,x_1)$, $B_i \ni (x_{i-1},x_i)$ for $i=2,\ldots,r$. Since $h \geq 3$ there exists an edge, say (x_1,x_{r+1}) in B_1 , with $x_{r+1} \neq x_r$ (because G is simple) ; x_{r+1} is not an articulation node of B_1 . So the triple (x_1,x_2,x_{r+1}) satisfies a) and b) since $(x_2,x_{r+1}) \notin U$.

Theorem of Brooks [5] : Let $G = (X,U)$ be a connected simple graph without articulation node and with maximum degree $h \geq 3$; if G is not a complete graph, $\gamma(G) \leq h$.

Proof : A) Let $(\bar{x},a,b)$ be a triple with the properties a) and b) of Proposition 3.4 .

Define $N_0 = \{\bar{x}\}$, $N_1 = \{y \mid y \neq a,b, \exists (\bar{x},y) \in U\}$ and for $j = 2,3,\ldots,$ $N_j = \{y \mid y \notin \{a,b\} \cup N_0 \cup \ldots\ldots \cup N_{j-1}, \exists (z,y) \in U$ with $z \in N_{j-1}\}$. Let q be the smallest index for which $N_q = \emptyset$; we let $N_q = \{a,b\}$.

B) From A , $X = N_0 \cup \ldots \cup N_q$ otherwise $\{a,b\}$ would be an articulation set. Order the nodes by taking first N_q , then

N_{q-1} and so on ; we have $x_n = \bar{x}$. Color the nodes sequentially. We have $\max_{i \leq n-1} d_{G(i)}(x_i) \leq h-1$ since for each node v in N_j there is an edge (u,v) with $u \in N_p$ $(p < j)$. So $G(n-1)$ is colored with at most h colors. $x_n = \bar{x}$ may be colored with one of these h colors since both $x_1 = a$ and $x_2 = b$ have color 1 .

<u>Theorem 3.2</u> : Let $S_1,\dots,S_k$ be a usual k-coloring of the nodes of G and let G(i) be the subgraph generated by the nodes of $S_1 \cup \dots \cup S_i$ and $d_i = \max_{x \in S_i} d_{G(i)}(x)$. Then $\gamma(G) \leq 1 + \max_{i \leq k} \min(d_i, i-1)$.

This result is easily obtained by using a sequential node coloring algorithm in G ; it is an extension of theorem 5 in [4 p 335] ; it may be generalized to hypergraphs.

4. HYPERGRAPH COLORING

A hypergraph H consists of a finite set X of n nodes and a family $E = (E_i | i \in I)$ of m nonempty subsets of X (edges) satisfying $\bigcup_{i=1}^{m} E_i = X$. Given a subset S of nodes of $H = (X,E)$ $s(E_i)$ will denote the cardinality of $S \cap E_i$. A set S of nodes is <u>stable</u> if $s(E_i) \leq |E_i| - 1$ for E_i 2. A <u>usual k-coloring</u> of the nodes of $H = (X,E)$ is a partition $(S_1,S_2,\dots,S_k)$ of X into k stable sets S_j . The <u>chromatic number</u> $\gamma(H)$ of H is the smallest k for which there exists a usual k-coloring.

A usual k-coloring of the nodes of a hypergraph $H = (X,E)$ may be obtained by using a sequential coloring algorithm in the same way as for graphs. We may assume that all edges of H are distinct and define the hyperdegree h(x) of a node x in the same way as Berge [4, p 429] . Notice first that (exactly as for graphs) whenever a node is removed from a hypergraph, all edges which contain this node are also to be removed. So we generally get a partial subhypergraph (p.s.h.); in the case of graphs we simply get a subgraph.

Here we may have isolated nodes in a hypergraph. Next let $x_1,\dots,x_n$ be an ordering of the nodes of H and let H(i) be the p.s.h. obtained by keeping only nodes $x_1,\dots,x_i$ (i.e. by removing nodes $x_{i+1},\dots,x_n$). Clearly if the nodes are colored consecutively we get the following bound of the chromatic number: $\gamma(H) \leq 1 + \max_{i\leq n} h_{H(i)}(x_i)$ where $h_{H(i)}(x_i)$ is the hyperdegree of node x_i in H(i). This bound may be improved by ordering the nodes as follows: x_n is a node of minimum hyperdegree in $H(n) = H$; for $i = n-1,\dots,1$ x_i is a node of minimum hyperdegree in $H(i)$.

<u>Proposition 4.1</u> : Let $H = (X,E)$ be a hypergraph and F the family of all p.s.h. $H' = (X',E')$ obtained by removing nodes from H . Then
$$\gamma(H) \leq 1 + \max_{H'\in F} \min_{x\in X'} h_{H'}(x) .$$

The proof is exactly the same as for graphs. (Similar results have also been obtained by P. Hansen)

A partition $(S_1,S_2,\dots,S_k)$ of the nodes of $H = (X,E)$ is a <u>p-bounded k-coloring</u> if $|s_a(E_i) - s_b(E_i)| \leq p$ for every edge E_i and every pair of colors a,b . If $p = 1$, the coloring is <u>equitable</u>. Also $(S_1,S_2,\dots,S_k)$ is a <u>good k-coloring</u> of the nodes of H if for every color a $s_a(E_i) \leq 1$ whenever $|E_i| \leq k$ and $s_a(E_i) \geq 1$ otherwise. Let $k(i) = |\{a|s_a(E_i) \geq 1\}|$.

Clearly if H is the dual of a multigraph G , any good (or equitable) k-coloring of the nodes of H defines a good (or equitable) k-coloring of the edges of G . The characterization of all hypergraphs H with $\gamma(H) = 2$ seems to be a difficult problem. Following C. Berge we consider here two generalizations of bipartite multigraphs.

H is <u>unimodular</u> if its edge incidence matrix A is totally unimodular. It follows from a theorem of A. Ghouila-Houri that H is unimodular if and only if every subhypergraph of H has an equitable bicoloring. Using this property we have obtained the following generalization of theorem 2.2 :

Theorem 4.1 [15] : For each integer $k \geq 2$ a unimodular hypergraph has an equitable k-coloring.

Proof : Let $(S_1,S_2,\ldots,S_k)$ be any partition of the nodes of $H = (X,E)$ into k subsets ; for each edge E_i and each pair of colors a,b we define $e_{ab}(E_i) = s_a(E_i) - s_b(E_i)$; let $e(E_i) = \max_{a,b} e_{ab}(E_i)$ for each E_i . If $e(E_i) \leq 1$ for all edges E_i , we have an equitable k-coloring. Otherwise let E_r be an edge with $e(E_r) \geq 2$ and suppose p,q are two distinct colors with $e_{pq}(E_r) = s_p(E_r) - s_q(E_r) = e(E_r) \geq 2$. The subgraph H' of H spanned by $S_p \cup S_q$ has an equitable bicoloring (S'_p,S'_q) ; let $S'_j = S_j$ for $j \neq p,q$. For $(S'_1,S'_2,\ldots,S'_k)$ we may define numbers $e'_{ab}(E_i)$ and $e'(E_i)$ exactly as previously.

For each edge E_i we have

$$\min_{j\leq k} s_j(E_i) \leq \min_{j\leq k} s'_j(E_i) \leq \max_{j\leq k} s'_j(E_i) \leq \max_{j\leq k} s_j(E_i)$$

i.e. $e'(E_i) \leq e(E_i)$; furthermore for E_r , the number of pairs a,b with $e'_{ab}(E_r) \leq e(E_r) - 1$ has increased by at least 1 since $e'_{pq}(E_r) = s'_p(E_r) - s'_q(E_r) \leq 1$. This procedure may be repeated until $e(E_i) \leq 1$ for every edge E_i .

A hypergraph $H = (X,E)$ is balanced if in every odd cycle $(x_1,E_1,x_2,E_2,\ldots,E_{2r+1},x_1)$ there is an edge containing at least 3 nodes of the cycle. A unimodular hypergraph is balanced and H is balanced if and only if every subhypergraph of H has a good bicoloring. A balanced hypergraph may not have an equitable k-coloring for each $k \geq 2$; however C. Berge has shown the following :

Theorem 4.2 [3] : For each integer $k \geq 2$ a balanced hypergraph has a good k-coloring.

Proof : We consider a partition $(S_1,S_2,\dots,S_k)$ of X ; if for some edge E_r , $k(r) < \min(k,|E_r|)$, there exists 2 indices p,q with $s_p(E_r) \geq 2$, $s_q(E_r) = 0$; recoloring the subhypergraph H_{pq} generated by $S_p \cup S_q$ we get a good bicoloring (S'_p,S'_q) of H_{pq} . Let $S'_j = S_j$ for $j \neq p,q$. Then for $(S'_1,S'_2,\dots,S'_q)$ we define numbers $k'(i)$; we have $k'(i) \geq k(i)$ for $i \neq r$ and $k'(r) = k(r) + 1$. By iterating this procedure, we shall get a good k-coloring of H .

J.C. Fournier and M. Las Vergnas [8] , [8a] have described other classes of bicolorable hypergraphs.

Another type of coloring will be useful in section 5 ; S is strongly stable in $H = (X,E)$ if $s(E_i) \leq 1$ $(i=1,\dots,m)$. A strong k-coloring of H is a partition of X into k strongly stable sets.

5. BALANCING THE COLORINGS

For each node x in $H = (X,E)$ let $d(x) = |\{i | E_i \ni x\}|$. $H(d)$ will denote a hypergraph where $\max_x d(x) = d$. If $d = 1$ all edges are disjoint; coloring problems are trivial in this case. So we will assume $d \geq 2$; s_i is the cardinality of S_i .

Theorem 5.1 : Let $(S_1,S_2,\dots,S_k)$ be a partition of the nodes of a hypergraph $H(d)$ with $\max s_j > 1 + (d-1) \min s_j$. Then there exists a partition $(S'_1,S'_2,\dots,S'_k)$ such that

a) $\max_j s'_j \leq 1 + (d-1) \min_j s'_j$

b) $\min_j s_j(E_i) \leq \min_j s'_j(E_i) \leq \max_j s'_j(E_i) \leq \max_j s_j(E_i)$

for every edge E_i .

Proof : A) We prove the theorem for $k = 2$; then the result follows for any $k > 2$ by successive applications of the interchange procedure described for the case $k = 2$.

Construct a simple graph G' whose nodes are those of $H(d)$. Its edges are obtained in the following way : we examine consecutively all edges E_i of $H(d)$. In each E_i we join by an edge as many disjoint pairs x,y of nodes as possible with $x \in S_1 \cap \cap E_i$, $y \in S_2 \cap E_i$ provided x and y have not been joined yet (2 pairs are disjoint if they have no common node). G' is a simple bipartite graph with maximum degree $\leq d$ since each node of $H(d)$ belongs to at most d edges E_i .

B) Suppose $s_1 = s_2 + K > 1 + (d-1)\, s_2$. G' has at most $d \cdot s_2$ edges and $s_1 + s_2 \geq d \cdot s_2 + 2$ nodes ; so it is not connected. Hence there must exist a connected component $G^* = (S^*_1 \cup S^*_2, U^*)$ of G' for which $s^*_2 < s^*_1 = s^*_2 + L \leq 1 + (d-1)\, s^*_2$. Observe that $0 < L \leq 1 + (d-2)\, s^*_2 \leq 1 + (d-2)\, s_2 < K$. Interchanging the nodes of S^*_1 and S^*_2 we obtain a partition $(\bar{S}_1, \bar{S}_2)$ of the nodes of $H(d)$ such that $|\bar{s}_1 - \bar{s}_2| < |s_1 - s_2|$ since $s_2 < \bar{s}_2 = s_2 + L < s_2 + K = s_1$ and $s_2 = s_1 - K < s_1 - L = \bar{s}_1 < s_1$. If (possibly after permutation of the indices) we still have $\bar{s}_1 > 1 + (d-1)\, \bar{s}_2$, we repeat the interchange procedure. Finally we get a partition (S'_1, S'_2) satisfying a) .

C) We show that b) holds after each interchange. Consider any edge E_i of $H(d)$. Let $r = \min(s_1(E_i), s_2(E_i))$; in G' there are r non adjacent edges (x_j, y_j) with $x_j \in S_1 \cap E_i$, $y_j \in S_2 \cap E_i$. Hence at most $|s_1(E_i) - s_2(E_i)|$ nodes of E_i are not adjacent to some edge of G' with both nodes in E_i . So, after each interchange we have $|\bar{s}_1(E_i) - \bar{s}_2(E_i)| \leq |s_1(E_i) - s_2(E_i)|$ for each E_i since if anyone of the r nodes x_j is removed from S_1 , it will be replaced by the corresponding y_j .

Notice that in the interchange process we have for any edge E_i $\bar{s}_1(E_i) = 0$ if and only if $s_1(E_i) = 0$ or $s_2(E_i) = 0$. As a consequence we may formulate : If a hypergraph $H(d)$ has a good or p-bounded k-coloring for some k, it also has a good or p-bounded k-coloring $(S_1,S_2,\dots,S_k)$ with $\max s_j \leq 1 + (d-1) \min s_j$.

Corollary 5.1.1 : For each integer $k \geq 2$ a unimodular hypergraph $H(d) = (X,E)$ has an equitable k-coloring $(S_1,S_2,\dots,S_k)$ such that $\frac{1}{d-1}(<|X|/k> -1) \leq s_j \leq (d-1)[|X|/k] + 1 \quad j=1,\dots,k$.

A similar result holds for good k-colorings of balanced hypergraphs.

When $H(d)$ is the hypergraph of maximal cliques of a simple graph G any strong k-coloring of $H(d)$ is a usual k-coloring of the nodes of G. We obtain :

Corollary 5.1.2 : Let G be a simple graph where no node belongs to more than d maximal cliques ; then for each $k \geq \gamma(G)$ there is a usual k-coloring $(S_1,S_2,\dots,S_k)$ of the nodes of G such that $\max s_j \leq 1 + (d-1) \min s_j$.

This result is best possible for $k = \gamma(G)$ as is seen by considering a star. However A. Hajnal and E. Szemeredi [9] have shown that there exists in G a usual $(h+1)$-coloring with $|s_j - s_i| \leq 1$ $(i,j \leq k)$ where h is the maximum degree in G.

Finally let $H(d)$ be the dual of a multigraph G ; then $d=2$. The interchange procedure of theorem 5.1 may be performed whenever S_1,S_2 satisfy $|s_1 - s_2| \geq 2$.

Theorem 5.2 [15] : If a sequence $(u_1,u_2,\dots,u_k)$ with $u_1 \geq u_2 \geq \dots \geq u_k$ represents the cardinalities in a k-coloring $(U_1,U_2,\dots,U_k)$ of the edges of a multigraph G then any sequence $(u'_1,u'_2,\dots,u'_k)$ such that

a) $u'_1 \geq u'_2 \geq \dots \geq u'_k$

b) $\sum_{i=1}^{r} u'_i \leq \sum_{i=1}^{r} u_i$ $(r=1,2,\dots,k)$ with equality for $r=k$

corresponds to a k-coloring $(U'_1, U'_2, \ldots, U'_k)$ of G where for each node x $\min_i u_i(x) \leq \min_i u'_i(x) \leq \max_i u'_i(x) \leq \max_i u_i(x)$.

Proof : Starting from $\hat{u} = (u_1, \ldots, u_k)$, any sequence $\hat{u}' = (u'_i, \ldots, u'_k)$ satisfying a) and b) may be obtained by iterated applications of the interchange routine.

Given a sequence $\hat{u} = (u_1, u_2, \ldots, u_k)$ with $u_1 \geq u_2 \geq \cdots \geq u_k$ we write $\hat{u} > \hat{u}'$ for each $\hat{u}'$ satisfying a) and b) . Let $C(\hat{u})$ be the set containing all these sequences. Clearly in $C(\hat{u})$ there is a unique sequence $\hat{u}^* = (u^*_1, u^*_2, \ldots, u^*_k)$ for which $u^*_1 - u^*_k \leq 1$.

Corollary 5.2.1 :If a sequence $\hat{u}$ corresponds to a good (or p-bounded) k-coloring of G , then any sequence $\hat{u}'$ of $C(\hat{u})$ corresponds also to a good (or p-bounded) k-coloring. In particular there exists a good (or p-bounded) k-coloring $(U^*_1, U^*_2, \ldots, U^*_k)$ with $|u^*_i - u^*_j| \leq 1$ $(i,j \leq k)$.

Consequently for each $k \geq 2$ a bipartite multigraph has an equitable k-coloring $(U_1, U_2, \ldots, U_k)$ such that $|u_i - u_j| \leq 1$ $(i,j \leq k)$ [17] . For each $k \geq 2$ a multigraph G has a 2-bounded k-coloring with $|u_i - u_j| \leq 1$ $(i,j \leq k)$; if $k \geq q(G)$, there is a usual k-coloring with this property.

The problem of determining whether a sequence $(u_1, u_2, \ldots, u_k)$ corresponds to a usual k-coloring of the edges of a given multigraph seems difficult. Partial results are given in [6] and [16].

The interchange routine of theorem 5.1 is very simple when $H(d)$ is the dual of a multigraph. In fact we have the following :

Proposition 5.1 : Let (U_1, U_2) be a bicoloring of the edges of a multigraph G with $u_1 \geq u_2 + 1$; then there exists an alternating chain C such that the extreme edges of C are in U_1 and the extreme nodes x,y of C satisfy $u_1(x) > u_2(x)$,

$u_1(y) > u_2(y)$ (or $u_1(x) > u_2(x) + 1$ if $x = y$) .

Proof : Pickup any edge e in $G = (X,U)$ and construct an alternating chain C' containing e ; we extend C' as far as possible. We remove C' from G and take another edge e' in $U-C'$. We repeat the construction as long as G contains edges.

Finally we will get a partition P of U into alternating chains and cycles. For each alternating cycle $\overline{C}$ we have $|\overline{C} \cap U_1| = |\overline{C} \cap U_2|$. Since $u_1 \geq u_2 + 1$ we must have in P an alternating chain C with $|C \cap U_1| = |C \cap U_2| + 1$. The extreme edges of this chain are in U_1 .

Since each alternating chain was extended as far as possible in the partitioning procedure, it is easy to see that each extreme node x of C will satisfy $u_1(x) > u_2(x)$ or $u_1(x) > u_2(x) + 1$ if the extreme nodes of C coïncide.

Corollary (R.Z. Norman, M.O. Rabin [11a]) : A covering U_1 is minimum if and only if there is no alternating chain whose extreme edges e,f are in U_1 and whose extreme nodes are adjacent to some edge of U_1 other than e,f .

Proof : Clearly if there is such a chain, then by interchanging the edges of U_1 and $U_2 = U - U_1$ in the chain we get a covering with smaller cardinality.

Conversely let U_1 be a covering which is not minimum and U_2 a minimum covering. $U'_1 = U_1 - U_2$ and $U'_2 = U_2 - U_1$ define a bicoloring of $G' = (X, U'_1 \cup U'_2)$; since $u'_1 > u'_2$ there exists an alternating chain C whose extreme edges are in U_1 and whose extreme nodes satisfy $u_1(x) \geq u'_1(x) > u'_2(x)$ (or $u_1(x) \geq u'_1(x) > u'_2(x) + 1$ if they coïncide) . If $u'_2(x) \geq 1$, then we have $u_1(x) \geq 2$ (or $u_1(x) \geq 3$) . Otherwise if $u'_2(x) = 0$, there is in $U_2 - U'_2 = U_2 \cap U_1$ an edge (x,y) since U_2 is a cover. Clearly $(x,y) \neq e,f$.

With an analogous argument we would show that a matching U_2 is maximum if and only if there is no alternating chain whose extreme nodes x,y satisfy $u_2(x) = u_2(y) = 0$.

A similar reasoning would provide conditions for a stable set in a graph to have maximum cardinality.

REFERENCES

1. C. Berge, "Sur certains hypergraphes généralisant les graphes bipartis", Comb. Theory and its Applic. Balatonfüred (P. Erdös, A. Rényi, V.T. Sós, ed.) North Holland, Amsterdam, 1970, p 119-133.

2. - , Balanced Matrices, Math. Progr., vol 2, 1972, p 19-31.

3. - , Notes sur les bonnes colorations d'un hypergraphe, cahiers C.E.R.O., vol 15, No 3, 1973, p 219-223.

4. - , Graphs and Hypergraphs, North Holland, Amsterdam, 1973.

5. R.L. Brooks, On colouring the Nodes of a Network, Proc. Cambridge Phil. Soc., vol 37, 1941, p 194-197.

6. J. Folkman and D.R. Fulkerson, "Edge Colorings in Bipartite Graphs", Comb. Math. and their Applic. (R.C. Bose, T.A. Dowling, ed.) Univ. of North Carolina Press, Chapel Hill, 1969.

7. J.C. Fournier, Colorations des arêtes d'un graphe, Cahiers C.E.R.O., vol 15, No 3, 1973, p 311-314.

8. J.C. Fournier and M. Las Vergnas, Une classe d'hypergraphes bichromatiques, Discrete Math., vol 2, 1972, p 407-410.

8a. - , Une classe d'hypergraphes bichromatiques II, Discrete Math., vol 7, 1974, p 99-106.

9. A. Hajnal and E. Szemerédi, "Proof of a Conjecture of P.

Erdös, Comb Theory and its Applic. Balatonfüred (P. Erdös, A. Rényi, V.T. Sós, ed.) North Holland, Amsterdam, 1970, p 601-623.

10. D.W. Matula, k-Components, Clusters and Slicings in Graphs, SIAM J. Appl. Math., vol 22, No 3, 1972, p 459-480.

11. D.W. Matula, G. Marble and J.D. Isaacson, "Graph Coloring Algorithms", Graph Theory and Computing (R.C. Read, ed.), Acad. Press, New York, 1972, p 109-122.

11a. R.Z. Norman, M.O. Rabin, An algorithm for the minimum cover of a graph, Proc. Am. Math. Soc., vol 10, 1959, p 315-319.

12. G. Szekeres and H. Wilf, An Inequality for the Chromatic Number of a Graph, J. Comb. Theory, vol 4, 1968, p 1-3.

13. V.G. Vizing, On an Estimate of the Chromatic class of a p-graph (Russian), Diskret. Analiz., vol 3, 1964, p 25-30.

14. D. Welsh and M. Powel, An upper bound for the chromatic number of a graph and its application to timetabling problems, Computer J., vol 10, 1967, p 85-87.

15. D. de Werra, Equitable Colorations of Graphs, R.I.R.O., R-3, 1971, p 3-8.

16. — , Investigations on an Edge Coloring Problem, Discrete Math., vol 1, 1971, p 167-179.

17. — , Decomposition of Bipartite Multigraphs into Matchings, Zeitschrift für Op. Res., vol 16, 1972, p 85-90.

**

Several computational algorithms have been proposed for determining the chromatic number of a graph. All these methods proceed by implicit enumeration of colorings; we shall just mention the following ones which we could not describe here because of the lack of space.

18. J. Randall Brown, Chromatic Scheduling and the Chromatic Number Problem, Manag. Sci., vol 19, No 4, 1972, p 456-463.

19. D.G. Corneil and B. Graham, An Algorithm for determining the Chromatic Number of a Graph, SIAM J. Comput., vol 2, No 4, 1973, p 311-318.

PROBLEMES EXTREMAUX CONCERNANT LE NOMBRE DES COLORATIONS DES SOMMETS D'UN GRAPHE FINI

I. Tomescu

Faculté de Mathématiques et de Mécanique,
Université de Bucarest, Roumanie

Une coloration du graphe G à k couleurs ou une k-coloration est une partition de ses sommets en k classes non-vides telles que deux sommets appartenant à une même classe ne soient pas adjacents [1]. Le plus petit nombre de classes d'une coloration de G est nommé nombre chromatique de G et il est noté par $\gamma(G)$. Les graphes G qui ont une seule coloration à $k = \gamma(G)$ couleurs ont été étudiés dans [2]. On peut déterminer le nombre chromatique d'un graphe fini G en résolvant un problème de couverture minimale des sommets de G par les ensembles intérieurement stables maximaux de G. Si l'on utilise l'algorithme de Petrick [3], on obtient aussi toutes les colorations minimales de G. Le nombre maximal des colorations d'un graphe G est donné par le résultat suivant [4] :

Théorème 1 : Le nombre maximal des (k+r)-colorations d'un graphe G ayant n sommets et de nombre chromatique k est égal à $C(n,k,r)$, le nombre des (k+r)-colorations du graphe composé d'un k-sous-graphe complet et de n-k sommets isolés, et ce graphe est unique avec cette propriété. Le nombre $C(n,k,r)$ est donné par l'expression :

$$C(n,k,r) = \sum_{p=r}^{n-k} \binom{n-k}{p} S(p,r)k^{n-k-p} \quad \text{pour} \quad 1 \leq k \leq n-k \quad \text{et}$$

$C(n,k,0) = k^{n-k}$ où $S(p,r)$ est le nombre de Stirling de deuxième espèce, c'est-à-dire le nombre des partitions d'un ensemble à p éléments en r classes.

La démonstration de ce théorème se fait par l'induction par rapport à n compte-tenu des relations de récurrence suivantes pour

B. Roy (ed.), Combinatorial Programming: Methods and Applications, 327–336.

les nombres $C(n,k,r)$ $(n \geq k$ et $0 \leq r \leq n-k)$:

$C(n,k,r) = C(n-1, k, r-1) + (k+r)\, C(n-1, k, r)$ pour $1 \leq r \leq n-k$
et $C(n,k,0) = k\, C(n-1, k, 0)$;

$$C(n,k,r) = \sum_{q=0}^{n-k-r} \binom{n-k}{q} C(n-1-q, k-1, r) \quad \text{pour } k \geq 2.$$

Si l'on note par $C_j(G_n)$ le nombre des j-colorations des sommets du graphe G_n à n sommets, alors le polynôme chromatique [5] de G_n vérifie les relations : $P(G_n ; \lambda) = 0$ pour tout $\lambda < \gamma(G_n)$ et si $\lambda \geq \gamma(G_n)$, alors :

$$P(G_n ; \lambda) = \sum_{j = \gamma(G_n)}^{\min(n,\lambda)} j\,!\, \binom{\lambda}{j} C_j(G_n)$$

d'où se déduit le résultat suivant :

<u>Corollaire 1.1</u> : Si nous notons :

$[\lambda]_k = \lambda(\lambda - 1) \ldots (\lambda - k+1)$,

alors $\max\limits_{\gamma(G_n)=k} P(G_n ; \lambda) = [\lambda]_k\, \lambda^{n-k}$ pour tout λ naturel et le maximum est atteint pour tout $\lambda \geq k$ seulement pour le graphe composé d'une k-clique et de $n-k$ sommets isolés.

<u>Corollaire 1.2</u> : Le nombre maximal des colorations minimales d'un graphe à n sommets est égal à :

$$\max_{r=[x],\{x\}} (r^{n-r})$$

où x vérifie l'équation $x(1 + \ln x) = n$

($[x]$ est la partie entière de x et $\{x\} = -[-x]$). Ce nombre, noté $C(n)$, croît vite avec n comme on le voit au tableau suivant [6] :

n	C(n)	n	C(n)
1	1	9	1024
2	1	10	4096
3	2	11	16384
4	4	12	78125
5	9	13	390625
6	27	14	1953125
7	81	15	10077696
8	256	16	60466176

Parce que le nombre maximal des k-colorations d'un graphe G à n sommets et de nombre chromatique égal à k est atteint seulement pour le graphe composé d'une k-clique et de $n - k$ sommets isolés, c'est-à-dire pour le graphe unique à n sommets ayant $\gamma(G) = k$ et un nombre minimal de $\binom{k}{2}$ arêtes, on peut supposer que dans un ensemble de graphes G_n à n sommets et de nombre chromatique $\gamma(G_n) = k$ le nombre maximal de k-colorations est atteint pour un graphe qui a le nombre minimal d'arêtes. Mais ce résultat n'est pas vrai, comme on voit pour les graphes notés $K_{1,1,4}$ et $K_{1,3,2} - x$ ayant 6 sommets.

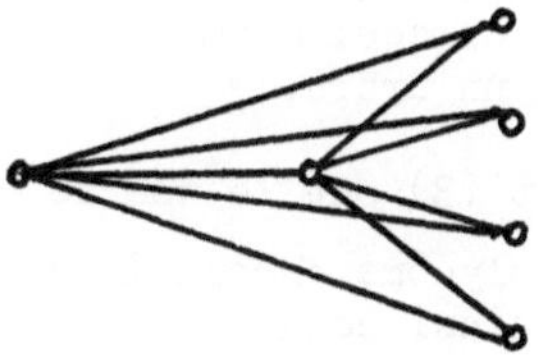

$K_{1,1,4}$

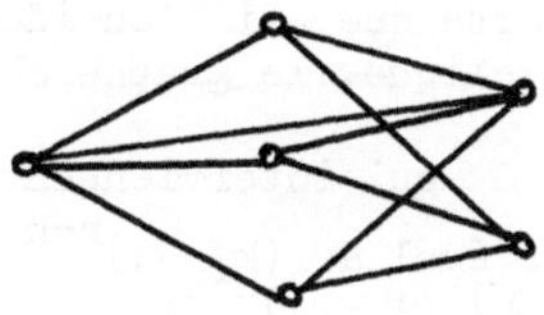

$K_{1,3,2} - x$

Ainsi $\gamma(K_{1,1,4}) = \gamma(K_{1,3,2} - x) = 3$, le nombre d'arêtes $m(K_{1,1,4}) = 9$, $m(K_{1,3,2} - x) = 10$ mais $C_3(K_{1,1,4}) = 1$ et $C_3(K_{1,3,2} - x) = 2$.

Dans ce qui suit, on présente quelques résultats partiels sur le nombre maximal de colorations d'un graphe connexe [7].

<u>Théorème 2</u> : Si le graphe G à $n \geq 3$ sommets est connexe et de nombre chromatique $\gamma(G) = 2$, alors $C_3(G) \leq 2^{n-2} - 1$, les seuls graphes connexes qui réalisent ce nombre maximal de 3-colorations étant les arbres à n sommets.

Théorème 3 : Le nombre maximal de 3-colorations d'un graphe connexe à n sommets et de nombre chromatique $\gamma(G) = 3$ est égal à $\frac{1}{3}(2^{n-1} - 1)$ pour n impair et à $\frac{2}{3}(2^{n-2} - 1)$ pour n pair.
Si n est impair, le seul graphe connexe qui réalise ce nombre maximal de 3-colorations est le polygone impair C_n ; et si n est pair, c'est celui composé du polygone C_{n-1} et d'un autre sommet relié par une arête à un sommet de C_{n-1}.
On peut démontrer ces deux théorèmes par induction sur n. On voit que pour les graphes connexes le nombre maximal de 3-colorations est atteint pour les graphes ayant un nombre minimal d'arêtes, compte-tenu de la caractérisation suivante [8] :

Théorème 4 : Le nombre minimal d'arêtes d'un graphe connexe G à n sommets et de nombre chromatique $k (2 \leq k \leq n)$ est égal à $\binom{k}{2} + n - k$.

Les graphes qui ont ce nombre minimal d'arêtes ont la forme suivante :

(1) pour $k = 2$, ils sont des arbres à n sommets ;
(2) pour $k = 3$, ils sont composés d'un cycle impair à p sommets $(3 \leq p \leq n)$ et de $n - p$ sommets de sorte que si l'on identifie à un seul sommet les sommets du cycle, le graphe obtenu est un arbre ;
(3) pour $k \geq 4$, ils sont composés d'une k-clique et de $n - k$ sommets de sorte que, si l'on identifie à un seul sommet les sommets de la k-clique, le graphe obtenu est un arbre.

Les graphes G qui interviennent au point (3) ont le nombre de k-colorations égal à $(k - 1)^{n-k}$ et le polynôme chromatique $P(G ; \lambda) = [\lambda]_k (\lambda - 1)^{n-k}$. Nous sommes ainsi conduits aux conjectures suivantes :

C1 - Le nombre maximal des k-colorations d'un graphe connexe G ayant n sommets et $\gamma(G) = k \geq 4$ est égal à $(k - 1)^{n-k}$, les seuls graphes qui ont ce nombre maximal de colorations ayant la forme (3).

C2 - Le nombre maximal des (k+r)-colorations d'un graphe connexe G ayant n sommets et le nombre chromatique $k \geq 4$ est atteint seulement pour les graphes ayant la forme (3) pour tout $0 \leq r < n - k$.

Ce nombre de (k+r)-colorations peut être obtenu de l'expression du polynôme chromatique des graphes de la forme (3). Evidemment, C2 implique C1.

Les graphes sans sommet isolé, de nombre chromatique donné, ayant le nombre minimal d'arêtes ont été caractérisés dans [9] sous la forme suivante :

Théorème 5 : Si G est un graphe sans sommet isolé, à n sommets, m arêtes et de nombre chromatique $\gamma(G) = k$, alors :

$$m \geq \binom{k}{2} + \left\{\frac{n-k}{2}\right\}$$

Pour $n - k$ pair, le graphe G qui a un nombre minimal d'arêtes est unique (jusqu'à un isomorphisme près) et il est composé d'un k-sous-graphe complet et de $n - k$ sommets qui sont reliés deux à deux par $\frac{n-k}{2}$ arêtes.

Pour $n - k$ impair, il y a deux types de graphes non-isomorphes qui ont un nombre minimal d'arêtes :

Un graphe composé d'une k-clique, de $n - k - 1$ sommets qui sont reliés deux à deux par $(n - k - 1)/2$ arêtes et d'un autre sommet x qui est relié par une arête à un sommet qui appartient à la k-clique.

L'autre graphe a la propriété que le sommet x est relié par une arête à un sommet qui n'appartient pas au sous-graphe complet à k sommets. Pour $k = 2$, ces deux types de graphes coïncident.

Le polynôme chromatique d'un graphe G caractérisé par le théorème 5 est égal à :

$$P(G ; \lambda) = [\lambda]_k \, \lambda^{[(n-k)/2]} \, (\lambda - 1)^{\{(n-k)/2\}}.$$

Nous sommes conduits aux conjectures suivantes :

C3 - Le nombre maximal des k-colorations d'un graphe G ayant n sommets, $\gamma(G) = k$ et qui n'a pas de sommets isolés est égal à $k^{[(n-k)/2]}(k - 1)^{\{(n-k)/2\}}$ et ce nombre est atteint seulement pour les graphes G caractérisés par le théorème 5.

C4 - Le nombre maximal des (k+r)-colorations d'un graphe G ayant n sommets, $\gamma(G) = k$ et qui n'a pas de sommets isolés est atteint seulement pour les graphes qui ont un nombre minimal d'arêtes pour tout $0 \leq r < n - k$.

Le polynôme chromatique du cycle à n sommets C_n est égal à $P(C_n ; \lambda) = (\lambda - 1)^n + (-1)^n (\lambda - 1)$ [5], d'où on obtient que le nombre des 3-colorations de C_n est égal à $(2^{n-1} - 1)/3$ pour n impair et à $(2^{n-1} - 2)/3$ pour n pair. Dans [10], on obtient le résultat suivant :

Théorème 6 : Le nombre maximal des 3-colorations d'un graphe hamiltonien G à n sommets et de nombre chromatique $\gamma(G) = 3$ est égal à $(2^{n-1} - 1)/3$ pour n impair et il est atteint seulement pour le cycle impair C_n et ce nombre maximal de 3-colorations est égal à $(2^{n-1} - 2)/3 - (2^{n-1} + 2^{2s} + 2^{n-2s} - 7)/9$ où $s = \left[\frac{n}{4}\right]$ pour n pair et ce nombre de colorations est atteint pour le graphe composé du cycle C_n et d'une corde qui relie deux sommets du cycle qui se trouvent à une distance maximale paire (égale à $2\left[\frac{n}{4}\right]$).

On voit que le nombre maximal des 3-colorations d'un graphe hamiltonien est atteint aussi dans la classe des graphes hamiltoniens G à n sommets, de nombre chromatique $\gamma(G) = 3$, qui ont un nombre minimal d'arêtes, compte-tenu de la caractérisation suivante [10] :

Théorème 7 : Le nombre minimal d'arêtes d'un graphe hamiltonien G à n sommets et de nombre chromatique k $(2 \leq k < n)$ est égal à : n pour $(k = 2 ; n$ pair$)$ ou $(k = 3 ; n$ impair$)$; $n + 1$ pour $(k = 3 ; n$ pair$)$; $\binom{k}{2} + n - k + 1$ pour $k \geq 4$.

Les graphes qui ont ce nombre minimal d'arêtes ont la forme suivante :

(1) pour $(k = 2 ; n$ pair$)$ ou $(k = 3 ; n$ impair$)$, ils sont des cycles C_n ;

(2) pour $k = 3 ; n$ pair, ils sont composés d'un cycle impair à p sommets $(3 \leq p \leq n - 1)$ et de $n - p$ sommets qui forment une chaîne reliée par ses extrémités à deux sommets consécutifs du cycle C_p ;

(3) pour $k \geq 4$, ils sont composés d'une k-clique et de $n - k$ sommets qui forment une chaîne reliée par ses extrémités à deux sommets différents de la k-clique.

La démonstration de ce théorème se fait par induction sur n en utilisant le théorème 4 et le fait que, pour tout graphe hamiltonien G, le sous-graphe obtenu de G par la suppression d'un sommet x est connexe.

Le polynôme chromatique d'un graphe G de la forme (3) est égal à [10] :

$$P(G ; \lambda) = [\lambda]_k \frac{(\lambda - 1)^{n-k+1} + (-1)^{n-k}}{\lambda}$$

et le nombre des k-colorations d'un tel graphe G est égal à $C_k(G) = ((k - 1)^{n-k+1} + (-1)^{n-k})/k$ $(k \geq 4)$.

Nous pouvons formuler les conjectures suivantes :

C5 - Le nombre maximal des k-colorations d'un graphe hamiltonien G à n sommets et de nombre chromatique égal à k $(k \geq 4)$ est égal à $((k - 1)^{n-k+1} + (-1)^{n-k})/k$ et ce nombre est atteint seulement pour les graphes G caractérisés par le théorème 7.

C6 - Le nombre maximal des (k+r)-colorations d'un graphe hamiltonien G à n sommets et $\gamma(G) = k$ est atteint seulement pour les graphes qui ont un nombre minimal d'arêtes pour tout $k \geq 4$ et $0 \leq r < n-k$.

Evidemment, C6 implique C5. Le nombre minimal de colorations d'un graphe à n sommets et de nombre chromatique k est atteint aussi pour un graphe ayant le nombre maximal d'arêtes parmi les graphes avec ces propriétés, à savoir pour le graphe de Turan, noté T(n, k) [11].

Le graphe T(n, k) est un graphe k-parti complet à n sommets pour lequel m parties contiennent t + 1 sommets et k - m parties contiennent t sommets où m est le reste de la division de n par k ($n = kt + m$ et $0 \leq m \leq k - 1$).

Ce graphe est le graphe unique (jusqu'à un isomorphisme près) à n sommets, de nombre chromatique k dont le nombre d'arêtes est maximal parmi les graphes ayant ces propriétés [11].

Le nombre des (k+r)-colorations du graphe T(n, k) est donné par l'expression :

$$D(n,k,r) = \sum_{\substack{n_1,\dots,n_k \geq 1 \\ n_1+\dots+n_k = k+r}} \prod_{i=1}^{m} S(t+1, n_i) \prod_{j=m+1}^{k} S(t, n_j)$$

Evidemment, $D(n,k,r) = 1$ pour $r = 0$ et $r = n - k$ et $D(n,k,r) = 0$ pour $r > n - k$.

Le polynôme chromatique d'un graphe composé de p sommets isolés est égal à $\lambda^p = \sum_{k=1}^{p} S(p, k) [\lambda]_k$. Compte-tenu de la méthode de R.C. Read [5], nous obtenons $P(T(n, k) ; \lambda) = (\sum_{p=1}^{t+1} S(t + 1, p) [\lambda]_p)^m (\sum_{q=1}^{t} S(t, q) [\lambda]_q)^{k-m}$ où, par définition, le produit $[\lambda]_p [\lambda]_q = [\lambda]_{p+q}$ pour tout p, q. Avec la formule du multinôme, on obtient $P(T(n, k) ; \lambda) = \sum \binom{m}{p_1,\ldots,p_{t+1}} \binom{k-m}{q_1,\ldots,q_t} \prod_{i=2}^{t} (S(t + 1, i))^{p_i} \prod_{j=2}^{t-1} (S(t, j))^{q_j} [\lambda]_{p \oplus q}$ où la somme est effectuée d'après toutes les partitions (ordonnées) : $p_1 + \ldots + p_{t+1} = m$; $q_1 + \ldots + q_t = k - m$ et $p \oplus q = p_1 + 2 p_2 + \ldots + (t + 1)p_{t+1} + q_1 + 2 q_2 + \ldots + tq_t$.

En particulier, on obtient l'expression du polynôme chromatique du graphe biparti complet $K_{p,q}$ [12] : $P(K_{p,q} ; \lambda) = \sum_{r=1}^{p} \sum_{s=1}^{q} S(p, r) S(q, s) [\lambda]_{r+s}$. Par exemple $P(T(8, 3) ; \lambda) = ([\lambda]_1 + 3[\lambda]_2 + [\lambda]_3)^2 ([\lambda]_1 + [\lambda]_2) = [\lambda]_3 + 7[\lambda]_4 + 17[\lambda]_5 + 17[\lambda]_6 + 7[\lambda]_7 + [\lambda]_8 = \lambda(\lambda - 1) (\lambda - 2) (\lambda^5-18 \lambda^4 + 136 \lambda^3-529 \lambda^2+1047 \lambda - 836)$.

Théorème 8 : Le nombre minimal des (k+r)-colorations d'un graphe G ayant n sommets et de nombre chromatique k est égal à $D(n, k, r)$ et, pour tout $0 < r < n - k$, le seul graphe qui a ce nombre minimal de colorations est le graphe $T(n, k)$.

La démonstration de ce résultat est directe, en utilisant une certaine construction et quelques inégalités portant sur les nombres de Stirling de deuxième espèce, comme par exemple :

Si $p \geq q$ et $u \geq v$, alors $S(p, u) S(q, v) \geq S(p, v) S(q, u)$ et si $p > q$ et $s \geq 3$, alors il y a l'inégalité :

$$\sum_{i+j=s} S(p + 1, i) S(q, j) > \sum_{i+j=s} S(p, i) S(q + 1, j).$$

Corollaire 8.1 : Les nombres $D(n, k, r)$ vérifient l'inégalité : $D(n, k, r) \leq S(n - k + 1, r + 1)$.

Corollaire 8.2 : Les polynômes chromatiques des graphes G_n à n sommets vérifient $\min_{\gamma(G_n)=k} P(G_n ; \lambda) = P(T(n, k) ; \lambda)$ pour tout λ naturel et le minimum est atteint pour tout $\lambda > k$ seulement pour le graphe $T(n, k)$.

On voit que le graphe $T(n, k)$ est connexe, sans sommet isolé pour $n \geq 2$ et hamiltonien pour tout $n \geq 3$ et $k \geq 3$. Pour $k = 2$ seulement le graphe $T(n, 2)$ avec n impair n'est pas hamiltonien. Mais un graphe hamiltonien G avec n sommets, n impair, a le nombre chromatique $\gamma(G) \geq 3$, donc $k \geq 3$.

Par conséquent, nous ne pouvons pas formuler des conjectures analogues à C1-C6 pour le nombre minimal des (k+r)-colorations des graphes connexes, sans sommet isolé, hamiltoniens.

REFERENCES

1. BERGE, C. - "Graphes et hypergraphes". Dunod, Paris, 1970.
2. HARARY, F. ; HEDETNIEMI, S.T. ; ROBINSON, R. - "Uniquely colorable graphs". J. Combinatorial Theory, 6, 1969, 264-270.
3. PETRICK, S.R. - "A direct determination of the irredundant forms of a Boolean function from the set of prime implicants". AFCRC-TR-56-110, Air Force Cambridge Research Center, 1956.
4. TOMESCU, I. - "Le nombre maximal de colorations d'un graphe". C.R. Acad. Sc. Paris, 272, 1971, 1301-1303.
5. READ, R.C. - "An Introduction to Chromatic Polynomials". J. Combinatorial Theory, 4, 1968, 52-71.
6. TOMESCU, I. - "Introduction à la combinatorique" (en roumain). Editura tehnica, Bucuresti, 1972.
7. TOMESCU, I. - "Le nombre maximal de 3-colorations d'un graphe connexe". Discrete Mathematics, 1, 4, 1972, 351-356.
8. TOMESCU, I. - "Le nombre des graphes connexes k-chromatiques minimaux aux sommets étiquetés". C.R. Acad. Sc. Paris, 273, 1971, 1124-1126.
9. TOMESCU, I. - "Une caractérisation des graphes k-chromatiques minimaux sans sommet isolé". R.A.I.R.O., 6e année, R-1, 1972, 88-91.
10. TOMESCU, I. - "Le nombre maximal des 3-colorations d'un graphe hamiltonien". (Non publié).
11. TOMESCU, I. - "Le nombre minimal de colorations d'un graphe". C.R. Acad. Sc. Paris, 274, 1972, 539-542.

12. SWENSON, J.R. - "The chromatic polynomial of a complete bipartite graph". The Amer. Math. Monthly, 80, 7, 1973, 797-798.

A FEW REMARKS ON CHROMATIC SCHEDULING

D. de Werra

Département de Mathématiques

Ecole Polytechnique Fédérale de Lausanne (Switzerland)

1. INTRODUCTION AND SUMMARY

Many scheduling problems may be solved by coloring graphs or hypergraphs. However in practice we have to take into account some supplementary constraints in order to get a good schedule. A property of colorings related to the so called good schedules is established for some hypergraphs and for multigraphs.

2. COLORINGS OF PARALLEL NODES

Two nodes of a hypergraph $H = (X,E)$ are <u>parallel</u> if they are contained in exactly the same edges. Parallelism is an equivalence relation on X ; let $N_1,N_2,\ldots,N_p$ be the different classes. If H is the dual of a multigraph G , parallel nodes of H correspond to parallel edges in G , i.e. edges joining the same pair of nodes. $H(d)$ denotes a hypergraph where no node belongs to more than d edges. Otherwise concepts not defined here can be found in C. Berge [1] .

<u>Theorem 2.1</u> : For each integer $k \geq 2$ a unimodular hypergraph $H(d) = (X,E)$ has an equitable k-coloring $(S_1,S_2,\ldots,S_k)$

B. Roy (ed.), Combinatorial Programming: Methods and Applications, 337–342.

satisfying

a) $\max_j s_j \leq 1 + (d-1) \min_j s_j$

b) $-1 \leq |N_r \cap S_j| - |N_r \cap S_i| \leq 1$

for every class N_r and every pair of colors i,j .

Proof : Let $(S_1, S_2, \ldots, S_k)$ be an equitable k-coloring of $H(d)$ satisfying a) . Such a coloring exists [2] . Let s_{ir} be the cardinality of $N_r \cap S_i$; for each N_r define $e(r) = \max_{i,j} |s_{ir} - s_{jr}|$; if $e(r) \leq 1$ for each class N_r we are done. Otherwise assume there is a class N_q and 2 colors a,b for which $e(q) = s_{aq} - s_{bq} \geq 2$. Consider the subhypergraph $\hat{H}$ generated by $S_a \cup S_b$ and remove from each class $\hat{N}_r = N_r \cap (S_a \cup S_b)$ the largest possible subset N_r^* of nodes with $|N_r^*|$ even. The remaining subhypergraph $\bar{H}$ still has an equitable bicoloring (S'_a, S'_b) satisfying a) . Reintroducing one half of each N_r^* into S'_a and the other into S'_b we get an equitable bicoloring of $\hat{H}$ satisfying a) and $|s'_{ar} - s'_{br}| \leq 1$ for each $\hat{N}_r$. Letting $S'_j = S_j$ for $j \neq a,b$ we get an equitable k-coloring $(S'_1, \ldots, S'_k)$ for which a) holds. We also have for each class N_r

$$\min_j s_{jr} \leq \min_j s'_{jr} \leq \max_j s'_{jr} \leq \max_j s_{jr} \quad \text{i.e. } e'(r) \leq e(r) .$$

The number of pairs i,j with $|s_{iq} - s_{jq}| = e(q)$ has decreased by at least 1 since $|s'_{aq} - s'_{bq}| \leq 1 < e(q)$. Hence by iterating this procedure we will finally get an equitable k-coloring satisfying a) and b) .

Remark : This property holds also for good k-colorings in balanced hypergraphs.

If $H(d)$ is the dual of a bipartite multigraph, then $d = 2$ and we obtain the following ($u_i(x,y)$ is the number of parallel edges in U_i joining nodes x and y) .

Corollary 2.1.1 : For each integer $k \geqslant 2$ a bipartite multigraph $G = (X,U)$ has an equitable k-coloring $(U_1,U_2,\dots,U_k)$ such that

a) $|u_i - u_j| \leqslant 1$ $(i,j \leqslant k)$

b) $|u_i(x,y) - u_j(x,y)| \leqslant 1$ $(i,j \leqslant k \; ; \; x,y \in X)$

However if G is not bipartite, it may not have an equitable k-coloring for each $k \geqslant 2$. But it is known that G has a 2-bounded k-coloring (i.e. $|u_i(x) - u_j(x)| \leqslant 2$ $(i,j \leqslant k \; ; \; x \in X)$).

For proving the next theorem we need the following :

Lemma : A connected multigraph G has an equitable bicoloring (U_1,U_2) with $|u_1 - u_2| \leqslant 1$ if and only if G is not an odd cycle. If G is an odd cycle there exists a 2-bounded bicoloring with $|u_1(x) - u_2(x)| = 2$ for one arbitrary node x and $u_1(y) = u_2(y)$ for all nodes $y \neq x$ (This is an immediate consequence of Proposition 2.1 and Corollary 5.2.1 in [2]).

Theorem 2.2 : Any k-coloring $(U_1,U_2,\dots,U_k)$ of a multigraph $G = (X,U)$ may be transformed into a k-coloring $(\overline{U}_1,\overline{U}_2,\dots,\overline{U}_k)$ such that

a) $|\overline{u}_i - \overline{u}_j| \leqslant 1$ $(i,j \leqslant k)$

b) $|\overline{u}_i(x,y) - \overline{u}_j(x,y)| \leqslant 2$ $(i,j \leqslant k \; ; \; x,y \in X)$

c) $\min_j u_j(x) \leqslant \min_j \overline{u}_j(x) \leqslant \max_j \overline{u}_j(x) \leqslant \max_j u_j(x)$ $(x \in X)$

Proof : A) We start from a k-coloring $(U_1,U_2,\dots,U_k)$ of G such that a) holds. Define for each pair of nodes x,y $e(x,y) = \max_{i,j} |u_i(x,y) - u_j(x,y)|$. Assume there are two nodes v,w and 2 colors a,b such that $e(v,w) = u_a(v,w) - u_b(v,w) \geqslant 3$. Consider the multigraph $G' = (X,U_a \cup U_b)$ and remove successively from each family $F(x,y)$ of parallel edges joining any two nodes x and y as many pairs of edges f,g as possible with $f \in U_a$, $g \in U_b$. In the remaining multigraph $G^* = (X, U_a^* \cup U_b^*)$, (U_a^*, U_b^*) is a bicoloring with $u_a^*(x) - u_b^*(x) = u_a(x) - u_b(x)$ for each node x .

B) Next we eliminate from each family $F^*(x,y)$ with $|F^*(x,y)| > 2$ an even number of edges in such a way that the remaining family $\overline{F}(x,y)$ satisfies $1 \leq |\overline{F}(x,y)| \leq 2$. Let $\overline{G}$ be the remaining multigraph. There is a 1-1 correspondence between the connected components C_i^* of G^* and those $(\overline{C}_i)$ of $\overline{G}$. Moreover $\overline{C}_i$ is an odd cycle if and only if C_i^* is an odd cycle.

C) We determine in $\overline{G}$ a bicoloring $(\overline{U}_a, \overline{U}_b)$ satisfying i) $|\overline{u}_a - \overline{u}_b| \leq 1$, ii) $|\overline{u}_a(x,y) - \overline{u}_b(x,y)| \leq |u_a(x,y) - u_b(x,y)|$ for each pair x,y , iii) $|\overline{u}_a(x) - \overline{u}_b(x)| \leq |u_a(x) - u_b(x)|$ for each node x : for each $\overline{C}_i$ which is not an odd cycle, there exists an equitable bicoloring satisfying i) and iii) from the lemma. Also for each odd cycle $\overline{C}_i$, there exists a node $z \in \overline{C}_i$ with $|u_a(z) - u_b(z)| \geq 2$ since C_i^* is also an odd cycle. We determine in this case a bicoloring $(\tilde{U}_a, \tilde{U}_b)$ of $\overline{C}_i$ with $|\tilde{u}_a(z) - \tilde{u}_b(z)| = 2 \leq |u_a(z) - u_b(z)|$, $|\tilde{u}_a(y) - \tilde{u}_b(y)| = 0$ for all nodes $y \neq z$ in $\overline{C}_i$ (so we have $|\tilde{u}_a - \tilde{u}_b| = 1$) .

Dealing with each connected component of $\overline{G}$ separately we get a bicoloring $(\overline{U}_a, \overline{U}_b)$ satisfying i) and iii) . Furthermore from A) ii) holds for any bicoloring of the partial graph $\overline{G}$ of G^* .

D) We reintroduce all edges which had been removed previously (one half of each family is put into $\overline{U}_a$ and the other half into $\overline{U}_b$) . $(\overline{U}_a, \overline{U}_b)$ is a bicoloring of G' satisfying i), ii) and iii) . Let $\overline{U}_i = U_i$ for $i \neq a,b$; then from C) , $(\overline{U}_1, \overline{U}_2, \ldots, \overline{U}_k)$ satisfies

$$\max_{i,j} |\overline{u}_i(x) - \overline{u}_j(x)| \leq \max_{i,j} |u_i(x) - u_j(x)|$$

for each node x .

Furthermore $\bar{e}(x,y) = \max_{i,j} |\bar{u}_i(x,y) - \bar{u}_j(x,y)| \leq e(x,y)$ for all pairs x,y . The number of pairs i,j with $\bar{u}_i(v,w) - \bar{u}_j(v,w) = e(v,w)$ has decreased by at least 1 since for a,b $|\bar{u}_a(v,w) - \bar{u}_b(v,w)| \leq 2 < e(v,w)$. Iterating this process we will finally get the desired k-coloring.

As a consequence of theorem 2.2 we see that if for some $k \geq 2$ a multigraph G has an equitable k-coloring, then G also has an equitable k-coloring satisfying a) and b) . This result is best possible : in a multigraph consisting of 2 triangles a,b,c and d,e,f with 2 parallel edges joining nodes a and d , we have $|u_1(a,d) - u_2(a,d)| = 2$ for each equitable bicoloring. However this multigraph has a 2-bounded bicoloring with $u_1(a,d) = u_2(a,d)$. In fact we have the following result :

<u>Theorem 2.3</u> : For each $k \geq 2$ a multigraph G has a 2-bounded k-coloring $(U_1,U_2,\ldots,U_k)$ satisfying

a) $|u_i - u_j| \leq 1$ $(i,j \leq k)$

b) $|u_i(x,y) - u_j(x,y)| \leq 1$ $(i,j \leq k \; ; \; x,y \in X)$

<u>Proof</u> : We start from any k-coloring satisfying a) and b). By using a recoloring procedure similar to that of theorem 2.2 , we obtain finally a 2-bounded k-coloring such that a) and b) hold.

3. APPLICATIONS

We mention an application in the area of course scheduling. Let X be a set of classes, Y a set of teachers, U a set of one-hour lectures; each lecture involving class x and teacher y is represented by an edge (x,y) in the bipartite multigraph $G = (X,Y,U)$. Let k be the number of working days in the week; an equitable k-coloring represents a balanced weekly schedule [3] :

for any class x (or teacher y) the number of lectures $u_i(x)$ and $u_j(x)$ (or $u_i(y)$ and $u_j(y)$) involving x (or y) during any 2 days i and j differ by at most 1 .

Generally one tries to spread all lectures of teacher x to class y as uniformly as possible throughout the week. If this has to be done for all pairs x,y the good schedules will correspond to the colorings of Corollary 2.1.1 . Note that we also have almost the same total number of lectures occurring each day.

Remark: We may also consider colorings of oriented graphs; if we define $u_i^+(x)$ (resp. $u_i^-(x)$) as the number of arcs in U_i whose initial (resp. terminal) endpoint is x and $u_i^+(x,y)$ as the number of arcs of the form (x,y) in U_i , then we have:

For each $k \geq 2$ there exists a k-coloring $(U_1,\ldots, U_k)$ of the arcs of a graph G such that

a) $|u_i - u_j| \leq 1$ $(i,j \leq k)$

b1) $|u_i^+(x) - u_j^+(x)| \leq 1$

b2) $|u_i^-(x) - u_j^-(x)| \leq 1$ $(i,j \leq k;\ x \in X)$

c) $|u_i^+(x,y) - u_j^+(x,y)| \leq 1$ $(i,j \leq k;\ x,y \in X)$

REFERENCES

1. C. Berge, Graphs and Hypergraphs, North Holland, Amsterdam, 1973.

2. D. de Werra, How to color a Graph (this volume).

3. —— , Balanced Schedules, INFOR J., vol 9, No 3, 1971, p 230-237.

MINIMIZING TOTAL COSTS IN ONE-MACHINE SCHEDULING

A.H.G. Rinnooy Kan°, B.J. Lageweg*, J.K. Lenstra*

°Graduate School of Management, Delft, The Netherlands
*Mathematisch Centrum, Amsterdam, The Netherlands

1. INTRODUCTION

Suppose we have n *jobs* $J_1,\ldots,J_n$ that arrive simultaneously at time $t = 0$ to be processed on a continuously available *machine* which can handle only one job at a time. J_i takes p_i time units to be processed; costs $c_i(t)$, non-decreasing in t, are incurred if J_i is completed at time t. We seek to find a schedule with associated completion times t_i that minimizes $\sum_{i=1}^{n} c_i(t_i)$.

The problem is trivial in the case of *linear* cost functions $c_i(t) = \alpha_i(t-d_i)$, where d_i can be interpreted as a due date for J_i; the optimal schedule has J_j preceding J_k if $p_j/\alpha_j \le p_k/\alpha_k$. The *general* problem is considerably more difficult: a special case where $c_i(t) = 0$ if $t \le d$, $c_i(t) = \alpha_i$ if $t > d$ belongs to Karp's list of *NP-complete* problems [8]. A polynomial-bounded algorithm for this problem would lead to efficient algorithms for a number of classic computational problems, and its existence seems highly unlikely.

Dynamic programming has been applied to solve the general problem [7,9], but most researchers have concentrated on the *weighted tardiness* function $c_i(t) = \alpha_i \max\{0,t-d_i\}$. This problem has been attacked by methods of implicit enumeration, notably of the *branch-and-bound* type [13], supported by *elimination criteria* that establish precedence relations between jobs [4,14]. Comparison of some of these methods [1] suggests that their rather poor performance may be due to the absence of strong lower bounds. We try to fill this gap by introducing an algorithm for the general problem, that performs satisfactorily in the special case of the weighted tardiness criterion. The algorithm and the computational experiments are described in more detail in [12].

B. Roy (ed.), Combinatorial Programming: Methods and Applications, 343–350.

2. DESCRIPTION OF THE ALGORITHM

In sections 2.1, 2.2 and 2.3 an *enumeration scheme*, *elimination criteria* and a *lower bound* are proposed that together define our *branch-and-bound* algorithm. We include some remarks on the implementation of the elimination criteria and the lower bound.

2.1. Enumeration scheme

Since an optimal solution without machine idle time always exists [11], the total time needed to process a set of jobs is independent of the processing order.

We create a search tree as follows. From the root node, where no jobs have been scheduled, n branches lead to n nodes on the first level, each of which corresponds to a particular job being scheduled in the n-th position. Generally, each node in the tree corresponds to a set $\{J_i | i \in S' \subset \{1,\dots,n\}\}$ filling the last $|S'|$ positions in a given order. By successively placing each job J_r ($r \in S = \{1,\dots,n\}-S'$) in the $|S|$-th position, $|S|$ new nodes are created. J_r then runs from $P(S)-p_r$ to $P(S)$, where $P(Q) = \sum_{i \in Q} p_i$ for any $Q \subset \{1,\dots,n\}$.

2.2. Elimination criteria

Successive application of the theorems in this section in each node of the tree will lead to sets $\{J_h | h \in B_i\}$ and $\{J_\ell | \ell \in A_i\}$ that respectively *precede* or *follow* J_i in at least one optimal schedule. We can then limit the search to schedules satisfying these precedence constraints. In the following, implications for the weighted tardiness criterion will be presented as corollaries.

THEOREM 1. *At least one optimal solution has* J_j *preceding* J_k ($j,k \in S$) *if (a)* $c_j(t)-c_k(t)$ *is non-decreasing in* t *on the interval* $(P(B_k)+p_k, P(S-A_j))$, *and (b)* $p_j \le p_k$.

Proof. If in any schedule J_k precedes J_j, with J_k starting at time C and J_j finishing at time D, consider the schedule obtained by interchanging J_k and J_j. The contribution to total costs by all jobs except J_k does not increase, because of condition *(b)*. As to the joint contribution of J_j and J_k, we have from condition *(a)* $c_j(D)-c_k(D) \ge c_j(C+p_k)-c_k(C+p_k)$, and from *(b)* $c_j(C+p_k) \ge c_j(C+p_j)$, together implying $c_j(D)+c_k(C+p_k) \ge c_j(C+p_j)+c_k(D)$. (Q.E.D.)

COROLLARY 1. *At least one optimal schedule has* J_j *preceding* J_k ($j,k \in S$) *if* $d_j \le \max\{d_k, P(B_k)+p_k\}$, $\alpha_j \ge \alpha_k$, *and* $p_j \le p_k$.

THEOREM 2. *At least one optimal schedule has* J_j *preceding* J_k ($j,k \in S$) *if (a)* $c_k(P(B_k)+p_k) = c_k(P(S-A_j)-p_k)$, *and (b)* $c_j(t)-c_k(t)$ *is non-decreasing in* t *on the interval* $(P(S-A_j)-p_k, P(S-A_j))$.

Proof. If $p_j \le p_k$, we can apply Theorem 1. If $p_j > p_k$ and J_k precedes J_j, with J_k starting at C and J_j finishing at D, consider the schedule obtained by putting J_k directly after J_j. The contribution to total costs by all jobs except J_k does not increase. As to the costs of J_j and J_k, we have from *(a)* $c_k(D-p_k) = c_k(C+p_k)$, and from *(b)* $c_j(D)-c_k(D) \ge c_j(D-p_k)-c_k(D-p_k)$, together implying $c_j(D)+c_k(C+p_k) \ge c_j(D-p_k)+c_k(D)$. (Q.E.D.)

COROLLARY 2. *At least one optimal schedule has* J_j *preceding* J_k *(*$j,k \in S$*) if* $d_k \ge P(S-A_j)-p_k$, $d_j \le d_k$, *and* $\alpha_j \ge \alpha_k$.

THEOREM 3. *At least one optimal schedule has* J_j *preceding* J_k *(*$j,k \in S$*) if* $c_k(P(B_k)+p_k) = c_k(P(S-A_j))$.

COROLLARY 3. *At least one optimal schedule has* J_j *preceding* J_k *(*$j,k \in S$*) if* $d_k \ge P(S-A_j)$.

THEOREM 4. *In at least one optimal schedule* J_k *(*$k \in S$*) comes last among* $\{J_j | j \in S\}$ *if* $c_k(p_k) = c_k(P(S))$.

COROLLARY 4. *In at least one optimal schedule* J_k *(*$k \in S$*) comes last among* $\{J_j | j \in S\}$ *if* $d_k \ge P(S)$.

Theorems 3 and 4 are special cases of Theorem 2. Corollary 1 is given in [13]. Corollaries 1, 2 and 3 are extended versions of Theorems 1, 2 and 3 in [4]. Our proofs, however, are more general and considerably simpler than the original ones. Corollary 4 is also known as *Elmaghraby's Lemma* [3].

The only problem arising with the *implementation* of these elimination criteria is the possible creation of *precedence cycles* whenever two theorems seemingly contradict each other. These cycles are avoided by constructing the *transitive closure* of the set of known precedence relations immediately after a new relation has been found and by only examining pairs (J_j,J_k) that are not yet related.

For a general cost function Theorems 1 to 4 can be applied in every node. In testing the algorithm on the weighted tardiness cost function, however, we applied Corollaries 1, 3 and 2 only in the root node, repeatedly running through them in the above order until no improvement was possible. Corollary 4 was checked in every node.

Precedence relations that are *a priori* given can be handled by the algorithm in an obvious way.

2.3. Lower bound

The lower bound LB on the costs of all possible schedules in a node has the form $LB = c(S')+LB^*$. Here $c(S')$ denotes the costs incurred by $\{J_i\}_{i\in S'}$, and LB^* is a lower bound on the costs c^* of an optimal schedule $\pi^* = (\pi^*(1),\ldots,\pi^*(m))$ for the jobs in $\{J_i\}_{i\in S}$, which are renumbered from 1 to m (= $|S|$).

If all p_i are equal, then the costs of putting J_i in position j are $c_{ij} = c_i(jp_1)$, and π^* is obtained from the solution (x^*_{ij}) to the following *linear assignment problem* (cf. [9]):

$$\min\{\textstyle\sum_{i=1}^m \sum_{j=1}^m c_{ij}x_{ij} \mid \sum_{j=1}^m x_{ij} = 1 \ (i = 1,\dots,m), \quad \sum_{i=1}^m x_{ij} = 1 \ (j = 1,\dots,m), \quad x_{ij} \geq 0 \quad (i,j = 1,\dots,m)\}. \tag{1}$$

If not all p_i are equal, this idea can be used to compute a lower bound, in two ways. Assuming all p_i are integers, we can treat each job J_i as p_i/g new jobs, where $g = \text{g.c.d.}(p_1,\dots,p_n)$, thus turning (1) into a $(P(S)/g)\times m$ *linear transportation problem*. However, it seems difficult to define effective cost coefficients for a general cost function (see [6] for a special case). Since job splitting can occur and the problem will often be large, we prefer a different approach. We define:

$$R_i(k) = \min_Q\{P(Q) \mid Q \subset \{1,\dots,m\}-(B_i\cup\{i\}\cup A_i), |Q| = k\};$$

$$t_{ij} = P(B_i) + p_i + R_i(j-|B_i|-1);$$

$$c_{ij} = \begin{cases} c_i(t_{ij}) & \text{for } |B_i| < j \leq |\{1,\dots,m\}-A_i|, \\ \infty & \text{otherwise.} \end{cases}$$

Solution of (1) now gives the desired lower bound LB^*, since c_{ij} is a lower bound on the costs of putting J_i in position j and since π^* is a feasible solution to (1):

$$c^* \geq \textstyle\sum_{j=1}^m c_{\pi^*(j)j} \geq LB^*.$$

We now turn to the *implementation* of this lower bound. In any node, the solution to (1) can also be evaluated as a schedule, which may lead to a decrease in the value UB of the best schedule found so far. If LB ≥ UB, the node can be eliminated. Otherwise, the jobs in $\{J_i \mid i \in S, S\cap A_i = \emptyset\}$ are candidates for position m. A complete solution of the assignment problems in these descendant nodes may be avoided by exploiting the solution (x^*_{ij}) to (1) and the soltuion (u^*_i,v^*_j) to its dual:

$$\max\{\textstyle\sum_{i=1}^m u_i + \sum_{j=1}^m v_j \mid u_i+v_j \leq c_{ij} \ (i,j = 1,\dots,m)\}.$$

Observing that $(u^*_i,v^*_j)_{i\neq r,j\neq m}$ is a feasible dual solution to the assignment problem, obtained from (1) by deleting row r and column m, we see that a simple lower bound on the costs of scheduling J_r in position m is given by:

$$LB_r = c(S'\cup\{r\}) + (LB^*-u^*_r-v^*_m) = LB + (c_{rm}-u^*_r-v^*_m) \geq LB.$$

Branches for which $LB_r \geq UB$ can be pruned immediately. From the remaining candidates, a job J_r with minimal LB_r is scheduled in position m. If application of elimination criteria does not further increase LB_r, we have to solve a new $(m-1)\times(m-1)$ assignment problem. Here we can still profit from (x^*_{ij}) and (u^*_i,v^*_j), in two ways.

(a) The earliest possible finishing times t_{ij} will not decrease, neither will the cost coefficients c_{ij}. So (u^*_i,v^*_j) provides a *feasible dual* solution to the new problem.

(b) (x^*_{ij}) provides a *partial primal* solution to the new problem, that can be made *orthogonal* to the given dual solution by resetting $x^*_{ij} = 0$ if $u^*_i+v^*_j < c_{ij}$.

Remark (a) suggests an alternative bounding mechanism, whereby the assignment problem is solved only in the root node and provides bounds throughout the whole search tree by sums of appropriate dual variables (cf. [6]). Although we obtained reasonable computational results with this approach, we preferred the stronger bound; even then the trees may become quite large for moderate size problems.

In selecting a method for solving the assignment problems, ideally we would like to have a fast algorithm, not requiring an initial basic solution and producing a sequence of non-decreasing feasible dual solutions each of which may lead to early elimination of the current node. Dorhout's dual method [2] turned out to be more suitable than primal methods such as the stepping-stone algorithm or primal-dual ones such as the Hungarian method.

Dorhout's algorithm works on a complete bipartite graph $G = (S,T,E)$ where S and T correspond to unscheduled jobs and unfilled positions; edge $e_{ij} \in E$ has weight $w_{ij} = c_{ij}-u_i-v_j$. A partial primal solution (x_{ij}), orthogonal to a feasible dual solution (u_i,v_j), defines a *matching* on G. The algorithm constructs the shortest augmenting path from any *exposed* vertex in S to the nearest exposed vertex in T, augments the matching and restores the orthogonality while the dual feasibility is maintained.

3. COMPUTATIONAL EXPERIMENTS

3.1. Tested algorithms

Our algorithm was tested on the weighted tardiness criterion and compared with Shwimer's algorithm [13] and a simple lexicographic method [10]. Both of them use the enumeration scheme described in section 2.1 and a lower bound corresponding to our LB_r.

Shwimer applies Corollary 4 and the static part of Corollary 1 (i.e. $d_j \le d_k$). His lower bound is given by:

$$LB'_r = c(S'\cup\{r\}) + \min_{i\in S-\{r\}}\{\alpha_i \max\{0,P(S-\{r\})-d_i\} + \min_{h\in S-\{r,i\}}\{\alpha_h\}\cdot T_{max}(S-\{r,i\})\},$$

where $T_{max}(Q)$ is the minimal maximal tardiness over all schedules of $\{J_h\}_{h\in Q}$, found by ordering the jobs according to increasing d_h (see [11]). This bound can be computed very quickly, but depends explicitly on a property of the tardiness function.

The lexicographic method always chooses from the remaining candidates a job J_r with maximal d_r, applies Corollary 4 and uses a lower bound $LB_r'' = c(S' \cup \{r\})$.

3.2. Test problems

Each test problem with n jobs is specified by n integer triples (p_i, d_i, α_i). Their distribution is determined by four parameters: ρ (correlation between processing times and due dates), s (relative variation of processing times), t (average tardiness factor), and r (relative range of due dates).

The α_i are generated from a uniform distribution over the interval (4.5,15.5). The p_i are generated from a normal distribution with mean $\mu = 100$ and variance $s\mu$. If $\rho = 0$, the d_i are generated from a uniform distribution with mean $(1-t)n\mu$ and variance $(rn\mu)^2/12$. If $\rho > 0$, each d_i is generated in a similar way by replacing μ by p_i; this leads to $\rho = (1-t)/\sqrt{\{(1+1/s^2)r^2/12 + (1-t)^2\}}$.

The parameters ρ, t and r were found to influence the performance of other tardiness algorithms [1]; s was introduced because of its possible influence on our lower bound. We would expect *a priori* problems with positive ρ (see [4, Corollary 1.3]), small s, very small or very large t (see [14]) and large r to be relatively easy for our method.

3.3. Computational results

We generated problems with 15 and 20 jobs, setting the parameters defined above to various values. The three algorithms were coded in ALGOL 60 and run on the CD 73-28 of the SARA Computing Centre in Amsterdam. The computational results can be found in Table 1.

The parameter t has a major influence on the performance of the algorithms, problems with t=.2 or t=.4 being "easy" and problems with t=.6 or t=.8 being "difficult". As to the other parameters, ρ has no detectable influence, and problems with s=.05 and r=.95 are indeed easier than problems with s=.25 and r=.20.

On the easy problems, the lexicographic method runs quickly through large search trees; Shwimer's algorithm also performs well. Our algorithm creates very small trees, but it seems hardly worth while to compute sophisticated lower bounds for these problems.

On the difficult problems, however, our algorithm is by far superior to the other methods. Both of them fail on all twelve problems with 20 jobs; our method finishes seven of them, while the best solutions to the remaining five are better than Shwimer's.

Recently, Fisher [5] developed a dual average tardiness algorithm that uses a subgradient approach to produce strong lower bounds. Our algorithm performs very well on his test problems. However, they are easy ones with t=.5 and r=1, and both methods cannot be compared from these data alone.

4. CONCLUDING REMARKS

Our main conclusion has to be that, although our elimination criteria and our lower bound turn out to be useful, this one-machine problem remains a very difficult one.

An easy extension of our algorithm would be to check all elimination criteria anew in every node. More criteria might be found by considering the effects of moving three or more jobs at a time.

Our lower bound could be strengthened by explicitly respecting known precedence relations in solving the assignment problem. It is difficult to predict the effectiveness of this approach.

The idea of computing lower bounds by solving assignment problems whose coefficients c_{ij} underestimate the costs of putting job J_i in position j, can be applied to a wider set of problems, e.g. to minimizing total costs in an m-machine flow shop. This seems an interesting topic for future research.

We think that it would be worth while to develop very sharp bounds for the upper levels of the search tree and gradually simpler ones as we move down the tree and more extensive enumeration becomes attractive. Although our first experiments with such a *gliding lower bound* were disappointing, the idea could become useful in the future.

In spite of all the work done so far, the problem of minimizing total costs on one machine is likely to remain a challenge to researchers for a long time to come.

number of jobs n		15				20			
tardiness	t	.2	.4	.6	.8	.2	.4	.6	.8
number of problems		12	12	12	12	6	6	6	6
median solution time	Our Alg.	.0	.8	6.3	45.6	.8	1.1	180.8	300 *
	Shwimer	.0	.6	76.7	300 *	.2	2.2	300 *	300 *
	Lex.Alg.	.0	.2	60 *	60 *	.1	1.8	60 *	60 *
maximum solution time	Our Alg.	.6	8.2	121.8	85.6	1.2	20.3	(2)*	(3)*
	Shwimer	.3	3.9	(3)*	(12)*	.3	10.2	(6)*	(6)*
	Lex.Alg.	.3	14.8	(10)*	(12)*	.2	21.6	(6)*	(6)*
median number of nodes	Our Alg.	1	44	647	4532	9	25	11105	-
	Shwimer	1	86	13066	-	12	281	-	-
	Lex.Alg.	1	305	-	-	105	3564	-	-
maximum number of nodes	Our Alg.	28	541	9564	9952	29	1206	-	-
	Shwimer	69	586	-	-	29	1130	-	-
	Lex.Alg.	572	36231	-	-	580	57671	-	-

Table 1. Computational results: solution time (in CPU seconds) and number of nodes (including eliminated nodes).

ℓ * : the median solution time exceeds the time limit ℓ.

(k)* : the time limit is exceeded k times.

ACKNOWLEDGEMENT

B. Dorhout's cooperation in making available his assignment code is gratefully acknowledged.

REFERENCES

1. K.R. BAKER, J.B. MARTIN, An Experimental Comparison of Solution Algorithms for the Single-Machine Tardiness Problem, *Nav.Res. Log.Quart.* 21(1974)187-199.
2. B. DORHOUT, Experiments with Some Algorithms for the Linear Assignment Problem, Report BW 39, Mathematisch Centrum, Amsterdam, 1974.
3. S.E. ELMAGHRABY, The One-Machine Sequencing Problem with Delay Costs, *J.Ind.Eng.* 19(1968)105-108.
4. H. EMMONS, One-Machine Sequencing to Minimize Certain Functions of Job Tardiness, *Opns.Res.* 17(1969)701-715.
5. M.L. FISHER, A Dual Algorithm for the One-Machine Scheduling Problem, Report 7403, Graduate School of Business, University of Chicago, 1974.
6. L. GELDERS, P.R. KLEINDORFER, Coordinating Aggregate and Detailed Scheduling Decisions in the One-Machine Job Shop: Part I. Theory, *Opns.Res.* 22(1974)46-60.
7. M. HELD, R.M. KARP, A Dynamic Programming Approach to Sequencing Problems, *J.SIAM* 10(1962)196-210.
8. R.M. KARP, Reducibility among Combinatorial Problems, pp.85-103 in R.E. MILLER, J.W. THATCHER (eds.), *Complexity of Computer Computations*, Plenum Press, New York-London, 1972.
9. E.L. LAWLER, On Scheduling Problems with Deferral Costs, *Man. Sci.* 11(1964)280-288.
10. J.K. LENSTRA, Recursive Algorithms for Enumerating Subsets, Lattice-Points, Combinations and Permutations, Report BW 28, Mathematisch Centrum, Amsterdam, 1973.
11. A.H.G. RINNOOY KAN, The Machine Scheduling Problem, Report BW 27, Mathematisch Centrum, Amsterdam, 1973; Report R/73/4, Graduate School of Management, Delft, 1973.
12. A.H.G. RINNOOY KAN, B.J. LAGEWEG, J.K. LENSTRA, Minimizing Total Costs in One-Machine Scheduling, *Opns.Res.* (to appear).
13. J. SHWIMER, On the *N*-Job, One-Machine, Sequence-Independent Scheduling Problem with Tardiness Penalties: a Branch-and-Bound Solution, *Man. Sci.* 18(1972)B301-313.
14. V. SRINIVASAN, A Hybrid Algorithm for the One-Machine Sequencing Problem to Minimize Total Tardiness, *Nav.Res.Log.Quart.* 18(1971)317-327.

THE QUADRATIC ASSIGNMENT PROBLEM: A BRIEF REVIEW*

E.L. Lawler

Department of Electrical Engineering and Computer Sciences, The University of California, Berkeley, CA, U.S.A.

ABSTRACT. The quadratic assignment problem, its applications, and various exact and inexact procedures for its solution are briefly reviewed. Certain special cases of the one-dimensional module placement problem, itself a special case of the quadratic assignment problem, are surveyed.

1. PROBLEM STATEMENT

The ordinary (linear) assignment problem is stated as follows. Given an $n \times n$ matrix $C = (c_{ij})$, find an $n \times n$ permutation matrix $X = (x_{ij})$ so as to

$$\text{minimize} \quad C \cdot X = \sum_{i,j} c_{ij} x_{ij} \ .$$

The quadratic assignment problem is stated as follows. Given n^4 coefficients c_{ijpq} $(i, j, p, q = 1,2,\ldots,n)$ find an $n \times n$ permutation matrix $X = (x_{ij})$ so as to

$$\text{minimize} \quad \sum_{i,j} \sum_{p,q} c_{ijpq} x_{ij} x_{pq} \ .$$

A more specialized form of the quadratic assignment problem, due to Koopmans and Beckmann [17] is stated as follows. Given two $n \times n$ matrices $D = (d_{ij})$ and $T = (t_{ij})$, find an $n \times n$ permutation matrix $X = (x_{ij})$ so as to

*The preparation of this paper was supported in part by the U.S. Air Force Office of Scientific Research, Grant AFOSR-71-2076.

B. Roy (ed.), Combinatorial Programming: Methods and Applications, 351–360.

minimize $D\cdot(XTX^t)$.

(Here we employ the dot product notation introduced above.)

Sometimes it is useful to introduce a linear term into the Koopmans-Beckmann objective function, i.e.

minimize $D\cdot(XTX^t) + C\cdot X$,

where C is a given $n \times n$ matrix.

The Koopmans-Beckmann problem is clearly a special case of the more general quadratic assignment problem, by noting that one can set $c_{ijpq} = d_{ip}t_{jq}$.

2. APPLICATIONS AND PROBLEM FORMULATIONS

The Koopmans-Beckmann problem is suggested by the following situation. Let it be required to assign n plants to n locations in such a way that the total cost of interplant transportation is minimized. Let

d_{ip} = the cost of transporting one unit of commodity from location i to location p,

t_{jq} = the number of units of commodity to be transported from plant j to plant q.

Each assignment of plants to locations is given by a permutation matrix $X = (x_{ij})$, where

x_{ij} = 1 if location i is assigned to plant j
= 0 otherwise.

A solution to the Koopmans-Beckmann problem yields an assignment for which the total transporation costs are minimized.

This type of problem formulation is often employed in the placement of electronic modules on a computer backplane. See Hanan and Kurtzberg [10].

A multicommodity version of the Koopmans-Beckmann problem can also be stated. Let $D^{(1)},T^{(1)},\ldots,D^{(m)},T^{(m)}$ be m pairs of matrices for different commodities. Then we seek to

minimize $\sum_k D^{(k)}\cdot(XT^{(k)}X^t)$,

which is equivalent to a quadratic form with

$$c_{ijpq} = \sum_k d_{ip}^{(k)} t_{jq}^{(k)} \ .$$

It is noteworthy that the traveling salesman's problem is a special case of the Koopmans-Beckmann formulation in which D is a matrix of distances between cities and T is a cyclic permutation matrix of the form

$$T = \begin{bmatrix} 0 & 1 & 0 & 0 \\ 0 & 0 & 1 & 0 \\ 0 & 0 & 0 & 1 \\ 1 & 0 & 0 & 0 \end{bmatrix} .$$

It is therefore not surprising that a variety of problems involving permutations and sequences can be formulated as quadratic assignment problems. For example, consider the following "candidates' problem", formulated in [19].

The presidential and vice-presidential candidates of one of the major American parties are planning their campaign itinerary. They decide that there are $2n$ cities that should be subjected to a full day's visit by one or the other of them during a particular n-day period. It does not matter which candidate visits any given city, or on what day within the n-day period he visits it. Each night during the period the two candidates will confer for a fixed length of time by long distance telephone. The day before his tour begins, the presidential candidate is scheduled to be in city P_0, and the day after in P_{n+1}. Similar engagements for the vice-presidential candidate are V_o and V_{n+1}.

The problem is to plan the tours for the two candidates in such a way that the total of the transportation costs and the telephone costs is minimized. Travel costs for the presidential candidate and his entourage are p cents per airline mile, and for the vice-presidential candidate v cents. Telephone charges are t cents per airline mile.

Let a $2n \times 2n$ matrix D represent the distance between the $2n$ cities. Also define a $2n \times 2n$ matrix T of the form

$$T = \left[\begin{array}{ccccc|ccccc} 0 & p & 0 & 0 & 0 & t & 0 & 0 & 0 & 0 \\ 0 & 0 & p & 0 & 0 & 0 & t & 0 & 0 & 0 \\ 0 & 0 & 0 & p & 0 & 0 & 0 & t & 0 & 0 \\ 0 & 0 & 0 & 0 & p & 0 & 0 & 0 & t & 0 \\ 0 & 0 & 0 & 0 & 0 & 0 & 0 & 0 & 0 & t \\ \hline 0 & 0 & 0 & 0 & 0 & 0 & v & 0 & 0 & 0 \\ 0 & 0 & 0 & 0 & 0 & 0 & 0 & v & 0 & 0 \\ 0 & 0 & 0 & 0 & 0 & 0 & 0 & 0 & v & 0 \\ 0 & 0 & 0 & 0 & 0 & 0 & 0 & 0 & 0 & v \\ 0 & 0 & 0 & 0 & 0 & 0 & 0 & 0 & 0 & 0 \end{array}\right]$$

The three nonzero quadrants are related to the presidential candidate's tour, the telephone conferences, and the vice-presidential candidate's tour, respectively.

The solution is represented by a $2n \times 2n$ permutation matrix $X = (x_{ij})$, whose elements are defined as follows:

For $i \leqq n$:

$x_{ij} = 1$ if the presidential candidate visits city i on the jth day,

$= 0$ otherwise.

For $i \geqq n+1$:

$x_{ij} = 1$ if the vice-presidential candidate visits city i on the $(j-n)^{th}$ day,

$= 0$ otherwise.

The quantity

$$D \cdot (XTX^t)$$

represents all costs except the travel costs to and from the cities P_o, P_{n+1}, V_o and V_{n+1}. For this purpose, define a $2n \times 2n$ matrix C, where

$c_{1j} = p$ times the distance from city P_o to city j,

$c_{n+1,j} = v$ times the distance from city V_o to city j,

$c_{nj} = p$ times the distance from city j to city P_{n+1},

$c_{2n,j} = v$ times the distance from city j to city V_{n+1}, and the remaining c_{ij} are zero. Then the objective of the problem is to minimize

$$D \cdot (XTX^t) + C \cdot X \ ,$$

which is a single commodity Koopmans-Beckmann problem with additional linear costs.

3. METHODS OF SOLUTION

Inasmuch as the traveling salesman's problem, and other hard problems, can be formulated as special cases of quadratic assignment, it is not surprising that no efficient procedure has been found to obtain exact solutions. See Karp [14]. In fact, it appears to be safe to say that little real progress has been made in the ten years or so since the problem began to receive widespread attention. Among the approaches which have been attempted are the following:

(1) Branch-and-bound methods, e.g. Gilmore [5] and Lawler [19]. These yield exact solutions in a reasonable amount of time for relatively small problems, e.g. $n \leq 15$.

(2) Formulation of equivalent integer linear programming problems, e.g. Lawler [19]. Actual computational experience with this approach is unknown to the author, and, in any case, prospects appear bleak.

(3) Obtaining an exact solution to a related continuous problem and then discretizing. See Kodres [16].

(4) Heuristic procedures, e.g. pairwise interchanges of plant assignments. Heuristics have been tested by many investigators, with varying degrees of success. For an excellent survey, see Hanan and Kurtzberg [10].

(5) Identification of special cases which can be solved efficiently. Some of these special cases may serve as adequate approximations to more general problems.

The first several approaches have been abundantly reported on in the literature. Accordingly, the remainder of this paper is devoted to the discussion of certain special cases which have been more recently identified and which are presumably not so well known.

4. ONE DIMENSIONAL MODULE PLACEMENT PROBLEM

Suppose n electronic modules are to be placed in a one dimensional array, at unit intervals. Let

t_{jq} = the number of wires connecting module j and module q.

The objective is to place the modules in such a way that the total wire length is minimized. Clearly, this is a Koopmans-Beckmann problem, with T matrix as given and $D = (d_{ip})$, where

$$d_{ip} = |i-p| .$$

A general dynamic programming solution to this problem is as follows. Let S be an arbitrary subset of the modules, i.e. $S \subseteq N = \{1,2,\ldots,n\}$. For each such subset S define a subproblem with $|S|+1$ modules in which all the modules in the complement of S, i.e. N-S, are contracted to a single module (graphical contraction) which is constrained to be placed at location 1. Let

F(S) = the minimum wire length for subproblem S,

and

$$t(S) = \sum_{i\in S} \sum_{j\in N-S} t_{ij} .$$

Then it is easily shown that

$$F(\emptyset) = 0,$$

$$F(S) = \min_{k\in S} \{F(S-k)\} + t(S) .$$

These equations can be solved for F(N) in $O(n2^n)$ running time. Exponentially growing running time is displeasing. However, we may note that simple recursive solutions are unknown for the two-dimensional problem, and the results in that arena are even less pleasing.

The solution method can easily be generalized to the case in which the one-dimensional module locations are at arbitrary, rather than unit, intervals. We leave this generalization as an exercise for the reader.

5. SPECIAL CASE DUE TO PRATT

A special case of the one-dimensional module location problem has been solved by Pratt [22], making use of a theorem on inequalities due to Hardy, Littlewood and Polya, and generalized by Knuth.

Suppose the matrix T of wire connections is of the form

$$t_{ij} = p_i p_j ,$$

where p_i is a nonnegative parameter assigned to module i. Assume $p_1 \leq p_2 \leq \cdots \leq p_n$. Then an optimal placement results when the modules are placed in "alternating order," i.e.

$$1,3,5,7,\ldots,8,6,4,2 .$$

Clearly this placement can be determined by a simple sorting of the p_i's, which requires only $O(n \log n)$ running time.

(Pratt's distance matrix can be somewhat further generalized beyond the simple one-dimensional problem, but this need not concern us here.)

The two-dimensional version of Pratt's problem has been studied by Karp, McKellar and Wong [15], who have shown that it is possible to obtain near-optimal solutions to that problem.

6. ANOTHER SPECIAL CASE: NETWORK FLOWS

Suppose the matrix $T = (t_{ij})$ is of such a form that there exists a symmetric flow network for which t_{ij} is the maximum attainable flow between i and j. It is well known [7] that necessary and sufficient conditions for a symmetric matrix T to be of this form are that the "triangle" inequalities,

$$t_{ij} \geq \min \{t_{ik}, t_{kj}\} ,$$

hold for all i, j, k. As a specific example, suppose p_i is a nonnegative integer assigned to module i and

$$t_{ij} = \min \{p_i, p_j\} .$$

Then $T = (t_{ij})$ satisfies the triangle inequalities.

It is also well known that any such matrix T of flow values can be realized by a symmetric flow network in the form of a path connecting the n nodes. We assert that the ordering of the nodes in this path is an optimal ordering of the nodes for the one-dimensional module placement problem.

For an arbitrary matrix T, the triangle inequalities can be verified in $O(n^3)$ running time, and this order of running time is also sufficient to obtain the desired optimal ordering.

7. THE SPECIAL CASE OF TREES

Suppose the intermodule connections have a tree structure. That is, there exists a tree spanning the n modules such that

$$t_{ij} = 1 \text{ if } (i,j) \text{ is an arc of the tree}$$
$$= 0 \text{ otherwise.}$$

Then it is possible to prove that there exists an optimal placement of the modules which satisfies the following properties:

(1) Locations 1 and n are occupied by leaves of the tree. Call these leaves s, t.

(2) Let P be the unique path between s and t in the tree. The modules in P occupy locations in the same relative positions as their order of occurrence in P. (Thus the contribution of the arcs in P to the objective function is exactly $n-1$.)

(3) The deletion of P from the tree yields one or more disconnected subtrees. The modules of each such subtree are optimally assigned to a contiguous set of locations, without regard to the remaining modules.

If there were some efficient means to determine the identity of the leaves s and t, then clearly the placement problem would unravel itself quite nicely. Unfortunately, no such means has been found. (A good, but not necessarily optimal, heuristic is to make s and t the endpoints of a longest path.)

Nevertheless, the properties stated above do suggest a procedure which is recursive over subtrees. Each subtree calls for an examination of no more than $O(n^2)$ alternatives, each of which requires $O(n)$ running time to evaluate. If the number of subtrees is t (where $t < 2^{n-1}$), then the overall running time is $O(n^3 t)$.

8. ROOTED TREES: A SPECIAL CASE OF ADOLPHSON AND HU

Now suppose the intermodule connections are represented by an arc weighted (directed) tree rooted from a point. Let

t_{ij} = the weight of arc (i,j), if (i,j) exists
= otherwise.

The modules are to be optimally placed, subject to the constraint that if (i,j) is an arc of the tree, then module i to be positioned to the left of module j. An O(n log n) computational procedure for this problem has been devised by Adolphson and Hu [1] who have also established that a machine sequencing problem solved by Horn [13] can be reduced to a placement problem of this type.

The sequencing problem of Horn has been solved by Sidney [24] for the more general case of "series parallel" precedence constraints, and it appears that it may also be possible to generalize the Adolphson-Hu procedure in this way.

REFERENCES

1. D. Adolphson and T.C. Hu, "Optimal Linear Ordering," SIAM J. Appl. Math. 25 (1973), 403-423.
2. P.S. Davis and T.L. Ray, "A Branch-Bound Algorithm for the Capacitated Facilities Location Problem," Naval Res. Logistics Qtrly 16 (1969), 331-344.
3. M.A. Efroymson and T.L. Ray, "A Branch-Bound Algorithm for Plant Location," Opns. Res. 14 (1966), 361-368.
4. J.N. Gavert and N.V. Plyter, "The Optimal Assignment of Facilities to Locations by Branch and Bound," Opns.Res. 14 (1966), 210-232.
5. P.C. Gilmore, "Optimal and Sub-optimal Algorithms for the Quadratic Assignment Problem," SIAM J. Appl. Math. 10 (1962), 305-313.
6. R.H. Glaser, "A Quasi-Simplex Method for Designing Suboptimal Packages for Electronic Building Blocks," Proc. 1959 Computer Applic. Symp., Armour Res. Found., Ill. Inst. Tech., 100-111.
7. R.E. Gomory and T.C. Hu, "Multi-Terminal Network Flows," SIAM J. Appl. Math. 9 (1961), 551-570.
8. G.W. Graves and A.B. Whinston, "An Algorithm for the Quadratic Assignment Problem," Mgt. Sci. 16 (1970), 453-471.
9. S.A. Graciano, "Branch and Bound Solutions to the Capacitated Plant Location Problem," Opns. Res. 17 (1969), 1005-1016.
10. M. Hanan and J.M. Kurtzberg, "A Review of the Placement and Quadratic Assignment Problems," SIAM Rev. 14 (1972), 324-342.
11. G. Henry, "Recherche d'un Reseau de Depots Optimum," Reuve Francaise d'informatique et de Recherche Operationnelle 2 (1968), 61-70.
12. F.S. Hillier and M.M. Connors, "Quadratic Assignment Problem Algorithms and the Location of Indivisible Facilities," Mgt. Sci. 13 (1966), 42-57.

13. W.A. Horn, "Single Machine Job Sequencing with Treelike Precedence Ordering and Linear Delay Penalties," SIAM J. Appl. Math. 23 (1972), 189-202.
14. R.M. Karp, "Reducibility Among Combinatorial Problems," in Complexity of Computer Computations, R.E. Miller and J.W. Thatcher, eds., Plenum Press, N.Y., 1972, 85-104.
15. R.M. Karp, A.C. McKellar, C.K. Wong, "Near-Optimal Solutions to a 2-Dimensional Placement Problem," IBM Research Tech. Report RC4740, February 1974.
16. U.R. Kodres, "Geometrical Positioning of Circuit Elements in a Computer," Conf. Paper 1172, AIEE Fall General Mtg., Oct. 1959.
17. T.C. Koopmans and M.J. Beckmann, "Assignment Problems and the Location of Economic Activities," Econometrica 25 (1957), 52-75.
18. A.H. Land, "A Problem of Assignment with Inter-related Costs," Opnl. Res. Qtrly 14 (1963), 185-199.
19. E.L. Lawler, "The Quadratic Assignment Problem," Mgt. Sci. 9 (1963), 586-589.
20. P.M. Morse, "Optimal Linear Ordering of Information Items," Opns. Res. 20 (1972), 741-751.
21. C.E. Nugent, T.E. Vollman and J. Ruml, "An Experimental Comparison of Techniques for the Assignment of Facilities to Locations," Opns. Res. 16 (1968), 150-173.
22. V.R. Pratt, "An N log N Algorithm to Distribute N Records Optimally in a Sequential Access File," in Complexity of Computer Computations, R.E. Miller and J.W. Thatcher, eds., Plenum Press, N.Y., 1972, 111-118.
23. T.C. Raymond, "A Method for Optimizing Circuit Module Placement," IBM Tech. Disclosure Bull. 13 (1970), 274-276.
24. J. Sidney, Ph.D. dissertation, University of Michigan, Ann Arbor, 1971.
25. K. Spielberg, "Plant Location with Generalized Search Origin," Mgt. Sci. 16 (1969), 165-178.
26. L. Steinberg, "The Backboard Wiring Problem: A Placement Algorithm," SIAM Rev. 3 (1961), 37-50.

FONCTIONS D'EVALUATION ET PENALITES POUR LES PROGRAMMES QUADRATIQUES EN VARIABLES 0-1

P. Hansen

Institut d'Economie Scientifique et de Gestion, Lille

RESUME. On propose une série de fonctions d'évaluation, de plus en plus précises, pour les programmes quadratiques en variables 0-1; ces fonctions d'évaluation sont obtenues grâce à des pénalités additives et non additives. On présente aussi les résultats d'essais comparatifs sur ordinateur de trois algorithmes utilisant une partie ou l'ensemble des fonctions d'évaluation et des pénalités obtenues.

1. INTRODUCTION

Considérons un programme quadratique en variables 0-1, écrit sous la forme suivante:

$$\text{Min} \sum_i \sum_j c_{ij}\, x_i x_j \qquad (1)$$

sous les contraintes

$$\sum_i \sum_j a_{ijk}\, x_i x_j - b_k \geq 0 \qquad (2)$$

et

$$x_j \in \{0,1\} \qquad (3)$$

$(i=1,2,...,n;\ j=1,2,...,n;\ k=1,2,...,m)$
où les c_{ij}, a_{ijk} et b_k sont des réels et l'on suppose, sans perte de généralité, que $c_{ij}=0$ et $a_{ijk}=0$ pour $i>j$.

B. Roy (ed.), Combinatorial Programming: Methods and Applications, 361–370.

Comme $x_j.x_j=x_j$ pour $x_j \in \{0,1\}$, les termes linéaires de (1) et (2) sont les termes $c_{jj}x_jx_j$ et $a_{jjk}x_jx_j$ pour $j=1,2,...,n$. Aucune restriction telle que la monotonicité ou la convexité n'est imposée à la fonction économique (1) ou aux membres de gauche des contraintes (2). Plusieurs auteurs [5][7]-[9][12][15][16][18][19] ont proposé des algorithmes lexicographiques ou des procédures d'optimisation par séparation et évaluation pour résoudre le problème (1)-(3), parfois avec quelques restrictions supplémentaires. Des applications ont été proposées dans les domaines des choix d'investissements [15][17][21][22], du choix des médias [3][5][23], de la statistique [2] et de la théorie des graphes [2][5][10]. Il est bien connu que l'efficience des procédures d'optimisation par séparation et évaluation dépend en grande partie de la précision des fonctions d'évaluation qu'elles utilisent. Dans la suite de cette note, on propose une série de fonctions d'évaluation plus précises que celles utilisées antérieurement (à l'exception, peut-être, de celles obtenues en [7] par l'étude des relations logiques entre couples ou triplets de variables impliquées par les contraintes du problème). Ces fonctions d'évaluation sont obtenues à l'aide de pénalités additives [11] et non additives. On présente aussi les résultats d'essais comparatifs sur ordinateur de trois algorithmes utilisant une partie ou l'ensemble des fonctions d'évaluation et des pénalités obtenues.

2. FONCTIONS D'EVALUATION ET PENALITES

Dans une procédure d'optimisation par séparation et évaluation, on effectue des séparations successives de l'ensemble de solutions du problème à résoudre, définissant ainsi des sous-problèmes, auxquels sont appliqués des tests. Si les séparations se font en fixant une variable à 0 ou à 1, le problème obtenu à une itération courante a la même forme que le problème de départ. Pour simplifier l'écriture on présentera les fonctions d'évaluation pour le problème (1)-(3) en supposant toutes les variables libres; la prise en compte des valeurs des variables fixées à 0 ou à 1 à une itération courante se fait sans difficultés. On notera $\underline{a}$ le minimum d'un réel a et de 0 et $\overline{a}$ le maximum de a et de 0.

Proposition 1:

$$\underline{z}^1 = \sum_i \sum_j \underline{c}_{ij} \qquad (4)$$

est un minorant des valeurs de la fonction économique (1) pour $X\in\{0,1\}^n$.

Théorème 1: Les pénalités

$$p_j^0=\underline{c}_{jj}-\sum_i \underline{c}_{ij}-\sum_j \underline{c}_{ji} \qquad (5)$$

et

$$p_j^1=\overline{c}_{jj}+\sum_{i\neq j|c_{ij}\cdot c_{ii}<0} \min(|c_{ij}|,|c_{ii}|)$$

$$+\sum_{i\neq j|c_{ji}\cdot c_{ii}<0} \min(|c_{ji}|,|c_{ii}|) \qquad (6)$$

peuvent être associées à l'évaluation $\underline{z}^1$.

Démonstration: Si $x_j=0$, il est clair que $\underline{z}^1$ s'accroît de p_j^0; si $x_j=1$, $\underline{z}^1$ peut s'accroître du fait du terme linéaire en x_j et du fait que les termes quadratiques $c_{ij}x_ix_j$ ou $c_{ji}x_jx_i$ contenant x_j s'ajoutent aux termes linéaires $c_{ii}x_ix_i=c_{ii}x_i$. Si $c_{ij}>0$ (ou $c_{ji}>0$) et $c_{ii}<0$, le nouveau coefficient $\underline{c}_{ii}$ sera égal à $c_{ii}-c_{ij}$ si $c_{ij}<-c_{ii}$ et à 0 autrement; si $c_{ij}<0$ (ou $c_{ji}<0$) et $c_{ii}>0$ le nouveau coefficient $\underline{c}_{ii}$ sera égal à $c_{ij}+c_{ii}$ si $-c_{ij}>c_{ii}$ et à 0 autrement; dans les deux cas $\underline{z}^1$ s'accroît de $\min(|c_{ij}|,|c_{ii}|)$ (ou $\min(|c_{ji}|,|c_{ii}|)$). Si c_{ij} et c_{ii} (ou c_{ji} et c_{ii}) sont de même signe $\underline{z}^1$ ne s'accroît pas du fait du terme quadratique $c_{ij}x_ix_j$ (ou $c_{ji}x_jx_i$).

Corollaire 1:

$$\underline{z}^2=\underline{z}^1+\max_j \min(p_j^0,p_j^1) \qquad (7)$$

est un minorant des valeurs de (1) pour $X\in\{0,1\}^n$.

Théorème 2: Les pénalités additives

$$p_j^{0\prime}=-\sum_i \alpha_{ij}\underline{c}_{ij}-\sum_i(1-\alpha_{ji})\underline{c}_{ji} \qquad (8)$$

où

$$0\leq\alpha_{ij}\leq 1 \quad (i=1,2,\ldots,n;\ j=1,2,\ldots,n) \qquad (9)$$

et

$$p_j^{1\prime}=\overline{c}_{jj} \qquad (10)$$

peuvent être associées à l'évaluation $\underline{z}^1$.

Démonstration: La fonction

$$\sum_j c_{jj}x_j+\sum_i\sum_{j\neq i}\underline{c}_{ij}x_ix_j \qquad (11)$$

minore la fonction (1) pour $X\in\{0,1\}^n$; la fonction

$$\sum_j \bar{c}_{jj}x_j+\sum_j \underline{c}_{jj}x_j+\sum_i \sum_{j\neq i} \alpha_{ij}\underline{c}_{ij}x_j+\sum_i \sum_{j\neq i} (1-\alpha_{ij})\underline{c}_{ij}x_i \qquad (12)$$

$$= \sum_j \bar{c}_{jj}x_j+\sum_j(\underline{c}_{jj}+\sum_{i\neq j} \alpha_{ij}\underline{c}_{ij}+\sum_{i\neq j} (1-\alpha_{ji})\underline{c}_{ji})x_j \qquad (13)$$

$$= \sum_j \bar{c}_{jj}x_j+\sum_j(\sum_i \alpha_{ij}\underline{c}_{ij}+\sum_i(1-\alpha_{ji})\underline{c}_{ji})x_j \qquad (14)$$

$$= \sum_j p_j^{1\prime}\ x_j-\sum_j p_j^{0\prime}\ x_j \qquad (15)$$

$$= \underline{z}^1+\sum_j p_j^{1\prime}\ x_j+\sum_j p_j^{0\prime}(1-x_j) \qquad (16)$$

minore la fonction (11) et donc la fonction économique (1) pour $X\in\{0,1\}^n$.

Corollaire 2:

$$\underline{z}^3=\underline{z}^1+\sum_j \min\ (p_j^{0\prime},p_j^{1\prime}) \qquad (17)$$

est un minorant des valeurs de (1) pour $X\in\{0,1\}^n$.

Posons, pour $j=1,2,...,n$:

$$q_j=p_j^{1\prime}-p_j^{0\prime}. \qquad (18)$$

Théorème 3: Les pénalités

$$p_j^{0\prime\prime}=-\underline{q}_j \qquad (19)$$

et

$$p_j^{1\prime\prime}=\bar{q}_j+\sum_{i\neq j|c_{ij}>0} \min(c_{ij},-\underline{q}_i)+\sum_{i\neq j|c_{ji}>0} \min(c_{ji},-\underline{q}_i) \qquad (20)$$

peuvent être associées à l'évaluation $\underline{z}^3$.

Démonstration: D'après le théorème 2 et le corollaire 2, la fonction

$$\sum_j q_jx_j+\sum_i \sum_{j\neq i} \bar{c}_{ij}x_ix_j \qquad (21)$$

minore la fonction (1) pour $X\in\{0,1\}^n$ et

$$\underline{z}^3= \sum_j \underline{q}_j; \qquad (22)$$

la suite de la démonstration est semblable à celle du théorème 1 et est omise ici.

Corollaire 3:

$$\underline{z}^4=\underline{z}^3+\max_j \min\,(p_j^{0''},p_j^{1''}) \tag{23}$$

est un minorant des valeurs de (1) pour $X\in\{0,1\}^n$.

Théorème 4:

$$\underline{z}^5=\underline{z}^3+\sum_i \sum_{j\neq i|c_{ij}>0} r_{ij} \tag{24}$$

où

$$r_{ij}=\min(c_{ij},-\beta_i^j\underline{q}_i,-\beta_j^i\underline{q}_j), \tag{25}$$

$$0\leq\beta_j^i\leq 1 \tag{26}$$

et

$$\sum_i\beta_j^i=1 \quad (i=1,2,\ldots,n;\ j=1,2,\ldots,n) \tag{27}$$

est un minorant des valeurs de (1) pour $X\in\{0,1\}^n$.

Démonstration: La fonction (21) qui minore la fonction (1) pour $X\in\{0,1\}^n$ est minorée par la fonction

$$\sum_i \sum_j \beta_j^i\underline{q}_jx_j+\sum_i\sum_{j\neq i}\bar{c}_{ij}x_ix_j \tag{28}$$

$$=\sum_j\underline{q}_j-\sum_i\sum_j\beta_j^i\underline{q}_j(1-x_j)+\sum_i\sum_{j\neq i}\bar{c}_{ij}x_ix_j \tag{29}$$

$$\geq\underline{z}^3+\sum_{i<j}\sum_j[\bar{c}_{ij}x_ix_j-\beta_j^i\underline{q}_j(1-x_j)-\beta_i^j\underline{q}_i(1-x_i)] \tag{30}$$

et comme

$$r_{ij}\leq\bar{c}_{ij}x_ix_j-\beta_j^i\underline{q}_j(1-x_j)-\beta_i^j\underline{q}_i(1-x_i) \tag{31}$$

pour x_i et $x_j\in\{0,1\}$, (24) est bien un minorant de (1) pour $X\in\{0,1\}^n$.

Posons, pour $j=1,2,\ldots,n$

$$q'_j=q_j+\sum_{i\neq j|c_{ij}>0} r_{ij}+\sum_{i\neq j|c_{ji}>0} r_{ji} \tag{32}$$

et pour tout i et j tels que $c_{ij}>0$

$$c'_{ij}=\bar{c}_{ij}-r_{ij}. \tag{33}$$

Théorème 5: Les pénalités

$$p_j^{0\,'''} = -\underline{q}'_j \qquad (34)$$

et

$$p_j^{1\,'''} = \overline{q}'_j + \sum_{i \neq j} \min(c'_{ij}, -\underline{q}'_i) + \sum_{i \neq j} \min(c'_{ji}, -\underline{q}'_i) \qquad (35)$$

peuvent être associées à l'évaluation $\underline{z}^5$.

Démonstration: D'après les théorèmes 3 et 4, la fonction

$$\sum_{i<j}\sum_j r_{ij} + \sum_j \overline{q}'_j x_j - \sum_j \underline{q}'_j (1-x_j) + \sum_i \sum_{j \neq i \mid c'_{ij} > 0} c'_{ij} x_i x_j \qquad (36)$$

minore la fonction (1) pour $X \in \{0,1\}^n$ et $\underline{z}^5$ égale la somme des coefficients négatifs de (36); la suite de la démonstration est semblable à celle du théorème 1 et est omise ici.

Corollaire 4 :

$$\underline{z}^6 = \underline{z}^5 + \max_j \min(p_j^{0\,'''}, p_j^{1\,'''}) \qquad (37)$$

est un minorant des valeurs de la fonction économique (1) pour $X \in \{0,1\}^n$.

Des évaluations par excès des valeurs des membres de gauche des contraintes (2) pour $X \in \{0,1\}^n$ peuvent être obtenues à l'aide de théorèmes semblables aux théorèmes 1 à 5.

3. ALGORITHMES ET ESSAIS SUR ORDINATEUR

Les fonctions d'évaluation $\underline{z}^3$ à $\underline{z}^6$ dépendent des valeurs des paramètres α_{ij} et les fonctions d'évaluation $\underline{z}^5$ et $\underline{z}^6$ dépendent des valeurs des paramètres α_{ij} et β_j^i. Le choix des valeurs à donner à ces paramètres devra se faire en tenant compte de la précision des évaluations obtenues et du temps nécessaire à les calculer. D'après [1][13][20] les valeurs des α_{ij} qui maximisent $\underline{z}^3$ peuvent être obtenues en minimisant (11) à l'aide de l'algorithme de Ford et Fulkerson [4] pour la recherche du flot maximum dans un réseau de transport. Pour des α_{ij} donnés, les valeurs des β_j^i qui maximisent $\underline{z}^5$ peuvent être obtenues par la programmation linéaire. Des méthodes de calcul plus simples ont été utilisées jusqu'ici.

Trois algorithmes, appelés BNL101, BNL102 et BNL103 ont été construits, programmés et essayés sur un ordinateur CDC 6400 [14]; ces algorithmes sont des P.S.E.S.

et utilisent une suite de tests directs et de tests conditionnels. Si l'évaluation $\underline{z}$ obtenue par un test direct dépasse ou égale la valeur f_{opt} de la meilleure solution précédemment obtenue on passe à l'étape de régression et sinon on continue en séquence. Si une variable est fixée à 0 ou à 1 par un test conditionnel on retourne après cette fixation au premier test direct. Si aucune variable n'est fixée après un passage par tous les tests on procède à une séparation en écartant d'abord l'ensemble de solutions candidates auquel correspond la plus grande évalution par défaut.
L'algorithme BNL101 utilise la fonction d'évaluation $\underline{z}^1$, les pénalités p_j^0 et p_j^1 (sans tenir compte des termes correspondant aux c_{ij} et c_{ji} dans p_j^1) et des fonctions d'évaluation et des pénalités semblables pour les membres de gauche des contraintes; les séparations se font d'après les valeurs des pénalités p_j^0 et p_j^1. L'algorithme BNL102 utilise en plus les fonctions d'évaluation $\underline{z}^3$ et $\underline{z}^4$, les pénalités additives $p_j^{0\prime}$ et $p_j^{1\prime}$ avec $\alpha_{ij}=\frac{1}{2}$ pour tout i et j et des fonctions d'évaluation et des pénalités semblables pour les membres de gauche des contraintes; les séparations se font d'après les valeurs de pénalités $p_j^{0\prime}$ et $p_j^{1\prime}$. L'algorithme

Tableau 1.

Problème N°	Nombre de variables	Temps de résolution(Secondes CDC6400) BNL101	BNL102	BNL103
1	6	0,165	0,112	0,206
2	8	0,530	0,353	0,566
3	10	0,975	0,340	0,407
4	12	5,522	1,156	3,169
5	14	3,618	0,551	1,243
6	16	6,811	0,521	1,556
7	18	7,854	1,901	5,240
8	20	21,188	1,300	2,533
9	22	22,161	0,757	1,862
10	24	127,690	6,785	14,962
11	26	413,126	8,298	8,018
12	28	1041,966	42,729	37,252
13	30	>1500,000	9,735	9,309
14	32		110,601	99,171
15	34		115,578	
16	36		162,138	
17	38		401,586	
18	40		729,236	

BNL103 utilise l'ensemble des résultats de la section précédente; les α_{ij} sont choisis égaux à $\frac{1}{2}$ et les β_j^1 sont choisis séquentiellement de façon à maximiser les r_{ij} successifs. Les séparations se font d'après les valeurs des pénalités p_j^{0}''' et p_j^{1}'''. Les trois algorithmes sont décrits en détail dans [14].

Dans une première série d'expériences on a considéré des problèmes de taille croissante avec de 6 à 40 variables et 4 contraintes. La fonction économique d'un problème ayant n variables contient n termes linéaires à coefficients positifs, $n/2$ termes quadratiques à coefficients positifs et $n/2$ termes quadratiques à coefficients négatifs, de même que chacune des contraintes. Les données des 13 premiers problèmes figurent dans [13] et les données complètes dans [14]. Les temps de calcul obtenus avec les algorithmes BNL101, BNL102 et BNL103 figurent dans le tableau 1. On voit clairement que l'usage de pénalités additives diminue très fortement le temps de calcul; l'usage des fonctions d'évaluation $\underline{z}^5$ et $\underline{z}^6$, précises et longues à calculer, ne se justifie que pour les plus grands problèmes.

Tableau 2.

Problème N°	Nombre de variables	Temps de résolution (Secondes CDC6400) BNL102	BNL103
1	6	0,043	0,089
2	8	0,089	0,212
3	10	0,282	0,586
4	12	0,769	1,723
5	14	0,864	1,739
6	16	2,147	4,291
7	18	3,990	6,147
8	20	11,049	15,298
9	22	16,904	12,954
10	24	63,511	41,445
11	26	143,911	95,567

Dans une seconde série d'expériences on a résolu à l'aide des algorithmes BNL102 et BNL103 une série de problèmes de taille croissante avec un nombre maximum de termes quadratiques - soit $\frac{n(n-1)}{2}$ pour un problème à n variables - dans la fonction économique et dans chacune des trois contraintes considérées. Les données complètes de ces problèmes figurent dans [14]. Les temps de calcul obtenus avec les algorithmes BNL102 et BNL103 figurent dans le tableau 2. Ils confirment l'intérêt de l'emploi des fonctions d'évaluation les plus précises pour résoudre les plus grands problèmes.

BIBLIOGRAPHIE

1. M.L. Balinski, On a Selection Problem, Manag.Sci. 17, 230, 1970.
2. J. de Smet, Le problème des signes de Thurstone, Revue Fr. Infor. Rech. Opér., 2, 33, 1968.
3. M. Despontin, D. Van Oudheusden and P. Hansen, Choix de médias par programmation quadratique en variables 0-1, dans les actes du colloque de l'AFCET Aide à la décision, tome 1, 1, 1974.
4. L. Ford and D.R. Fulkerson, Flows in Networks, Princeton, 1962.
5. V. Ginsburgh et A. Van Peetersen, Un algorithme de programmation quadratique en variables binaires, Revue Fr. Infor. Rech. Opér., 3, 57, 1969.
6. P.L. Hammer, Pseudo-Boolean Remarks on Balanced Graphs, Technion, 1969.
7. P.L. Hammer and P. Hansen, Quadratic 0-1 Programming, CORE discussion paper 7219, 1972.
8. P.L. Hammer and A.A. Rubin, Quadratic Programming with 0-1 Variables, Technion, 1969.
9. P.L. Hammer and A.A. Rubin, Some Remarks on Quadratic Programming with 0-1 Variables, Revue Fr. Infor. Rech. Opér., 4, 67, 1970.
10. P.L. Hammer and Rudeanu, Boolean Methods in Operations Research and Related Areas, Springer, Heidelberg, 1968.
11. P. Hansen, Pénalités additives pour les programmes en variables 0-1, Comptes-Rendus Acad. Sci. Paris, 273, 175, 1971.
12. P. Hansen, Quadratic 0-1 Programming by Implicit Enumeration, in Numerical Methods in Nonlinear Optimization, ed. by F.A. Lootsma, Academic Press, New-York, 1972.
13. P. Hansen, Minimisation d'une fonction quadratique en variables 0-1 par l'algorithme de Ford et Fulkerson, papier présenté au colloque Structures Economiques et Econométrie, Lyon, 1973.
14. P. Hansen, Programmes Mathématiques en Variables 0-1, thèse d'agrégation de l'enseignement supérieur, Université Libre de Bruxelles, 1974.
15. F.S. Hillier, The Evaluation of Risky Interrelated Investments, North-Holland, Amsterdam, 1969.
16. D.J. Laughhunn, Quadratic Binary Programming with Applications to Capital Budgeting Problems, Oper. Res., 18, 454, 1970.

17. D.J. Laughhunn and D.E. Peterson, Capital Expenditure Programming and Some Alternative Approaches to Risk, Manag. Sci., 17, 320, 1971.
18. E.L. Lawler and M.D. Bell, A Method for Solving Discrete Optimization Problems, Oper. Res., 14, 1098, 1966.
19. J.C.T. Mao and B.A. Wallingford, An Extension of Lawler and Bell's Method of Discrete Optimization with Examples from Capital Budgeting, Manag.Sci., 15, 51, 1968.
20. J. Rhys, A Selection Problem of Shared Fixed Costs and Network Flows, Manag. Sci., 17, 200, 1970.
21. M. Schecter and P.L. Hammer, A Note on the Dynamic Planning of Investment Projects, Eur. Econ. Rev., 2, 111, 1970.
22. H.M. Weingartner, Capital Budgeting of Interrelated Projects, Manag. Sci., 12, 485, 1966.
23. W. Zangwill, Media Selection by Decision Programming, J. of Adv. Res., 5, 30, 1965.

SOLUTION OF THE MACHINE LOADING PROBLEM WITH BINARY VARIABLES

C.Sandi

IBM Scientific Center - Pisa

ABSTRACT. In this paper the machine loading problem, i.e. the problem of the optimal assignment of n jobs to m machines of limited capacities, is considered with the further constraint that each job has to be performed using one machine only. The problem may be formulated as an integer 0,1 LP problem, for which an implicit enumeration method of solution is suggested. This method draws advantage from: i) a proposed heuristic solution, to have a good initial "ceiling" (often the optimal solution itself!), ii) an "a priori" criterium to widely reduce the set of solutions to be inspected, iii) a special method to get bounding functions and branching criteria. A wide computational experience allows a good insight into the method.

1. INTRODUCTION

The problem considered here originated from the need of assigning, in some optimal fashion, the monthly production to the available paper machines in a paper industry. The main purpose was to assign "homogeneous productions" (i.e. paper of the same quality, colour, substance, etc.) to the same paper machine. And this because of the exceedingly high cost involved at each change of production in a paper machine (stop, clean, reset, load, etc. operations requiring even days!). After dividing the monthly production into n "homogeneous products", the problem was simplified to allow the mathematical formulation given in section 2; i.e. the classical machine loading problem, with the further constraint that each product has to be made using one machine only. The same problem also arises when the reels produced by the paper machine have to be cut according to the established cutting schedules. Because of

B. Roy (ed.), Combinatorial Programming: Methods and Applications, 371–378.

the high cost involved in changing cutting schedule, here again "homogeneous productions" (i.e. requiring the same cutting schedule) have to be assigned to the same cutting machine.

As formulated in section 2, the problem is equivalent to a transportation problem where each destination has to be supplied by one source only; under this form, two approaches have already been tried. The first is an implicit enumeration approach [1] [2], using multi-branching [3] or single-branching [4] techniques. The second approach is a classical branch and bound method [5] , which uses the optimum value of the continuous solution as bounding function, and the non-integer valued variables in the continuous solution as branching variables [6].

In this paper a combination of the two approaches is suggested. Using the terminology of [7] , "separation" is based on an implicit enumeration technique of a single-branching type, in order to reduce core storage requirement; "relaxation" of the integrality constraints gives the continuous LP problem, to be used for "fathoming" and for achieving branching information. On forward steps the optimal solution to the relaxed problem is easily obtained from the one of the previous step; the same is true for backward steps, when core storage limitation prevents the storage of intermediate continuous solutions. Finally the method draws advantage from a proposed heuristic solution according to [8] , and from an "a priori" criterium to reduce the set of solutions to be inspected, to get the optimal solution (see [9]).

2. THE PROBLEM

The special class of machine loading problems described in section 1 may have the following mathematical formulation. Let's define:

$l_i > 0$ capacity of machine i (i=1,m)

$q_j > 0$ amount of product j required (j=1,n)

$c_{ij} \geqslant 0$ cost if product j is made on machine i

x_{ij} fraction of product j made on machine i;

then the problem, P say, is to find x_{ij} such that:

(1.1) $$\Sigma_i \Sigma_j c_{ij} x_{ij} = \min$$

subject to:

(1.2) $$\Sigma_j q_j x_{ij} \leqslant l_i \quad (i=1,m)$$

(1.3) $$\Sigma_i x_{ij} = 1 \quad (j=1,n)$$

(1.4) $$x_{ij} \in \{0,1\}$$

where for feasibility reasons $\Sigma_i \ l_i \geqslant \Sigma_j q_j$.

Problem P stated by (1.1) - (1.4) is an integer LP problem with m x n binary variables x_{ij} (i=1,m; j=1,n) and m + n constraints given by (1.2), (1.3). With realistic values of m and n, this problem may have thousands of binary variables and several hundreds of rows, so that the general purpose methods of solution for integer programming problems may be unpractical. For this reason an "ad hoc" method is suggested, which draws advantage from the strong structure of the problem matrix.

A small numerical example of problem P with m = 4 and n = 10 follows, together with its solution.

3	5	10	1	2	3	5	3	8	2	q_j / l_i
13	9	1	(3)	14	15	(7)	(9)	15	8	9
13	(9)	20	6	17	(7)	9	16	17	(1)	10
18	15	(11)	14	(13)	8	18	12	(17)	12	20
(5)	4	19	2	6	15	19	4	15	20	3

Fig.1 Numerical example of problem P. Circled costs correspond to optimal assignment.

3. THE METHOD

The method is described in precise mathematical terms by the algorithm below. The notation P, l_i, q_j, c_{ij}, x_{ij}, m, n, has the same meaning as in section 2. Furthermore let's define:

$$I = \{1, 2, \ldots, m\} \; ; \quad J = \{1, 2, \ldots, n\}$$

$$P' \begin{cases} \Sigma_i \Sigma_j c_{ij} x_{ij} = \min \\ \text{s.t. } \Sigma_j q_j x_{ij} \leqslant l_i \quad i \in I \\ \Sigma_i x_{ij} = 1 \quad j \in J \\ 0 \leqslant x_{ij} \leqslant 1 \quad i \in I, \ j \in J \end{cases}$$

$$P^\circ \begin{cases} \sum_i \sum_j c_{ij} x_{ij} = \min \\ \text{s.t.} \sum_i x_{ij} = 1 \quad j \in J \\ x_{ij} \in \{0,1\} \quad i \in I, \ j \in J \end{cases}$$

P' is the relaxation of P obtained by substituting to the integrality constraints (1.4) the "continuous" constraints $0 \leqslant x_{ij} \leqslant 1$; practically P' is equivalent to a classical (un)balanced transportation problem. P° is also a relaxation of P obtained from P by dropping the capacity constraints (1.2). Let's define:

F(P)	the set of the feasible solutions for P
X,X',X°	the (m x n) assignment matrix for P, P', P°
z,z',z°	the optima for P, P', P° respectively,
z^h	the value of an heuristic solution for P;

where obviously: $z^\circ \leqslant z' \leqslant z \leqslant z^h$. In what follows the c_{ij}'s are supposed to be such that $c_{ij} = \infty$ if $q_j > l_i$. According to [1] , [9] let's introduce also the string A of indicial pairs of "assigned" or "fixed" variables, ranked according to the index r. We can now describe the 7 steps of the algorithm.

<u>Step 1a</u> <u>Start step</u>: Set $z = \infty$. For each $j \in J$ determine the index i_j such that:

$$c_{i_j j} = \min_{i \in I} \{c_{ij}\}$$

In case of ties the choice is arbitrary (a suggestion may be to choose the index i_j for which l_{i_j} is maximum). For each $j \in J$ set:

$$x_{i_j j} = x^\circ_{i_j j} = 1 \ ; \ x_{ij} = x^\circ_{ij} = 0 \quad i \in I - \{i_j\}$$

X° represents an optimal solution to P°, and will be the starting point of the search for an optimal solution to P. If $X = X^\circ \in F(P)$ go to step 5; otherwise:
<u>1b</u> Solve P' and store the optimal solution found in X'. If $X' \in F(P)$ set X=X' and go to step 5; otherwise a lower bound z' to z can be displayed (if desired).
<u>1c</u> Try method [8] to get an heuristic solution to P. If one is found set $z = z^h$ and an upper bound z^h on z can be

displayed (if desired); otherwise

1d Set $r = 0$ and form the sets:

$$I_j = \{ i \mid x_{ij} = 0 , \quad i \in I \} \quad j \in J$$

$$J_i = \{ j \mid x_{ij} = 1 , \quad j \in J \} \quad i \in I$$

Step 2a Branching step. Compute for each $i \in I$ the quantities:

$$s_i = l_i - \Sigma_j x_{ij} \ ; \quad d_i = s_i + \sum_{j \in J_i} q_j x_{ij} \ .$$

Form the sets:

$I^- = \{ i \mid s_i < 0, \quad i \in I \}$; $I^+ = I - I^-$

Since $X \notin F(P)$, I^- (and therefore I^+) is non-empty. Indicating with $w_{ij} = c_{ij} / q_j$ $(i \in I, \ j \in J)$ the relative costs, let's define the minimization operation:

$$\begin{cases} w_{\hat{k}\hat{j}} - w_{\hat{i}\hat{j}} = \min \{ w_{kj} - w_{ij} \} \\ i \in I^- \ ; \ j \in J_i \ ; \ k \in I^+ \cap I_j \ ; \ q_j \leqslant d_k \end{cases}$$

2b Look for a triplet $(\hat{i},\hat{k},\hat{j})$ under the condition $x'_{kj} = 1$. If one is found (for ties the choice is arbitrary) go to step 3. Otherwise:

2c Look for a triplet $(\hat{i},\hat{k},\hat{j})$ under the condition $x'_{kj} \neq 0$. If one is found (for ties the choice is arbitrary) go to step 3; otherwise:

2d Look for a triplet $(\hat{i},\hat{k},\hat{j})$. If none is found go to step 6; otherwise:

Step 3 Fathoming test: Solve problem P" obtained from P' by adding the constraint $x'_{\hat{k}\hat{j}} = 1$; and indicate with X" and z" the optimal solution and the optimum found (X" and z" may be easily obtained from X' and z' applying the method described in [11]). Now if $z'' \geqslant z$ go to step 6; otherwise set $z' = z''$ and $X' = X''$.

Step 4 Forward step: set $r = r+1$, $A(r) = (\hat{k},\hat{j})$; $x_{\hat{k}\hat{j}} = 1$, $x_{\hat{i}\hat{j}} = 0$; $J_{\hat{i}} = J_{\hat{i}} - \{\hat{j}\}$; update problem P' adding to P' the constraint $x'_{\hat{k}\hat{j}} = 1$. If $X \notin F(P)$ go to step 2a; otherwise:

Step 5 Feasible solution: If $z > \Sigma_i \Sigma_j c_{ij} x_{ij}$ a better feasible solution X for P is displayed; set $z = \Sigma_i \Sigma_j c_{ij} x_{ij}$ and go to step 6. Otherwise:

Step 6 Backward step: if $r = 0$ go to step 7. Otherwise let $(i,j) = A(r)$. If x_{ij} is "fixed" to the value 0, set:
$r = r-1$, $I_j = I_j \bigcup \{i\}$; drop from P' the constraint $x'_{ij} = 0$ and go to step 6 again. If x_{ij} is "assigned" (i.e.) $x_{ij} = 1$) set: $x_{ij} = 0$, $x_{i_j j} = 1$ (remember the definition of i_j in step 1a); $I_j = I_j - \{i\}$;
$J_{i_j} = J_{i_j} \bigcup \{j\}$; update problem P' dropping the constraint $x'_{ij} = 1$ and adding the constraint $x'_{ij} = 0$.
Go to step 2a.

Step 7 End step: If $z \neq \infty$, the last feasible solution displayed is optimal for P. Otherwise the problem has no feasible solution.

A few comments on the method follow: i) On forward steps, only one column j of the assignment matrix X is changed; in this column the 1 is shifted from its original row i_j (which becomes $\hat{i}$ in the notation of step 2a) to a new row $\hat{k}$ where $\hat{i} \in I^-$ and $\hat{k} \in I^+$. This means a wide "a priori" reduction on the number of forward steps (see [9]). ii) Fathoming is eliminated, if the branch variable $x_{\hat{k}\hat{j}}$ is such that $x'_{\hat{k}\hat{j}}$ is already 1 in the optimal solution of P'; and resolving P' with the added constraint $x'_{\hat{k}\hat{j}} = 1$ is equivalent to solving a small sequence of shortest path problems in a directed network of m nodes and at most $(m - 1)(m - 2)+1$ arcs (see [11]). iii) A good heuristic solution can be found using the method described in [8]; in most cases deviations less than 1% from the optimum can be found. iv) A lower bound z' to z can be associated at each open branch.

4. COMPUTATIONAL EXPERIENCE

To test the algorithm described in section 3, a code has been written in Fortran 1V language and several problems have been solved using this code on an IBM 360/67. The problem sizes have been chosen as follows: $m \in \{2, 3, 5, 10\}$ and $n \in \{20, 30, 50, 100\}$. A uniform random number generator has been used to obtain q_j and c_{ij} values in the interval (1, 100). Two runs have been made, according to the method chosen to generate the 1_i's. The results of the first run are summarized in Table 1; for this run each 1_j was set to $(.7) \times \max_{i \in I} \{\sum_j q_j x_{ij}\}$, as in ref [4] , (direct comparison with computational experience of ref [4] is not possible since in that paper the more general case of q_{ij} depending also on i is considered rather than the simpler case where $q_{ij} = q_j$, $i \in I$). The results of the second run have been summarized in Table 2; in this second run the l_i's were obtained as follows: let $Q = 1.1 \times \sum_j q_j$; $u_1\ u_2 \ldots u_{m-1}$ uniform random numbers in (0,Q); $v_1\ v_2 \ldots v_{m-1}$ the same numbers sorted in ascending order; $v_o = 0$ and $v_m = Q$; then finally $l_i = v_i - v_{i-1}$, $i \in I$ (the l_i's obtained in this way have the cumulative probability distribution function $F(l) = 1-(1-l/Q)^{m-1}$. The solution times reported in Tables 1 and 2 were measured with an accuracy of 1/60 milliseconds and do not include time for input, data generation, problem set up, and output: in each row of the Tables, means,standard deviations, etc. are taken over 10 problems of the same size.

M,N	TIME(SEC.) MEAN	TIME(SEC.) S.D.	TIME(SEC.) MIN	MAX	ITERATIONS MEAN	ITERATIONS S.D.	ITERS MIN	MAX
2, 20	0.00	0.00	0.0	0.02	1.3	0.5	1	2
2, 30	0.00	0.00	0.0	0.00	1.0	0.0	1	1
2, 50	0.00	0.01	0.0	0.03	1.3	0.9	1	4
2,100	0.00	0.00	0.0	0.00	1.0	0.0	1	1
3, 20	0.01	0.01	0.0	0.03	1.9	1.0	1	4
3, 30	0.01	0.02	0.0	0.07	2.5	2.3	1	7
3, 50	0.05	0.10	0.0	0.33	4.7	8.0	1	28
3,100	0.00	0.00	0.0	0.00	1.0	0.0	1	1
5, 20	0.03	0.04	0.0	0.12	4.1	4.2	1	14
5, 30	0.20	0.27	0.0	0.97	15.1	16.7	1	59
5, 50	0.32	0.54	0.0	1.60	22.2	35.8	1	97
5,100	0.42	0.70	0.0	2.42	24.8	40.0	1	137
10, 20	10.78	26.31	0.0	88.63	302.5	634.1	1	2094
10, 30	18.38	29.18	0.0	88.98	617.9	879.8	1	2404
10, 50	6.32	14.26	0.0	48.22	251.0	529.8	1	1781
10,100	16.29	25.68	0.0	77.58	719.8	1100.2	1	3147

TABLE 1

M,N	TIME(SEC.) MEAN	TIME(SEC.) S.D.	TIME(SEC.) MIN	MAX	ITERATIONS MEAN	ITERATIONS S.D.	ITERS MIN	MAX
2, 20	0.00	0.01	0.00	0.03	1.5	0.7	1	3
2, 30	0.02	0.03	0.00	0.10	2.2	2.4	1	8
2, 50	0.04	0.07	0.00	0.23	2.9	3.1	1	10
2,100	0.08	0.09	0.00	0.25	4.8	3.7	1	12
3, 20	0.12	0.11	0.00	0.37	12.6	11.1	1	36

M,N	TIME(SEC.) MEAN	TIME(SEC.) S.D.	TIME(SEC.) MIN	MAX	ITERATIONS MEAN	ITERATIONS S.D.	ITERS MIN	MAX
3, 30	0.59	1.22	0.00	4.17	28.9	53.4	2	184
3, 50	0.52	1.08	0.00	3.67	27.9	53.3	1	183
3,100	16.64	15.88	0.00	42.65	367.5	346.4	1	895
5, 20	1.66	2.23	0.08	7.27	117.7	146.9	6	476
5, 30	2.00	2.04	0.00	6.00	110.6	102.8	2	297
5, 50	17.72	13.59	0.03	33.02	735.9	587.0	3	1553
5,100	121.52	97.15	0.47	280.50	2437.1	1563.0	21	4140
10, 20	70.39	50.31	1.12	144.88	3095.9	2055.8	98	6005
10, 30	78.08	66.18	0.40	195.62	3464.0	2889.3	27	8805
10, 50	256.84	166.07	7.42	596.63	8125.9	4925.6	259	16616

TABLE 2

5. BIBLIOGRAPHY

1. E.Balas, "An Additive Algorithm for Solving Linear Programs with Zero-One Variables", Opns. Res. 13, 517-546 (1965).
2. E.Balas, "Discrete Programming by the Filter Method", Opns. Res. 15, 915-957 (1967).
3. A.De Maio and C.Roveda, "An All Zero-One Algorithm for a Certain Class of Transportation Problems", Opns.Res. 19, 1406-1418 (1971).
4. G.T.Ross and R.M.Soland, "A Branch and Bound Algorithm for the Generalized Assignment Problem", Research Report n.CS138, Center for Cybernetic Studies, The University of Texas, Sept. 1973.
5. A.H.Land and A.G.Doig, "An Automatic Method of Solving Discrete Programming Problems", Econometrica 28,497-520 (1960).
6. V.Srinivasan and G.Thompson, "An Algorithm for Assigning Uses to Sources in a Special Class of Transportation Problems", Opns. Res. 21, 284-295 (1973).
7. A.M.Geoffrion and R.E.Marsten, "Integer Programming Algorithms: a Framework and State-of-Art Survey", Management Sci. 18, 465-491 (1972).
8. C.Sandi, "Heuristic Solution to the Transportation Problem with Binary Variables", Technical Report n.513-3528, IBM Italy Pisa Scientific Center, July, 1974.
9. C.Sandi, "Reduction in the Search Solving a Certain Class of 0,1 IP Problems by Enumerative Methods", Technical Report n.513-3511, IBM Italy Pisa Scientific Center, June 1972.
10. N.P.Tuan, "A Flexible Tree-Search Method for Integer Programming Problems", Opns. Res.19, 115-119 (1971).
11. C.Sandi, "Transportation Problem Solved by a Sequence of Shortest-Path Problems", Technical Report n.513-3529, IBM Italy Pisa Scientific Center, June 1974.

THE ROLE OF PUZZLES IN TEACHING COMBINATORIAL PROGRAMMING

H. Müller-Merbach

Fachgebiet Betriebswirtschaftslehre (Operations Research)
Technische Hochschule Darmstadt, D-61 Darmstadt, Germany

ABSTRACT: Solving combinatorial problems requires a great deal of experience with this type of problem. Combinatorial type puzzles can to some extent serve the purpose of making the student familiar with combinatorial problems and the methods used to solve them. In this paper it will be discussed which type of puzzles could be used in this context, how the various methods can be applied to them, and what educational experience can result.

1. THE USE OF PUZZLES IN TEACHING COMBINATORIAL PROGRAMMING

Problem solving in the sense of Operations Research consists roughly of the following four steps: (i) stating the real problem; (ii) building a formal problem (model); (iii) solving the formal problem; (iv) transferring the solution to reality. Each of these steps is equally important.

Education in problem solving, therefore, includes emphasis on all the four steps. It may be advantageous at the first level though, to teach these steps separately. At a higher level of education, the whole process of problem solving should be considered, not the single steps themselves.

Separate teaching of the single steps may be of particular importance in the field of combinatorial problems. This is due to the many different methods which can be applied to each problem. It is also due to the great sensitivity of the efficiency of the methods to the structure of the problem. For this reason I put particular emphasis on step (iii), i.e. solving the formal problem, in combinatorial programming. And I have found that combinatorial

B. Roy (ed.), Combinatorial Programming: Methods and Applications, 379–386.

type puzzles are a splendid tool to train students in using the methods of combinatorial problem solving. Examples shall be given in this paper.

The puzzles have several advantages over real problems. (1) They have already a structure like formal problems. (2) The problem is immediately clear. (3) There are no difficulties with the collection of data. (4) In some cases the content is a bit jocular which may motivate the student to solve the problem. (5) New problems can easily be generated (or found in newspapers or magazines) so that there are no limitations to train oneself.

As examples, three types of puzzles shall be considered in this article.

The appropriate techniques to solve these puzzles as well as many other combinatorial problems are: (i) integer programming; (ii) branched discursion (enumeration, trial and error, branch and exclude or branch and bound, dynamic programming; whatever name is preferred); (iii) graph theory.

2. NUMBER PUZZLES (ARITHMOGRIPHS)

Many German magazines publish number puzzles (in Zeit-Magazin also called "arithmogriphs"). Two examples are given in the sections 2.1 - 2.2. They consist of nine integer numbers with 1 to 4 digits each. The numbers are connected by six equations. The digits are represented by letters, the values of which are to be found. Each letter represents a different digit.

Due to the structure of the single number puzzle and due to the skill of the problem solver, different approaches are advantageous. Branched discursion will in any case yield the solution (section 2.1). In many cases a specific graph-theoretic structuring method (section 2.2) is more efficient.

2.1 Branched discursion

The first problem (taken from: Zeit-Magazin 19/1972) is the following:

(I)	ISE	+	EID	=	ALK
	−		+		−
(II)	RAS	−	KL	=	RUM
	=		=		=
(III)	ERR	+	MDR	=	LLM
	(IV)		(V)		(VI)

In some examples, the values of the single letters can directly be detected one after another; this may be called "linear discursion" and is based on simple arithmetic rules. If e.g. R=2 could be detected, linear discussion would yield M=4 (eq.III), E=3 (eq.V), K=8 (eq.VI) etc.

If the values of the single letters can not subsequently be detected, then a trial and error process (or enumeration process or branched discursion process) has to be started in which a single letter is replaced by arbitrary digits, one after another. This process leads to a tree structure which is typical for all branch and bound techniques.

Such branching is necessary in the above example, since the value of no letter can be detected in the beginning. Therefore, one letter has to be chosen for the trial and error process. It is obvious that a letter of great influence (number of appearances) will tend to keep the process efficient. Therefore, in this case R (5 times) will be taken. As the following trial and error tree shows, R=0 and R=1 lead to contradictions, while R=2 starts a chain of linear discursion yielding the desired solution.

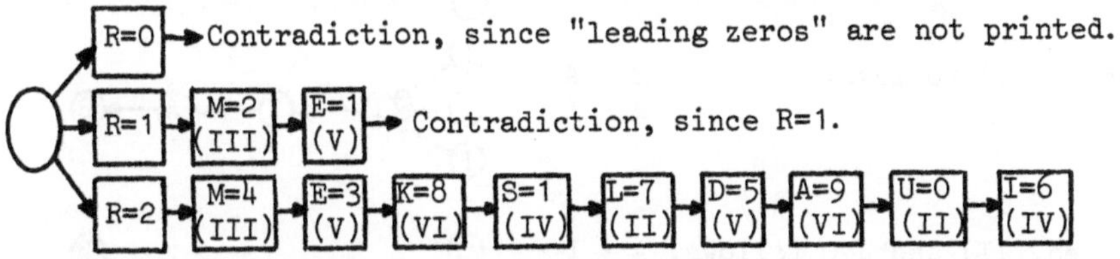

In many cases the trial and error tree is much bigger in terms of branches and in terms of nodes. In this fortunate case the third trial already yielded the solution, and no further branching was necessary.

2.2 Specific graph theoretic approach

A very efficient second method to solve most number puzzles is to derive as many "less"-conditions as possible and connect them in the form of a graph. Through systematically doing so, the values of the variables can be found almost automatically. One may switch to linear discursion after the first values have been detected.

This technique will be demonstrated by the following example (taken from: Hör Zu 17/1972):

```
(I)       ABCD : EFG =  HC
            -     .     +
(II)       FHA -  IG  = FJD
            =     =     =
(III)     AHBE -ACFE  = FAJ
          (IV)   (V)   (VI)
```

"Less"-conditions can be easily derived from the leading letters of the single equations as follows:

From eq.(III) follows: J = 0 (linear discursion)

From eq.(VI) and J=0 follows: A = H+1

The arc of the graph with the indication 1 means that H is 1 less than A.

From eq.(II) and J=0 follows: I = H - 1

From eq.(III) follows: C < H, F < H

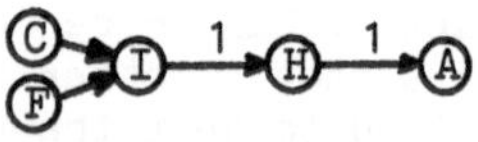

From eq.(IV) follows: F < B, H < B

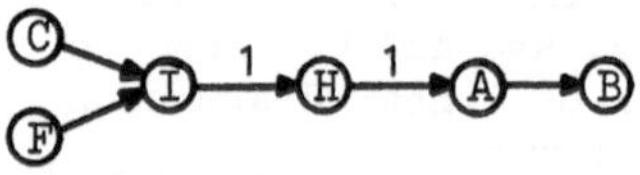

From eq.(I) follows: E < A, H < A

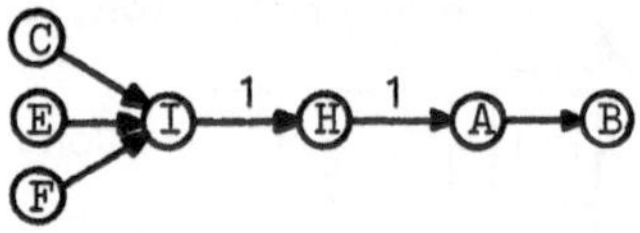

From eq.(II) and J=0 follows: A < D, A < G

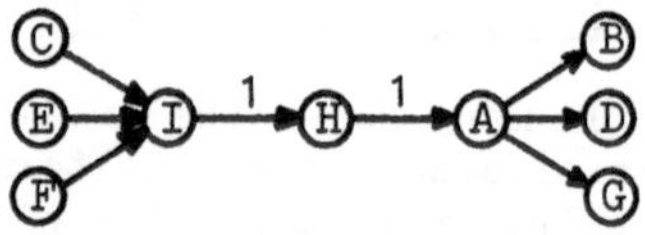

From this graph it follows immediately: I = 4, H = 5, and A = 6.

These values can now be used to find the values of all the other letters by linear discursion: E = 1 (I); D = 7 (IV); C = 3 (VI); G = 9 (II); F = 2 (III); B = 8 (III).

This method of structuring a problem by means of a graph has the advantage over linear and branched discursion that the relations between the letters become very clear. It can very quickly be carried out since the 6 equations can be examined one after another. The knowledge of some basic algebraic rules is sufficient.

2.3 Educational goals

What the student can learn from solving such number puzzles and from developing the techniques mentioned is:

(i) There can be many ways to solve a specific problem even if the problem is already stated in mathematical terms.

(ii) Combinatorial problems of the same type can be so different that no method may in general be advantageous over another method.

(iii) By developing the method of branched discursion the student will see how important the proper choice of the branching letter is and also how important the look ahead skill (linear discursion) is.

(iv) By developing the graph theoretic approach the student will find how efficient such simple structuring is; in addition, he will need creativity to develop arithmetic rules for the detection of "less"-conditions.

3. A DISCRETE STEP DYNAMIC PROCESS

Much closer related to real problems than the number puzzles are dynamic process puzzles like the following "filling problem" which successfully can be used in the very first lecture on enumerative techniques:

A wine merchant has three barrels, one exactly 8 gallons in size full of wine, and two empty barrels 5 gallons and 3 gallons in size, respectively. A customer asks for 4 gallons of wine. How can these 4 gallons be measured if only the three barrels are available? Therefore, the wine has to be poured from one barrel into another until one barrel contains exactly 4 gallons. Exact measurement is only possible if in each case of pouring wine from one barrel to another either the one barrel becomes completely full or the other barrel becomes completely empty.

In the first step either 5 gallons can be poured into the 5 gallons barrel or 3 gallons into the 3 gallons barrel. There are three subsequent states after step two, two steps after step 3 etc. The following enumeration tree contains all the possible states. This is a tree "with memory" which means that each state is generated only once. As in dynamic programming, all the new states of each step are generated in parallel. The states in this example are represented by the fillings of the large (top), the middle, and the small (bottom) barrel (See next page). Step 6 of the first branch leads to the desired 4 gallons.

The puzzles of the discrete step dynamic process type are very different in detail. Therefore, the enumeration or trial and error process requires an individual development in each case. What makes these problems valuable for students is that they can learn the first steps of combinatorial programming before proceeding to real world problems.

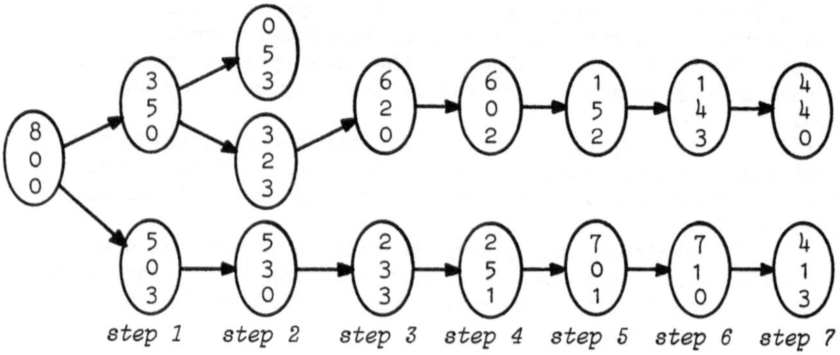

4. PUZZLES WITH TRUE AND FALSE INFORMATION (LIAR PUZZLES)

Among the many types of combinatorial puzzles those with true and false information (liar puzzles) can be used very nicely to develop the students' ability to develop enumerative or trial and error techniques (branched discursion techniques). Since these problems can often be formulated jocular, the students' motivation to solve them can even be increased. The following problem illustrates this type:

The state "Semiparadise" is called after the relativ trustworthiness of its politicians. In contradiction to all the other states of the world where only 10 percent of the statements of politicians are true, the politicians of Semiparadise have a rate of exactly 50 percent true statements. More precisely every second statement of each individual politician is true while every other statement is a lie.

Party ALPHA has 73, party BETA has 74 seats in the parliament. At a recent ballot of extreme importance it happened though that party ALPHA received 74 votes, party BETA only 73. And some reporters wrote that they found out that Mr. INCORRUPT, member of BETA, voted for ALPHA, after ALPHA paid him 50 million pernunzas for this purpose. Immediately, a parliamentary committee was established to find out the truth. It was clear to the committee that if the money was payed at all the source of the 50 million pernunzas was the unknown treasurer of the secret funds of the party ALPHA. The committee invited five members of ALPHA. Each of them made two statements (one of which was true and the other a lie):

Mr. A said: "Neither of us five party members is the treasurer of the secret funds of the party ALPHA. But I know that the 50 million pernunzas for Mr.INCORRUPT went from Mr. D via Mr. C to Mr. B."

Mr. B said: " The pernunzas were indeed paid to Mr. INCORRUPT. Mr. C is the treasurer of the secret funds of the party ALPHA."

Mr. C said: "The second statement of Mr. A is true. The second statement of Mr. B is also true."

Mr. D said: "Mr. INCORRUPT received no money at all from our party. I am the treasurer of the secret funds of the party ALPHA."

Mr. E said: "Mr. D is not the treasurer of the secret funds of the party ALPHA. I received the 50 million pernunzas from Mr. B and forwarded them to Mr. INCORRUPT."

How can the committee find the truth from this mosaic of truth and lies? Branched discursion (enumeration, trial and error or whatever name is preferred) helps. Since many statements concern the position of the treasurer this may be a good point to begin the solution process which is illustrated by the following tree. The numbers after the names refer to the first or second statement of each politician (t=true; f=false).

If A1 is true (no treasurer), then B2 is false (C is treasurer). In this case, both statements of C are false (since both, A2 and B2 are false) which is a contradiction to the assumptions. Therefore, one of the politicians is the treasurer (A1 is false), and the money passed from D via C to B (A2 is true). Let C be the treasurer (B2 is true). In this case, both statements of C are true which again contradicts with the assumptions. Therefore, C is not the treasurer (B2 is false). This is in accordance with C. Since B1 is true, D1 must be false. Therefore, D is the treasurer (D2 is true). It follows that E1 is false and, therefore, E2 is true.

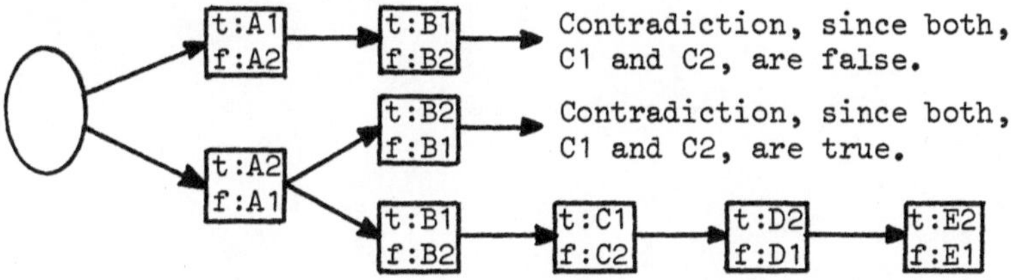

The result is that, indeed, Mr. INCORRUPT received the 50 million pernunzas (B1 is true). The money was provided by Mr. D, the treasurer (D2 is true). The money passed from Mr. D via Mr. C via Mr. B via Mr. E to Mr. INCORRUPT (A2 and E2 are true). Therefore, only Mr. A did not participate in the financial part of this fine operation.

5. CONCLUSIONS

It was not the objective of this paper to show that puzzles can be solved by enumerative methods. Rather, it was the objective to stimulate all those who are teaching combinatorial programming to use puzzles of different kinds to help students become familiar with the structure of enumerative approaches to combinatorial problems. What can be taught very efficiently by means of the puzzles is how the enumerative process can be developed for each specific type of problem.